THE IDEA OF DEMOCRACY

The idea of democracy

Edited by

DAVID COPP, JEAN HAMPTON, and JOHN E. ROEMER

CAMBRIDGE
UNIVERSITY PRESS

Published by the Press Syndicate of the University of Cambridge
The Pitt Building, Trumpington Street, Cambridge CB2 1RP
40 West 20th Street, New York, NY 10011-4211, USA
10 Stamford Road, Oakleigh, Melbourne 3166, Australia

First published 1993
First paperback edition 1995
Reprinted 1995

Printed in the United States of America

Library of Congress Cataloging-in-Publication Data is available.

A catalogue record for this book is available from the British Library.

ISBN 0-521-48326-3 paperback

Contents

Notes on the contributors

RICHARD J. ARNESON is Professor of Philosophy at the University of California at San Diego. He has held visiting appointments at the California Institute of Technology and the University of California at Davis. He writes on political theory and moral philosophy.

PRANAB BARDHAN is Professor of Economics at the University of California at Berkeley. He has published many articles in the areas of international and development economics, economics of institutions, and political economy of development. His books include *Conversations Between Economists and Anthropologists* (1989), *The Political Economy of Development in India* (1984), and *Land, Labor and Rural Poverty* (1984).

SAMUEL BOWLES is Professor of Economics at the University of Massachusetts at Amherst, where he teaches microeconomic theory and political economy. With Herbert Gintis, he wrote *Democracy and Capitalism: Property, Community, and the Contradictions of Modern Social Thought* (1986) and *Schooling in Capitalist America* (1976).

THOMAS CHRISTIANO is Assistant Professor of Philosophy at the University of Arizona. He has published papers in the areas of democratic theory, distributive justice, and the theory of value. He is currently working on books on democratic institutions and on the foundations of democracy.

JOSHUA COHEN is a Professor of Philosophy and Political Science at the Massachusetts Institute of Technology. Coauthor of *On Democracy* (1983), he is currently working on books on the importance of intermediate associations in democratic governance and on the role of the injustice of slavery in explaining the demise of slavery.

DAVID COPP is Professor of Philosophy at the University of California at Davis. His published articles are mainly on topics in moral and political philosophy. He coedited *On the Track of Reason* (1992),

Morality, Reason and Truth (1985), and *Pornography and Censorship* (1983), and he is currently completing a book on the foundations of morality. He is an Associate Editor of *Ethics*.

DAVID ESTLUND is Assistant Professor in the Department of Philosophy at Brown University. He has published several philosophical articles on democracy, including "Democracy Without Preference" in *The Philosophical Review*, July 1990.

JOHN FEREJOHN is a Senior Fellow at the Hoover Institution and Patrick Suppes Family Professor in Humanities and Sciences and Professor of Political Science at Stanford University. His primary areas of scholarly interest are positive political theory and political institutions and behavior. He wrote *Pork Barrel Politics* (1974), is a coauthor of *The Personal Vote* (1987), and is working on a book concerning coattail voting in the United States.

DAVID GAUTHIER is Distinguished Service Professor of Philosophy at the University of Pittsburgh. His principal writings include *Moral Dealing: Contract, Ethics, and Reason* (1990), *Morals by Agreement* (1986), and *The Logic of Leviathan* (1969). He is currently developing a theory of rational commitment, and a reading of Rousseau linking the philosophical and autobiographical works.

HERBERT GINTIS is Professor of Economics at the University of Massachusetts at Amherst. He is coauthor with Samuel Bowles of *Democracy and Capitalism: Property, Community, and the Contradictions of Modern Social Thought* (1986) and *Schooling in Capitalist America* (1976). He is currently working on the microfoundations of political economy.

JEAN HAMPTON is Professor of Philosophy at the University of Arizona. She has published *Hobbes and the Social Contract Tradition* (Cambridge, 1986) and (with Jeffrie Murphy) *Forgiveness and Mercy* (Cambridge, 1988). She has also published papers on ethics, political philosophy, philosophy of law, and feminist theory and has recently been awarded a Pew Fellowship.

RUSSELL HARDIN is the Mellon Foundation Professor of Political Science, Philosophy, and Public Policy Studies at the University of Chicago. He is the author of *Morality Within the Limits of Reason* (1988) and *Collective Action* (1982).

STEPHEN HOLMES is Professor of Political Science and Law at the University of Chicago and has published *Anatomy of Liberalism* (1992),

Rethinking the Liberal Tradition (1992), and *Benjamin Constant and the Making of Modern Liberalism* (1984).

MICHAEL S. MCPHERSON, the W. van Alan Clark Third Century Professor of Economics at Williams College, is one of the founding editors of the journal *Economics and Philosophy*. He is a coauthor of *Keeping College Affordable: Government and Educational Opportunity* (1991). His coauthored essay "Taking Ethics Seriously: Economics and Contemporary Moral Philosophy" is to be published in the *Journal of Economic Literature*.

KARL OVE MOENE is Professor of Economics in the Department of Economics at the University of Oslo. His work is related to the impact of alternative institutional designs. Presently, he is working on two projects: "Wage Formation and Unemployment" and "Poverty and Development."

CHRISTOPHER W. MORRIS, Associate Professor of Philosophy at Bowling Green State University, is also Senior Research Fellow at the Social Philosophy and Policy Center at Bowling Green and Research Associate at the Centre de Récherche en Epistémologie Appliquée at the Ecôle Polytechnique (Paris). He is coeditor with R. G. Frey of *Violence, Terrorism, and Justice* and *Liability and Responsibility* (both Cambridge, 1991).

JOHN RAWLS is Professor of Philosophy Emeritus at Harvard University. He is the author of *A Theory of Justice* (1971).

JOHN E. ROEMER is Professor of Economics and Director of the Program on Economy, Justice and Society at the University of California at Davis. He has written in the areas of Marxian economics, economic theory, distributive justice, welfare economics, and political economy. His most recent book is *Free to Lose: An Introduction to Marxist Economic Philosophy* (1988).

DEBRA SATZ is Assistant Professor of Philosophy at Stanford University. She has published papers on Marxism and on various topics in social and political philosophy.

JOHN D. STEPHENS is Professor of Political Science and Sociology at the University of North Carolina, Chapel Hill. He is the author of *The Transition from Capitalism to Socialism* (1979) and a coauthor of *Capitalist Development and Democracy* (1992) and *Democratic Socialism in Jamaica* (1986).

ROBERT SUGDEN is Professor of Economics at the University of East Anglia in Norwich, England. He has written on welfare economics and social choice, particularly from a contractarian perspective. He also works on game theory, choice under uncertainty, and the evolution of conventions.

CASS R. SUNSTEIN is Karl N. Llewellyn Professor of Jurisprudence in the Law School and the Department of Political Science at the University of Chicago. He is the author of *After the Rights Revolution* (1990), a coauthor of *Constitutional Law* (2d ed., 1991), and the author of *The Partial Constitution* (in press).

Introduction

The extraordinary political events of recent years, in which people around the globe, particularly in Eastern Europe, have clamored for democratic forms of government, have made reflection on the nature of democracy not merely appropriate but important. The essays in this volume take up fundamental questions that advocates for democracy would be wise to reflect upon more fully. What is democracy and what is its point? How have democracies originated? Are they always or even usually preferable to nondemocratic forms of polity? If so, on what grounds? How should a democracy respond to the preferences of its citizens? How can a democracy remain unified and animated by tolerance if it is composed of groups whose members accept different and even conflicting religious and moral views? Must a democratic polity be linked to capitalism, or is something that could be called "democratic market socialism" a viable and attractive possibility for many modern societies? And is this form of polity appropriate not only for governments but also for firms?

In presenting essays that address these questions, our aim has been not merely to publish a set of philosophy papers but to craft a volume that looks at democracy from a number of different disciplines. The contributors include philosophers, economists, historians, political scientists, and law professors, and the contributions are in two forms: First, there are the main essays, which take up a variety of questions about the nature and justification of democracy. Second, each main essay is followed by at least one commentary that further pursues, criticizes, or evaluates the issues raised in the essay, and which often has been written by a theorist from a discipline other than that of the essay's author. The result, we hope, is a diverse and rich presentation of interests, concerns, and methodologies that bear on questions about democracy, which we believe will profit philosophers and social scientists alike.

The book is divided into five sections, according to the main themes of the essays. But the most important issues are addressed in most of the essays. For example, although the first section is on the justification of democracy, most of the book's essays address this in one way or another; and although Part III is called "Democracy and Public Reason," several essays in the first and second parts also address the role of public reason and public debate and reasonableness in democracy. Finally, most of the essays have something to say about economics and make claims about actual cases of democratic government.

Part I. The point of democracy

The three pairs of essays and commentaries in Part I attempt, in different ways, to identify reasons for favoring democracy. That is, they address the question of why or whether democracy is a better political system than other systems. This question is also addressed, although with different emphases, in the essays and commentaries in Parts II and III. Some of the essays in Part I also address issues about democracy and economics that are addressed in Part IV and issues about public reason that are addressed in Part II.

It is fitting to begin the volume with an analysis of Tocqueville's *Democracy in America*, which contains a rich and complex evaluation of democracy in the nineteenth-century United States. Stephen Holmes describes Tocqueville's position as "paradoxical" and "labyrinthine," and his aim in his essay is to determine to what extent it can be made coherent. Tocqueville spoke of the "one pregnant thought" that unified his book, and Holmes thinks he most likely had in mind the idea that "extreme democracy forestalls the dangers of democracy." Holmes explains that Tocqueville distinguished between democracy in the sense of a democratic political system, or a set of institutions through which rulers are held responsible to electoral majorities, and democracy in the sense of a social system in which there is an absence "of legally maintained class hierarchies." Tocqueville's thesis is that political democracy can defuse some of the social conflict that might otherwise result from the emergence of a democratic social system. As Holmes puts it, Tocqueville viewed America as "a counterrevolutionary's dream" and thought that political democracy could help stabilize French society. In the end, however, Tocqueville said that the "main object" of his book was to explain the stability of political democracy in the United States. He concluded that political democracy could not easily be transplanted to France, since American democracy owed its stability partly to social, geographical, and historical circumstances that could not be duplicated in France.

One of the more interesting features of Tocqueville's analysis, in light of recent developments in Eastern Europe, is his view of the relationship between political democracy and commerce. This issue is taken up again in Part IV of the present book. Holmes describes Tocqueville as holding that commerce and political democracy are interdependent and must be in balance. The argument is complex, and Holmes finds aspects of it contradictory. In brief, a flourishing economy is essential to the stability of democracy, since it gives defeated politicians an alternative, which makes them more likely to accept defeat rather than attempt illegally to hold on to office. On the other hand, a lively democratic political culture counteracts the excessive individualism that might otherwise result in a society occupied mainly with commerce.

Debra Satz emphasizes Tocqueville's views about commerce in her discussion of Holmes's analysis. She claims that Holmes does not sufficiently emphasize a pessimistic strand in Tocqueville's thought, namely, the worry that "commerce and democratic politics can produce opposing social psychologies." She argues that Tocqueville perceived a tendency of commerce to undermine political democracy and that he sensed that the balance between the two may depend on the persistence of the small-scale commercial activity and property ownership that was characteristic of America at the time he wrote. Unequal wealth tends to undermine real political equality, and the division of labor undermines the individual autonomy that is necessary for a healthy democracy.

Tocqueville's support for democracy was qualified and conditional, as Satz and Holmes point out. He certainly did not have deep theoretical reasons for advocating it. He did not argue, for example, that it is intrinsically fair or that it promotes civic virtue. Rather, he thought that its advantages in the historical circumstances of mid–nineteenth-century America outweighed its disadvantages, such as the incompetence with which democratic governments tend to handle public business.

The incompetence of democratic governments and the alleged political ignorance of voters are the starting points of David Estlund's argument in "Making Truth Safe for Democracy." Estlund's inquiry is motivated by his desire to defend an *epistemic* conception of democracy, by which he seems to mean a conception of democratic institutions as justified by their ability to discover the political truth, or the truth about what society ought to do in order to deal with social problems. He realizes that this conception is threatened by the long-standing objection that most voters lack knowledge of the political truths. Moreover, if there is an elite that has political expertise, then the Socratic principle that knowledge justifies power implies that that elite ought to govern society. Estlund considers the possibility of avoiding the argument by denying that there are political truths. One might hold, for example, that the best that government can do is register the merely conative preferences of the voters. Estlund views this approach as too exotic; and it is not one that is open to him, since he aims to defend the idea that citizens can debate substantive political beliefs and are not restricted to voting their preferences. He therefore proposes a different strategy for avoiding the objection, one that invokes the ignorance of the masses about the identity of the people who have political expertise. He contends that even if some people have political expertise, their mere possession of such expertise cannot justify their holding political power. Their empowerment would not be morally legitimate if a reasonable member of society might nevertheless fail to recognize their knowledge. And he thinks that some reasonable people may always fail to recognize the wisdom of the elite. Hence rule by the wise cannot be justified. Estlund concludes his essay by posing a problem for the epistemic conception of democracy. How could democratic procedures have epistemic virtues "that it is unreasonable to deny"? Estlund's discussion of "reasonableness" bears on the notion of "public reason," which is addressed in Part III.

In his commentary, David Copp argues against Estlund's epistemic conception of the justification for democracy. Copp does not reject the idea that democratic debate and voting are to be understood cognitively, as concerned with the truth of various political claims, and not merely with the tabulation of preferences. But, he argues, it is implausible to suppose democracy can be justified as a method for discovering truths about what society ought to do; for if there are political truths, government by the intelligentsia would be better designed by its nature than democracy to lead to their recognition. Copp sorts out some of the issues raised in Estlund's essay and analyzes the argument about expertise and power. He claims that Estlund has misdiagnosed the objection and that Estlund's proposed answer to it is not satisfactory. For according to Estlund's position, if the wise were recognized as such by all the reasonable members of society, then rule by the wise would be legitimate. Yet Copp urges that systems of government have to be evaluated for their overall consequences and for their intrinsic fairness and not simply on the basis of the accuracy with which they are able to identify what society ought to do. Democracy may well be the preferable form of government because of its fairness or its overall good consequences even if there is an elite whose political wisdom has been widely recognized. If it has wisdom, a democrat would say, the elite ought to agree that democracy is preferable.

Estlund and Holmes both argue, however, that democracy cannot cogently be defended on the basis of indirect social effects that are not intended. Tocqueville claimed that industry, prosperity, and energy are among the beneficial effects of democracy, but Holmes claims that a defense of democracy on the basis of unintended side effects of this kind would violate a publicity condition to the effect that "the true reason an institution is valuable should be precisely the reason the institution is widely accepted." Estlund claims that democracy would not in fact have the alleged good effects on the character of citizens if they did not believe it would yield good decisions about social problems. Copp defends the Tocquevillean argument against Estlund's objection, and also, by implication, against Holmes's.

Richard Arneson also offers a consequentialist argument in favor of democracy. He claims in particular that rights of democratic participation have the function of protecting more fundamental rights, such as rights to privacy, freedom of expression, economic equality, and the like. He restricts attention, then, to the consequences of political systems for the protection of fundamental rights, and he views political rights as merely instrumental to protecting these rights. In his view, there is no fundamental right to participate in democratic institutions, and democracy is not itself a requirement of fairness, even though it might affect the fairness of society in other respects. Arneson's position has at least the following interesting features: First, he thinks that democracy is a second-best solution. If it were possible to identify reliably the people with political expertise or moral competence, and to ensure that they are not corrupted, he thinks it would be best to give political power to them rather than to have democracy, for this would maximize the chance of fundamental rights' being protected. In this argument, Arneson is, like Estlund, restricting attention to the decisions and policies that emerge from the political process and is not taking into account all of the other "Tocquevillean" effects that a political process can have. Second, since rights of democratic participation are justified on the basis of their effect on fundamental rights, there is clearly, in Arneson's view, a justification for restricting democracy, if doing so is necessary to protect fundamental rights. In this way the protective account of democracy that Arneson proposes can explain why a political democracy should be "substantively constitutional." It can explain, that is, why democracy should be limited constitutionally by devices such as the Bill of Rights in the U.S. Constitution. The justification for anti-democratic limits on majority rule is the same as the justification for rights of democratic participation, namely, that they are designed to protect fundamental rights. Finally, Arneson argues that democracy in the workplace is not on the same footing as democracy at the national level. His idea is that since the only justification for rights of democratic participation is protective, then, if fundamental rights are protected by democracy at the national level, there may be no justification for democracy in the workplace.

Robert Sugden challenges Arneson's view that there is no content to the idea that certain procedures are intrinsically fair. He points out that the common idea that it would be best if those with political or moral expertise were given political power, assuming they could be reliably identified and immunized against corruption, is not inconsistent with the idea that representative democracy is the best political system. For it may be that the voters ought to elect people with such expertise. Most important, Sugden attacks Arneson's distinction between procedural and fundamental rights. Arneson holds, for instance, that the right that parents have to raise their own children is merely a *procedural* right, which must be justified by its consequences. Yet Sugden asks why this right should be viewed as procedural. More generally, it is not clear that there is a sound basis for the distinction between procedural and fundamental rights. Sugden asks why Arneson does not adopt the indirect consequentialist position that no rights are fundamental and all must be justified by their consequences. The result of such a thoroughgoing consequentialism, however, would be to bring into consideration all the consequences of democracy, including side effects of the kind that interested Tocqueville.

Part II. Democracy and preferences

Part II addresses the idea that the aim of democracy is to determine the collectively preferred or best social policy as a function of the preferences of individual citizens. This idea can lead to the welfarist conception of democracy that is criticized in Cass Sunstein's essay or to the public choice theoretical conception that is explained in Russell Hardin's essay and criticized in Thomas Christiano's reply.

The public choice theoretical conception is that democratic institutions define procedures for aggregating individual preferences about social options into a collective preference. Russell Hardin argues, in "Public Choice Versus Democracy," that the chief results of public choice theory imply that "majoritarian democracy is both conceptually and motivationally flawed." One set of results from public choice theory includes both Condorcet's problem of cyclical majorities and Kenneth Arrow's celebrated impossibility theorem. Arrow's theorem is about so-called social choice rules that take as input any profile of individual preferences over complete social worlds and give as output a so-called social preference over those worlds. The theorem says that there is no rule of this kind that meets a given set of apparently acceptable normative and conceptual criteria. As Hardin expresses the result, there is no aggregation rule that meets all of the criteria in question and is such that "every society, no matter how lacking in agreement, can follow [that rule] for the social ordering of all its alternative whole [social worlds]." Some of the criteria invoked by Arrow are unrealistic. But Hardin argues that "more realistic assumptions will not block the conclusion that public choice procedures are normatively incoherent if they are to translate individual into collective choices, as majoritarian democracy is supposed to do." The second set of results from public choice theory defines what Hardin calls the collective action problem. It is illustrated by the Prisoners' Dilemma. The problem, Hardin explains, is that even if we knew which option would be collectively preferred or best, narrow self-interest might prevent us from implementing that option voluntarily. Coercion might enable us to implement the option, of course, but we must wonder about the justice of coercing those who do not agree with the choice that is being implemented. Moreover, there are collective action problems that arise in connection with coercion, for the narrow self-interest of those who are to coerce the rest of us may lead them to coerce us to their own ends rather than to the ends we intended. Hardin concludes that democratic theory and practice have "grievous foundational flaws."

Thomas Christiano rejects most of Hardin's claims about democracy in his reply, "Social Choice and Democracy." He argues that the public choice theoretical conception of democracy is mistaken for a variety of reasons. Most important, he argues that democratic procedures are not social choice rules in Arrow's sense, and that this means that Arrow's impossibility theorem has no clear normative significance. In particular, democratic majority rule should not be understood simply as an implementation of a function from individual preferences to a social preference. A benevolent and omniscient dictator could implement a majoritarian function, but the government in that case obviously would not be majoritarian. Instead of the public choice conception, Christiano advocates a "distributive conception," according to which a voting procedure assigns to people the resource of voting power. In democracy, the distribution of this resource is equal. A *fully* egalitarian collective decision-making process would be designed to distribute equally *all* resources relevant to determining the outcome, not merely voting power. So understood, democracy – and political egalitarianism more generally – can be defended as a requirement of egalitarian justice, just as equality in the distribution of other resources can be defended as a requirement of justice. Christiano concludes his commentary by explaining some of the details, such as the relation between political egalitarianism and economic egalitarianism. Christiano's commentary is an attempt to justify democracy as intrinsically fair.

In "Democracy and Shifting Preferences," Cass Sunstein criticizes the welfarist idea that democracies must take the preferences of their citizens as "givens," to be satisfied as extensively as possible. Calling this position "subjective welfarism," Sunstein contends that its advocates assume that by treating "preferences as sovereign" the political society "is most likely to promote both individual freedom, rightly conceived, and individual or social welfare." But Sunstein thinks that there is a way in which Plato is right that politics is the "art whose business it is to care for souls," and he proposes that we embrace, instead of subjective welfarism, a "republican" vision of democratic life, in which citizens participate in government in order to improve the moral life of the community. Liberalism, he claims, ought to be understood to sanction certain interferences in the private preferences of the citizenry, particularly by virtue of the fact that many of our preferences are "endogenous," that is, self-generated and adaptive to a range of factors. Through such interference, the government will be able to foster not only citizens' welfare but also their autonomy. Sunstein notes that no less liberal a thinker than John Dewey argued for something like this view of the function of liberal-democratic government. So for Sunstein, respecting autonomy is not simply respecting preferences, no matter what they may be, but also encouraging certain kinds of preferences even while discouraging, prohibiting, or constraining others through the regulation of societal institutions that effect the generation of preferences. And he catalogs examples of cases in which it seems right to argue that considerations of both autonomy and welfare justify government interference in preference formation, even while subjective welfarism would disallow such interference.

In his commentary, John Ferejohn replies that Sunstein has failed to appreciate the extent to which subjective welfarism can also sanction governmental interference in preferences and preference formation, namely, in circumstances where those preferences are misinformed. Ferejohn maintains that a person's preferences should not be understood superficially to include choices for such items as breakfast foods; rather, he argues we should make "a distinction between fundamental things over which genuine preferences are defined and constructed entities over which induced preferences are defined." He then argues that subjective welfarists could advocate public intervention in the formation of nonfundamental or *induced* preferences, as long as it was possible to believe such intervention would be effective (and he notes that it is at least arguable that it would be so in some situations, e.g., in cases of human addiction). But Ferejohn worries that democracies continually face the problem of ensuring that government officials are properly controlled by, and answerable to, those who have elected them, and he notes that as long as this problem is unresolved, "there is reason to be skeptical about the efficacy and purpose of public intervention in preference formation." In any case, he contends that because both subjective welfarists and Sunstein's "republicans" can justify interference in preference formation, we will not be able to choose between these two positions by noting that there are individual preferences that "seem not to deserve respect."

Part III. Democracy and public reason

Ferejohn concludes his commentary by noting that subjective welfarism is an instance of "liberal neutrality," which denies to "the public or to the state any morally separate stance from which to intervene in genuinely private conceptions of good lives," and which he believes is a theory that helps to further the freedom of members of a democracy by blocking interference in their choices of how to live their lives. The essays and commentaries in Part III explore, either directly or indirectly, how far the doctrine of liberal neutrality can serve to unify and render just those democracies in the modern world with very diverse populations. The first is John Rawls's essay "The Domain of the Political and Overlapping Consensus," in which Rawls further clarifies and defends a thesis he has advanced in recent years in a number of essays, namely, that modern pluralist democracies must be united by a common allegiance to what he terms an "overlapping consensus." This consensus is understood by Rawls to set out certain basic rights and liberties that members agree will prevail in their political community. Each member takes the content of this consensus to be correct, given his or her own comprehensive moral and political views, but because these particular comprehensive views are not built into the consensus itself, its content can be accepted by all without disrupting or threatening their diverse beliefs. But does this mean that an overlapping consensus is some kind of modus vivendi, arrived at by political debate and compromise, which members accept only as a means of securing union with others who hold moral views they cannot accept? And if so, doesn't this make that consensus merely a product of politics, which could change as the composition of society changed and which might have little to do with what many would consider to be *justice*?

In his essay in this volume, Rawls is concerned to deny this interpretation of the overlapping consensus and defend the idea that such a consensus in modern democratic societies could claim to be constituted by principles of justice. Specifically, he argues that the consensus must be understood to contain only what it would be appropriate to consider a *reasonable* framework of principles and values, "which apply to basic political institutions" and which "normally outweigh any values that may conflict with them." It is, therefore, not a consensus that every member of the society, no matter what his or her views, could endorse; it is only a consensus that those members whose views are *reasonable* could endorse. With this position Rawls hopes to be able to explain how a pluralistic society can and does remain unified using only tolerant rather than coercive means, even while explaining how this tolerant unifying device can still claim to be a public charter of *justice* and not a mere political compromise whose content might easily make us morally queasy (or worse). If he is successful, Rawls will have pulled off the remarkable theoretical feat of explaining how a democratic society can remain unified via a conception of justice and yet do so in a way that is "morally neutral" and thus respectful of the moral diversity of views in its pluralist population. His theory would be attractive to those, such as Arneson and Ferejohn, who wish, as far as possible, to keep the state out of the business of judging and interfering in the decisions of individuals determining what a good life is like.

In his commentary on this essay, "Moral Pluralism and Political Consensus," Joshua Cohen sympathetically expands on, and attempts to bolster, this Rawlsian understanding of the overlapping consensus. He begins by showing how the concept of the overlapping consensus can be used to answer certain questions left unaddressed in Rawls's book *A Theory of Justice*. In particular, it allows Rawls to explain how a society can generate a *realistic* norm of justice, one that can actually be used to govern the kinds of pluralist democracies that exist in the world today (and Cohen argues that this is an issue that also concerned past theorists such as Hegel, Rousseau, and Marx). Cohen then develops arguments to support Rawls's contention that an overlapping consensus in any of these democracies is not a modus vivendi – a mere accommodation to those groups or interests in society who happen to be powerful and whose views may not conform to the standards of what we intuitively recognize as justice – but, rather, a consensus that is and must be *reasonable*. We are not required, Cohen maintains, to adjust the consensus to accommodate those with unreasonable views; instead, we are required to accommodate only those views that "are the natural consequence of the free exercise of practical reason," and he goes on to discuss how we can define and recognize such views.

In her commentary however, "The Moral Commitments of Liberalism," Jean Hampton questions whether a genuine consensus of existing views that could serve as a public charter for the existing pluralistic communities in democratic societies can be fully satisfactory as a conception of justice. Like Cohen, she focuses on Rawls's use of the term "reasonable," but she claims that Rawls actually uses two senses of that word in his essay. She argues that he sometimes uses "reasonable" to describe those beliefs – possibly incorrect – that are nonetheless permissibly arrived at in real, less-than-ideal situations where information is limited; and sometimes, she claims, he uses it to describe beliefs that would result from ideal reasoning, that is, reasoning in morally and epistemically ideal circumstances. Hampton contends that when Rawls argues for the creation of an overlapping consensus that respects the diversity of (only) reasonable beliefs, he uses that word in the first sense, to characterize the variety of beliefs we would consider permissible in our less than ideal world. But she claims that when he insists that the overlapping consensus can only be considered "reasonable" (and a *just* public charter) if it includes the idea that all people are equal and free, he has shifted to an appeal to the conclusions of what he takes to be ideal human reasoning. And since conceptions of ideal reasoning are informed by a whole variety of normative – and, in particular, moral – ideas that are eminently disputable by individuals who have grown up in a world that is less than ideal, then, to the extent that Rawls's theory is informed by these ideas, it is, in his own terms, only a partially comprehensive view. Hence, were it to be used in a liberal society, that society would be theoretically partisan rather than neutral. Hampton concludes that Rawls must choose between (1) an interpretation of the overlapping consensus that makes it morally neutral but impossible to justify apart from a political appeal to what people happen to believe and (2) an interpretation that grants it a powerful nonpolitical justification that is not morally neutral.

Hampton's own view is that the latter option is preferable, and in this respect she agrees with Sunstein that a democratic state ought to be interested not merely in respecting preferences but also in *correcting* them when they might encourage unjust behavior. Both believe that a liberal democracy cannot be neutral but must side with a certain kind of moral conception of what a society should be like. The debate between Hampton and Sunstein, on the one hand, and Ferejohn, Rawls, and Cohen, on the other, shows that advocates of democracy are not yet in agreement about exactly how a democratic regime must respect the interests of the citizenry whose collective will is taken to legitimize it.

David Gauthier's attempt to understand the unity of modern democratic societies in his essay "Constituting Democracy" looks, at first glance, even more political than Rawls's theory. Gauthier takes it that a political society is legitimate insofar as it rests on the legitimizing collective will of the people in that society, and he maintains that in the United States this principle of legitimation was made explicit in the creation of the U.S. Constitution. The creation of that constitution, however, did not, according to Gauthier, involve the kinds of strategic debates and behavior that characterize normal politics but, rather, involved what he calls "deliberative reasoning" intended to reveal or define what is in the public interest, and in which people interact with one another as "civic friends." This way of reasoning represents each individual's interests equally and fairly, so that the resulting consensus "is a *privileged* act of popular will." And this privileged act of will not only legitimizes and defines the structure of the political regime but also counts as a *just* consensus by virtue of the deliberative reasoning process from which it has arisen. So Gauthier presumably would say to Rawls that if we were to regard the U.S. Constitution as the Rawlsian "overlapping consensus" in the United States, then this consensus could indeed count as a representation of justice because of the *nonpolitical* way in which it has been defined: "The procedure of deliberative politics is thus informed by the standards that its outcome must satisfy."

In his commentary "On Contractarian Constitutional Democracy," Christopher Morris doubts that Gauthier's remarks in his essay can be successfully reconciled with his views in his book *Morals by Agreement*. Why, asks Morris, should the author of that book insist on the importance of civic friendship and equal respect, when his own arguments in *Morals by Agreement* appear to show that they are neither necessary nor sufficient for political order and stability? Moreover, asks Morris, hasn't Gauthier also shown that justice must be defined only by an ideal, fully informed bargain among fully rational individuals with equal bargaining power? Since the process of creating the U.S. Constitution has never (and will never) match this ideal, why should we take it to be constitutive of justice? Morris also puzzles over the fact that although Gauthier considers the U.S. government to be legitimized by the *real* consent of the people as delivered in the Constitution – the vehicle of the popular will – nonetheless, rather late in the essay he calls the Constitution something that the people "would have agreed upon" had each of them been fully able to engage in the deliberative reasoning that produced it. As Morris puts it: "That something might be the best justification for some arrangement is compatible with its being, in fact, no justification at all."

All of the essays and commentaries in Part III challenge the reader to reflect on how democratic regimes can simultaneously consider themselves to be both *just* regimes and also regimes that are adequately stable, even while being tolerant of, and responsive to, the diverse interests of their citizenries.

Part IV. Democracy and economics

The essays by John Roemer and by Samuel Bowles and Herbert Gintis take two different approaches to what a democratic socialist economy should look like. For Bowles and Gintis, the emphasis is on industrial democracy, that is, the control of firms by workers, whereas Roemer's democracy consists in the equal division of profits and in the control citizens exercise over the use of the economic surplus.

Roemer argues for the feasibility of market socialism, a system in which markets are used to allocate essentially the same class of goods as is allocated by markets under advanced capitalism but in which profits of firms are distributed equally among citizens. In particular, firms maximize profits; the right to profits, however, cannot be purchased with money in a stock market but is assigned by political (democratic) decision. The socialist aspects of this system are two: the intervention by the government in the investment process, necessary because of externalities and the incompleteness of futures markets, and the somewhat egalitarian income distribution achieved by means of a somewhat equal division of profits. Roemer reports on the work with his collaborators regarding the effectiveness of different methods of state intervention in the investment process. He concludes that intervention would be at least as successful if carried out by manipulating interest rates as it would be if more direct, quantity-allocation methods were used. Thus effective *planning* need not be implemented via commandist and *centralized allocation* methods.

The second major question addressed is whether a system of incentives can be designed that would motivate firms' managements to maximize profits when there are no individuals who own large shares of any firm. Roemer argues that this is possible, reporting here on a proposal by Bardhan in which a limited stock market would exist where firms could trade the stock of other firms. The monitoring would be carried out mainly by banks, much as in the Japanese *keiretsu* system.

Roemer raises two other questions: Would a market socialist economy have the same tendencies in regard to unemployment as capitalist economies, and would the tendency of capitalism to produce various pernicious "public bads" be reduced in a market socialist economy? The answers offered are no and yes, respectively. The argument establishing the reduction of public bads under market socialism does not depend on people's having different preferences under socialism than under capitalism, but only on the economic consequences of an egalitarian distribution of corporate profits. Hence Roemer claims that the "quality of life" would improve in his system, without a cultural revolution that changes the preferences of citizens.

There is a link between Sunstein's ideas about the formation of preferences, and Roemer's view that the democratic process can decide the main contours of investment policy. Roemer argues that political parties would compete in democratic market socialism by proposing different plans for investment. The "Chicago school" of economics opposes using the electoral process to decide economic matters, because, it maintains, an individual will vote "irresponsibly," as his or her vote has no consequences for the individual's pocketbook. Sunstein, however, sees the democratic process as a forum for the education of citizens, and believes they can make responsible economic decisions in this forum.

In commenting on Roemer's essay, Michael McPherson distinguishes between two approaches for testing the feasibility of a proposed economic system of the type Roemer proposes: the Walrasian and the institutional. The Walrasian approach makes certain assumptions (e.g., that firms maximize profits, that agents behave as price takers) and studies the properties of equilibriums of well-specified models; the institutional approach pays more attention to whether these "Walrasian" assumptions are reasonable, given the kinds of institution that are likely to exist in an actual economy, but it does not construct models. With the current state of economic theory, a trade-off is involved in the choice of these approaches: To date, there is no model capable of giving the precise answers that Walrasian equilibrium theory gives and also of representing these institutional concerns in a general way. McPherson argues that Roemer's essay is an instance of this trade-off. The study of investment planning is precise and "Walrasian," but the institutional discussion, concerning the environment of firm managers, is sketchy. McPherson believes that the most interesting questions regarding the feasibility of market socialism are institutional, and that Roemer's analysis leaves much to be done in this regard.

McPherson also distinguishes between the attainability of an economic system and its sustainability once attained. The question of attainability concerns whether it is possible to move from here to there, and that of sustainability concerns whether, if there, the system will reproduce itself or will unravel. Roemer's essay deals entirely with the latter question, but the former is surely at least as important.

Samuel Bowles and Herbert Gintis begin their chapter by arguing that the standard neoclassical model is not the right one for analyzing the relative merits of capitalist and worker-owned firms, for that model ignores market imperfections, which are of the essence in the comparison. There are, in particular, two salient market imperfections: The capital market is not perfect, so workers who lack collateral cannot easily borrow to set up a firm; and the labor process is not easy to monitor, so capitalist firms face a problem in extracting labor from workers. Bowles and Gintis argue that democratically run firms are socially preferable to capitalist firms for reasons of accountability and efficiency: Both kinds of reasons arise from market imperfections.

The argument for accountability hinges on the claim that capitalists exercise "short-side power" over workers in their firm. The exchange of labor for the wage is contested, in the sense that the duties the worker must perform cannot be precisely specified, and so, on the job, there is a struggle between worker and boss over the performance of labor. Nor is it possible to monitor that performance costlessly or to seek third-party arbitration of conflicts. Employers solve this problem by paying workers an "employment rent," a bonus over the wage (or utility level) the worker could get at the next best opportunity. (In particular, the workers are better off than they would be if unemployed.) This "rent" makes it costly for the workers to lose their jobs, and hence they will exert effort even when not being constantly monitored by their employer, so long as there is some chance of being caught shirking. Because they pay a rent to the workers, the employers can force them to do things they would not do were they able to move with ease to another job with the same pay: the workers are on the "short side" of this power relation, because there are unemployed workers waiting to take their jobs. Bowles and Gintis provide four arguments for why the workplace should be democratically run; the central argument is that, in relations involving power, those who exercise power should be accountable to those over whom they exercise it.

The authors also argue that democratic firms are likely to be more technologically efficient than capitalist firms, but also more risk-averse. For example, since the workers in a democratic firm are the residual claimants, they will have an incentive to monitor each other, saving the money that capitalist owners must expend on monitoring. The democratic firm will be more risk-averse than the capitalist firm because its workers will have all their assets tied up in the firm, as opposed to capital owners, who can diversify their portfolios. Manager-run capitalist firms are also more risk-averse than is socially optimal because managers have most of their assets tied up in the firm, but one would expect that socially suboptimal bias toward risk aversion would be even worse in worker-owned firms.

Karl Moene contests Bowles and Gintis's claim that the essence of capitalist power consists in the short-side power employers have over workers, owing to the impossibility of perfect monitoring. He argues that, historically, in situations where capitalists have been able to monitor workers easily, workers have been exploited more: The employer makes the workers a take-it-or-leave-it offer and drives their utility down to a point almost as low as it would be were they unemployed. The employment rent that workers receive in situations where monitoring is difficult, which in the Bowles–Gintis argument is a stratagem on the part of the employer, can perhaps be more convincingly explained as a consequence of workers' bargaining power: You pay us more than the reservation wage of unemployed workers or we shirk. Moene also argues that, in the relation between corporate managers and stockholders, it is the managers who have power over stockholders, not the other way around as the theory of contested exchange would have it. The evidence is the body of empirical literature that attests to the difficulty stockholders have in controlling managers, a group Moene dubs the "nomenklatura of the West." Moene concludes by agreeing with Bowles and Gintis that worker-controlled firms can be both more democratic and more efficient than capitalist firms, but he does not think the contested-exchange argument strengthens the assertion.

Part V. Democracy: case studies

John Stephens's essay begins by outlining two prominent theories of the origins of democracy, those of Seymour Lipset and Barrington Moore. In Lipset's modernization theory, economic development brings about democracy by bringing about urbanization, literacy, and, concomitantly, the moderation of economic demands. Without a strong middle class, the ruling classes fear the power democracy would give to the poor and the workers; hence they oppose democracy. But with development, economic inequality diminishes. The poor become less poor and hence more moderate, and a sizable middle class develops with moderate interests; these developments reduce the opposition of the ruling classes to democracy. Then democracy becomes politically feasible. The middle class is the moving force in the movement toward democracy in this theory.

Barrington Moore's theory, which Stephens calls a class-analytic approach, argues that there is no necessary relation between economic development and democracy. The (virtually) necessary and sufficient condition for the development of democracy is the absence of a strong coalition among (1) large landowners who depend on labor-repressive methods in agriculture, (2) the state, and (3) a politically dependent bourgeoisie of medium strength. The strength of the working class is not an important variable if this coalition exists. The key factor for Moore is the strength of the bourgeoisie. If it is strong and independent, then it becomes a force for democracy. Stephens also refers tangentially to the views of "many Marxists and liberals" that the bourgeoisie is the dominant force for democracy.

Stephens's hypothesis is that the strength of the working class is the key variable. Capitalist development is associated with democracy because it is associated with the strengthening of the working class and the weakening of the landowning class.

In the book Stephens summarizes in his essay, cross-national studies are reported that have been conducted to test which of these theories offers the best explanation of the origins of democracy. The essay summarizes the evidence from Europe, Central America, and the Caribbean. The evidence supports Stephens's theory. Modernization theory is shown to be a weak hypothesis because there are many historical cases in which the middle class supported authoritarianism (e.g., interwar Austria and Germany). The theories in which the bourgeoisie is the key force (Moore and Marxist) are contradicted by many cases in which the bourgeoisie did not support democracy *ex ante* but only *ex post facto*. According to Stephens, the only class that consistently supports democracy is the working class. Alone, however, it cannot bring about democracy; it requires allies in the middle class.

In discussing the Caribbean case, Stephens addresses the correlation between British colonial rule and success of democracy. He attributes it to the fact that the British were in control of the state apparatus and did not ally themselves with the landed class, which wanted to repress the peasantry. Thus, the alliance between the landed class and the state that chokes off working-class power did not materialize. "The imperial power was a brake on the exploitative aims of the planter class."

The kiss of death of democracy occurs if the working class raises demands that are too radical, when it has enough power to win but does not have a significant base for those demands among the middle class. The fall of Allende in Chile is an instance.

In conclusion, Stephens raises the question of whether, in fact, democracy as he defines it (universal suffrage, election of a parliament, and civil rights) is correlated with increased representation of the *interests* of the disadvantaged classes. He characterizes Leninism as saying it is not (i.e., as saying that formal democracy is a sham under capitalism).

Stephens disagrees with the "Leninist" view but does not study the question here.

Pranab Bardhan concurs with Stephens's class-analytic approach, but he questions Stephens's claims that the working class has always been the key actor in bringing democracy about, by pointing out that there are examples (1) where capitalism brought about democracy but not a strong working class and (2) where it brought about a strong working class but one that was not prodemocracy. Bardhan points to a set of examples where democracy was brought about either as a stratagem of the ruling class to weaken the working class by offsetting its votes with the votes of the more conservative peasantry or as a mechanism for settling rivalries among equipotent sectors of the ruling class in an efficient (nonviolent) way. India, a case not discussed by Stephens, is the prime example of the latter.

Conclusion

The essays in this volume leave a variety of issues in need of further attention. There are questions about the justification of democracy: Can democracy be defended as the best political system, and if so, on what grounds? Is its justification epistemic, consequentialist, or a matter of its intrinsic fairness? Is its justification compatible with the antidemocratic or antimajoritarian devices we see in actual functioning democratic political systems, including such varied institutions and practices as constitutional bills of rights, vote trading, coalition building, and parliamentary representation by districts rather than in proportion to the votes cast for political parties? Some of the questions concern how a democracy can ensure its legitimacy and stability in the face of political pluralism: How is pluralism to be taken into account without either risking the central interests of minorities, or excessively curtailing the power of majorities, or risking democracy itself through misplaced tolerance? Must the justification of democracy be addressed in some sense to all of the various comprehensive political conceptions represented in a given society, or can democracy properly be advocated on the basis of one or a few of these conceptions, even if some citizens would reject democracy for their own reasons? There are also questions about the very conception of democracy: Is it best viewed as a device for protecting rights, a device for aggregating mere preferences, a device for distributing power, or a device for identifying political truths? Some of the questions concern the relation between political egalitarianism and economic justice, and the relation between democracy and capitalism or socialism. And there are questions about the "scope" of democracy: Is it enough if the central government is democratic, or must all levels of government and administration be answerable to the people they serve or govern? Must democracy be extended into all institutions? Does the rationale for democracy also extend to workplace democracy? Finally, what are the prospects for democracy? It has been stable in a few societies for a few tens of decades. What explains this, and can democracy be sustained into the indefinite future?

DAVID COPP
JEAN HAMPTON
JOHN E. ROEMER

Part I

The point of democracy

1

Tocqueville and democracy

STEPHEN HOLMES

At the beginning of *Démocratie en Amérique*, Alexis de Tocqueville asserts, with no clarifying explanation, that his book is unified by *une pensée mère*, translated ingeniously into English as "one pregnant thought."[1] There is plenty of room for disagreement about this key idea, this *fil conducteur* purportedly woven through a long, kaleidoscopic, detour-studded, and loosely organized work. Perhaps the master concept, tying Tocqueville's cascade of insights together, is a memorable descriptive claim: that *mœurs* are all-important,[2] that a society's starting point determines its subsequent fate, or that the abolition of primogeniture and legal inequalities has revolutionized the old European world, leaving nothing unchanged. But given Tocqueville's turn of mind, especially his addiction to eye-catching paradoxes, the most likely candidate for the book's leading thought is this: "Extreme freedom corrects the abuse of freedom, and extreme democracy forestalls the dangers of democracy."[3]

Unless you exaggerate, Tocqueville believed, no one will understand what you have to say.[4] So, the question readers must ask is: What does this particular exaggeration mean?

A democratic cure for a democratic disease

The word "democracy," in Tocqueville's first and greatest work, is systematically ambiguous.[5] It specifies, on the one hand, a social arrangement and, on the other hand, a political system. "Democracy" sometimes refers to social leveling or the collapse of legally maintained class hierarchies. At other times, it refers to self-government or the institutions guaranteeing that rulers remain responsible to electoral majorities. Tocqueville underscores the difference between these two species of "democracy" by insisting that democracy in a social sense is inevitable, an inescapable feature of the modern world, while

This essay is the unripe fruit of an ongoing collaboration with Jon Elster on Tocqueville's political psychology and social thought.

democracy in a political sense is a product of human freedom, a matter for prudence or choice.

The two forms of "democracy" are causally related, it turns out. In a society where class differences are legally enforced, the lower orders glimpse their superiors only from a courteous distance. This lack of contact and opportunity for observation (outside the shuttered sphere of the household) gives rise, in rigidly stratified societies, to poetic illusions.[6] Legal inferiors imagine that their unapproachable legal superiors also excel them morally, intellectually, and humanly. This misconception, fostered and perpetuated by ignorance, encourages them to bend their knees, heteronomously, to authority from above. As legal classes are abolished, however, opportunities for revealing glances into the lives of the preeminent increase. When one individual eyeballs another, even a wealthy one, up close, delusions about intrinsic superiority vanish. After legal stratification is abolished, as a consequence, ordinary citizens lose their immemorial readiness to do whatever would-be masters prescribe.[7] In this way, social leveling naturally produces a predilection for democratic self-rule. The cave-in of legal classes allows the formerly lower orders to scrutinize the high and mighty close at hand. Clarity of perception destroys the psychological conditions for deference and submission. Legal equality makes citizens "suspicious of all authority and soon suggests the notion and the love of political liberty."[8]

To explore in this way the causal relations between his two forms of "democracy," Tocqueville keeps them sharply distinct conceptually.[9] His striking proposal (to tame democracy by more democracy) is intelligible only if we keep the double meaning of "democracy" in mind. Interpreted in this light, his seemingly paradoxical thesis means simply that democratic *lois politiques* can forestall the most distasteful consequences of a democratic *état social*. Clever legislators can deploy *virtú* against *fortuna*, using self-government to rechannel the unstoppable egalitarian flood. If they are adroit, they can engage democratic politics to protect, say, private property, which would otherwise be threatened by a general tendency toward social leveling.

Démocratie en Amérique, especially Volume I, can be read as a sociological portrait of American culture and institutions. But what thematic coherence does it have? To answer this question, we must look at the political purpose with which Tocqueville began his book. We cannot grasp the unifying thread to which he draws our attention if we slight his initial reformist or propagandistic aim. In a letter composed in America toward the end of 1831, he wrote that France "is the subject of nearly all my thoughts."[10] The book he eventually wrote, in fact, is pervaded by an obsession with French political instability. At the outset, at least, he thought he could do something about it. Thus, at times, Tocqueville's language veers revealingly close to that of a social engineer.[11] He suggests that democratic institutions should be "introduites prudemment dans la société."[12] Embarking on his mission, he pictured himself not as a mere observer but as a reformer, considering practical alternatives, proposing change. He draws attention explicitly to this original motivation behind his book. He did not go to America simply to satisfy his curiosity, he claims: "I sought there lessons from which we might profit."[13] What were these lessons? And what, at first, was Tocqueville's practical design?

To understand what Tocqueville was for, we must understand what he was against – what he was up against. His central argument is directed against a very specific audience, against men who, despite their refined manners and honorable character, were intractable "enemies of all progress."[14] These backward-looking individuals had hopelessly misjudged "the great democratic revolution," that is, the breakdown of land-based aristocracy, that was completed in late eighteenth-century France. They "think it a new thing and, supposing it an accident, hope that they can still check it."[15] They do not see the roots of legal equality in the remote past. They believe absurdly that they can reverse the flow of history. Explicitly invoking his dual concept of "democracy," Tocqueville notes that "there are many men in France who regard equality of conditions as the first of evils and political liberty as the second."[16] One may doubt if there were actually "many" Frenchmen of this sort. But, whatever their actual numbers, they played a disproportionately important role in Tocqueville's own mental world. He was arguing principally against these men, against a group of militant reactionaries with whom he had close family connections. They were fiercely opposed to democratization in both senses. They had bitterly condemned the oath of allegiance Tocqueville had sworn to Louis-Philippe. He set out to show them just how wrong they were.

He used rhetoric against them, of course. Since they were religious men, he suggested that opposition to democracy (in the social sense) is an act of insurrection against God.[17] Since they found conspiracy theories of the French Revolution wholly convincing, he insisted that the Revolution had been in preparation for centuries. It was not the work of one generation and could not be reversed by another. Since they were men "for whom the word democracy is synonymous with anarchy, upheaval, spoliation, and murder,"[18] he hammered ceaselessly on the nonidentity of democratic government and revolution. Political democracy is not dangerous and unstable, but completely safe. It is perfectly compatible with property, religion, and social stability.

The weightiest piece of evidence Tocqueville produces in support of his democracy-is-harmless claim – an idea that was confusing and almost unthinkable to reactionaries – is the United States itself. "Almost the whole of Europe has been convulsed by revolutions," he wrote in 1848, while "America has not even suffered from riots."[19] Or even more emphatically: "There is no country in the world harboring fewer germs of revolution than America."[20] A flourishing and nonrevolutionary United States was a crushing counterexample for the Right. The center-piece of French conservative thought was that social order is impossible without legal inequality. America, therefore, completely shattered the ultraroyalist worldview. It demonstrated once and for all that democracy does not entail anarchy, upheaval, spoliation, and murder. Furthermore, the United States provides a model for imitation. "The Americans," we read, "have applied remedies, of which so far they alone have thought, to the ills common to all democratic peoples; and though they were the first to attempt this, they have succeeded."[21] Not the same cure, exactly, but a similar one, could certainly be tried in France.

America reveals what democracy can be like when freed from the futile and counterproductive resistance of reactionary forces. Democracy has been so irritable and threatening in France because, among other things, conservatives continue to wage war against it. Even when they are resigned to the abolition of legal privileges, they remain vehemently opposed to political democratization. But "drawing the line" is a fatal mistake. Intransigence exacerbates the situation. If the old aristocracy continues to adopt a rigidly hostile attitude toward political liberalization, the whole social order, including respect for property, will explode. Instead of opposing popular government, conservatives should support it. They should encourage democratic political institutions because such institutions can compensate for the moral and human losses accompanying the collapse of legal hierarchy. Democratic government can also help prevent another revolution. At the heart of *Démocratie en Amérique*, or so it seems at first, lies a recipe for damage limitation. The collapse of land-based aristocracy is irreversible. But its noxious aftereffects can be mitigated by the deft introduction of popular self-rule. Democracy in a political sense can relieve the agony caused by democracy in the social sense.

The inherent defects of democratic government

On the other hand, that popular government, as Tocqueville describes it, could offer an efficient remedy to a massive problem appears highly unlikely. Political democracy itself, after all, is massively deficient on almost every conceivable dimension. Tocqueville denies being hostile to democratic politics. But he cannot prevent himself from being "sincère."[22] His sincerity takes the form of a scathing exposé of democratic political life.

He explains, for starters, that democratic governments tend to handle public business with lavish incompetence: "It is incontestable that the people often manage public affairs very badly."[23] As a legislative system, representative democracy is woefully inadequate: "its laws are almost always defective or untimely."[24] This is not surprising, since the vast majority of human beings are chronically myopic and exhibit little self-control. Thus, "the American people let themselves get intoxicated by their passions and carried away by their ideas."[25] But if this is true, how can there be a democratic remedy for a democratic ailment? Will not the cure be worse than the disease?

The paradox deepens as Tocqueville's analysis unfolds. Elections are simply another forum in which people give free rein to "the democratic sentiment of envy."[26] Admirable qualities are rare among elected officials in the United States. A lack of leisure time for forming an accurate assessment of the candidates and even a lack of ability to distinguish the able from the incompetent obstruct the emergence of gifted leaders. But envy of the talented – which, incidentally, presupposes a capacity to recognize who they are – is also involved: "the natural instincts of democracy lead the people to keep men of distinction from power."[27] The problem of mediocre elected officials is heightened by the unwillingness of talented men to throw their hats into the ring. In an egalitarian and commercial society, individuals of great ambition would prefer to pursue wealth rather than political power – except, interestingly enough, in times of emergency or national crisis.[28]

In any case, the politicians who are ordinarily elected have no ability to lead. They are almost wholly passive and enslaved. Anxious to polish the royal apple, courtiers once volunteered their wives and daughters as mistresses to the king. American politicians go them one better. Before the sovereign majority, they prostitute themselves.[29] This is not surprising because "in America, the people are a master who must be indulged to the utmost possible limits."[30] Andrew Jackson in particular is singled out as the majority's predictably ill-mannered creature.[31]

The ultimate source of the defects of popular government is the obtuseness of the majority itself. The majority urges its elected officials to attack the national bank without having the slightest idea of what the national bank is or does.[32] Because the majority is chronically impulsive, majoritarian politics leads to legislative and administrative instability.[33] Part of the problem is that new representatives are elected every term, rinsing away all memory of what the government has been doing even in the recent past: "After one brief moment of power, officials are lost again amid the everchanging crowd."[34]

But the source of the problem, Tocqueville repeats, lies within the majority itself, with its psychological immaturity and rashness. It is shortsighted and unable to formulate long-term goals.[35] When it makes plans, it fails to stick to them. It is unable to act in a regular or methodical manner.[36] The majority cannot make continuous efforts. It cannot withstand "over a long period the great storms that beset a nation's political existence."[37] Focusing on the future, it forgets the past, building new prisons, for example, leaving the old ones unreformed.[38] Summing up, Tocqueville says: "A democracy finds it difficult to coordinate the details of a great undertaking and to fix on some plan and carry it through with determination in spite of obstacles. It has little capacity for combining measures in secret and waiting patiently for the result."[39] Democratic government can never accomplish great deeds. Described in this way, representative democracy certainly sounds more like a problem than a solution.[40]

The diagnosis becomes grimmer, and the paradox more paradoxical, when Tocqueville turns to consider the cornerstone of democratic politics, "publicity." Public discussion, he asserts, has a tendency to intensify social conflicts: "In the heat of the struggle each partisan is driven beyond the natural limits of his own views by the views and excesses of his adversaries, loses sight of the very aim he was pursuing, and uses language which ill corresponds to his real feelings and to his secret instincts."[41] Freewheeling and wide-open debate does not guarantee the triumph of truth. Instead, it encourages political polarization, ideological intransigence, and a general loss of contact with reality.

To this dangerous side effect of public discussion must be added the problems of information overload that accompany full freedom of communication. Tocqueville claims, remarkably enough, that "there is a sort of ignorance which results from extreme publicity."[42] Democratic citizens are exposed to so many opinions and so many facts that they are reduced to choosing at random. Rather than increasing the rationality of collective decisions, publicity forces citizens into making choices on wholly arbitrary grounds.

Thus far, I have focused on the incompetence and disorderliness of democratic government. But Tocqueville also has another concern: the potential oppressiveness of democratic rule. The theme of the "tyranny of the majority" will not be discussed fully here, but Tocqueville's position can be summarized as follows: There is no intellectual pluralism in the United States, and thus no serious public debate. (The passage about the dangers of public debate cited earlier refers explicitly to France.) American society is dominated by a monolithic power that cannot be escaped: "I know no country in which, generally speaking, there is less independence of mind and true freedom of discussion than in America."[43] No Molières, mocking the court before the courtiers' own eyes, have a chance to succeed in the United States.[44] Dissenters and nonconformists are swiftly brought into line: "the majority has such absolute and irresistible sway that one must in a sense renounce one's rights as a citizen and, so to say, one's status as a man when one wants to diverge from the path it has marked out."[45] What is repugnant about America is the scarcity of guarantees erected against such stifling tyranny.[46]

Reading passage after passage of this sort in which democratic government is dissected and denounced, we begin to think that Tocqueville has either forgotten his political aim or never took it seriously in the first place. Undressed in this way, American democracy appears an unlikely model for the French to imitate. How can something as defective as democratic politics solve the fundamental problems produced by social leveling?

Yet, despite all its highly visible defects, "democratic liberty applied to the state's internal affairs brings blessings greater than the ills resulting from a democratic government's mistakes."[47] The advantages of democracy are great enough to overcome democracy's formidable flaws. How is this possible? Egalitarian societies, Tocqueville believes, are liable to four distinct ills for which democratic government, although incompetent and potentially tyrannical, provides a partial cure. These ills are (1) a deficit of authority, (2) the prestige of radical factions, (3) Bonapartist dictatorship, and (4) the psychological torpor that results from an exclusive concentration on private life.

Creating obedience to the law

With the progressive erosion of religious piety and class deference, why will most people feel obliged to abide by the law? This was a central question posed by reactionary theorists in France. To them Tocqueville answered that political democracy, despite its drawbacks, does one thing very well: It motivates ordinary citizens to obey the law. Laws are ineptly drafted in a democracy, but at least people observe them.[48] No one will attack the institution of private property if he owns some property himself. Similarly, the less fortunate members of society can be induced to respect authority simply by being given a piece of authority.

If allowed to participate in governance, through public discussion and the periodic election of public officials, they will voluntarily comply with governmental decisions.[49] If French elites envy the law-abidingness of Americans, they should consider its cause: "The Americans rightly boast of their obedience to the laws. But one must add that in America legislation is made by the people and for the people."[50] For one thing, even indirect participation in lawmaking increases the chances that ordinary citizens will know the content of the law.[51] Moreover, self-government produces a psychological tendency to obey the law which cannot be explained simply by the fact that democratic laws serve the interests of the governed. Indeed, "however annoying a law may be, the American will submit to it, not only as the work of the majority but also as his own doing; he regards it as a contract to which he is one of the parties."[52] People are emotionally attached to their government because they take part in it.[53] They take an interest in the prosperity of their country not only because it is personally beneficial, but also because *they* have created it.[54] Democratic citizens, and this includes those who are outvoted, feel implicated in the laws passed by a popularly elected assembly. These are *their* laws, to which they, and everyone else, must submit.

Democratic government would be impossible, of course, if the losers in electoral politics were not willing to acquiesce in the decisions made by the winners. Focusing on this point, Tocqueville assures his readers that, in the United States, "all parties are ready to recognize the rights of the majority because they all hope one day to profit themselves by them."[55] Anticipation of one day becoming members of a winning coalition leads all citizens to treat the majority's right to decide as something precious that must be preserved. They obey others in the hope of being eventually obeyed themselves.

Reactionary theorists, such as Joseph de Maistre and Louis de Bonald, argued that laws will be respected only if ordinary subjects consider them to be necessary or inevitable, to be expressions, for example, of God's immutable will. When popular government is well established, Tocqueville replies, the opposite is the case. People obey the law not because it is necessary, but because it is contingent. They submit to the law today because they know they could change it tomorrow.[56] It is easier to tolerate a nuisance if one knows that, with enough effort, it could be removed. (Notice that the contrary thesis – that burdens become heavier when we perceive them as contingent – is the core argument of *L'Ancien régime*.) Analogously, ordinary people defer to the authority of public officials because they know they could oust them from office in the next election.[57]

Domesticating radical factions

Probably the most striking example of Tocqueville's attempt to subvert reactionary ideology is his argument about universal suffrage. He admits, first of all, that universal suffrage hands the fate of society over to the poor.[58] This is exactly what the opponents of extending the right to vote most feared. To chip away at their opposition, he first contends that halfway solutions are intrinsically unstable. By the 1830s, the suffrage had already been extended to affluent members of the middle class. Once traditional restrictions on the franchise have been lifted, however, there is nothing that can stop them from being abolished altogether.[59] But his real argument appeals not to the necessity but rather to the utility of universal suffrage – its utility from a conservative and counterrevolutionary point of view.

The most persuasive argument against political freedom is that it permits the growth of violent and uncompromising factions. Tocqueville himself suggests as much in his remarks about public discussion just cited. In any case, French reticence about a right of association (there was no such right in France until 1901) stirred him to argue that "freedom of political association is not nearly as dangerous to public peace as is supposed."[60] For one thing, if associations are legally accepted, secret societies, very difficult for the police to monitor, will disappear "in countries where associations are free, secret societies are unknown. There are factions in America, but no conspirators."[61] The diffusion of liberties, paradoxically enough, makes society easier to control.

In a modern nation such as France, public opinion is going to make itself felt in one way or another. If public opinion cannot express itself through political associations, newspapers, and electoral politics, then it will be channeled into mob violence. Referring to *l'opinion publique*, Tocqueville states that "in America it works through elections and decrees, in France by revolutions."[62] Popular government, in other words, is a safety valve. It vents public steam, and prevents society from blowing up.

Universal suffrage must be seen in the same light. As the experience of 1793–4 revealed, the most dangerous faction is one that acts in the name of the majority of citizens. In any egalitarian society, the will of the majority necessarily has enormous moral prestige. A crazed minority faction, such as the Jacobins, persuasively confiscating the name of the majority, can perpetrate unthinkable atrocities. How can this problem be solved? The only effective solution is to construct political institutions that make it impossible for minority factions convincingly to claim the right to speak for the majority. Only one institution can do this: universal suffrage.

Perhaps universal suffrage is the most powerful of all the elements tending to moderate the violence of political associations in the United States. In a country with universal suffrage the majority is never in doubt, because no party can reasonably claim to represent those who have not voted at all. Therefore associations know, and everyone knows, that they do not represent the majority.[63]

In the absence of universal suffrage, faction leaders claim to speak for the people as a whole.[64] And who can prove that they do not?

Where the franchise is severely restricted, moreover, factions become conspiratorial, aggressive, and swollen with a sense of their own holy mission. They operate according to "military ways and maxims."[65] They become Leninist, one might say. Universal suffrage changes all this, cordializing militant factions into democratic parties, ready to compromise. Above all, when the franchise is extended, radical factions "lose the sacred character belonging to the struggle of the oppressed against the oppressor."[66] Universal suffrage will not only make impossible the dictatorship of Paris over France. It will desacralize radical groups, diminishing their prestige in the public eye. Not ultimate values, it will appear, but group interests alone are at stake.

The chance to achieve one's aims through persuasion and electioneering is a social sedative. It takes the wind out of radical sails. Similarly, the more frequently elections are held, the less bitterness and frustration will the losers feel.[67] And the less inclined will they be to destroy the entire system by insurrection. In sum, Tocqueville has turned ultraroyalism upside down: The more democratic the system, the less revolutionary it will be.

Preventing Caesarism

Popular government generates social loyalties and a widespread willingness to obey the law. It also dampens the zeal and undermines the status of political militants and radicals. Its third function, in Tocqueville's eyes, is to prevent the reappearance of a Bonapartist dictatorship: "I foresee that if the peaceful dominion of the majority is not established among us in good time, we shall sooner or later fall under the *unlimited* authority of a single man."[68] Of all four arguments advanced for the desirability of political democratization, this one is the least fully developed. Caesarism was less frequently on his mind in the 1830s than it became with the sudden return of Bonapartism in the early 1850s, when he was writing the *Ancien régime*. In any case, his basic claim is simple to state. If citizens become wholly absorbed in private life, particularly in economic affairs, they will leave the political stage free to be taken over by an ambitious strongman. "Greed for prosperity," he says, "hands over" privatized citizens "to the first master who offers himself."[69] When citizens focus exclusively on their private advantages, these private advantages, too, may be lost. Unlike France, America is protected against incipient Bonapartism by the intensity of popular attention to public affairs.[70]

This argument could obviously have appealed to a much broader spectrum of French public opinion than the first two. Archreactionary and militantly antidemocratic forces were not the only ones who might have feared a new Napoleon. Thus, it is revealing that Tocqueville mentions this idea in passing but devotes to it none of the careful elaboration he provides for his other arguments. This imbalance suggests, once again, that French conservatives and reactionaries were the principal audience he had in mind.

The "greatest advantage" of democratic government

John Stuart Mill claimed that, taken together, freedom of the press, public discussion, periodic elections, and a broad suffrage will produce political decisions that are more intelligent than decisions made by closed and autocratic regimes.[71] Tocqueville would have heartily disagreed. Representative democracies consistently produce foolish decisions. What makes such regimes valuable are not their policies and laws, but their indirect social effects. To perceive these hidden advantages, of course, takes acute vision, which most observers lack: "The vices and weaknesses of democratic government are easy to see; they can be proved by obvious facts, whereas its salutary influence is exercised in an imperceptible and almost secret way. Its defects strike one at first glance, but its good qualities are revealed only in the long run."[72] This is a typically Tocquevillean passage. Democracy is good, but not for the reasons its ridiculous advocates believe. Tocqueville can reveal the true advantages of democratic government, because he, unlike most other observers, attends to hidden, indirect, and long-term consequences.

Of public men Tocqueville wrote condescendingly that "in democracies they bring about good results of which they have never thought."[73] A hidden hand was at work within the political domain itself. Today, the justification of democratic processes by invoking side effects that are unnoticed and unintended by the parties involved seems deeply unsatisfactory. We tend to believe that justifications of public institutions should themselves be "public." The true reason an institution is valuable should be precisely the reason the institution is widely accepted. Tocqueville, however, lived in a somewhat different moral world. He

took for granted justification by secret and unintended side effects. At
the time, the most common example of justification by an unintended
(and unintendable) result was religion. Religion is socially useful. It
reconciles the poor to their poverty and provides morally feeble individuals with an anesthetic against the pangs of mortality. These are
powerful justifications for admiring religion as a social institution, but
they cannot possibly be reasons for an individual to accept religion as
true. Tocqueville's justifications of democracy have a similar structure.
They, too, violate the "publicity condition" for moral legitimacy.

What, then, according to Tocqueville, is "le plus grand avantage du
gouvernement démocratique"? What is the main unintended side effect
that makes democratic government so desirable, despite its multiple
flaws? He formulates his point this way: "It is certainly not the elected
magistrate who makes the American democracy prosper, but the fact
that the magistrates are elected."[74] By electing their rulers and indirectly making their laws, democratic citizens produce mediocre governance
and shoddy legislation. But they simultaneously transform themselves
into more energetic and active individuals: "Democracy does not provide a people with the most skillful of governments, but it does that
which the most skillful government cannot do: it spreads throughout the
body social a restless activity, superabundant force, and energy never
found elsewhere, which, however little favored by circumstance, can do
wonders. *Those are its true advantages.*"[75] Democratic government does
everything less well, but it does more things.[76] And it disseminates a
tremendous energy throughout the social world. What you find in
America is not competent administration or stability of views, scrupu-
lous attention to details or well-oiled procedures; "what one does find is
a picture of power, somewhat wild perhaps, but robust, and a life liable
to mishaps but full of striving and animation."[77] What justifies representative democracy is this effervescence penetrating into all spheres of
life: "That constantly renewed agitation introduced by democratic government into political life passes, then, into civil society. Perhaps,
taking everything into consideration, that is the greatest advantage of
democratic government."[78] The main benefit of government through
popularly elected representatives is social vitality. Democracies are not
good at marshaling their resources or using them efficiently. They even
tend to confiscate acquired wealth. But what they do, by way of compensation, is to produce many more resources and much more wealth
than any other kind of government.[79] They do this indirectly, by defus-
ing a spirit of activity and cooperative adventurism throughout civil
society.

In his "Conclusion' to the first volume of *Démocratie*, Tocqueville contemplates the glorious expansionism of the "English race" in North America. It is spreading unstoppably across the continent. In "lower Canada," by contrast, a few hundred thousand Frenchmen huddle together pathetically, sticks-in-the-mud. What accounts for this difference, so humiliating to the French? Tocqueville's answer is that traditions of local self-government were missing among his countrymen: "Free peoples accustomed to municipal government find it much easier than do others to establish flourishing colonies. The habit of thinking for oneself and governing oneself is indispensable in a new country, where success is bound to depend in great measure on the individual effort of the colonists."[80] The British came to the New World with habits of self-reliance formed in the context of town government.[81] Political participation energized the British character, preparing Britain's victory in the great European contest to colonize the New World.

We should take a moment to admire the structure of Tocqueville's argument thus far. Although both societies are based on legal equality, the United States is superior to France along two dimensions. America is both safer and more energetic than France. It is both less revolutionary and more on the move. Democracy, in the social sense, has brought political instability and psychological torpor to France. In the United States, by contrast, legal equality has been associated with political stability and a kind of heroic restlessness. What is the source of the difference? France has succumbed to the worst consequences of social leveling because it has continued to resist democracy in the political sense. Resistance to liberalization has made the country more dangerous politically and less vital economically. America, by contrast, has muffled the damaging impact of legal equality by introducing political self-rule. It has found a democratic cure for a democratic disease.

The paradox of political associations

The idea of a political cure for social ills, of a democratic remedy for a democratic disease, is probably what Tocqueville had in mind when he referred to the "mother idea" unifying *Démocratie en Amérique*. Nevertheless, the book is much too rich in disconnected insights to be boiled down to a single formula. The therapeutic role Tocqueville ascribes to religion, for example, does not fit comfortably into the "democracy cures democracy" scheme.[82] But the way Tocqueville supplements, deviates from, and eventually subverts his central thesis can best be explored by looking first at his famous chapter on the relation between political and economic associations.

Rulers in countries such as France, where legal equality has been

established, are deeply suspicious of political associations but are warm-
ly supportive of associations in the economic sphere. The former appear
dangerously conspiratorial, a threat to the government's monopoly on
power. The latter, by contrast, seem beneficial for two reasons: (1) They
distract men's minds from public affairs, and (2) they discourage revolution by getting people involved in delicate and long-term projects for
which public tranquility is essential.[83] But the contrary attitudes they
display toward these two sorts of association simply reveal how inept
today's rulers are at causal thinking. They fail to perceive "le noeud
caché" (the hidden link) connecting political and economic associations.[84] Thus, "in avoiding one dangerous ill they deprive themselves of
an efficacious remedy."[85] Cooperation is contagious. Daily experience
of political associations gives citizens the idea of civil associations.[86] In
other words, "when a people has a political life, the idea of associations
and eagerness to form them are part of everybody's everyday life."[87]
Democratic cooperation helps overcome the "natural distaste" people
feel for working in common.[88] In sum, "politics spread a general habit
and taste for association."[89] And, if rulers were up to the occasion, this
beneficial side effect could prove to be useful indeed.

The idea that people can become immensely powerful if they act in
concert is not self-evident. How can such an important lesson be
learned? Only by democratic politics. The palpable advantages people
gain by political cooperation teach them the value of association in
general. (This analysis, incidentally, assumes that democratic government is much less incompetent than Tocqueville had earlier claimed.)
Citizens are drawn together politically, and the personal contacts they
make in the political arena are easily renewed for the purpose of
establishing economic cooperation. It is easy to introduce people to the
values of association this way, because nobody worries about losing
money when they join a political association.[90] Once inside such a body,
individuals learn how to make a large group function effectively (what
procedures to adopt, etc.), and they learn how to subordinate themselves for a common purpose. As a result, "one may think of political
associations as great free schools to which all citizens come to be taught
the general theory of association."[91]

Notice that a selective banning of political associations, leaving economic associations free, will not be effective. For one thing, the public
stigma attached to political associations will discredit economic associations in the public mind. Ordinary people will interpret a government
prohibition as a sign that there is something disreputable about associations in general.[92] True, the government can give them the opportunity
to associate economically; but they will have lost the desire to do so.

The inclination to associate for any reason whatsoever will have been killed by the prohibition of political associations.[93]

If all associations, including political ones, are permitted, by contrast, people will come to think of association as a normal affair. They will then rush eagerly to join economic associations, becoming distracted from public affairs and engaged in long-term ventures that require public tranquillity. The validity of this analysis is confirmed by America, a counterrevolutionary's dream. Americans are single-mindedly at work on complex projects "which would be thrown into confusion by the slightest revolution."[94] The result should make every French ruler green with envy: "these people who are so well occupied have no temptation to disturb the state or to upset the public calm by which they profit."[95]

The causal chain leading to this marvelous result is easy to trace. Through political associations, the Americans have not only learned the art of economic association, they have also gained a taste for it. They transport their associative habits, inclinations, and skills "into the affairs of civil life and put them to a thousand uses."[96] On the basis of this subtle analysis, Tocqueville is able to formulate his remarkable paradox of political associations, another thumb in the reactionary eye: "By the enjoyment of a dangerous liberty, the Americans learn the art of rendering the dangers of freedom less formidable."[97] The cure for freedom is more freedom. At some historical moments and in the short run, perhaps, political associations can be dangerous. But, in general, "the freedom of political association favors the welfare and even the tranquillity of the citizens."[98]

Democratic politics and commercial life

Participation in political associations favors public tranquillity by driving citizens into private life! More politics produces less politics! This strange argument is just another, more memorable version of Tocqueville's general thesis that political energies, created by republican institutions, will spill over into civil society. He had already presented the claim quite eloquently in these terms in Volume I. Democratic politics will certainly lead to "prodigious industrial expansion."[99] As a participant in collective efforts, each citizen is psychologically encouraged to invest in his own property: "Daily new improvements to communal property are suggested to him, and that starts him wishing to improve his own."[100] Putting the experience of political associations to use in the commercial sphere leads to quick results: "great political freedom improves and spreads the technique of association. Thus freedom [in ages of equality] is particularly favorable to the production of wealth."[101] In sum, democratic politics brings prosperity and makes commercial society thrive. Taken alone, this argument seems plausible enough. But when Tocqueville elaborates on the idea, as he does in Volume II, it assumes a quite different shape. To describe the main accomplishment of public involvement in politics as the eventual withdrawal of citizens from the political realm is, without doubt, to carry the art of paradox to a new height.

Unfortunately, according to Tocqueville's own analysis, the absorption in private affairs which guarantees tranquillity will also expose society to a Bonapartist *coup* and even to the politics of arbitrary confiscation. An active polity spawns an active economy. But if the economy becomes all-absorbing, citizens will cease participating in politics altogether. After all, there are only twenty-four hours in a day. Economic success, as a result, necessarily cuts into the energy that can be allocated to public affairs. Privatization may solve the problem of revolution, but it produces the problem of Caesarism. The more robust, lively, and time-consuming economic life becomes, the greater is the threat it poses to political freedom and, indirectly, to economic prosperity as well.

Perspectives on commercial society

Tocqueville's whole analysis of the relation between democratic government and commercial life displays more richness than coherence. Before delving further into the subject, in any case, I want to make two preliminary points.

First of all, in his criticism of *Démocratie*, J. S. Mill said that Tocqueville had confused "commercialism" with "equality." The two are not necessarily linked. England, which combines a powerful class system with a booming commercial economy, is only the most obvious example. Whatever the virtue of this criticism, it focuses attention usefully on an important feature of Tocqueville's analysis. When Tocqueville says that democratic politics can solve the problems of "democracy" in a social sense, he means to include, without further explanation, the problems of commercial society. I have already mentioned some of these problems, especially the unwanted political and economic effects of excessive privatization. But Tocqueville probably puts greatest emphasis on the destructive effects of commercialism on the individual's soul. One great virtue of democratic politics, in his eyes, is that it can solve this problem, can re-elevate the debased character of commercial man.

Second, Tocqueville did not approach the problems of commercial society in a value-neutral way. Biblical and chivalric norms (inconsistent among themselves) conspired to produce in his mind a general feeling of revulsion toward commercial activity. The romantic movement, always in the background, had a similar effect. Commerce may not be the worst thing one person can do to another; but it is selfish, petty, tawdry, and low. The *Kulturkritik*, the nose-in-air critique of commercial civilization, running throughout the book has a significant effect on the shape of Tocqueville's argument.

Political cures for commercial ills

Among its other virtues, democratic politics rescues modern individuals from the degrading focus on their own well-being encouraged by commercial society. A succinct formulation of this thesis is the following: "The Americans have used liberty to combat individualism born of equality, and they have won."[102] The main defect of a commercial or hyperindividualistic society is a general pettiness of soul. Democratic politics provide a cure for the disgraceful personal traits typical of a commercial people. How can we get individuals today to rise above their selfishness and greed? There is but one persuasive answer: "it is only passion for freedom, habitually enjoyed, which can do more than hold its own against a habitual absorption in well-being."[103] The beneficial effects of political participation on the individual far outweigh the defects of majoritarian government. True, ordinary people are certain to bungle the handling of public affairs, "but their concern therewith is bound to extend their mental horizon and shake them out of the rut of ordinary routine."[104] Democratic government is a machine for awakening, stretching, and enlivening the mind. It lifts individuals above themselves and engages them in the concerns of others, in the problems of the whole community.

Taken by itself, this analysis is clear enough. It becomes incredibly confusing, however, when we try to integrate it with what Tocqueville says elsewhere about the relationship between democratic government and economic life. The basic contradiction in Tocqueville's approach to this question, reduced to its essentials, is that democratic government has two effects: (1) It launches citizens into the exciting adventure of commerce, and (2) it rescues them from the filthy ditch of commerce. Political participation both propels energized individuals *into* the economic domain and rescues enervated individuals *from* the economic domain. There may be a way to make these two claims coherent, but Tocqueville provides no clue of how this might be done. Moreover, the commercialism–democracy pattern he traces is even more complex than this apparent contradiction suggests.

For one thing, Tocqueville does not consistently describe the economic sphere as degraded. He does not stick to the idea that commercial and industrial activity is wholly devoid of meaning. Notice the striking claim: "For an American the whole of life is treated like a game of chance, a time of revolution, or the day of battle."[105] When Tocqueville refers to the whole of life here, he principally means economic life. The American, in fact, puts "a sort of heroism in his greed for gain."[106] For much the same reason, Tocqueville writes, bizarrely, of "grandeur commerciale." Grandeur is wholly incompatible with ordinary venality; so Tocqueville discovers greatness of soul in Americans only because "in the end they come to love enterprises in which chance plays a part. This draws them to trade not only for the sake of promised gain, but also because they love the emotions it provides."[107] Here commercial life is motored by what Tocqueville calls an "immaterial interest." Economic activity is not instrumental but consummatory. Even without politics, it gives meaning to life. In commerce as well as politics, people love the activity more than the result. In general, Americans do not consider their economic efforts as "costs" that must be repaid by corresponding "benefits." On the contrary, in America, effort expended is counted among the benefits: "No men are more attached to their own way of life, which would lose its savor if they were relieved of the anxieties which harass them. They love their cares more than aristocrats love their pleasures."[108] This statement expresses clearly Tocqueville's refusal to stigmatize economic life as a sphere of meaningless drudgery from which individuals must be heroically rescued by democratic politics.

Commercial cures for political ills

The appropriateness of analyzing the commercialism–democracy relation according to an asymmetrical cures–ills scheme is also thrown into doubt by another aspect of Tocqueville's analysis. In some situations, commercialism may provide an indispensable remedy for the defects of political democracy itself. Consider one of the problems presented by frequent elections. Those in office will have a large incentive to subvert the entire system if, on being ousted, they will not be able to land a suitable job. Luckily, "in the United States it is so easy to establish an independent position that the official who loses his place may be deprived of the comforts of life but not of the means of subsistence."[109] In other words, a lively economy provides an essential prop for a democratic polity.

Even more important is the way commercialism helps quell the danger of democratic factionalism. Commerce is a social coolant. Americans are political active, without being revolutionary, because "they carry a trader's habits over into the business of politics."[110] The commercial ethic has more or less the same effect on the political temperature as universal suffrage. It demilitarizes factions and domesticates them into parties ready to compromise: "Love of wealth therefore takes the place of ambition, and prosperity quenches the fire of faction."[111] Involvement in economic ventures is "an efficacious remedy" for revolutionary ambitions; it distracts men from politics, and, "getting them more and more occupied with projects for which public tranquillity is essential," it discourages "thoughts of revolution."[112] Economic prosperity also increases social mobility. Rapid upward and downward mobility (from rags to rags in three generations) may seem chaotic; but it actually softens potential social cleavages, making class warfare more unlikely.

Mutual support of the public and private realms

What all this suggests is that being saved from commerce by politics may be desirable in some situations. In other settings, however, people may instead need to be saved from politics by commerce. Tocqueville, however, seldom presents his insights in such a "balanced" way. He prefers the extreme and one-sided formulation, the exaggeration that catches fire in the reader's eye. Nonetheless, with the commentator's advantage, we can see that he must have meant something of this sort. The escape from commerce into democratic politics is good, but not too good. It should definitely not be carried to an extreme. The same could be said about the escape from democratic politics into commerce. The ideal society is one in which a balance is struck between economic and political life.

This happy coexistence of public and private spheres, strikingly enough, is precisely what Tocqueville found in the United States. Democratic politics and a commercial economy are mutually supportive. There is "a close and necessary link between these two things, that is, freedom and industry."[113] America is a commercial republic. It encourages energetic participation in both economic and political life. This is the unusual behavior Tocqueville observed: "An American will attend to his private interests as if he were alone in the world; the moment afterward, he will be deep in public business as if he had forgotten his own."[114] In America, there is no inherent contradiction or incompatibility between the public and the private. That is one reason why the United States is wholly unlike the classical republics of the ancient world.[115] The value of political participation is not premised on the disvalue of economic life. Indeed, Americans do not enter into politics to leave their economic concerns behind. No romantic "transcending" of self-interest is involved. Rather, Americans are mobilized politically to protect their interests, materially understood.[116] Political democracy does not require citizens to transcend their interests. On the contrary, it guarantees coincidence of the interests of the governors and the governed.[117] Thus, it is not surprising that "American legislation appeals mainly to private interest."[118] Just as each individual is the best judge of his own interests, so is each electoral district.[119] A concern for oneself does not lead to a neglect of one's neighbor only because each citizen is aware of "the close connection between his private profit and the general interest."[120] Tocqueville asks the question, "how does it come about that each man is as interested in the affairs of his township, of his canton, and of the whole state as he is in his own affairs?"[121] His answer is that the citizens take an interest in democratic politics because democratic politics serves their interests.

There is nothing about *this* discussion to suggest any sort of disdain or distaste for self-interest as such. For example, Americans are praised as being "enlightened, awake to their own interests, and accustomed to take thought for them."[122] Democratic legislation may be poorly formulated, but it nevertheless tends to benefit mankind.[123] There is something universalistic about a regime founded in this way on self-interest: "The moral authority of the majority is also founded on the principle that the interest of the greatest number should be preferred to that of those who are fewer."[124]

The mutually supportive relation of public and private action explains why Tocqueville can describe Americans, in a way that seems contradictory at first, as wholly devoted to both politics and money. On the one hand, "I know of no other country where love of money has such a grip on men's hearts."[125] Similarly, "the passions that stir the Americans most deeply are commercial and not political ones."[126] On the other hand: "It is hard to explain the place filled by political concerns in the life of an American. To take a hand in the government of society and to talk about it is his most important business and, so to say, the only pleasure he knows."[127] Moreover, the meaning of life in America is derived wholly from politics: "If an American should be reduced to occupying himself with his own affairs, at that moment half his existence would be snatched from him; he would feel it as a vast void in his life and would become incredibly unhappy."[128] Life in the United States is neither too public nor too private. The American citizen is a hybrid creature: an economicopolitical man.

Straddling two traditions

What sets Tocqueville apart from other theorists, then, is that he refuses to rely on political or economic mechanisms alone, but insists on seeing them in tandemn. To speak anachronistically, but illustratively, Tocqueville does not view politics, as Hannah Arendt does, as merely a beautiful alternative to the base economic sphere. And unlike Milton Freidman, he does not view commercial life as a self-sufficient realm, flourishing best when wholly freed from the damaging intrusions of politics. Tocqueville takes a middle road between liberal economics and classical politics. That is what makes his position unique.

Another way to describe the singularity of his standpoint is this: He straddled the eighteenth and nineteenth centuries. Like Stendhal, he had one foot in the Enlightenment and the other in the Romantic movement. In the eighteenth century, it is crude but not wholly inaccurate to say, "enthusiasm" was a derogatory term. Hot passions were looked upon as highly dangerous and, as Albert Hirschman has shown, positive attitudes toward commerce were partly due to a sense that the cool and steady passion of self-interest could help suppress volatile and violent passions such as vengefulness, malice, and yearning for glory. Tocqueville certainly retains this idea, as several citations have already shown. But he combines it with an entirely new and, to some extent, opposite idea – an idea characteristic of the romantic reaction against the Enlightenment. The trouble with the modern age, he repeatedly says, is that it is *boring*. Our passions are tepid. What we need is a reawakening of "great passions."

It is impossible to imagine a mainstream Enlightenment author, such as David Hume, expressing nostalgia for heroic passions. But Tocqueville's romantic critique of American commercialism bursts forth repeatedly. Consider this: "There is nothing more petty, insipid, crowded with paltry interests – in one word, antipoetic – than the daily life of an American."[129] Alternatively, the American people are "the coldest, most calculating, the least militaristic, and if one may put it so, the most prosaic in all the world."[130]

So where do Tocqueville's final sympathies lie? With the Enlightenment or with Romanticism? Does he want peace or excitement? Tranquillity or grandeur? Are passions a problem or a solution? Is self-interest a source of political stability or a sign of moral degradation? Is commerce an exhilarating adventure or a stream of sewage? These questions spin in the reader's head. Tocqueville answers them all with both/and.

The basic pattern of relations which Tocqueville traces between commercial and political life is quite complex; but it is, at least provisionally, susceptible to a synoptic or schematic presentation. In brief, commerce and democratic politics are mutually interdependent. Each solves problems produced by the other. And each encourages the formation of habits that, when carried into the other domain, have beneficial consequences.

Political cures for political ills

Another aspect of the paradox of political associations can now be considered. The pattern Tocqueville describes in that case does not refer to a political cure for a social ill. The ill in question is itself political (dangerous political associations), while the cure is directly political (complete freedom of political association) and indirectly economic (the proliferation of industrial and commercial associations). To say that Tocqueville is proposing *a cure for a cure* may sound confusing. But it accurately conveys the labyrinthine quality of the argument he makes.

Tocqueville obviously believes that democratic government is plagued by defects. Consolation can be drawn, of course, from its beneficial side effects, especially economic prosperity. But Tocqueville is not satisfied with this consideration. He also draws our attention to various ways in which the problems of democratic government can be *solved*. He is especially concerned with a number of mechanisms by which democracy's tendency to majority tyranny can be thwarted: "freedom is in danger when [the sovereign people] finds no obstacle that can restrain its course and give it time to moderate itself."[131] To preserve freedom, obstacles must be set up. Cures must be found for the ills of democratic government itself.

Recall, in this regard, Tocqueville's discussion of the "anticipation effect" whereby members of an outvoted minority respect the majority's decision in the hope and expectation that they, too, will someday be part of a winning coalition and will then need minority compliance. When advancing that argument, Tocqueville surprisingly does not mention the contrary effect. Members of an electoral majority might also treat the outvoted minority with tenderness, expecting one day to fall into the minority themselves and to have need of majority self-restraint. This omission could be a sign that he believes most people to be fundamentally optimistic. In discussing jury trials, however, he explicitly mentions the way decision makers are inhibited by anticipating that the tables will eventually be turned: "Juries teach men equity in practice. Each man, when judging his neighbor, thinks that he may be judged himself."[132] This passage makes all the more anomalous the omission of a corresponding argument in the discussion of majority rule. By neglecting this self-inhibiting mechanism, Tocqueville makes majoritarian politics seem more unshackled than it actually turns out to be. Why would he have done this?

One reason may be that American conformism solves a key problem of democratic politics. Wide-open debate produces ideological polarization and fuels factional animosity. In the United States, conformist pressures guarantee that there is no real debate. This may seem deplorable, but it is actually advantageous. Conformism makes Americans dull; but it also provides a social cure for a terrible political ill.

Implicitly, moreover, Tocqueville *does* rely on the argument that a majority in power will be self-limiting. Consider a passage, late in the book, where it appears. Here again, he suggests a democratic cure for a democratic disease: "a democratic education is necessary to protect women against the dangers with which the institutions and mores of democracy surround them."[133] His basic argument is this: In the new egalitarian and commercial society, female chastity cannot be protected in the old authoritarian manner, by giving girls a cloistered education, sheltering them totally from the world. It is much more effective to habituate young girls to take responsibility for themselves. If you expose them to the dangerous consequences of their own unwise choices at an early age, you will induce habits of sobriety and self-control that will be useful later on, when you are no longer around to hold their hands.[134] Substitute "the people" for "young girls" here, and you have an argument for the self-restraint learned by majorities that are thrust into decision-making roles. Liberalization is safe. Authoritarianism is dangerous. The best way to control the mass of Frenchmen is to give them access to political power.

He applies this argument quite explicitly to democratic government. Following Edmund Burke, French conservatives typically condemned the French revolutionaries for their abstract rationalism. Exploiting this conservative obsession, and transforming it ingeniously into an argument for democratic reform. Tocqueville argues that ordinary people will be cured of abstractions once they are saddled with day-to-day responsibility for the governance of their communities. Self-government produces fact-minded and practical citizens. For complex psychological reasons, all egalitarian societies promote abstract thinking. But "the best possible corrective" for this dangerous proclivity is "to make the citizens pay daily, practical attention" to public affairs.[135] The cure is distasteful, but effective. "That is how democratic institutions which make each citizen take a practical part in government moderate the excessive taste for general political theories which is prompted by equality."[136] To awaken reactionary sympathies, Tocqueville portrays democratic institutions as saddles strapped onto the sagging backs of the lower orders. Democracy *compels* subjects to be involved in political decision making, and thereby mitigates the noxious side effects of egalitarian culture. It does not merely allow commoners access to some hitherto forbidden fruit.

Antidemocratic cures for democratic ills

Tocqueville also describes various constitutional and semiconstitutional devices as essential mechanisms for inhibiting the tyrannical potential of majoritarian politics. In America, the executive branch is wholly unfit to limit the enormous power of Congress: "Beside the legislature, the President is an inferior and dependent power."[137] Above all, the Constitution guarantees that he cannot lead. Because he is "reeligible . . . the President of the United States is only a docile instrument in the hands of the majority."[138] So the executive branch provides no obstacle to democratic tyranny.

Bicameralism, by contrast, with an upper chamber that is *indirectly elected*, is a perfect example of a tyranny-prevention device. By such an arrangement, the majority's will is respected, but also "in some sense refined."[139] The people are represented, but in a nicely discriminating fashion. In national politics, moreover, *federalism* helps preserve public tranquillity by obstructing the rapid communication of mass hysteria: "Political passions, instead of spreading like a sheet of fire instantaneously over the whole land, break up in conflict with individual passions of each state."[140] Surprisingly enough, compartmentalization makes the union more stable.

(Note, parenthetically, that in the case of the American Indians, federalism was a tool of majority tyranny. What did the federal government do with the Indians? It "handed them over as subjects to the legislative tyranny of the states."[141] But that is not the whole story. The federal and state governments actually cooperated in the mass extermination of the aboriginal population of North America. The states brutally harassed the Indians and drove them westward, while the national government enticed them to leave peacefully by offering them promises of free land: "The states' tyranny forces the savages to flee, and the Union's promises make flight easy."[142] Federalism, in other words, was a kind of nice guy–tough guy routine whereby the Indians were cajoled into doing the white man's bidding at the lowest possible cost to the European settlers.)

In any case, the most important device for suppressing the tyrannical potentials of majoritarian politics is the judiciary: "The extension of judicial power over the political field should be the correlative to the extension of elected power."[143] Not judges alone, but lawyers, too, and even legal culture itself, help remedy the defects of democratic government: "the prestige accorded to lawyers and their permitted influence in the government are now the strongest barriers against the faults of democracy."[144] Unlike other elites, lawyers are trusted by the people.[145] This feeling is not exactly mutual, for lawyers have "a great distaste for the behavior of the multitude and secretly scorn the government of the people."[146] Their appetite for formality clashes rudely with the attitudes of most people.[147] They are "naturally strongly opposed to the revolutionary spirit and to the ill-considered passions of democracy."[148] In this sense, lawyers reinforce the moderating influence of commercialism, universal suffrage, indirect elections, bicameralism, and so forth. They do not want to overthrow democracy, however, but merely to "guide it."[149] In summarizing these points, Tocqueville cannot restrain himself from another memorable exaggeration: "In the United States . . . the legal body forms the most powerful and, so to say, the only counterbalance to democracy."[150]

It is immediately on the heels of this remarkable passage about lawyers as the unique counterweight to democracy that Tocqueville inserts his famous discussion of the jury system. Juries have several functions, according to Tocqueville. On the one hand, they improve the soul: "By making men pay attention to things other than their own affairs, they combat that individual selfishness which is like a rust in society."[151] Here again, jury verdicts are not particularly intelligent. But even if this system is not good for the litigants, it is good for the jurors themselves. (Once again, Tocqueville runs afoul of the "publicity" requirement. For moral benefits to the jurors, regardless of the effects on the plaintiff and defendant, cannot possibly be a public justification for the jury system.)

The jury system also has a political effect. It apparently gives those who serve an education in the laws, and teaches them responsibility as well. Thus, Tocqueville can conclude his discussion with the ringing statement that "the jury is the most effective way of establishing the people's rule and the most efficient way of teaching them to rule."[152] The jury system, seen from this perspective, is the cradle of popular sovereignty.

Tocqueville's explanation of what actually happens during a jury trial, however, does not support this inspiring conclusion. True, the jury is a school of virtue; but the schoolmaster is always present to lead his pupils around by the nose. What is the relation between the judge and the jurors in a civil trial? "He has almost unlimited influence over them," and "his intelligence completely dominates theirs."[153] The reason for his preeminent role is that the common law is simply too complicated for laymen to understand. There is no suggestion here that this asymmetry could ever be overcome by periodic jury duty. The judge will always stage-manage the trial and secretly control the jury's verdict. In this school, you might say, the students are never allowed to graduate. The jury system, in fact, is an example of pseudo democracy. The pretence of popular power is merely the screen for keeping power in the hands of an antidemocratic elite: "the jury, though seeming to diminish the magistrate's rights, in reality enlarges his sway, and in no other country are judges so powerful as in those where the people have a share in their privileges."[154] What looks like popular power is actually the power of a judicial elite.

In summary: Tocqueville's analysis of the jury system is irreducibly ambiguous because it suggests (1) that, as they become educated by judges, the people learn to rule themselves; and (2) that the heterono-mous arrangement whereby "the jurors pronounce the decision made by the judge"[155] will and should last forever. Like political associations, the jury system is a democratic cure for a democratic ill. Like the con-stitutional "obstacles" to majority tyranny it is, simultaneously, an antidemocratic cure for a democratic ill.

Local government

That Tocqueville believed it possible to "regulate" postaristocratic soci-ety constitutionally is beyond question. But he always coupled legal regulation with regulation by habits and moral character, noting that "the Americans have shown that we need not despair of regulating democracy by means of laws and mœurs."[156] Here, it seems, is a prime lesson for the French to learn: "My aim has been to show, by the American example, that laws and more especially mores can allow a democratic people to remain free."[157] What the example of the United States shows is that *moeurs* themselves can be introduced by laws, in particular by laws establishing local government. By giving local author-ities power over important questions, the lawmaker shapes the emotion-al attachment of citizens, for "in general, men's affections are drawn only in directions where power exists."[158]

Tocqueville frequently stresses the tyranny-preventing function of decentralized power. Referring to "excesses of despotism," he states that "a democracy without provincial institutions has no guarantee

against such ills."[159] Similarly, "municipal bodies and county administrations are like so many hidden reefs retarding or dividing the flood of
the popular will."[160] On this account, local government has a purely
negative and countermajoritarian function. Municipal institutions are
antidemocratic obstacles to the popular will. Indeed, according to Tocqueville's "reoccupation thesis," political associations and municipal
government "take the place" occupied by the nobility in the Middle
Ages. From this point of view, such institutions have a purely power-
checking and antidemocratic purpose. But Tocqueville claims that local
government is a remedy for license as well as for absolute power.[161] This
addition suggests that decentralized decision-making bodies have a positive function, alongside their negative one. Besides checking or hinder-
ing individuals, they can enlist and mobilize them: "The diverse municipal laws struck me as being so many barriers restraining the citizens'
restless ambition within a narrow sphere *and turning to the township's*
profit those very passions which might have overthrown the state."[162]
This passage seems promising, but vague. The whole gist of Tocqueville's argument, however, especially his emphasis on the morally uplifting
effect of participation in local politics, shows the inadequacy of the
negative or antimajoritarian interpretation of local government.

In an important passage, Tocqueville says explicitly that the decentralized system grew up in American by an historical sequence that
cannot possibly be reproduced in France.[163] In the legislative assembly
of 1849, a fellow deputy introduced a proposal for strengthening local
government, asserting that political participation at the local level was a
key to educating Frenchmen in the tasks of democracy. Interestingly
enough, Tocqueville dismissed the proposal as naive and impracticable.
This suggests that he was ultimately pessimistic about the possibility of
introducing decentralized schools of political virtue in France.[164]

The transition to democracy

Tocqueville's ultimate doubts about the usefulness in France of the
American model are expressed most persuasively in his account of the
transition to democracy in the two cases. French reactionaries tended to
draw conclusions about democracy itself from observations about the
revolutionary transition to democracy.[165] Traits of the transition,
however, should be distinguished clearly from traits of the state reached
after the transition. The fact of equality should not be confused with the
revolution that brings it about. Counterrevolutionaries are right to point
out the terrible social strains involved in moving from an aristocratic to a
democratic social state. Such a dramatic change is bound to be difficult:

"There can be no doubt that the moment when political rights are granted to a people who have till then been deprived of them is a time of crisis, a crisis which is often necessary but always dangerous."[166] But conservatives are wrong to conclude that this dangerous situation will persist after democracy is firmly established. Political instability owes as much to the lack of experience of democracy as to democracy itself.

By singling out the transition to democracy as a special social condition, deserving separate consideration, Tocqueville was inevitably drawn to examine the different way France and America accomplished the transit. He sums up his findings in a memorable sentence: "The Americans have this great advantage, that they attained democracy without the sufferings of a democratic revolution and that they were born equal instead of becoming so."[167] The French achieved legal equality by a bloody civil war. The decade 1789–99 brought *une violente révolution . . . chez un peuple très civilisé.*[168] French democracy was founded by forcing a king, an ecclesiastical establishment, and an aristocracy to give way. This end could not be achieved without "a prolonged struggle" and "in the course of that struggle implacable hatreds have been engendered between the classes."[169] The Americans achieved it more peacefully: A branch of the British tree simply broke off, floated across the Atlantic, and established roots in the ideal soil of North America. The colonists were middle-class dissenters who left king, established church, and landed nobility behind, and "men equal among themselves came to people the United States."[170] This unusual origin, according to Louis Hartz, is responsible for the remarkable absence of violent class struggle in American history. One egalitarian society was born amid violence, tumult, and sharp political polarization; the other came into being with fewer birth pangs, in a much less dramatic way.[171]

For anyone committed to the usefulness of the American model in France, this entire analysis is far from consoling. The two societies developed in totally different ways. Assuming that the outcome is "path dependent," it is unlikely that France has any important lessons to learn from the United States.

François Guizot said of Tocqueville: *C'est un vaincu qui accepte sa défaite* ("He is a defeated man who accepts his defeat"). This was not always true, although it became so. Tocqueville began his book with high hopes. At the outset, when he was barely twenty-five years old, his aim was to save France. It was this aim, combined with personal ambition, that propelled him to write *Démocratie.* As he progressed in his analysis, however, he saw the rescue of France become more and more remote. Accordingly, the book's "mother idea" underwent a subtle transformation. Increasingly aware of the many differences between the two countries of his concern, Tocqueville insisted that "one can imagine a democratic nation organized in a different way from the American people."[172] But his hope for reform was definitely on the wane. In several key passages his ultimate fatalism and resignation broke unmistakably through. Perhaps the most important of these passages is this:

> If ever a democratic republic similar to that of the United States came to be established in a country in which earlier a single man's power had introduced administrative centralization and had made it something accepted by custom and by law, I have no hesitation in saying that in such a republic despotism would become more intolerable than in any of the absolute monarchies of Europe. One would have to go over into Asia to find anything with which to compare it.[173]

The Bourbonist and Bonapartist legacies doomed French democracy to an unhappy course. Strategies for damage limitation were essentially a waste of time.

If he could no longer save France, what was Tocqueville able to do? Only one thing: satisfy his curiosity about the success of democratic politics in the United States, the failure of democratic politics in France. This is the puzzle Tocqueville wants to crack, as he tells us in the clearest possible terms: "The United States goes on being a democratic republic, and *the main object of this book* is to make clear the reason for this phenomenon."[174] Here was a "mother idea" that a pessimistic reformist manqué could fully embrace. Why was the United States able to maintain a stable democracy while other countries found this so difficult to achieve? The main factors Tocqueville mentions are these: (1) cheap land, which reduced the pressures on the political system from the poor; (2) the absence of any significant military threat;[175] (3) no tradition of hostility between republicanism and religion; (4) no city comparable in size, centrality, and population to Paris; (5) no aristocratic past needing to be overthrown by violence; and (6) the existence of the frontier, as an outlet for the ambitions of restless citizens.[176] This list could probably be extended. But the main point to note is that none of these conditions for a successful democracy could be imitated in France. Just so, America's "cultural fragment" method of making the crucial transition to legal equality was wholly beyond imitation. Eliminating reactionary resistance to political liberalization could have little effect compared to such a massive array of social conditions and causal forces. In the end, the "principal aim" of *Démocratie* became a gloomy one: to show that reform along the lines of American democracy was wholly impossible in France.

In some ways, the United States serves the same function in Tocqueville's thinking as Sparta served in the thought of Rousseau. It is Tocqueville's image of an ideal society that, for various reasons, cannot be imitated in France. He began to describe America as would a reformer, encouraging imitation. He ended up describing it in a much more pessimistic, though still analytically brilliant, way. The Americans have discovered a democratic cure for a democratic disease. This is what the French have been looking for. This is what the French will never be able to find.

Tocqueville concludes his chapter on civil and political associations in precisely this spirit. He cites two passages from Volume I in which he had argued that, on balance, the freedom of political association is simply too dangerous to be accepted in any pure or unlimited form. He had begun by asserting that the Americans have benefited immensely from "an unlimited freedom of political association."[177] But he ends on a skeptical note: "I even doubt whether there has ever been at any time a nation in which it was wise not to put any limits to freedom of association."[178] Freedom of political association would certainly bring great benefits; it has already brought them in the United States. But in France it would probably promote internal disorder, contempt for the law, and political instability. Fear of such calamities fully justifies important restrictions on the right to form political associations. So Tocqueville is clearly not proposing reform. The intellectual merits of his analysis are apparent, but what is left of his practical aim? In the end, he merely wants to make sure that his countrymen know what a terrible political and economic price they have to pay, to avoid anarchy, as they have to do: "To save a man's life, I can understand cutting off his arm. But I don't want anyone to tell me that he will be as dexterous as without it."[179] America is not a model to imitate. It is a barbaric land, in a way, but it is also an image of an unreachable perfection. Its function is not to motivate reform but simply to make Frenchmen wince with the painful recognition of how badly off they are, and will remain.

Notes

1 "Ceux qui voudront y regarder de près retrouveront, je pense, dans l'ouvrage entier, une pensée mère qui enchaîne, pour ainsi dire, toutes ses parties." *De la Démocratie en Amérique* (Paris: Gallimard, 1961), vol. 1, p. 13; 20. (Unless otherwise indicated, all citations will be of this edition, followed by the corresponding page number of the Lawrence translation.)
2 1, 322; 308.
3 Lawrence trans., 195; "l'extrême liberté corrige l'abus de la liberté, et . . .

l'extrême démocratie prévient les dangers de la démocratie" (1, 200). My assumption throughout is that Tocqueville's reputation for political wisdom is largely unearned. The idea cited here, for example, is too coquettish to be wise. But it does provide Tocqueville an opportunity to display his real talent – not his wisdom but his genius, his unmatched sociological imagination.

4 "Il ne faut pas oublier que l'auteur qui veut se faire comprendre est obligé de pousser chacune de ses idées dans toutes leurs conséquences théoriques, et souvent jusqu'aux limites du faux et de l'impracticable" (1, 13; 20).

5 Raymond Aron, *Main Currents of Sociological Thought* (Harmondsworth: Penguin, 1968), vol. 1, pp. 185–8.

6 That is: "les différentes classes dont un peuple aristocratique se compose étant fort séparées les unes des autres et se connaissant mal entre elles, l'imagination peut toujours, en les représentant, ajouter ou ôter quelque chose au réel" (2, 78; 484).

7 In his words, "dans un pays où les citoyens, devenus à peu près pareils, se voient tous de fort près, et, n'apercevant dans aucun d'entre eux les signes d'une grandeur et d'une supériorité incontestables, sont sans cesse ramenés vers leur propre raison comme vers la source la plus visible et la plus proche de la verité" (2, 12; 430).

8 Lawrence trans., p. 667; the independence born of equality "les dispose à considérer d'un œil mécontent toute autorité, et leur suggère bientôt l'idée et l'amour de la liberté politique" (2, 295).

9 The causal relation is loose, according to Tocqueville's account, because, among other reasons, equality creates a countervailing desire to *submit* to authority.

10 4 December 1831, to Hyppolyte de Tocqueville, *Selected Letters on Politics and Society*, edited by Roger Boesche (Berkeley: University of California Press, 1985), p. 66

11 Remember that he and Beaumont went to America officially, in a Benthamite spirit, in order to conduct research for prison reform in France.

12 1, 324; "prudently introduced into society" (310).

13 Lawrence trans., 18; "j'ai voulu y trouver des enseignements dont nous puissons profiter" (1, 11).

14 Lawrence trans., 17; "ennemis de tous les progrès" (1, 10).

15 Lawrence trans., 9; referring to the "grande révolution démocratique," he wrote that some people "la considèrent comme une chose nouvelle, et, la prenant pour un accident, ils espèrent pouvoir encore l'arrêter" (1, 1).

16 Lawrence trans., 513; "Beaucoup de gens en France considèrent l'égalité des conditions comme un premier mal, et la liberté politique comme un second" (2, 112).

17 "Vouloir arrêter la démocratie paraîtrait alors lutter contre Dieu même" (1, 5; 12); this is a striking proposition when juxtaposed to the ultraroyalist claim, found in Joseph de Maistre, for example, that the *proponents* of democracy had declared war against God.

18 *Selected Letters*, p. 66.

19 Preface to the twelfth edition, Lawrence trans, p. xiv; "Presque toute l'Europe était bouleversée par des révolutions; l'Amérique n'avait pas même d'émeutes" (xliv).

20 Lawrence trans., 182; "L'Amérique est peut-être en ce moment le pays du monde qui renferme dans son sein le moins de germes de révolution" (1, 187).

21 Lawrence trans., 311; "Les Américains . . . ont appliqué des remèdes dont eux seuls, jusqu'à présent, se sont avisés; et quoiqu'ils fussent les premiers à en faire l'essai, ils ont réussi" (1, 325).

22 2, 8; 418; when Americans read his account, they will reject it loudly, in apparent shock and disgust; but in their hearts they will know he is right.

23 Lawrence trans., 243; "Il est incontestable que le peuple dirige souvent fort mal les affaires publiques" (1, 254).

24 Lawrence trans., 232; "ses lois sont presque toujours défectueuses ou intempestives" (1, 242).

25 Lawrence trans., 268; "le peuple américain se laisee enivrer pas ses passions, ou se livre à l'entraînement des ses idées" (1, 280).

26 Lawrence trans., 310; "le sentiment démocratique de l'envie" (1, 325).

27 Lawrence trans., 198–9; "les instincts naturels de la démocratie portent le peuple à écarter les hommes distingués du pouvoir" (1, 205). This passage is difficult to reconcile with Tocqueville's claim that the population elects a candidate because "elle a conçu une très vaste idée de son mérite" (2, 94; 498).

28 1, 211; 204–5. There is a mistranslation in the Lawrence text here, suggesting that the Americans certainly would elect talented men if these men only presented themselves; Tocqueville actually says he does not know if they would (cf. *Souvenirs*).

29 1, 270; 259.

30 Lawrence trans., 64; "Le peuple, en Amérique, est un maître auquel il a fallu complaire jusqu'aux dernières limites du possible" (1, 60).

31 1, 410; 393.

32 1, 182; 178; see also 1, 406; 388–9.

33 For example, "L'instabilité législative est un mal inhérent au gouvernement démocratique" (1, 260); 249; see also the reference to "une mutabilité singuilière dans la législation" (1, 209; 202).

34 Lawrence trans., 207; 1, 214; for this and other reasons, representative democracy keeps poor records, making competent administration impossible.

35 1, 233; 223.

36 "Democratic freedom does not carry its undertakings through as perfectly as an intelligent despotism would; it often abandons them before it has reaped the profit" (Lawrence trans., 244; 1, 255).

37 Lawrence trans., 223, 1, 232.

38 1, 261; 250.

39 Lawrence trans., 229; "la démocratie ne saurait que difficilement coordonner

les détails d'une grande entreprise, s'arrêter à un dessein et le suivre ensuite obstinément à travers les obstacles. Elle est peu capable de combiner des mesures en secret et d'attendre patiemment leur résultat" (1, 238–9).

40 Corruption of democratic leaders is contagious.

41 Lawrence trans., 16; "Animé par la chaleur de la lutte, poussé au delà des limites naturelles de son opinion par les opinions et les excès de ses adversaires, chacun perd de vue l'objet même de ses poursuites et tient un langage qui répond mal à ses vrais sentiments et à ses instincts secrets" (1, 9). This "publicity trap" became a central theme in the *Souvenirs*.

42 Lawrence trans., 610; 2, 231.

43 Lawrence trans., 254–5; "Je ne connais pas de pays où il règne, en général, moins d' indépendance d'esprit et de véritable liberté de discussion qu'en Amérique " (1, 266).

44 1, 267; 256.

45 Lawrence trans., 258; 1, 269.

46 1, 263; 252. Note that Tocqueville follows Madison here in his discussion of oppression by factious majorities (260); but he *never* mentions Madison's solution to the problem, the role of the central government in tempering majority factionalism in the states.

47 Lawrence trans., 228; "la liberté démocratique appliqué aux affaires intérieures de l'Etat produit plus de biens que les erreurs du gouvernement de la démocratie ne sauraient amener de maux" (1, 238).

48 1, 251; 240–1.

49 1, 249; 238.

50 Lawrence trans., 224; "On vante avec raison l'obéissance que les Américains accordent aux lois. Il faut ajouter qu'en Amérique la législation est faitre par le peuple et pour le peuple" (1, 234).

51 "C'est en participant à la législation que l'Américain apprend à connaître les lois; c'est en gouvernant qu'il s'instruit des formes du gouvernement" (1, 318; 304).

52 Lawrence trans., 241; "Quelque fâcheuse que soit la loi, l'habitant des Etats-Unis s'y soumet donc sans peine, non seulement comme à l'ouvrage du plus grand nombre, mais encore comme au sien propre; il la considère sous le point de vue d'un contrat dans lequel il aurait été partie" (1, 251); this argument should be compared with the claim, advanced later, that women who enter into marriage on a wholly voluntary basis are more tightly bound by the marriage contract – and will be socially sanctioned in a more severe manner if they break it – than those whose marriages are arranged and compelled (2, 209–11; 592–4).

53 1, 67; 70 and 1, 247; 237.

54 The average American exhibits this paternal pride, in addition to his concern for private advantage: "il s'intéresse à la prosperité de son pays, d'abord comme à une chose qui lui est utile, et ensuite comme à son ouvrage" (1, 246; 236).

55 Lawrence trans., 248; "Aux Etats-Unis . . . tous les partis sont près à

reconnaître les droits de la majorité, parce que tous ils espèrent pouvoir un jour exercer à leur profit" (1, 259); also "celui qui aujourd'hui ne fait pas partie de la majorité sera peut-être demain dans ses rangs" (1, 251; 240).

56 "Au reste, le peuple en Amérique n'obéit pas seulement à la loi parce qu'elle est son ouvrage, mais encore parce qu'il peut la changer" (1, 252; 241).

57 "Dans les démocraties, la majorité pouvant chaque année enlever le pouvoir des mains auxquelles elle l'a confié, ne craint point non plus qu'on en abuse contre elle. Maîtresse de faire connaître à chaque instant ses volontés aux gouvernants, elle aime mieux les abandonner à leur propres efforts que de les enchaîner à une règle invariable" (1, 212; 205).

58 That is, "le vote universel donne donc réellement le gouvernement de la société aux pauvres" (1, 281; 210).

59 "Lorsqu'un peuple commence à toucher au cens électoral, on peut prévoir qu'il arrivera, dans un délai plus ou moins long, à le faire disparaître complètement" (1, 56; 59).

60 Lawrence trans., 523; "la liberté d'association en matière politique n'est point aussi dangereuse pour la tranquillité publique qu'on le suppose" (2, 125).

61 Lawrence trans., 193; "dans les pays où les associations sont libres, les sociétés secrètes sont inconnues. En Amérique, il y a des factieux, mais point de conspirateurs" (1, 198).

62 Lawrence trans., 124; "en Amérique, il procède par des élections et des arrêts; en France par des révolutions" (1, 126).

63 Lawrence trans., 194; "Mais de toutes les causes qui concourent aux Etats-Unis à modérer les violences de l'association politique, la plus puissante peut-être est le vote universel. Dans le pays où le vote universel est admis, la majorité n'est jamais douteuse, parce que nul parti ne saurait raisonnablement s'établir comme le repréntant de ceux qui n'ont point voté. Les associations savent donc, et tout le monde sait qu'elles ne représent point la majorité" (1, 200).

64 "En Europe, il n'y presque point d'associations qui ne prétendent ou ne croient représenter les voluntés de la majorité" (1, 200; 194–195).

65 Lawrence trans., 195; 1, 200.

66 Lawrence trans., 195; 1, 201.

67 1, 208; 202.

68 Lawrence trans., 315; "je prévois que si l'on ne réussit point avec le temps à fonder parmi nous l'empire paisible du plus grand nombre, nous arriverons tôt ou tard au pouvoir *illimité* d'un seul" (1, 330).

69 Lawrence trans., 539; 2, 146–7.

70 "The political activity prevailing in the United States is something one could never understand unless one had seen it" (242; 1, 253).

71 *On Liberty* and *Considerations on Representative Government*.

72 Lawrence trans., 231; "Les vices et les faiblesses du gouvernement de la démocratie se voient sans peine; on les démontre par des faits patents, tandis

que son influence salutaire s'exerce d'une manière insensible, et pour ainsi dire occulte. Ses défauts frappent du premier abord, mais ses qualités ne se découvrent qu'à la longue" (1, 241).

73 235; "ils produisent le bien sans en avoir la pensée" (1, 245).

74 Lawrence trans., 512; "Ce n'est point le magistrat élu qui fait prospérer la démocratie américaine; mais elle prospère parce que le magistrat est électif" (2, 112).

75 Lawrence trans., 244, my emphasis; "La démocratie ne donne pas au peuple le gouvernement la plus habile, mais elle fait ce que le gouvernement le plus habile est souvent impuissant à créer; elle répand dans tout le corps social une inquiète activité, une force surabondante, une énergie qui n'existent jamais sans elle, et qui, pour peu que les circonstances soient favorables, peuvent enfanter des merveilles. Là sont ses vrais avantages" (1, 255).

76 "La liberté démocratique . . . fait moins bien chaque chose, mais elle fait plus de choses" (1, 255; 244).

77 Lawrence trans., 92–3; "ce qu'on y trouve, c'est l'image de la force, un peu sauvage il est vrai, mais pleine de puissance; de la vie, accompagnée d'accidents, mais aussi de mouvements et d'efforts" (1, 92–3).

78 Lawrence trans., 243; "Cette agitation sans cesse renaissante, que le gouvernement de la démocratie a introduite dans le monde politique, passe ensuite dans la société civile. Je ne sais si, à tout prendre, ce n'est pas là le plus grand avantage du gouvernement démocratique" (1, 254).

79 Lawrence trans., 224; 1, 233 and 1, 216; 209.

80 Lawrence trans., 409; "les peuples libres et habitué au régime municipal parviennent bien plus aisément que les autres à créer de florisante colonies. L'habitude de penser par soi-même et de se gouverner est indispensable dans un pays nouveau, où le succès dépend nécessairement en grande partie des efforts individuels des colons" (1, 426n).

81 "A l'époque des premièrs émigrations, le gouvernement communal, ce germe fécond des institutions libres, était déjà profondément entré dans les habitudes anglaises" (1, 28; 33).

82 That politics, and politics alone, must provide the solution to the problems of commerce is by no means obvious from Tocqueville's account (2, 140–1; 534–5).

83 2, 125; 523.

84 2, 125; 524.

85 Lawrence trans., 523; "en évitant un mal dangereux ils se privent d'un remède efficace" (2, 125).

86 Notice that the spillover effect *does* go both ways: "Les associations civiles facilitent donc les associations politiques" (2, 122; 521); although Tocqueville considers this reverse effect of little importance.

87 Lawrence trans., 521; "Quand un peuple a une vie publique, l'idée de l'association et l'envie de s'associer se prédentent chaque jour à l'esprit de tous les citoyens" (2, 122).

88 Lawrence trans., 521; 2, 122.
89 Lawrence trans., 521; "la politique généralise le goût et l'habitude de l'association" (2, 122).
90 2, 123; 521.
91 Lawrence trans., 522; "Les associations politiques peuvent donc être considérées comme de grandes écoles gratuites, où tous les citoyens viennent apprendre la théorie générale des associations" (2, 123).
92 "Being in doubt, people steer clear of them altogether, and in some vague way public opinion tends to consider any association whatsoever as a rash and almost illicit enterprise" (522; 2, 124).
93 "En vain leur laisserez-vous l'entière liberté de s'occuper en commun de leur négoce; ils n'useront que nonchalamment des droits qu'on leur accorde" (2, 124; 523).
94 Lawrence trans., 523; 2, 125.
95 Lawrence trans., 523; "ces gens si bien occupés ne sont point tentés de troubler l'Etat ni de détruire un repos public dont ils profitent" (2, 125).
96 Lawrence trans., 524; "Ils transportent ensuite dans la vie civile les notions qu'ils ont ainsi acquises et les font servir à mille usages" (2, 126).
97 Lawrence trans., 524; "C'st donc en jouissant d'une liberté dangereuse que les Américains apprennent l'art de rendre les périls de la liberté moins grands" (2, 126).
98 Lawrence trans., 524; "la liberté d'association en matière politique est favorable au bien-être et même à la tranquillité des citoyens" (2, 126).
99 Lawrence trans., 244; 1, 255.
100 Lawrence trans., 244; "On lui indique tous les jours de nouvelles améliorations à faire à la propriété commune; et il sent naître le désir d'améliorer celle qui lui est personnelle" (1, 254–5).
101 539; "La liberté, dans ces siècles, est donc particulièrement utile à la production des richesses" (2, 147).
102 Lawrence trans., 511; "Les Américains ont combattu par la liberté l'individualisme que l'égalité faisait naître, et ils l'ont vaincu" (2, 110).
103 Lawrence trans., 663; "il n'y a que la passion et l'habitude de la liberté qui puissent lutter avec avantage contre l'habitude et la passion du bien-être" (2, 290).
104 Lawrence trans., 244; "mais le peuple ne saurait se mêler des affaires publiques sans que le cercle de ses idées ne vienne à s'étendre et sans qu'on ne voie son esprit sortir de sa routine ordinaire" (1, 254).
105 Lawrence trans., 404; "Pour un Américain, la vie entière se passe comme une partie de jeu, un temps de révolution, un jour de bataille" (1, 422).
106 Lawrence trans., 347; "une sorte d'héroïsme dans son avidité pour le gain" (1, 363).
107 Lawrence trans., 553; the Americans "finissent par aimer toutes les entreprises où l'hazard joue un rôle. Ils sont donc tous portés vers le commerce, non seulement à cause du gain qu'il leur promet, mais par l'amour des émotions qu'il leur donne" (2, 162).

108 Lawrence trans., 610; "Ils trouveraient la vie sans saveur, si on les délivrait des soins qui les tourmentent, et ils se montrent plus attachés à leurs soucis que les peuples aristocratiques à leurs plaisirs" (2, 230).

109 Lawrence trans., 130; "Aux Etats-Unis, il est si facile de se créer une existence indépendante, qu'ôter à un fonctionnaire la place qu'il occupe, c'est quelquefois lui enlever l'aisance de la vie, mais jamais les moyens de la soutenir" (1, 132).

110 Lawrence trans., 285; "ils transportent dans la politique des habitudes du négoce" (1, 298).

111 Lawrence trans., 306; "L'amour des richesses y prend donc la place de l'ambition et le bien-être y éteint l'ardeur des partis" (1, 320). Perhaps a slack commercial life explains why democratic government is so unsuccessful in South America, despite the geographical advantages and well-drafted constitutional rules, so similar to those found in North America (1, 235–6; 226).

112 Lawrence trans., 523; "les engageant de plus en plus dans des projets qui ne peuvent s'accomplir sans la paix publique, les détournent des révolutions" (2, 125).

113 Lawrence trans., 539; "Il y a donc un lien étroit et un rapport nécessaire entre ces deux choses: liberté et industrie" (2, 146).

114 Lawrence trans., 541; "Un Américain s'occupe de ses intérêts privés comme s'il était seul dans le monde, et, le moment d'après, il se livre à la chose publique comme s'il les avait oubliés" (2, 148).

115 1, 316; 302.

116 1, 66; 69.

117 It is essential, he says, that "les gouvernants n'aient point d'intérêts contraires ou différents de la masse des gouvernés" (1, 243; 233).

118 Lawrence trans., 79; "Mais c'est surtout à l'intérêt particulier que la législation américaine en appelle" (1, 78).

119 The logical inference from this premise to a federalist conclusion is quite striking: "chacun est le meilleur juge de ce qui n'a rapport qu'à lui-même, et le plus en état de pouvoir à ses besoins particuliers. La commune et le comté sont *donc* chargés de veiller à leurs intérêts spéciaux" (1, 81, my emphasis; 82).

120 Lawrence trans., 511; 2, 111.

121 Lawrence trans., 236; "d'où vient que chacun s'intéresse aux affaires de sa commune, de son canton et de l'Etat tout entier comme aux siennes mêmes?" (1, 247).

122 Lawrence trans., 90–1; "le peuple est éclairé, éveillé sur ses intérêts, et habitué à y songer" (1, 90).

123 Les lois de la démocratie tendent, en général, au bien du plus grand nombre" (1, 242; 232).

124 Lawrence trans., 247; "L'empire moral de la majorité se fonde encore sur ce principe, que les intérêts du plus grand nombre doivent être préférés à ceux du petit" (1, 258).

125 Lawrence trans., 54; 1, "je ne connais même pas de pays où l'amour de l'argent tienne une plus large place dans le cœur de l'homme" (1, 50).

126 Lawrence trans., 285; "Les passions qui agitent le plus profondément les Américains sont des passions commerciales et non des passions politiques" (1, 298). Tocqueville goes on to qualify this statement with a phrase cited above to the effect that Americans rather transport commercial habits into politics.

127 Lawrence trans., 243; the essential sentence is: "Se mêler du gouvernement de la société et en parler, c'est la plus grande affaire et pour ainsi dire le seul plaisir qu'un Américain connaisse" (1, 253–4).

128 Lawrence trans., 243; "Du moment, au contraire, où l'Américain serait réduit à ne s'occuper que de ses propres affaires, la moitié de son existence lui serait ravie; il senterait comme un vide immense dans ses jours, et il deviendrait incroyablement malhereux" (1, 254).

129 485; "On ne saurait rien concevoir de si petit, de si terne, de si rempli de misérables intérêts, de si antipoétique, que la vie d'un homme aux Etats-Unis" (2, 79).

130 Lawrence trans., 278; the American people "est, à coup sûr, le plus froid, le plus calculateur, le moins militaire, et, si je puis m'exprimer ainsi, le plus prosaïque de tous les peuples du monde" (1, 290).

131 Lawrence trans., 251–2; "je crois la liberté en péril lorsque ce pouvoir ne trouve devant lui aucun obstacle qui puisse retenir sa marche et lui donner le temps de se modérer lui-même" (1, 263).

132 Lawrence trans., 274; "Le jury . . . enseigne aux hommes la pratique de l'équité. Chacun, en jugeant son voisin, pense qu'il pourra être jugé à son tour" (1, 286).

133 Lawrence trans., 592; "il faut une éducation démocratique pour garantir la femme des périls dont les institutions et les mœurs de la démocratie l'environnent" (2, 208).

134 *Souvenirs*.

135 Lawrence, 442; 2, 26.

136 Lawrence trans., 442; "C'est ainsi que les institutions démocratiques, qui forcent chaque citoyen de s'occuper pratiquement du gouvernement, modèrent le goût excessif des théories générales en matière politique, que l'égalité suggère" (2, 26).

137 Lawrence trans., 124; "Le président est placé à coté de la législature, comme un pouvoir inférieur et dépendant" (1, 126).

138 Lawrence trans., 138; "Rééligible . . . le président des Etats-Unis n'est qu'un instrument docile dans les mains de la majorité" (1, 140).

139 Lawrence trans., 201; 1, 208.

140 Lawrence trans., 162; "Les passions politiques, au lieu de s'étendre en un instant, comme un nappe de feu, sur toute la surface du pays, vont se briser contre les intérêts et les passions individuelles de chaque Etat" (1, 166–7). Within each of the states, municipal and local governments have a similar effect (1, 64; 67).

141 Lawrence trans., 387; "il les livra comme des sujets à la tyrannie législative des Etats" (1, 405).

142 Lawrence trans., 337; "Les Etats, par leur tyrannie, forcent les sauvages à fuir; l'Union, par ses promesses et à l'aide de ses ressources, rend cette fuite aisée" (1, 352–353).

143 Lawrence trans., 75; "L'extension du pouvoir judiciare dans le monde politique doit donc être corrélative à l'extension du pouvoir électif" (1, 73).

144 Lawrence trans., 263; "l'autorité qu'ils ont donnée aux légistes, et l'influence qu'ils leur ont laissé prendre dans le gouvernement, forment aujourd'hui la plus puissante barrière contre les écarts de la démocratie" (1, 274–5).

145 He calls them "la seule classe éclairée dont le peuple ne se défie point" (1, 281; 269).

146 Lawrence trans., 264; "ils conçoivent un grand dégoût pour les actions de la multitude et méprisent secrètement le gouvernement du peuple" (1, 275).

147 "Men living in democratic centuries do not readily understand the importance of formalities and have an instinctive contempt for them" (Lawrence trans., 698; 2, 331).

148 Lawrence trans., 264; they are "naturellement fort opposés à l'esprit révolutionnaire et aux passions irréfléchies de la démocratie" (1, 275).

149 Lawrence trans., 266; 1, 277.

150 Lawrence trans., 268; "le corps de légistes forme dans ce pays le plus puissant, et, pour ainsi dire, l'unique contrepoids de la démocratie" (1, 280).

151 Lawrence trans., 274; "En forçant les hommes à s'occuper d'autre chose que de leur propres affaires, il combat l'égoïsme individuel, qui est comme la rouille des sociétés" (1, 286).

152 Lawrence trans., 276; "Ainsi le jury, qui est le moyen le plus énergique de faire régner le peuple, est aussi le moyen le plus efficace de lui apprendre à régner" (1, 288).

153 Lawrence trans., 275; "son intelligence domine entièrement la leur" and "Son influence sur eux est presque sans bornes" (1, 287).

154 Lawrence trans., 276; "Le jury, qui semble diminuer les droits de la magistrature, fonde donc réellement son empire, et il n'y a pas de pays où les juges soient aussi puissants que ceux où le peuple entre en partage de leurs privilèges" (1, 288).

155 Lawrence trans., 275; "Les jurés prononcent l'arrèt que le juge a rendu" (1, 287).

156 Lawrence trans., 311; "les Américains ont montré qu'il ne faut pas désespérer de régler la démocratie à l'aide des lois et des mœurs" (1, 325).

157 Lawrence trans., 315; "Mon but a été de montrer, par l'exemple de l'Amérique, que les lois et surtout les mœurs pouvaient permettre à un peuple démocratique de rester libre" (1, 329).

158 Lawrence trans., 68; "les affections des hommes ne se portent en général que là où il y a de la force" (1, 65).

159 Lawrence trans., 96; "Un démocratie sans institutions provinciales ne possède aucune garantie contre de pareils maux" (1, 96).

160 Lawrence trans., 263; "Les corps municipaux et les administrations des comtés forment donc comme autant d'écueils cachés qui rétardent ou divisent le flot de la volonté populaire" (1, 274).

161 "Ceux qui craignent la licence, et ceux qui redoutent la pouvoir absolu, doivent donc également désirer le développement graduel des libertés provinciales" (1, 96–97).

162 Lawrence trans., 311, my emphasis; "Leurs diverses lois municipales me parurent comme autant de barrières qui retenaient dans une sphère étroite l'ambition inquiète des citoyens, et tournaient au profit de la commune les mêmes passions démocratiques qui eussent pu renverser" (1, 325).

163 1, 404–5; 396–7.

164 The possibility that Tocqueville is actually a fatalist or pessimist about France is not contradicted but reinforced by his wholly unrealistic ideas about the soul-shaping powers of legal regulation. Tocqueville sounds disturbingly like Rousseau or even Robespierre, for example, when claiming that "laws can make men care for the fate of their countries. It depends on the laws to awaken and direct that vague instinct of patriotism which never leaves the human heart, and by linking it to everyday thoughts, passions, and habits, to make it a conscious and durable sentiment. And one should never say that it is too late to attempt that; nations do not grow old as men do. Each fresh generation is new material for the lawgiver" (Lawrence trans., 94–5; 1, 94–5).

165 In one and only one case, Tocqueville claims that the effects of the transition to democracy are superior to the effects of democracy itself. Striking is the accomplishment of great progress in the exact sciences at the very moment when the French were destroying the remains of the old feudal order. The achievement here was due neither to democracy, nor to the transition to democracy, but, rather, to the *violence* of the transition (2, 48; 460).

166 Lawrence trans., 239; "On ne peut pas douter que le moment où l'on accorde des droits politiques à un peuple qui en a été privé jusqu'alors ne soit un moment de crise, crise souvent nécessaire, mais toujours dangereuse" (1, 250); similarly, "Ce qui nous porte à ne voir dans la liberté d'association que le droit de faire la guerre aux gouvernants, c'est notre inexpérience en fait de liberté" (1, 199; 194).

167 Lawrence trans., 509; "Le grand avantage des Américains est d'être arrivés à la démocratie sans avoir à souffrir de révolutions démocratiques, et d'être nés égaux au lieu de le devenir" (2, 108).

168 2, 47; 460.

169 Lawrence trans., 508; "Une aristocratie ne succombe d'ordinaire qu'après une lutte prolongée durant laquelle il s'est allumé entre les différentes classes des haines implacables" (1, 107).

170 Lawrence trans., 248; the United States was "peuplés par des hommes égaux entre eux" (1, 259).

171 Louis Hartz, *The Liberal Tradition in America* (1955).
172 Lawrence trans., 309; "on peut supposer un peuple démocratique organisé d'une autre manière que le peuple américain" (1, 324).
173 Lawrence trans., 263; "S'il venait jamais à se fonder une république démocratique comme celle des Etats-Unis dans un pays où le pouvoir d'un seul aurait déjà établi et fait passer dans les habitudes, comme dans les lois, la centralisation administrative, je ne crains pas de le dire, dans une semblable république, le despotisme deviendrait plus intolérable que dans aucune des monarchies absolues de l'Europe. Il faudrait passer en Asie pour trouver quelque chose à lui comparer" (1, 274).
174 Lawrence trans., 277, my emphasis; "La république démocratique subsiste aux Etats-Unis. Le but principal de ce livre a été de faire comprendre les causes de ce phénomène" (1, 289).
175 "L'Union américain n'a point d'ennemis à combattre" (1, 320; 306); "Les Américains n'ont pas de voisins, par conséquent point de grandes guerres, de crise financière, de ravages ni de conquête à craindre" (1, 290; 278).
176 1, 295; 282.
177 Lawrence trans., 520; "Il n'y a sur la terre qu'une nation où l'on use chaque jour de la liberté illimitée de s'associer dans des vues politiques" (2, 123).
178 Lawrence trans., 524; "je doute même que, dans aucun pays et à aucune époque, il fût sage de ne pas poser des bornes à la liberté d'association" (2, 126).
179 Lawrence trans., 524; "Que pour sauver la vie d'un homme, on lui coupe un bras, je le comprends; mais je ne veux point qu'on m'assure qu'il va se montrer aussi adroit que s'il n'était pas manchot" (2, 126).

Tocqueville, commerce, and democracy

DEBRA SATZ

In his essay, "Tocqueville and Democracy," Stephen Holmes rightly focuses our attention on the paradoxical nature of Tocqueville's thought; he points out, in particular, that Tocqueville's worry about the excesses of democracy (in the social sense) led him to advocate excessive democracy (in the political sense). Other Tocquevillean paradoxes include: the observation that as individuals in a democratic social state become more alike, they become more isolated; the idea that aristocratic societies and institutions necessarily preserve liberty whereas democracies do not; the idea that social mobility and freedom produce monotony and mediocrity. In fact, Holmes's own presentation of Tocqueville is paradoxical: Holmes portrays Tocqueville as an extremist (a lover of startling and exaggerated formulations)[1] *and* as a "man of balance," a straddler between two centuries who sought a "middle road between liberal economics and classical politics,"[2] between virtue and commerce.

I intend to focus here on Holmes's argument that Tocqueville views democratic politics and commercial society as mutually reinforcing each other. I agree with Holmes that there are many passages where Tocqueville insists not only that commerce and democratic politics are two interdependent spheres, but also that each sphere transforms the other in beneficial ways.[3] However, I think this picture of two mutually supporting and interdependent spheres is oversimple: Sometimes Tocqueville worries that the spheres can come violently into conflict. In particular, he worries that commerce and democratic politics can produce opposing social psychologies.

Is this conflict inevitable? Can we separate the "spirit" of commercialism which Tocqueville admired from commerce itself? Or, rather, does the very success of commerce undermine the energetic ethos which created it? I will argue that Tocqueville believed the latter (and thereby anticipated an argument which Schumpeter gives in *Capitalism, Socialism and Democracy*). The possibility of avoiding conflict between the spheres of commerce and democratic politics depends on the existence of social conditions which, while perhaps true of America in the mid-nineteenth century (and indeed some historians have denied this), are not true of our own times. The "middle road" between commerce and virtue vanishes with the defeat of small-scale property ownership at the end of the nineteenth century. Today, we need to be much more sensitive to the ways in which commercial society and democratic society do not work in tandem.

To develop this argument, I begin with some definitions. How does Tocqueville conceive of democracy, equality, and liberty?

As Holmes points out, democracy in *Democracy in America* is not primarily a political concept, but one which is used to characterize an egalitarian social arrangement. Democracies are incompatible with legally maintained class hierarchies and caste distinctions. They are not incompatible with tyranny or the suppression of popular rule. Thus, in Tocquevillean democracy, equality is taken as a necessary condition while liberty is viewed as a problematic one. For Tocqueville, equality is the essential characteristic of a democracy. What is the nature of Tocquevillean equality? It does not entail equality of distribution of resources or welfare. It does entail, as I have suggested, formal equality, in the sense of equality before the law. But it is not limited to equality before the law. Tocqueville seems to have in mind two other characteristics of democratic equality. The first is that although an equal society can be composed of distinct social classes, there must be a non-zero probability of social mobility from one class to another. There may not be substantive equality of opportunity, but the equality of opportunity must be more than merely formal. It is, however, considerably weaker than the equality enjoined by John Rawls's fair equality of opportunity. Sometimes Tocqueville writes as if American society approximates substantive equality of opportunity; sometimes he recognizes that it does not.[4]

The second characteristic of equality is harder to specify; it concerns something like a cultural sentiment of equality. Examples of this sentiment include the expectation that one will be treated without regard to family background or social status, and the belief that differing cultural assets (including educational background, accent, and birthplace) will not translate into fixed privileges. This sentiment is supported by consumption norms which regulate acceptable manners of dress, language use, and leisure activities.

Finally, for Tocqueville liberty is primarily political liberty: Most fundamentally, it is the liberty to control the conditions of one's life and social association. This liberty is to be exercised equally by all. Lawyers, however, have a special status.[5]

To a large extent, democratic liberty, equality, and commerce can be mutually reinforcing, primarily through their psychological effects. Political participation conveys certain benefits on commercial activity:

1. political participation corrects for the privatizing effects of pursuing material interests. It creates new preferences in individuals, especially preferences for association.
2. As political participation instills in individuals the value of association, it promotes the growth of economic associations in which individuals work together toward common goals.
3. Democratic politics promotes economic expansion, by giving individuals culture and skills which are useful for commerce.

Conversely, commerce supports democratic politics. Holmes mentions two ways in which Tocqueville believes that commercialism corrects for the deficiencies of democracy:

1. Material prosperity makes political usurpation less likely by providing defeated politicians with avenues for "exit."
2. Commerce domesticates conflict; it "discourages thoughts of revolution." Commerce funnels passions into the pursuit of nonpolitical economic interests.

In addition, I think that there is a third way in which Tocqueville believes that commerce provides a support for political liberty: It creates a commercial actor who acts as an individual decision maker (autonomous from corporate groups). Tocqueville stresses the way in which commerce provides for an equalization of certain capacities (in particular, capacities of autonomous choosing) which culturally fit with the institutions of political democracy, for example, with the institution of "one person, one vote." The idea here is that commercial undertakings shape human development in a manner which cultivates individual choice, through the reliance on systems of distribution characterized by decentralization and by the possibility of exit by substantial numbers of participants.

Holmes concludes that Tocqueville's ideal society is one in which a balance is struck between economic and political life[6] and that this is precisely what Tocqueville found in America. Now most people would not dispute that commerce and political liberty can be mutually beneficial. But this mutual benefit is not necessarily the case, as Tocqueville was well aware. It depends on the presence of specific factors drawn from outside the realms of commerce and political liberty.

I have a more pessimistic reading of Tocqueville's belief in the possibility of a "middle way" between virtue and self-interest.

While commerce equalizes certain capacities between individuals (capacities of individuals as autonomous choosers), it simultaneously creates vast inequalities of wealth. Not only does unequal wealth tend to corrupt democracy, it also undermines the equal autonomous capacities of individuals that commerce initially creates.

Holmes cites Tocqueville's positive comments on commerce as a sphere of heroic activity.[7] Successful commerce, Tocqueville believes, involves more than calculation. Something more like entrepreneurial risk-taking. But it is interesting to note that Tocqueville's praise of American merchants stresses the low level of development of the division of labor:

[The American] does not find himself part of a society expertly organized to satisfy them [his desires]; consequently he often has to provide himself with the various things that education and habit have made necessary for him. In America it sometimes happens that one and the same man will till his fields, build his house, make his tools, cobble his shoes, and with his own hands weave the coarse cloth that covers him. This is bad for improving craftsmanship, but greatly serves to develop the worker's intelligence. An extreme division of labor, more than anything else whatsoever, tends to turn men into machines and to deprive the things made of any trace of soul.[8]

Now, the merchant's heroism may be partly the result of commerce (through the mechanism which creates for an autonomous actor). In the passage just cited, however, the "heroism" results from the self-reliance of the American merchant, a self-reliance fueled by commerce but incompatible with a highly developed division of labor. An extreme division of labor turns men and women into appendages to machines.

What is the relationship among commerce, inequality, and the division of labor? Inequality and the division of labor are not necessarily directly correlated. For example, under feudalism, a high degree of inequality of wealth was associated with a very undeveloped division of labor. But Tocqueville believes that, in a capitalist society without fixed limits for commercial activity, inequality and the division of labor develop together. Tocqueville mentions two "axioms" of capitalist commerce:

1. Increasing the division of labor increases the efficiency of production.
2. There are economies of scale.

The effects of these axioms are twofold: On the one hand, there is an increasing concentration and centralization of wealth. On the other, mobility in the class structure tends to decrease as the division of labor degrades the intelligence of the workers and undermines their self-reliance. Democracy becomes threatened by a new aristocracy of indus-trialists. Both axioms tend to undercut the economics of a small-scale property-owning democracy.

The autonomy which commercial activity promotes depends on the self-reliance of the commercial actor. But this self-reliance is under-mined when the commercial actor becomes a wage worker who is chained to the performance of a single, simple task. The possibility of mutually supportive interaction between commerce and liberty depends on the existence of background social conditions – in particular, on a widespread dispersion of property, which offers possibilities for a work-er's exit from degrading work conditions.

In his writings, Tocqueville tended to dismiss the threat posed by growing inequality and increasing division of labor, on four grounds:

1. The operation of these axioms is exceptional to the general condi-tion of social equality.
2. The industrialists cannot constitute themselves as a class, having no common traditions or corporate spirit.
3. Even under conditions of capital concentration and centralization, workers are free to move from one employer to another, and thus some sense of independence might be maintained.
4. There is no culture of mutual obligations that binds workers to owners, and thus no reason for workers to consent to conditions of servitude.

Is Tocqueville's dismissal of the threat commerce poses to democracy warranted? I think not. Tocqueville's response exaggerates the causal significance of cultural constraints, especially in the absence of institu-tional support. In particular, Tocqueville underestimates the extent to which workers' formal freedoms are undermined by the fact that work is no longer a sphere for the realization of autonomous capacities. The autonomous chooser created by commerce has become a part of the machine. Moreover, with the concentration and centralization of capital in private hands, the worker becomes in reality less free. For now private interests with larger resources acquire "a preponderant weight in settling social questions"[9] and the equal political liberty of citizens, a product of their more or less equal social conditions, is eroded.

In conclusion, I maintain that Tocqueville was well aware of the potential destructive effects of commerce on democratic liberty. I have pointed out the paradoxical effects commerce has on American society: It initially creates an individual who is capable of acting as an auton-omous chooser, but the development of the division of labor under-mines this capacity. Furthermore, the success of commerce erodes the small-scale property-owning basis of democracy. Unfortunately, Tocqueville provides no theory as to what kinds of economic arrangements are presuppositions for political liberty. For Tocqueville is not really even a theorist of democracy. As Holmes notes, Tocqueville's advocacy of democracy is equivocal and ambivalent; it is simply the best solution historically available to help us resolve certain dilemmas of modern society. Tocqueville's endorsement of democracy is thus not very systematic; it doesn't rest on a defense of democracy as a sphere for the development of distinctive virtues (e.g., autonomy, self-government) such as that given by Aristotle; or as an institution on which all rational agents would converge such as that proposed by those in the social contract tradition, nor does it rest on welfarist or consequentialist grounds. As Holmes emphasizes, Tocqueville's endorsement of democracy is qualified and path-dependent: The choices open to a society have a great deal to do with its historical starting points, especially its mores, or culture. Democracy is desirable only at certain points; it is not a universal ideal. Holmes ends his essay by pointing to Tocqueville's growing skepticism that his "new political science" could provide a democratic liberal model for France.

Can American society in the mid-nineteenth century provide a democratic liberal model for today? Surely Tocqueville is a great theorist of the connections between institutions and social psychology, of the culturally specific aspects of rationality. For example, his observations on the relationship between the sexes, on race, and on the links between conformism and a frenetic social openness are still trenchant and useful. Furthermore, the ideal of a small-scale property-owning democracy may be a reasonable one. But because Tocqueville says so little about the economic presuppositions of this democracy, and because he fails to deal with the effects of the Industrial Revolution on its stability, I do not think he is helpful for theorizing about democracy, at least for the United States of the present.

Notes

1 Stephen Holmes, "Tocqueville and Democracy," p. 1. All page citations refer to Holmes's original paper.
2 Holmes, p. 26.
3 Holmes, p. 27.
4 Cf. his discussion in *Democracy in America* (Garden City, N.Y.: Doubleday, Company, 1969), 54–6.
5 Cf. *Democracy in America*, 268ff.
6 Holmes, p. 24.

7 Holmes, p. 22.
8 Tocqueville, *Democracy in America*, 403.
9 John Rawls, *A Theory of Justice* (Cambridge, Mass.: Harvard University Press, 1971), 225–6.

2

Making truth safe for democracy

DAVID ESTLUND

One of the longest-standing objections to democracy alleges the ignorance of the masses.[1] Sometimes the insult is aimed at a specific group or
class of citizens, such as the *demos* of ancient Athens, but that is not the
core of the objection. Class distinctions aside, since some people are
likely to be wiser or more skilled than others on political matters, it can
seem absurd to base political decisions on the sheer number of citizens
that favor or oppose them, without regard to their relative abilities to
make such decisions well. Democrats will want to challenge the inference from the (difficult to deny) unequal distribution of political wisdom
to the superiority of authoritarian political institutions.

One way to deny it would be to resort to skepticism, to deny either
that there is normative political truth or that anyone knows it (better
than anyone else). Another way would be to emphasize the valuable
effects of democratic institutions on the character of the citizens, and
argue that these decisively favor democracy, however superior the social
decisions of more authoritarian arrangements. Instead, I will recommend, as a superior objection, an epistemic difficulty with authoritarianism, one that can be successfully pressed without resorting to
skepticism. Roughly, the problem is, Who will know the knowers? No
knower is knowable enough to be accepted by all reasonable citizens.
While the concept of reasonableness here makes the point partly a
moral one, it is still epistemological in an important way.

It may seem that the more serious problem with the idea of rulers as
moral experts is that even if they did know what ought to be done, they
may yet not try to do it. For example, there are pressures from special
interests, temptations to favor oneself, and mechanisms of self-
deception that serve to rationalize what is (otherwise) known to be
wrong. Since the self-deception point is still about the leaders' cognitive
credentials, it may be regarded as incompatible with one's having superior normative political wisdom. Outside pressures, and selfish temptations, are surely obstacles in the way of the conscientious exercise of

power. They are not, however, always insurmountable. The right combination of circumstances, institutional arrangements, and personal character apparently can often minimize the ill effects. These pressures and temptations are serious concerns if leaders are to be justified as moral experts, but they do not undermine that conception at as deep a level as I believe can be done.

The broader question that drives this inquiry is how far anti-authoritarian and other objections to the possibility of objective normative political truth should be thought to undermine the possibility of an epistemic conception of democracy, of democratic institutions as capable of ascertaining such political truths. No full theory of normative truth is developed, nor is an account of democracy's epistemic properties provided. Truth is not here *made* safe for democracy; this is only a step in that direction.

I. Normative Epistemic Authoritarianism

There is a natural association between the ideas of *truth* and *knowledge* on the one hand, and on the other hand the ideas of *expertise* and *authority*, and in turn *elite* and *power*. Socrates even argued, in an explicitly political context, that knowledge *is* power.[2] He also held the distinct view that knowledge justifies power – that the wise have a special claim to rule.[3] Socrates was no authoritarian, because he denied that anyone was wise in the requisite way.[4] Consider, though, the authoritarian position that is barely kept at bay. Call it *Normative Epistemic Authoritarianism* (sometimes I shall use the simpler name, "authoritarianism"). It includes the following three tenets:

1. *The Cognitivist Tenet*: Normative political claims (at least often) are true or false.
2. *The Elitist Epistemic Tenet*: Some (relatively few) people know the normative political truth significantly better than others.
3. *The Authoritarian Tenet*: The normative political knowledge of those who know is a strong moral reason for their holding political power.

Socrates avoids authoritarianism by denying the second tenet, but it would be avoided as well by denying either of the other tenets. I propose to criticize these three strategies, in order to call attention to a fourth tenet, which is, I believe, a more adequate place to criticize Normative Epistemic Authoritarianism.

II. No truth

It is not surprising to see democratic culture adopt nonobjective views, especially in the context of value. Such views as that the truth is constituted by rational consensus, that the good is constituted by rational individual desire, and that the common good is constituted by expression of a majority preference, might hope to deny authoritarianism's elitist epistemic tenet, that some few have special access to the truth. Similar motives may be at work in many current theories of democratic voting, and may partly explain the fact that a certain very natural conception of voting is not the standard one. Democratic voting could naturally be thought to be the culmination of a process of rational discussion about what is best for the community, with votes understood as opinions on the common good, having been potentially shaped and altered in response to reasoning employed in public discussion. That view of voting, however, is not typical. Votes are usually thought to be without cognitive content altogether. The received view of voting is that it is an expression of preference, the manifestation of a disposition to favor or choose one policy over another.[5] Why this noncognitive interpretation, despite the naturalness of a cognitive interpretation of voting as the culmination of public discussion?

Noncognitivism is a well-known position in moral philosophy, asserting that moral judgments are neither true nor false but, rather, express emotions, or recommend or prescribe actions, or have significance of some other nondescriptive kind. One reason for taking such a position is that the idea of a ground for cognitive moral judgments seems more problematic than for cognitive judgments of other kinds, such as those about easily verified matters of empirical fact. Similar reasons could be offered for noncognitivism about voting, since what society ought to do, or what is in the common interest, seems problematic in the same ways. A cognitive interpretation of voting must deal with this issue at some point.

There are, however, further reasons that might help explain noncognitivism in the case of voting, and I shall concentrate on these. Distinctively political worries are raised by the possibility of objective grounds for judgments about the common good, or about what society ought to do. If such judgments can be objectively correct or incorrect, then some might have better knowledge than others of these matters, and that would seem to give some people a special claim to political authority. Even though it would not be a conclusive claim, since moral issues other than expertise might be relevant, it would be a claim of some importance. If some know what we ought collectively to do, then there is a strong reason for thinking they ought to be given the power to see that we do it.

If, on the other hand, the idea of rule by an expert elite seems morally absurd, as it does to many today, the mistake might be taken to lie in the premise that there is any common good or other objective ground to be known for such political judgment. If there is none, then votes must not be opinions about what the common good is, or any other cognitive matter. They must be (like moral judgments generally, the view might go) noncognitive expressions of preference.

The no-truth view would be damaging to authoritarianism, even though its tendency to support democracy is so far an open question. As with the "no knowledge" option to be discussed below, it simply would preclude epistemic justifications of political arrangements. Whether democracy would prevail on other grounds would remain to be seen.

There is more about normative political truth and its denial in the next section. Here, the point is not that political truth must be admitted, but rather that denying political truth is deep and exotic business, and to that extent is not a robust case against authoritarianism. This will be especially significant if the strategy recommended below is agreed to depend on less deep and exotic premises. The objection here, then, is not to political noncognitivism as a philosophical position (although that will also be considered later), but to the strategy of resting the case against authoritarianism on that exotic and eternally controversial view.

III. Political truth and its democratic critics

The idea of an independent normative political truth has long been associated with the classical view that there are prescriptive laws in nature that are permanent and universal to which human-made laws are subordinate. The natural-law tradition has often conjoined with theological doctrines that place the authority of any law in the will of god(s).[6] There is, then, a historical association between the idea of truth as an independent standard of political choices, and the idea of our being constrained by the authority of a boss. It is possible to see much of the opposition to normative political truth as, at root, anti-authoritarian.

Anti-authoritarian conviction can be generalized beyond the resistance to personal authorities such as gods and kings, to oppose the very idea of entities external to the judgment and will of moral agents, which are nonetheless morally authoritative for them. John Rawls, in his doctoral dissertation, objects to the appeal to "exalted entities" such as God, the state, the course of nature, ethical realism, essential human nature, and the real self, as sources of moral authority. He characterizes any such theory as "authoritarian."[7] This is a morally or politically based resistance to the idea of independent moral or political truth.

One form of reaction to the idea of exalted entities, which informs a wide range of political positions from left-wing to right-wing, is to posit a morally based conception of freedom, often called "autonomy." On this view, the very existence of independent moral or political truths would violate freedom or sovereignty even if they are in no way constraints on what a person or polity is *able* to do.

Pushing this moral conviction in a right-wing direction, political libertarianism often holds that since there is no independent higher law that earthly law could be in the service of, only very limited state power could be legitimate. Political libertarianism has had considerable influence in the fields of economics and political science, especially under the methodological umbrella of "public choice theory." Public choice theorists have rejected the idea of normative political truth in different ways. One of the founders of "social choice theory" (an important precursor to public choice theory), Duncan Black seems to use a verificationist criterion for the cognitive content of propositions (propositions are meaningless unless they could in principle be verified through sensory experience) in order to conclude that votes could not have cognitive content.[8] But these writers seem to rely on political premises as much as on epistemological ones. Kenneth Arrow, also a founder of social choice theory, seems to base his rejection of the "Platonic realist" theory "that there exists an objective social good defined independently of individual desires" partly on its being "meaningless" "to the nominalist temperament," but partly on its ability to justify "government by the elite, secular or religious."[9] He declares as well that "for the single isolated individual there can be no other standard than his own values."[10] He thus intends to reject any independent standard for either individual or social decisions. This conclusion is endorsed by at least several of the leaders of public choice theory with its predominantly libertarian political implications.[11]

As a philosophical attempt to undermine the possibility of moral or political truth, a strong empirical criterion of meaningfulness is simply not plausible unless one has independent reason to deny meaningfulness to value statements. Otherwise, they stand among the best counterexamples to such a criterion. As for the political motives behind such views, the idea of individual moral autonomy is insufficient for libertarians' antistatism once the philosophical moves of verificationism and noncognitivism are rejected, as shown by the prominent role of autonomy in nonlibertarian theories of Rawls and others.

Indeed, there is an important affinity between libertarians and many liberals and socialists on the repugnance of morally authoritative exalted entities, and so on the doctrine of moral autonomy. This partly accounts for reticence about the idea of political truth that can be found in a number of theorists across the political spectrum. The challenge for nonlibertarians who, nonetheless, share the anti-authoritarian critique of exalted entities is to develop a basis for state legitimacy without exalting the state's moral authority. Noncognitivism appears to preclude the sort of moral foundation this project would require, and so is a natural opponent of the nonlibertarians.

Consider the views of Jürgen Habermas and John Rawls, both of whom have elaborate nonlibertarian theories of political legitimacy. Their shared rejection of the application of "true" and "false" to political principles reflects their sympathy with the libertarian refusal to appeal to moral authority of exalted entities. Still, both defend the possibility of objective validity of political principles. Habermas even regards his theory as "cognitivist." Clearly, this is a politically motivated resistance to political truth that neither rests on verificationism or non-cognitivism, nor purports to undermine the legitimacy of all substantial states. In what sense is "truth" rejected, and is the rejection compelling?

Habermas regards his views about moral theory as "cognitivist," although he denies that moral judgments are true or false.[12] This will puzzle some, since it is not uncommon to define ethical "noncognitivism" as the thesis that moral statements lack "cognitive content," the property of being either true or false. Habermas's point is that while moral judgments cannot "be true or false in the same way that descriptive statements can be true or false," (52) "normative claims to validity are *analogous to truth claims*." The aim is to resist noncognitivism and its skeptical and libertarian implications, without exalting any independent moral facts in the way that, for example, the intuitionists had done.[13]

While his official view is apparently that it is best not to regard moral and political principles as true or false, he regards the analogy to truth as so strong that the terminological question is not crucial. He is willing to let them be called true, so long as important differences from scientific or descriptive truth are kept in mind, but he prefers to speak of the *analogy* to truth.[14]

Furthermore, Habermas's explicit argument that normative validity is analogous to truth *rather* than an instance of it is unsatisfying. In effect, the argument is that truth and rightness each operate logically as modal operators on propositions.[15] This is supposed to show that acts are not right or wrong in the way that tables are yellow. We can go from, "one ought to lie," to "it is right that [one lies]," while there is no similar move from "the table is yellow," to "it is yellow that . . ." The closest thing is "it is true that [the table is yellow]." This point, if correct, would show that nonnormative propositions can have two distinct kinds of validity: truth and normative rightness. This does nothing to show that normative propositions cannot be true. Habermas seems to argue as if he has shown that truth and rightness are second-order predicates (taking "is yellow" as a first-order predicate), when all the argument would show is that they are higher-than-first-order predicates. If they can be third-order predicates, then he has done nothing to show that second-order propositions such as "it is right that [first-order proposition]" could not be true. What is wrong with "It is true that, it is right that . . ."? After all, we have been given no reason to question third-order truth predicates such as "It is true that, it is true that . . ." This argument against normative political truth, then, is not adequate.

John Rawls defends a "constructivist" account of political morality according to which what is just, unjust, right, and wrong are constituted by a hypothetical agreement among hypothetical agents. "It seems better to say that in constructivism first principles are reasonable (or unreasonable) than that they are true (or false)." "Apart from the procedure of constructing the principles of justice, there are no moral facts."[16] This may seem to reject the idea of moral and political truth. Like Habermas, Rawls is partly motivated by a wish to distinguish his views from intuitionism, which posits nonnatural properties (exalted entities) that are apprehended by a quasi-perceptual faculty of intuition. These, however, are points about moral *reality*, and moral *knowledge*, that seem to leave open what to say about the possibility of moral *truth*, and it is not yet clear why he should avoid or reject it.

It is natural to think that Rawls's resistance to the idea of truth for political principles is a consequence of his "constructivist" methodology. This is a mistake. In two contexts other than the political, Rawls recognizes the appropriateness of describing principles arrived at through constructivist methods as "true." First, in moral, as distinct from political theory he describes the first principles of morals arrived at through Kant's constructivism as "true statements about what kinds of considerations are good reasons for applying one of the three basic concepts [the right or just, the good, and moral worth of character]."[17] Second, in philosophy of mathematics Rawls does not quarrel with the idea that "possibilities of construction" might be an adequate account of mathematical truth, and he models his account of the validity of political principles on such theories: We may see them "as analogous to the way in which an infinity of primes is viewed (in constructivist mathematics) as a possibility of construction."[18] The resistance to truth is special to his *political* constructivism rather than resting on constructivism as such. A brief description of his conception of political justification will bring out the ideas that are germane to his avoidance of "truth."

Rawls argues that justification must proceed from *consensus* even as it attempts to reconcile *disagreement*. Since modern democracies contain a wide variety of deep, yet reasonable disagreements that are not likely to disappear without oppression, political justification can neither appeal to, nor hope to conclude with, any of these contending world views. Instead, it must appeal to the overlapping consensus that exists on several values that can form the basis for political life. The consensus is limited to the political domain, and so political justification must avoid depending on any wider doctrines (so far as possible). Outside of political matters, divergent reasonable world views are to be tolerated.[19]

Why not call the principles that are derived from the overlapping consensus "true"? The reason seems to be that there is no collective comprehensive conception of which they are a part. Since something is true only as a part of a comprehensive conception, there is no collective standpoint from which the principles could be held to be true. They are accepted by *each* individual as true (or reasonably close), but this cannot be the basis on which they are accepted by *all*, since not all believe them for the same reasons. The shared basis for their acceptance, Rawls suggests, ought to be the fact that they are the focus of a reasonable consensus – this is a fact that can be collectively acknowledged. The public basis of their validity, then, is their being reasonable in that sense. This is supposed to be compatible with each endorsing other, controversial grounds of the principles' validity as well – grounds derived from within controversial comprehensive conceptions.

Rawls recognizes that political principles can be true, as part of the best comprehensive conception. However, consider those comprehensive conceptions that endorse the political principles on controversial grounds, grounds other than reasonable consensus. Either the normative validity of the principles necessarily rests on reasonable consensus, or such consensus is not required for their validity. If the consensus criterion is not necessary for the normative validity of political principles, then all individuals might be politically bound by principles many of them cannot accept, contrary to the liberal heart of Rawls's theory of justification. If the principles' validity must indeed rest on reasonable consensus, then the views that endorse them on other grounds must be mistaken. No other grounds could be sufficient for their validity. Many of the comprehensive views making up the overlapping consensus must be mistaken in thinking otherwise.

The fact that many of the comprehensive conceptions would be mistaken is not in itself a difficulty. The theory can accommodate them so long as they are reasonable. Rather, the problem is that the overlapping consensus criterion *depends* on the presence of a number of views that ascribe other, mistaken, grounds to the validity of the political principles. If the overlapping consensus criterion were publicly accepted, it would find no overlappers. All would converge on the higher-level consensus criterion, waiting, for that reason, but in vain, for a lower-level overlapping consensus. There would not exist the overlapping set of lower-level views which the consensus criterion requires unless some mistakenly failed to apply that criterion. The consensus criterion is, in this respect, incompatible with its own publicity, a predicament involving well-known moral, practical, and perhaps logical difficulties.[20]

The problem is closely related to our topic, normative political truth. It is a consequence of trying to provide a common or public basis of validity, which would, as we have seen, necessitate moving from the true to the reasonable. The problem would be avoided by settling for the grounds of validity each gives to the principles from within their own comprehensive view. Each accepts the principles as true, even if for different reasons. It is possible, then, publicly to appeal to their truth as the basis of their validity. The appeal is not to the truth conceived in a certain way, but to the truth whatever it might be. In this way there is no appeal to anything that must be seen by anyone as conflicting with their own comprehensive view, with its view of the basis of the validity of the political principles.

It is not possible to consider here how the overall theory of justification is affected by this adjustment. The limited point is that Rawls's argument for regarding political principles as reasonable rather than true is not compelling. On the contrary, it is tied to what may be a deep difficulty with the overlapping consensus approach to political justification, namely, that it may contradict the potential components of any substantive consensus.

The point is not to criticize or endorse Rawls's or Habermas's overall theories of political justification. They are noteworthy here for their attempt to reject noncognitivism and skepticism without admitting "exalted entities." Neither one is persuasive in taking the rejection of exalted entities to require the rejection of normative truth. There is a more general idea behind this criticism. Unless a theory raises no moral or political standard that is independent of our actual choices or inquiries, it can have a place for moral and political truth even while rejecting the simple intuitionist–correspondence metaphysics and epistemology. The rejection of certain models of truth and knowledge is not yet the same as rejecting the applicability of those notions altogether.

The raising of political standards, whether or not these are timeless, independent, universal, or necessary, involves an idea of political truth. The standard itself yields practical objectivity (which is not yet truth) since action may fall short of the standard. Theoretical or cognitive objectivity is given by the fact that there is that standard. The presence of an appropriate target – an objective – gives practical objectivity, whether or not there are different targets for different situations, since the target might be missed. The cognitive objectivity here consists in the appropriateness of the target. Just as it is a practical error to miss the appropriate target, it is a cognitive error to aim at the wrong target. Assuming that knowledge implies at least true belief, where there is cognitive success or error, truth and falsity are applicable. Political truth, then, seems possible even without ultimate (timeless, independent, universal, necessary) truth. Rawls's constructivism and Habermas's discourse ethics may help show how the idea of nonultimate political truth is coherent, their protestations notwithstanding. The point about the connection between practical objectivity and normative truth, however, applies more generally.

IV. No knowledge

Socrates held not that there was no politically relevant truth, but rather that no one knew it. The anti-authoritarian implications are obvious, though again these are not by themselves a positive case for democracy. Furthermore, these political benefits of the view that no one knows the political truth do nothing to show that it is the case. It is a difficult issue, and since no single philosophical treatment could remove the deep controversy that exists about it the issue will be avoided here as far as possible. Socrates' way of avoiding authoritarian politics through skepticism is too exotic to be generally persuasive, whatever its philosophical merits. At the very least, it is more exotic than necessary if authoritarianism can be criticized on simpler grounds as I will argue it can. Similar considerations count against the "no truth" strategy just discussed, since, for example, the prevalent view that there is such a thing as political wisdom implies the view that there is political truth. Neither form of skepticism is a widely acceptable premise and should be avoided if possible. Accordingly, let it be allowed that there is political truth and knowledge.

V. Do some have more political wisdom than others?

Socratic skepticism is not the only way to resist the Elitist Epistemic Tenet. It might be held that while there is political knowledge, there are no elites in this respect; it is distributed equally.

However, even the elitist component of the Elitist Epistemic Tenet is, I believe, difficult to deny. If it is controversial, this may be partly owing to its being taken to claim more than it actually claims. It *does* claim that some relatively few have better normative political wisdom than others. It *does not* claim that this distinction is available to justify giving the wiser more political power.

There is a puzzle about how to argue for the Elitist Epistemic Tenet. It will not do to appeal to individuals or groups who are generally agreed to have superior normative political wisdom. This will likely fail since there are probably no examples that would receive such general agreement. This failure should not count against the tenet, since it does not claim that anyone would attract such general agreement. The only way to use examples is indirectly, by encouraging the reader to provide his or her own. They needn't be agreeable to anyone else, since no claim about their agreeability is implied by the Elitist Epistemic Tenet.[21]

A second line of objection is the temptation to think that the Elitist Epistemic Tenet must be denied by the tradition that asserts the equality of all people. It is often noted that this tradition does not assert intellectual or physical equality, but moral equality. However, this is still vague as stated, and in ways that might lead to confusion about the distribution of political wisdom. We may distinguish three things that moral equality might be taken to mean – that all are:

1. Worthy of equal moral and political regard
2. Equally capable of virtue
3. Equally morally and politically wise

That all are worthy of equal moral and political regard is certainly intended by the tradition that asserts human equality. It is so abstract that, as formulated, it does not clearly conflict with the view that some few have superior moral or political wisdom. A different but related position is that, in the words of Seneca, "virtue closes the door to no man."[22] This still does not entail equal distribution of normative political wisdom. It does not even entail equal virtue. It asserts, more weakly, universal *capacity* for virtue.

The suggestion that all are equally morally or politically wise is not, I believe, part of the commitment to human moral equality. Indeed, some moral egalitarians explicitly reject the idea. This is true of the Federalists, who could not plausibly be thought to dissent from Jefferson's declaration that "all men are created equal." *Federalist* No. 78, for example, defends an unlimited term of office for high judges on the grounds that "the government can have no great option between fit characters." There are few enough who can master the body of knowledge required, but "the number must be still smaller of those who unite the requisite integrity with the requisite knowledge."[23]

VI. Character effects

Democracy might be held to have virtues of a nonepistemic kind that are conclusive in its favor, denying the Authoritarian Tenet that the knowers have a special claim to rule. Democracy is often thought to have profound and morally significant beneficial effects on the character of the citizens such as fostering public spiritedness, or self-respect. Could these be sufficient to recommend democracy over authoritarianism independent of the quality of the social decisions these institutions produce?

The character effects attributed to democracy depend causally on whether the citizens believe that democracy yields good social choices. If we assume that our normative democratic theory must be consistent with its being publicly believed, we cannot appeal to democracy's character effects while denying that democratic social choices have anything independently to recommend them. If that were believed by the citizens, widespread participation either would not occur or would not produce the alleged virtues. For democracy to have the alleged good character effects, it is apparently a psychological fact that citizens must believe in the value of the process on independent grounds. It matters a great deal to the participants, and so to normative theory, whether democracy's social choices are as good as those of more authoritarian arrangements.[24]

The argument is that a political system must have some public point independent of educative effects of participation, otherwise participation won't have substantial educative effects. One might object that all that is required is that each *individual* have some aim other than self-development.[25] This is compatible with the main (public) point of a democratic system of social choice being the educative effects on citizens. If democracy is a system that tends to produce citizens who pursue their own aims and convictions, and who can get educative benefits out of doing so, then this is a perfectly good defense of democracy, one might argue.

We should notice that this defense of democracy, addressed to prospective participants, fails to speak to any of their aims and values other than self-development. It is true, each citizen will (we assume) have other aims, but these are taken as valuable in this argument only as part of a technique for achieving self-development, which is, alone, presented as valuable. This doesn't go so far as to doubt or denigrate the participants' other values, but the argument puts that question aside for the purpose of promoting the value of self-education. The standard difficulty with this form of argument is that it requires, for its purported effects, that the participants pursue goals other than those promoted by the argument itself – in this case, goals other than self-development. This raises the question whether the participants could still behave as required while accepting the public, self-development form of justification for the democratic system.

This case is importantly different from, for example, David Wiggins's critique of noncognitivist theories of the meaning of life.[26] Those views say or imply that the "participant" values are entirely illusory, but then rely on their attendant satisfactions as a crucial part of "meaning." People with this view of meaning would have a difficult time achieving the satisfactions in question. But in the democracy case, the self-development argument is a public political reason for democracy, in terms of the satisfactions of participant values, that doesn't denigrate or debunk those participant values. It puts them in less than a central place (by emphasizing the value of self-development instead) not because they are doubtful (as in noncognitivism) but because they vary widely from one person to the next. It hopes to be a reason that carries weight for adherents of a wide variety of reasonable value schemes by not aligning itself with any of the relevant schemes to the exclusion of others. Because the educative argument need not denigrate the participant values, it needn't be "forgotten" or ignored in order for the pursuit of those values to occur or be beneficial. Its being accepted does not automatically undermine the stance required for self-educative participation to take place.

However, although the connection is less direct, self-educative participation does seem to depend on what might be called *system-based hope*, the hope that one's highest aims might be well served by the system in which one participates. This is analogous to what we might call *agency-based hope*, the hope that one's acting will well serve the aims for which one acts. Agency-based hope may or may not be required for agency itself, but it is apparently necessary for the development of certain traits and attitudes such as a sense of responsibility, self-esteem, perseverance, and so on. In the very specific form of agency that is participation in a publicly accepted political system, agency-based hope depends importantly on system-based hope. If a person has no basis for hope that his or her aims will be well served by the political system, then one is not likely to have a basis for hope that one's agency *as* a participant in that system will serve those aims well either. As a result, important character effects will be missed.

The argument, then, ought not to be that the self-development justification cannot be accepted simultaneously with (because, e.g., it denigrates) participant values whose pursuit is required for self-education. Rather, the self-education justification is too thin to support agency-based hope of citizens as democratic participants. Without some further public reasons for a democratic system other than self-development, citizens are likely to lack reasons and motivation for the form of activity that would be educative. Or if they are somehow motivated by the self-educative argument itself, without system-based hope, their activity is unlikely to be educative.

A separate difficulty about basing democracy's value on character effects is that there is so much at stake in politics that democracy's tendency to produce autonomous or lively citizens, even if granted, could be overwhelmed by the superior quality of the decisions of some other system such as an authoritarian one. If many atrocities and gross injustices could be avoided by authoritarian arrangements, this advantage would be difficult to gainsay on the basis of even considerable character effects of democracy.

VII. Who will know the knowers?[27]

There is a fourth tenet implied by Normative Epistemic Authoritarianism if it is offered as a genuine practical program:

> 4. *The Second-Order Epistemic Tenet*: The knowers can be known by sufficiently many nonknowers to empower them, and to practically and morally legitimate their power.

This, I believe, is authoritarianism's most vulnerable claim. Unlike noncognitivism or Socratism, which espouse what we might call two versions of first-order epistemic unavailability, and are therefore exotic, consider this argument from second-order unavailability:[28] Even if some have knowledge, others have no way of knowing this unless they can know the same thing by independent means, in which case they have no use for the other's expertise.

I am interested in this second-order unavailability only with regard to knowledge about such things as what society ought to do, or what is in the common interest of the community. Even in this limited political domain, the problem might be denied. Certain methods might be thought to allow ranking some people as probably better than others even without independent access to the truth. For example, people who have thought about the questions at hand might be presumed to be more competent than those who have not, or the experienced to be better than the inexperienced. However, even those equally educated and experienced (or whatever the observable criterion is supposed to be) are likely to disagree among themselves. This is not to doubt that experience or thought are epistemically helpful. It is not that skeptical. Again it is instead the second-order (and interpersonal) point: Even if there are forms of thought and experience that improve a person's competence on some issues, they are not sufficiently identifiable by others in particular instances. The evident differences between the qualifications of putative experts, such as their place of education, or the experience they have, are typically insufficient to determine their relative reliability. Therefore, disagreements among *apparently* equally expert individuals are probably inevitable. Any differences that are not apparent are unavailable.

A slightly different suggestion for avoiding this second-order epistemic problem would be to estimate expertise on the basis of the person's past success. If one car mechanic has managed to make your car run smoothly, and another has failed, this seems a good ground for attributing greater expertise to the successful mechanic. The example assumes, plausibly, that it is known to be better for a car to run smoothly, other things equal. But our problem is to identify the experts in politics, and here the criteria of success are less obvious. There are certainly things that some politicians can do more effectively than others, such as raise or lower taxes, build friendly or suspicious relationships with foreign rivals, lighten or intensify public retribution against convicted criminals, increase or decrease commercial influence on government, and so on. Unlike the case of the car mechanic, the kind of expertise we are seeking here involves knowing which of these things to do, and under what circumstances, as well as knowing how to do it. The very goals of politics are under constant political contention. We are assuming that the goals are not given to all in advance, and so there is no clear way to judge a putative expert on the most important matters in terms of success.

VIII. Second-order skepticism?

The problems of second-order knowledge have so far been presented as though a full skepticism is warranted at that level (though I have avoided that term). Skepticism about first-order knowledge seemed unnecessarily exotic and controversial, however, and the same is apparently true of second-order skepticism. It is surely less controversial to say that it is impossible to know the knowers than to say that it is impossible to know anything. Yet it is common to think that it is not futile, even though it is difficult, to try to determine who is wiser on political matters. Second-order *skepticism*, then, is no more generally acceptable as a premise for normative political theory than first-order skepticism.

Apparently, though, it would be acceptable to hold that second-order knowledge is sufficiently difficult that on any given second-order issue *many* will fail, even if it is possible that some will succeed. This weaker skepticism still has some promise as an argument against authoritarianism, since epistemic authority cannot be regarded as publicly established unless more than a few can recognize it. But how many must be able to recognize it? The answer depends on which of several potential problems is being pressed against authoritarianism.

Before considering the more germane problem of moral legitimacy, consider two practical problems: empowerment and practical legitimacy. First, the installation of the wise into positions of predominant power is likely to require that their wisdom is known to more than a few. The very attainment of power will often require a wide base of popular support, though not always. To the extent that second-order knowledge is difficult (even if not impossible) there is a problem of empowerment facing any scheme of rule by the wise.

Second, even if power is achieved by the wise without their wisdom being widely recognized, there is the closely related issue of practical legitimacy. Once in power, a leader typically requires the allegiance of more than a few of the subjects in order to exercise the power of his or her position. This can sometimes be done without, as when, for example, the use of violence or threats can accomplish the intended purposes, but limited political support is typically a severe constraint on the exercise of political power.

Political support and so practical legitimacy might be obtained under false pretenses of various kinds, and so the problems of second-order knowledge are not insuperable on this score. Bread and circuses or lies deception might do as well from the standpoint of practical legitimacy. Similarly, the empowerment problem might be solved by coercion rather than by establishing epistemic authority. The avoidance of the practical problems of second-order knowledge by violent or deceptive means, however, raises obvious moral questions. Even if empowerment and practical legitimacy are achieved, there are questions of moral legitimacy.

Moral legitimacy does not require that the wisdom of the rulers be known and acknowledged by everyone, since some may have impaired abilities, or ulterior motives or may be unreasonable in some other way. Acceptable reasons are morally owed to the reasonable. We don't need a detailed theory of reasonableness here. Let the term stand for those to whom acceptable reasons are morally owed, assuming this is a proper subset of all people in the community. According to this principle of moral legitimacy, the problem of second-order knowledge poses a problem of moral legitimacy for authoritarianism so long as some reasonable people may fail to recognize the epistemic authority in question. For there to be a problem of moral legitimacy, it need not be held that second-order knowledge is impossible, but only that it is generally something on which reasonable people might disagree. Even though the idea of reasonableness is, so far, quite vague, the problem of second-order knowledge does appear to be at least this severe. Notice that saying so falls short of second-order *skepticism*, since it can be allowed that some individuals can achieve second-order knowledge.[29] Normative authoritarianism, then, cannot survive the fact of *second-order unavailability*.

Second-order unavailability is preferable to second-order skepticism since it is a weaker claim. It is also weaker than first-order skepticism, but the idea of *first-order unavailability* has not been considered. Could the argument against authoritarianism just as well be located there, in the denial that relevant *truths* could be beyond reasonable dispute? First, even if no relevant truths could be accepted by all reasonable people, this would not defeat authoritarianism so long as some knowers were beyond reasonable challenge. Second-order unavailability is required to rule this out. Second, it seems less clear that no relevant normative truth (e.g., principles) could meet with reasonable consensus than that no individual's epistemic authority could do so, although this cannot be pursued here.

The uncontroversial idea that some relevant truths are open to reasonable disagreement, plays an important role in the issue of what may be legitimately offered as public political reasons for proposals. Some theorists of liberalism have urged that claims or doctrines that are open to reasonable dispute are not available as legitimate public reasons. Below I try to show how this appeal to first-order unavailability is as insufficient in that context as it was in this – that second-order unavailability must also be assumed. Consideration of the liberal doctrine of public reason also provides an occasion to note how epistemology enters the account in ways some have seemed to deny.

First, however, the relevance of epistemology to the argument against authoritarianism could be challenged.

IX. Is it merely a problem of agreement?

It might be argued that second-order unavailability is really more a problem of agreement than of knowledge. The problem is not that the knowers cannot be known at all. It is that there is no one whose normative epistemic authority can be agreed to by all reasonable people (those to whom acceptable reasons are owed).[30] However, to say of some proposition or subject matter that being a reasonable person does not guarantee that one knows the truth, is to state certain limits on its *knowability*. It does not deny that it can be known; it is a more moderate limit than that. It is, however, an epistemological claim. In this way, it is an epistemological claim to say that no one's normative epistemic authority is such that it could not be doubted by reasonable people. The problem of second-order unavailability is a problem that rests on an epistemological limitation. *No knower is so knowable as to be known by all reasonable people.*

We should return briefly to Hobbes's argument to the effect that no one's political wisdom is appreciably greater than anyone else's. Hobbes's position is quite parallel to the one defended here, with the exception that in the context of his larger theory, the problem *is* primarily one of agreement rather than of knowledge.

Hobbes seems not to operate with the idea of anyone's being owed acceptable reasons. In Hobbes, the primary aim is to promote peace by persuading people to agree with one another on a certain collective arrangement. He employs prudential reasons as an appropriate persuasive tool where the audience is assumed to have in common that they are concerned with self-preservation and their own well-being.[31] The goal is to get agreement on some stable arrangement or other. For Hobbes, the real problem with the idea of knowers as leaders, then, is that none can be agreed to. Hobbes takes this as evidence that there is none who has significantly superior wisdom, but he neither establishes this, nor does he need to. Whether there are superior knowers or not, *agreement* is impossible.

Agreement does not play the same role in the argument presented here. The primary aim is not agreement one with another, but the provision to each of reasons he or she is owed (some being owed acceptable reasons, others not). The problem about knowing the knowers, is not that no knowers will be *agreed* upon, but that empowering any proposed knower *will leave some people without the reasons they are individually owed*. It is an epistemological point to say that some will be left out in this way even where the proposed knower is genuine.

The conception of justification according to which people (if reasonable) are owed acceptable reasons for the political power of others over them, may be fairly called liberal. As such it is not a mode of argument that is likely to persuade many authoritarians. Still, it would be wrong to think this begs the question against Normative Epistemic Authoritarianism. For instance, it does not deny the Authoritarian Tenet that political wisdom is a strong moral reason for power, though it denies that it is morally sufficient. It adds the requirement that such reasons be acceptable to all reasonable people. This does not in any way assume that no one's epistemic authority could be so acceptable; that is entirely a separate point.

X. Epistemic authority and liberal public reason

If the argument against Normative Epistemic Authoritarianism is importantly epistemological, ought it to be eschewed by recent liberal theories that hope to avoid epistemological premises?[32] Rawls's theory on this matter is the most fully articulated. However, the preceding discussion allows us to detect moderate epistemological premises in his own theory. The epistemological content of second-order unavailability is no more divisive or problematic than the epistemological content of his theory of "burdens of reason." Indeed, it will emerge below that Rawls's doctrine of public reasons (as I will call it) actually requires a version of second-order unavailability.

By the "doctrine of public reason," I mean the view that it is improper, in public political justification, to assume or appeal to views about which there is reasonable controversy. Rawls says that to appeal to controversial doctrines as true fails to acknowledge that there is room for reasonable disagreement. Thomas Nagel says that doing so is, in effect, appealing merely to the fact that one believes the claim in question, as though this should have special epistemic weight.[33] Neither wishes to rely on a general skepticism, and so it must be allowed that some people may really have the truth. The question is why even the knowers may not appeal to it as the truth.

Rawls relies on the implications of the moral notion of reasonableness.[34] The liberal doctrine of public reason is then interpreted as precluding the appeal in public political discussion (about constitutional essentials, a wrinkle I shall ignore for present purposes) to the alleged truth of any doctrine about which reasonable people could and do disagree. There are two parts here: first, there are certain controversial claims about which reasonable people could disagree. Second, the assertion of such claims as reasons in public political discussion fails to regard those who disagree as reasonable. This is not a *purely* epistemic

criterion for public reasons since it is limited to consideration of what must be accepted by people in a certain *moral* category – the reasonable. The difference, then, between reasons that are public and those that are not is not just a matter of how "knowable" they are. Still, the distinction is partly epistemological. The difference between views that all reasonable people must accept and those they needn't accept is apparently an epistemological difference. This is evident from Rawls's (partial) list of factors that explain how disagreement on certain matters is compatible with the reasonableness of the disputants. Examples include the complexity of relevant evidence, differences over the relative weight of relevant considerations, and the inherent vagueness of important concepts.[35] Rawls describes these as "burdens of reason," "the many hazards involved in the correct (and conscientious) exercise of our powers of reason and judgment in the ordinary course of political life."[36] In order to avoid relying on the strong skeptical views either that there is no truth on such matters or that even if there is truth there is no knowledge of it, one must explain disagreement as an *epistemic failure* of at least some people to know things that may be knowable. The admittedly moral claim that one needn't be unreasonable to fail in this way does not remove the epistemological character of this failure. It only concentrates attention on the epistemic difficulty[37] of these matters specifically for reasonable people. *The burdens of reason represent first-order epistemic difficulties* over a certain range of issues. They postulate no impenetrable epistemic barrier, and so do not constitute a form of skepticism, but a form of unavailability, as we have been using those terms. However, first-order unavailability is not sufficient support for the doctrine of public reason.

Reasonable people, it is said, could disagree. This is importantly ambiguous. One sense in which someone might disagree with me is to believe false what I believe true. A second kind of disagreement is to believe false what I believe true, *knowing that I so believe*. The second, unlike the first, rejects my putative epistemic authority. To clarify the difference consider an example where disagreement (the first kind) is reasonable, but knowing disagreement (the second kind) is not. Suppose it is not unreasonable[38] for others to think I am not feeling well. I may be behaving in a way that makes that one possible conclusion for reasonable observers. It would, however, be unreasonable for them to maintain that belief in full knowledge of the fact that I don't believe it. It would be unreasonable not to defer to my belief on this matter even if it is not otherwise unreasonable to hold the opposite view from mine. It can be reasonable to disagree, but unreasonable *knowingly* to disagree.

Suppose there were analogous examples in political discussion, of people with whom reasonable people cannot knowingly disagree on certain matters about which it is otherwise reasonable to disagree. Such people would not transgress the bounds of public reason if they asserted controversial truths as reasons in public political discussion. This is because doing so would enter the fact that *they believe* these controversial propositions. In general, of course, the fact that a certain person believes a certain controversial view is less important in political discussion than whether it is true.[39] But where the person's authority cannot reasonably be doubted, as in this example, the fact of their belief has whatever importance the truth of the proposition itself would have (plus whatever importance the fact of belief has in the case of less credible people). Marking off a category of issues that are controversial and outside of public reason will not establish that *assertions* of such views are precluded by public reason, since such assertions introduce the public reason that certain putative experts believe them. So long as the possibility of such authority is allowed, the doctrine of public reason will have no implications for public political speech.[40]

The fact that the asserted doctrine is something about which reasonable people could disagree (its first-order unavailability) does not, then, show that its assertion by a certain speaker could never make it unreasonable knowingly to disagree. Until the latter claim is established, the assertion of such doctrines in public political discussion cannot be assumed to go beyond public reason. Such assertions can be interpreted as entering the doctrine into public reason (by authority it is unreasonable to deny) and (then) appealing to it.

To avoid this result, the possibility of knowledge on certain matters might be denied. Or one could reject the idea that such knowers, if any, could be known. As we have seen, though, these are strong and controversial epistemological claims. To avoid such skepticism it must be granted that there might be such knowers, and that they might be known by at least some. Granting this, there is the prospect that those knowers are not unreasonable to assert their epistemic authority by appealing to the truth as such.

If this possibility is also to be avoided, and the doctrine of public reason is to have any practical application, it must be denied that anyone is ever to be deferred to on the matters in question by all reasonable people. The possibility of having knowledge must be granted, as must the possibility of its being known by at least some others, if skepticism is to be avoided. What can be insisted upon is that for any alleged epistemic authority on these matters, reasonable people can disagree over whether the authority is real. *If deference can always be reasonably withheld on those matters, then appeal to one's own epistemic authority in public political discussion transgresses the bounds of public reason.* There would remain no reason to regard appeals to alleged truths on controversial matters as appeals to any public reasons. This involves appealing to the problem of second-order unavailability elaborated earlier.

The conclusion of this section, then, is that while adherents of the doctrine of public reason have good reason for resisting appeals to strong, controversial epistemological views, especially some forms of skepticism, that doctrine, at least as developed by Rawls, cannot eschew epistemology altogether. The burdens of reason already make a partly epistemological point. More strikingly, the doctrine requires that no knowers can be known by all reasonable people. This puts the view in no position to object to the epistemological content of the second-order unavailability argument against authoritarianism. In fact, it is fair to say the two are of a piece. They are anti-authoritarian on the basis of a view of justification which places second-order epistemic obstacles in the way of a defense of anyone's status as a knower.

XI. Epistemic problems with strongly epistemic voting

If rule by a knowing elite is unavailable, and yet normative political truth is allowed, the question is how politics might legitimately be guided by that truth. This raises a special challenge for the theory of democracy – a system where (at least certain) decisions are made by citizens in general regardless of their relative individual wisdom. How could democratic procedures have an epistemic authority that is unreasonable to deny? Only one kind of answer can be explored, and rejected, here. Consider the Rousseauean view that voting is capable of discovering an independent truth about the common good. We may distinguish the "strongly epistemic" view, that voting has epistemic virtues of its own, from the "weakly epistemic" view, that it has epistemic virtues derived from some other practice or institution, such as public discussion. I consider only the strong view here, and only one version of it. The central account of how voting could have epistemic virtues of its own is Condorcet's Jury Theorem.[41] This is a mathematical result showing that if independent voters are, on average, better than chance at getting the correct answer to any class of yes–no questions (such as "is x in the common interest?"), then the chance of at least a majority being correct on such questions goes up rapidly with the size of the group. Even if voters are only barely better than chance, the group as a whole is virtually infallible in groups the size of realistic political communities.[42]

	Uniform individual competence			
	.505	.51	.525	.55
Number of voters				
1,000	.6241	.7365	.9433	.9993
10,000	.8413	.9772	.9999	.9999
1,000,000	.9999	.9999	.9999	.9999

Group competence under majority rule

A full discussion of this theorem and its relevance for democratic theory is not possible here. One important detail, however, is that the competence of the group drops if the average individual competence is below .5, approaching zero just as rapidly as it approaches 1 when individuals are above .5. There are several difficulties in trying to apply this model to democratic voting, one of which is especially related to the problems of epistemic authority.[43] It is a crucial question whether average individual competence on some relevant class of social questions is above .5. The problem raised by the .5 threshold, though, is not that this is higher than the actual average competence. It is rather that *we don't know whether it is or not*. It may be that the average competence is above .5 and that properly held voting procedures would be virtually infallible about the common good. The problem is that even if this is so, it seems impossible to establish publicly without independent access to the truth.[44]

This problem with democratic application of the Condorcet model precisely mirrors the original problem we discussed about rule by knowledgeable individuals or elites. First, the objection does not depend on denying the existence of political truth, even though some have denied it in precisely this context.[45] Nor is it a Socratic skepticism about whether anyone *has* the relevant knowledge. It is the cluster of second-order problems about publicly *establishing* that they do. The Condorcet Jury Theorem gives us no epistemic mileage unless we can first publicly establish, in a way that is unreasonable to deny, that the average individual competence is above .5. There is no reason why it could not be so, but it is hard to see how such a thing could be established without independent public knowledge of the answer key – the very facts we hoped to use democratic voting to reveal.[46] This second-order unavailability is a grave difficulty for the Condorcetian conception of voting as strongly epistemic.

There is an important respect in which a Condorcetian approach to democracy has authoritarian tendencies, and so it is not a coincidence that it is subject to the same objection. If it were possible to know whether the average individual competence is above .5, it seems likely that it would be possible to know at least something about who was more competent than whom. Depending on the numbers, there are many circumstances in which the group competence would be improved by disenfranchising the less competent. First, those who are worse than .5 contribute nothing to the group competence under any circumstances. Second, even those above .5 may, depending on the circumstances, still be holding the group competence back because they are not as competent as others. In other words, if we had enough information to know that a Condorcetian model could be applied, we would very likely have enough information to limit suffrage to a subset of citizens, which is nothing but an authoritarian elite. The result is reminiscent of John Stuart Mill's proposal to give multiple votes to the more competent and educated voters,[47] which suffers from the same second-order difficulty. My argument against the model is not the moral premise that such authoritarian arrangements are objectionable. If epistemic authority could be established in the way that application of the Condorcet model would require, it is not clear whether authoritarianism would be objectionable. However, the problem lies in publicly establishing that epistemic authority. If we don't have enough higher-order knowledge for authoritarianism, then we don't have enough for Condorcetian democracy or its close authoritarian relatives, such as Millian multiple voting.

XII. Conclusion

We do not need to deny that there is an objective normative political truth, or that anyone could know it better than others in order to object to the view that the knowers ought to rule. There are difficulties about knowing the knowers. It is not that they could not be known by anyone; grant that they could. One problem is that they will not attract sufficient agreement to maintain or successfully exercise their power, as Hobbes emphasized. A deeper problem is that any putative knower could be doubted by some reasonable people, and so knowledge cannot give moral legitimacy to political power. Some despair of having society governed by any truth that is independent of actual bargains struck by individual maximizers, and this can give rise to a certain conception of democracy.[48] However, if there is a truth according to which some such bargains could be morally illegitimate, one might hope it could be given political influence. If so, it will have to be in a democratic way, since no individual or elite can defend, in a morally sufficient manner, their claim to epistemic authority. Whether or how democracy might have epistemic authority of its own, in a way that avoids the objections to authoritarianism, is an important question that must await another occasion.

Notes

1 Ancestors of this chapter were presented as papers and helpfully discussed at the Conference on Democracy at the University of California, Davis, May 4–5, 1990, Philosophy Colloquia at the University of California, Irvine and Davis campuses, at Brown University, and at the Central Division APA meetings in Chicago in April 1991. I am grateful for useful discussions with Tom Christiano, David Copp, Jean Hampton, Alon Harel, Greg Kavka, Andy Levine, William Nelson, John Rawls, and Paul Warren. This work was supported by a fellowship for recent Ph.D.s from the American Council of Learned Societies that is partially funded by the National Endowment for the Humanities.

2 *Gorgias* 466b–468e.

3 Supporting texts include *Crito* 47c9–d2, *Laches* 184e8–9, *Gorgias* 463d1–465e1, *Republic* I 341c4–342e11. This is also Richard Kraut's interpretation in *Socrates and the State* (Princeton, N.J.: Princeton University Press, 1984), pp. 231–44. Kraut calls this Socratic view authoritarian, but that seems inappropriate when the view is conjoined with another Socratic view (as Kraut agrees) that it is a permanent human fact that there are no experts of the relevant kind. At most, we could say that it is one of authoritarianism's central claims, although it is not by itself authoritarian.

4 Gregory Vlastos argues that precisely what Socrates meant when he denied that he or anyone had wisdom is a matter of some subtlety (and irony). See his, "Socrates' Disavowal of Knowledge," *Philosophical Quarterly* 35, no. 138 (January 1985). Vlastos argues that Socrates was a supporter of Athenian democracy, in "The Historical Socrates and Athenian Democracy," *Political Theory* 11 no. 4 (November 1983).

5 It is important to note that voters are not in a position to choose social actions, but can only choose which way to vote. Social choice over a set of alternatives cannot be composed of individual choices over the same alternatives. The ubiquity of the possibility of strategic misrepresentation of preferences reflects this fact. It is proven in Alan Gibbard, "Manipulation of Voting Schemes: A General Result," *Econometrica* 41 (1973), and M. A. Satterthwaite, "Strategy Proofness and Arrow's Conditions," *Journal of Economic Theory* 10 (1975). I argue for the interpretation of votes as opinions on the common interest, in "Democracy Without Preference," *Philosophical Review* (July 1990).

6 See Edward S. Corwin, *The "Higher Law" Background of American Constitutional Law* (Ithaca, N.Y.: Cornell University Press, 1988; first published 1928).

7 *A Study in the Grounds of Ethical Knowledge: Considered with Reference to Judgments on the Moral Worth of Character*, doctoral dissertation, Princeton University, 1950, pp. 317–35. On page 1, Rawls characterizes all such theories as "authoritarian." The role of appeals to a Kantian doctrine of autonomy in *A Theory of Justice* (Cambridge, Mass.: Harvard University Press, 1971) and the later work is complicated by Rawls's increasing reluctance to rely on any

esoteric metaphysical views. Still, that Kant would regard appeals to any of the "exalted entities" as heteronomous continues to be central to the defense of Rawls's own version of constructivism. See "Kantian Constructivism in Moral Theory," *Journal of Philosophy* 77, no. 9 (September 1980): 559.

8 Quoted in note 45.

9 Kenneth Arrow, *Social Choice and Individual Values* (New Haven, Conn.: Yale University Press, 1951, 1963 [first and second editions]), pp. 22–3.

10 "Values and Collective Decision-Making," in F. Hahn and M. Hollis, eds., *Philosophy and Economic Theory* (Oxford: Oxford University Press, 1979), p. 114.

11 James M. Buchanan and Gordon Tullock, *The Calculus of Consent* (Ann Arbor: University of Michigan Press, 1962), pp. 11–12: "We shall reject at the outset any organic interpretation of collective activity. . . . Only some organic conception of society can postulate the emergence of a mystical general will that is derived independently of the decision-making process in which the political choices made by the separate individuals are controlling."

Gordon Tullock, "Public Choice in Practice," in Clifford S. Russell, ed., *Collective Decision Making: Applications from Public Choice Theory* (Baltimore: Johns Hopkins University Press, 1979), pp. 31, 33 (cited in Jane Mansbridge, *Beyond Self-Interest* (Chicago: University of Chicago Press, 1990): "The traditional view of government has always been that it sought something called 'the public interest,' [but] with public choice, all of this has changed. . . . the public interest point of view still informs many statements by public figures and the more old-fashioned students of politics."

William Riker, *Liberalism Against Populism* (San Francisco: W. H. Freeman, 1982), p. 244: "Social choice theory forces us to recognize that the people cannot rule as a corporate body in the way the populists suppose. Instead officials rule, and they do not represent some indefinable popular will."

The libertarian content of much Public Choice work is difficult to demonstrate briefly. Indeed, it constantly denies that it is a "normative" as distinct from a "positive" discipline. Suffice it to say that its thorough reduction of value to individual preference, and its critique of bureaucracies and social choice mechanisms as inefficient, combine to support a strong (though defeasible) preference for unfettered individual market activity over centralized institutions such as the state.

12 *Moral Consciousness and Communicative Action* (Cambridge, Mass.: MIT Press, 1990), especially pp. 50–7, 120, 197; hereafter, "MCCA."

13 Like Rawls, Habermas take the intuitionist views of W. D. Ross, G. E. Moore, and others as the central moral-philosophical representatives of exalted entities.

14 In "Wahrheitstheorien," in *Wirklichkeit und Reflexion: Walter Schulz zum 60 Geburtstag* (Pfullingen: Neske, 1973), he rejects both the view that "normative statements can be true in the same sense as descriptive statements," and the view that "normative statements cannot be true at all" (p. 226). See also "Discourse Ethics," p. 56 in MCCA.

15 Habermas usually speaks of utterances rather than propositions as the truth bearers. This is not possible here, since the moral claim that it is right that *p*, does not involve any utterance of *p*.

16 "Kantian Constructivism in Moral Theory," pp. 569 and 519 respectively.

17 "Themes in Kant's Moral Philosophy," in Eckhart Förster, ed., *Kant's Transcendental Deduction* (Stanford, Calif.: Stanford University Press, 1989), p. 95, emphasis added. See also "Kantian Constructivism," p. 569, where he says that the usage, in the political conception, of "reasonable" rather than "true" "does not imply that there are no natural uses for the notion of truth in moral reasoning."

18 *Political Liberalism* (New York: Columbia University Press, 1993), Lecture III, section 7, p. 123.

19 See, for example, "The Idea of an Overlapping Consensus," *Oxford Journal of Legal Studies* 7, no. 1 (1987).

20 Rawls himself is the most influential recent proponent of publicity in political philosophy. See, for example, *A Theory of Justice*, p. 133.

It is not entirely clear whether Rawls endorses what I have called the publicity criterion of validity. There are (arguably) some hints in recent work that overlapping consensus may be more epistemic than constitutive. However, interpreting him in that way involves difficulties of its own, as does such a theory itself. It is relevant that Kant saw reasonable consensus as epistemic of objectivity rather than constitutive. See, for example, the Canon of Pure Reason, sec. 3, esp. first and second paragraphs (A 820–821; B 848–849), in *The Critique of Pure Reason*.

21 Hobbes claims that all are relatively equal in qualities of body and mind (with the exception of very abstract or technical thought). See *Leviathan*, chap. 13, first paragraph. His argument, though, is based on a failure of agreement about who the knowers are. He takes this as evidence that there are none, even though the disagreement is composed of everyone thinking they are one. Hobbes's views are considered in Section IX of this essay.

22 Cited by S. Benn in "Equality," *Encyclopedia of Philosophy*, Paul Edwards, ed. (New York: Macmillan, 1967).

23 *The Federalist Papers* (New York: Mentor Books, 1961), p. 471.

24 See Jon Elster's definitive treatment of this point in *Sour Grapes* (Cambridge: Cambridge University Press, 1983), pp. 91–100, sec. II.9.

25 I benefited from discussion of this objection with Tom Christiano. See his brief version of the objection in "Freedom, Consensus, and Equality in Collective Decision Making," *Ethics* 101, no. 1 (October 1990).

26 "Truth, Invention, and the Meaning of Life," in Geoffrey Sayre-McCord, ed., *Essays in Moral Realism* (Ithaca, N.Y.: Cornell University Press, 1988).

27 Thanks to Greg Kavka for noting the similarity to the traditional problem of who will watch the watchers.

28 I avoid the term "skepticism" here for reasons that will emerge, but that is roughly the idea.

29 A further complication appears if we consider the possibility that despite the

difficulties of first- and second-order knowledge, all reasonable people would know who the second-order knowers are, which would avail them of the first-order knowledge as well. Suppose, that is, that there is no similar problem of third-order knowledge. (Obviously, a similar situation could arise at any higher order.) If this were so, epistemic authority could apparently be established with all reasonable citizens. However, without special circumstances it is clear that third-order, or higher-order, knowledge will be at least as difficult as second-order, and almost certainly more difficult.

30 This is a minimal definition of reasonableness that tries to avoid certain complexities. Rawls's fuller definition is quoted below, in note 34.

31 It is not that this is all anyone cares about, but that this is something they all care about.

32 To emphasize the difference between his constructivism and rational intuitionism, Rawls says that "justifying a conception of justification is not primarily an epistemological problem" ("Kantian Constructivism"); and "the aim . . . is practical, not metaphysical or epistemological" ("Justice as Fairness: Political, Not Metaphysical," *Philosophy and Public Affairs* 14, no. 3 [Summer 1985]: 223–51). Charles Larmore seems to take the point more broadly against the relevance of epistemology when discussing the question of why we may not appeal to a controversial conception of the good in public political reasoning. "The inadequacy of skepticism as an answer to this question suggests that the reasons for the ideal of neutrality are not primarily *epistemological*. My view is that they are basically *moral*." See Larmore, "Political Liberalism," *Political Theory* 18, no. 3 (August 1990): 342. Thomas Nagel, on the other hand, explicitly recognizes the epistemological dimension of the problem, although his discussion is limited to what I call first-order unavailability, and does not take up the second-order issue in the context of either authoritarianism or public reason. See Nagel, "Moral Conflict and Political Legitimacy," *Philosophy and Public Affairs* 16, no. 3 (Summer 1967): 229–31.

33 John Rawls, "The Domain of the Political and Overlapping Consensus," *New York University Law Review* 64, no. 2 (May 1989): 238–9 (hereafter, "Domain"). The essay is also reprinted in the present volume. See also Nagel, "Moral Conflict."

34 Reasonable people, he says, are "persons who have realized their two moral powers [a capacity for a sense of justice and a capacity for a conception of the good] to a degree sufficient to be free and equal citizens in a democratic regime and who have an enduring desire to be fully cooperating members of society over a complete life" (Domain 236). The point I am after does not depend on the details of this notion.

35 Domain 235–8. On the avoidance of skepticism, see *A Theory of Justice*, p. 214, and "The Idea of an Overlapping Consensus," 12–15. The reason for avoiding skepticism is itself partly motivated by the need to appeal to public reasons.

36 Domain 236.

37 Rawls appeals to the "hardness," "difficulty," or in one case "complexity" of such matters in his explication of six listed burdens of reason, Domain 237.

38 This will not be the same notion of reasonableness as Rawls's, but an analogous notion for the purposes of this analogy. The difference does not affect the argument, which does not depend on the analogy.

39 Thomas Nagel makes this point in "Moral Conflict."

40 It is true that the reason appealed to in such cases is not simply the truth of the asserted doctrine. It is first an appeal to the fact of the speaker's belief as a reason for others also to believe. The speaker, however, is then free to regard the truth of the doctrine as available to public reason. It should be accepted by all reasonable people, since they should accept the speaker's authority. Such assertions of p by putative experts seem to have this dual structure: an appeal to one's own authority as a reason to believe p, and then an appeal to p itself.

41 For the connections, historical and theoretical, between these views of Rousseau and Condorcet, and some critical discussion of the democratic application of the Jury Theorem, see Bernard Grofman and Scott Feld, "Rousseau's General Will: A Condorcetian Perspective," *American Political Science Review* (July 1988), and the separate replies by Jeremy Waldron and David Estlund with a rejoinder by Grofman and Feld, collectively titled, "Democratic Theory and the Public Interest: Condorcet and Rousseau Revisited," *APSR* (December 1989).

42 These numbers assume homogeneous competence rather than average competence, but the results aren't changed appreciably. See Guillermo Owen, Bernard Grofman, and Scott Feld, "Proving a Distribution-free Generalization of the Condorcet Jury Theorem," *Mathematical Social Sciences* 17 (1989). The numbers in the table are taken from Nicholas Miller, "Information, Electorates and Democracy: Some Extensions and Interpretations of the Condorcet Jury Theorem," in Bernard Grofman and Guillermo Owen, eds., *Information Pooling and Group Decision Making* (London: JAI Press, 1983).

43 A separate issue, about whether the Jury Theorem's requirement of voter independence could be met in voting situations is taken up in Estlund, "Opinion Leaders, Independence, and Condorcet's Jury Theorem," forthcoming. It also contains a nontechnical proof of the Jury Theorem.

44 The threshold is precisely the competence of a coin flip: 50–50. It may seem hard to imagine the average competence on any question being lower than this, but it is actually quite possible. People use methods, principles, and previous experience to answer such questions. If they did not, they would be no better or worse than random. But these very factors that make it possible for humans to be better than random also allow them to be worse. The possibility of systematic correctness brings with it the possibility of systematic error. If our methods or principles or experiences happen to be incorrect rather than correct, we will be less competent than a coin flip.

45 Duncan Black challenges the Condorcetian assumption that there is any political truth which could render a vote correct or incorrect: "When a judge, say, declares an accused person to be either guilty or innocent, it would be possible to conceive of a test which, in principle at least, would be capable of telling us whether his judgement had been right or wrong. But in the case of elections no such test is conceivable; and the phrase 'the probability of the correctness of a voter's opinion' seems to be without definite meaning" (*The Theory of Committees and Elections* [Cambridge University Press, 1958], p. 163).

46 It is sometimes possible to estimate individual competence without independent access to the truth by, for example, comparing the individual answers to those of some Condorcetian majority. But knowing the base majority is Condorcetian requires knowing their individual competences, and the problem reemerges. Various such strategies are discussed in Bernard Grofman and Scott Feld, "Determining Optimal Weights for Expert Judgement," in Grofman and Owen, eds., *Information Pooling*. None of those strategies avoids, I think, the problem of second-order unavailability.

47 Mill, however, explicitly criticizes the application of Condorcet's Jury Theorem to democratic voting (*A System of Logic*, Book III, chap. 18, sec. 3).

48 See, for example, David Gauthier's essay in this volume. I criticize Gauthier's claim there to have a deliberative conception of constitutional democracy in "Who's Afraid of Deliberative Democracy: The Strategic-Deliberative Dichotomy in Recent Constitutional Jurisprudence," *Texas Law Review*, forthcoming.

Could political truth be a hazard for democracy?

DAVID COPP

Suppose there are truths about what society ought to do, or "political truths," as I shall call them. Suppose, that is, that many of the significant problems faced by society have morally correct solutions and that there are corresponding true propositions to the effect that society ought to implement these solutions. Could this supposition somehow be the basis of an argument against democracy?

Taken by itself, of course, the thesis that there are political truths leaves completely unaddressed the substantive question of how society ought to be governed. Perhaps, for example, one of the political truths is that society ought to be governed democratically. The thesis that there are *no* political truths also leaves unaddressed the question of how society ought to be governed. The idea that there are no political truths could take the form of an assertion that all political propositions are false, or more plausibly, it could take the form of a noncognitivist thesis to the effect that political judgments are prescriptions that, logically, are not candidates for a truth value. But either way, we would still need to know what form of government to favor. In short, we may conceptualize matters by thinking of there being truth in this domain, or we may conceptualize matters in some less natural way, which would deny truth but still permit us to debate what society ought to do. But nothing in the theory of democracy turns on our choice. Whether we view normative claims as putative truths or simply as injunctions that lack truth value, we may assert the characteristic principle held by democrats: "Society's formal procedures for determining the decisions of government or the membership of government ought to give (most of) the adult members of society power over those decisions or over the membership, power

Versions of this essay were presented to the May 1990 Conference on Democracy that was held at the University of California, Davis, and to the Philosophy Department at Simon Fraser University. I thank those who participated in the discussion on those two occasions, as well as Carl Cranor, David Dolinko, John Fischer, Jean Hampton, Craig Ihara, Christopher W. Morris, Steve Munzer, Michael Otsuka, and Mark Ravizza, for their helpful comments and suggestions.

equal to that enjoyed by any other (qualified) member."[1] I will refer to this as the "democratic principle."

A standard complaint against democracy, however, is that democracy unjustifiably gives equal political power to citizens regardless of their expertise in political matters. On one reading, the objection is that if there are political truths, and if some people have better access to them than do the rest of us, then these people ought to have more political power than the rest of us, other things equal. For they are in a better position than the rest of us to recognize the correct solutions to social problems. As David Estlund points out in "Making Truth Safe for Democracy," the objection depends on a version of the Socratic principle that "knowledge justifies power – that the wise have a special claim to rule."[2] I call this principle in its various formulations the "knowledge and power principle." Given this principle, if there are political truths, and if there is knowledge of these truths that is not enjoyed equally by all citizens, then we seem to have an argument against the democratic principle.[3] For these three premises seem to entail that the ruling power ought not to be given to all members of society in equal measure, but ought instead to be given to those who know what society ought to do.

Estlund favors an "epistemic conception of democracy," a conception of "democratic institutions as capable of ascertaining . . . political truths."[4] He therefore needs to defeat the objection from expertise without rejecting the idea of political truth. Moreover, he views the knowledge and power principle as intuitively quite plausible. He seems at least to concede that if some other form of government were *known* to be more successful than democracy at ascertaining political truths, and if we could implement it in a justified manner, it would then be difficult to justify democracy. Yet he thinks that we cannot justifiably implement rule by the wise, for those with expertise cannot be widely enough known for them to be legitimately empowered. That is, Estlund argues, those with special political expertise would have to be widely known to possess such expertise in order for their empowerment to be legitimate; their possession of expertise would have to be much more widely known than could in fact be the case. Hence, rule by the wise would be illegitimate.

On Estlund's position, as I shall explain, it seems that rule by the wise would be legitimate in circumstances of the sort Plato had in mind when he advocated rule by the philosophers. If we want to reject Plato's ideal, then I think we must not rest our support for democracy on a belief in its epistemic virtues. We must not rest our support for it on the belief that no other system of government could be known to do better at identifying the political truths. Instead, as I shall briefly suggest, our support for democracy should rest on familiar arguments either about the justice or fairness of democracy or else about its beneficial indirect effects. I shall defend arguments of the latter kind from an influential objection of Jon Elster's to the effect that they are "self-defeating."[5]

I begin by exploring the objection from political expertise. I show that a democrat has nothing to gain from denying that there are political truths, nor from denying that there is political knowledge. For a version of the argument can be constructed that does not depend on the thesis that there are political truths. I argue that a democrat must deny the knowledge and power principle. The key issue is whether the arguments about the indirect effects of democracy provide adequate reason to deny it.

1. The objection from political expertise

As stated so far, the objection combines the knowledge and power principle with the following two premises:

(1) There are political truths.
(2) The members of a small intelligentsia have much better knowledge of the centrally important political truths than anyone else.

In this section I claim that a democrat cannot avoid the objection by denying either premise.

The argument does not depend on any form of "realism" about political truth; it requires only that one's conception of political truth leave open the possibility of political expertise. Estlund is mistaken to think that what he calls "nonobjective" views of political truth rule out this possibility. He mentions, as two examples of nonobjective theories, the view that "the truth is constituted by" what would "emerge" in a "rational consensus" and the view that "the common good is constituted by expression of a majority preference."[6] I believe that each of these theories leaves open the possibility that certain groups may count as especially successful knowers of political truths.

The rational consensus theory leaves open the possibility that there is a group whose actual beliefs tend to coincide with the hypothetical rational consensus on a wider range of issues than is typical. The people in this group may accept the theory about rational consensus and therefore may refrain from accepting a political proposition unless they have reason to believe it would be the focus of rational consensus. The political beliefs of this group would be more likely to count as knowledge according to the theory than would the political beliefs of most people. Not even the majority preference theory rules out political expertise. Notice that democratic voting may not be the best way to ascertain the majority preference on a given issue, for there is always the possibility of strategic voting in a way that misrepresents one's preference. Moreover, even if the common good is constituted by the majority preference, it is a separate question whether society ought to implement the common good in every case. Some may know the truth about this better than others. They might also be able to do better than most people at determining what the majority would prefer, as distinguished from how the majority would vote. These people could develop expertise in this matter on their own, or rely on the assistance of specialists. In either case, according to the theory, they would be more likely than most people to qualify as having political knowledge. Therefore, neither the rational consensus theory nor the majority preference theory rules out elitism about political knowledge.

As Estlund recognizes, a democrat could deny premise (1) of the argument by adopting noncognitivism, which entails that there are no political truths at all.[7] But this is not a way to avoid the most general form of the objection from expertise, for there is a formulation of it that does not depend on a cognitivist construal of normative political claims.

Cognitivism and noncognitivism are meta-ethical theories that differ in how they interpret the semantics of normative moral and political claims. For example, noncognitivism would interpret the knowledge and power principle as prescription or injunction that lacks truth value. I do not want to go into the details. There are different theories about this. The important point is that cognitivism and noncognitivism are simply different theories about the meaning and logic of normative claims and arguments.

Now, the argument we are considering includes the cognitivist tenet of premise (1), but this premise could be replaced by the following normative claim, which is neutral between cognitivism and noncognitivism:

(1′) There are certain things that society ought to do, programs it ought to implement, legislation and policies it ought to adopt, and so forth.

The second premise could be reformulated accordingly:

(2′) The members of a small intelligentsia have a much better ability than anyone else to identify what it is that society ought to do.

Combined with an appropriate version of the knowledge and power principle, these premises give us a revised version of the objection from expertise, the "primed version," one that lends itself to either a cognitivist or a noncognitivist interpretation.

Let me illustrate this by showing roughly how the objection would be interpreted by the noncognitivist theory recently proposed by Allan Gibbard.[8] According to Gibbard's theory, a person who proposed the objection from political expertise could be viewed as expressing her acceptance of a system of norms N and a set of factual beliefs B with the following properties: (1″) Given the actual circumstances of the society, there are certain things that N requires the society to do. (2″) There is a proper part of society each member of which is such that, to a much closer approximation than in the case of anyone outside the group, given his factual beliefs, his system of norms requires the society to do the things that N requires the society to do given the actual circumstances of the society. And (3″) there is a justification for a person to hold political power if and only if he is part of a group, each member of which accepts a system of norms with the property that, to a closer approximation than in the case of anyone outside the group, given his factual beliefs, the system requires the society to do the things that N requires the society to do given the actual circumstances of the society.

In short, since there is a noncognitivist construal of the primed version of the argument, the argument cannot be escaped by opting for noncognitivism. Anyone who accepts premises (1′) and (2′) and an appropriate variant of the knowledge and power principle is committed to the primed version of the argument, whether it be construed in cognitivist or noncognitivist terms.

Nor can one easily avoid being committed to premises (1′) and (2′), at least on a noncognitivist interpretation. Premise (1″) is the reading of (1′) given by Gibbard's theory. Virtually anyone will count as having a system of norms that requires society to do or not to do certain things. For virtually anyone will have structured pro attitudes and con attitudes toward certain social policies, and his having such attitudes will standardly amount to his accepting such a system of norms. Moreover, any *democrat* accepts a system of norms of this kind, for a democrat accepts the democratic principle, which means that he accepts a system of norms that requires an equal distribution of political power. And as for premise (2″), it seems highly unlikely that anyone who accepts a system of norms that applies to social policy will find more than a minority of his fellow citizens agreeing with him in every case as to what society ought to do. Hence, almost every citizen, and all democrats, are committed to premises (1′) and (2′) in at least the noncognitivist interpretation that would be offered by Gibbard. In what follows. I ignore noncognitivist construals of the argument and ignore the primed interpretation.

The upshot of this discussion is that a democrat can avoid the objection from expertise in its most general form only if she is prepared to reject the knowledge and power principle in formulations appropriate to both versions of the argument, the primed version and the original version.

2. The knowledge and power principle

If the original argument is to entail that the democratic principle is false, the knowledge and power principle must be strengthened beyond the simple formula that knowledge justifies power. For this formula does not purport to *exclude* anyone from playing a role in choosing the government. A person who favors representative democracy could therefore accept it, but insist that democracy is the most reliable method to empower those with knowledge. If the voter sees that certain people have political expertise, she can exercise her vote in an effort to elect those people to office.[9] To overcome this reply, an authoritarian must either strengthen the knowledge and power principle or argue with Estlund that the average citizen cannot reliably recognize those with political expertise or would not reliably vote for them.

Estlund formulates the knowledge and power principle as the doctrine that "the normative political knowledge of those who know is a strong moral reason for their holding political power."[10] But this formula is actually weaker than Socrates's doctrine that knowledge *justifies* power, for it merely says that knowledge is one of perhaps many kinds of reason that would justify a person's holding power. And Estlund adds that it does not even mean that knowledge is a *sufficient* reason for power.[11] Hence, a democrat could accept Estlund's version of the knowledge and power principle together with premises (1) and (2). Estlund thinks that the authoritarian must add the following premise to the argument: "The knowers can be known by sufficiently many non-knowers to empower them, and to practically and morally legitimate their power."[12] But a person who favors representative democracy could accept this premise and add that democracy is the most reliable method to empower those with knowledge. I therefore think that a democrat could accept all of the premises of the argument, as Estlund formulates it. Estlund is incorrect to think the democrat is forced to resist the argument.

In order to yield an argument against the democratic principle, the knowledge and power principle could be strengthened to read as follows:

> If someone has knowledge of the centrally important political truths, and is not otherwise disqualified, then she has a claim to share in the ruling of society, and no one who lacks such knowledge has any such claim.

I shall treat this as the definitive formulation of the principle for the rest of this commentary. Clearly we have an argument against democracy if we combine this version of the knowledge and power principle with the original premises (1) and (2):

(1) There are political truths.
(2) The members of a small intelligentsia have much better knowledge of the centrally important political truths than anyone else.

The argument goes through provided that some members of the intelligentsia are not disqualified from holding power by, for example, craziness or corruption. For it follows that

(4) The qualified members of the intelligentsia, and they alone, have a claim to share in the ruling of society.

Of course, a democrat would want to deny the knowledge and power principle. For a democrat does not believe that a citizen's claim to an equal share of political power depends on her having knowledge of the political truths. A democrat would be in favor of democracy (other things being equal) even if political knowledge happened to be distributed unevenly in society. But on what basis would a democrat argue against the knowledge and power principle? I begin with the strategy suggested in Estlund's paper.

3. The second-order epistemic tenet

Estlund thinks that authoritarianism is vulnerable to an argument based on the proposition that those with political knowledge cannot be known by sufficiently many others "to empower them, and to practically and morally legitimate their power."[13] Let us refer to this claim as the "second-order epistemic tenet." I think that Estlund can be read as arguing from this tenet against the definitive formulation of the knowledge and power principle. I shall read him as arguing in effect that, given the tenet, the definitive formulation of the principle must be abandoned in favor of his weaker formulation. But the definitive formulation is required by the argument against democracy. Hence, a democrat can defend her position against the objection from expertise if she can defend the second-order epistemic tenet.

But how is Estlund's argument supposed to work? I can see two lines of reasoning in Estlund's paper. The first concerns the practical problems of empowerment. In order to empower the wise, the wise must be recognized by sufficiently many people with the ability to bring about their empowerment. But this problem is not germane to the present philosophical debate, as Estlund recognizes. For even if the problem of empowerment were insuperable, which it is not, the knowledge and power principle might still be true. The authoritarian could still maintain that only the qualified members of the intelligentsia have a moral claim to share in the ruling of society.[14]

Estlund's second line of reasoning concerns the moral legitimacy of government. A form of government need not be justified to every member of the society, since "some may have impaired abilities, or ulterior motives or may be unreasonable in some other way." He proposes that a system of government is morally legitimate only if acceptable reasons for it can be given to "the reasonable." He adds that he wants to let the term "reasonable" "stand for those to whom acceptable moral reasons are morally owed." And he concludes, "this principle of moral legitimacy" means that rule by the intelligentsia is not morally legitimate if, as the second-order epistemic tenet implies, "some reasonable people may fail to recognize" the special knowledge of those who belong to the intelligentsia.[15]

The argument seems to rest on a methodological principle to the effect that any proposal about the distribution of political power must be justified by reasons that could be offered to all reasonable members of society. This principle would imply, of course, that the knowledge and power principle must be justified to the reasonable. It would also imply that any distribution of power to people who allegedly qualify for power in virtue of their special knowledge would itself have to be justified to the reasonable. It would require an authoritarian who accepted the knowledge and power principle to justify any allocation of power to those with special expertise by giving reasons to the reasonable members of society. It seems to be on this basis that Estlund appeals to the second-order tenet.

The methodological principle implies that the knowledge and power principle is not acceptable as it stands. For the latter says that the political knowledge of the qualified is necessary *and sufficient* for them to have a claim to share in ruling society. But the methodological principle implies that there is an additional requirement, if the power of the qualified knowers is to be justified, namely, that reasons can be given to the reasonable for thinking that the knowers know and deserve on that basis to rule. It implies that the knowledge and power principle must be weakened.

What kind of reasons must be given to the reasonable? Estlund requires that the reasons be sufficient to *ensure* that all reasonable people *would* recognize the knowers and their claim to rule.[16] This is an unreasonable demand. Of course, a defender of the knowledge and power principle could satisfy it trivially by defining the "reasonable" in a question-begging way as "all and only the members of the intelligentsia who also accept the knowledge and power principle." All of *these* people could be given reasons sufficient to ensure that they would recognize the knowers and their claim to rule. But unless the question is begged in some other way, no specification of the category of reasonable persons would *guarantee* that the reasonable would recognize the knowers and their claim to power. This is not a special problem for the knowledge and power principle, however. For it is also true that the reasonable cannot be guaranteed to accept the democratic principle, unless the category of the "reasonable" is defined in a question-begging manner.[17]

Estlund would not be on firmer ground if he demanded only that the reasonable *could* be brought to agree in their recognition of the knowers and their claim to power. For although there is deep and persisting disagreement about political matters in our own society, this is a contingent matter. Even if it is difficult to recognize the knowers, if they really are *knowers*, as we are assuming for the sake of argument, then we must concede that "the reasonable" *could* be brought by argument and evidence to recognize them as such. It is possible, even if not guaranteed, that agreement would be the result of argument. And unless we beg the question, we must also concede that the reasonable could be brought to agree to the knowledge and power principle. Hence, an authoritarian could apparently meet the requirement that he give reasons that *could* bring the reasonable to recognize the knowers and their claim to rule.

We need an interpretation of the methodological principle whereby it implies that the knowledge and power principle must not only be weakened, but weakened in a way that removes the sting of the argument from political expertise. If the methodological principle demanded that reasons be given that would *ensure* agreement by the reasonable, then no political proposal could be justified. But if it merely demanded that reasons be given that *could* lead to agreement by the reasonable, then the knowledge and power principle and rule by the intelligentsia could be justified. The argument would still go through. The solution to the problem is surely to read the principle as demanding simply that *good* reasons be given, that reasons be given that *ought* to lead the reasonable to agree. No work is done here by the notion of the reasonable; everything rests on the availability of good arguments. This means, in effect, that the methodological principle is merely reminding us that an argument must be given to justify both the knowledge and power principle and any proposed distribution of power to those alleged to have special expertise. Hence, Estlund still needs an argument to show why we should not accept the knowledge and power principle in its definitive formulation.

Consider, moreover, Estlund's position that rule by those with political expertise would be illegitimate unless they could be known by the "reasonable" to have such expertise. This position does not yet explain why, for example, there would not be good reasons for rule by the intelligentsia in circumstances of the kind Plato had in mind when he advocated rule by the philosophers. Imagine a society in which the political philosophers have knowledge of the political truths. They have true political belief combined with a sophisticated understanding of the basis of what they believe. Imagine that among the nonphilosophers, most people have some political beliefs, but few of them have knowledge of political matters, for their beliefs are not justified by any argument of which they have an appreciation. Imagine, however, that there is widespread agreement that the philosophers have political knowledge, and imagine it is widely known that they have a sophisticated understanding of the basis of their beliefs about the common good. Hence, people believe and have good reason to believe that the philosophers' political beliefs are well justified and that the philosophers have political knowledge. They could plausibly be said to *know* that the philosophers have political knowledge.[18] This is a society in which the intelligentsia alone have political knowledge and in which it is known that the intelligentsia have political knowledge. In this situation, Estlund appears to have no reply to the claim that the philosophers ought ideally to rule. But a democrat would surely say that in order to know whether rule by the wise would be warranted in a situation of this kind, we would need to know a good deal more about the situation, about the psychology of the wise, and about the nature of the social problems faced by society and the nature of the best solutions to the problems. It seems to me that in many circumstances of the kind I have described, if the philosophers were reasoning correctly, they would conclude in favor of democracy and against the knowledge and power principle.

4. Why democracy?

I shall look briefly at a few defenses of democracy, both consequentialist and nonconsequentialist defenses. Let me begin, however, by considering an argument in favor of the knowledge and power principle.

It may seem that it would be a virtue of a type of political system if, because of its nature, it could be expected to yield decisions to bring about the things that society ought to bring about. But in order to arrive at correct decisions about what society ought to do, except by chance, the government must to be able to recognize the correct solutions to social problems. This suggests that it would be a virtue of a type of political system if, by its very nature, it promised to provide access to the truth about what society ought to do. Government by those with the relevant political knowledge would by its very nature provide access to the political truths, and it is hard to imagine how any other system could do better. Hence, we might conclude, other things being equal, an ideal system would give the ruling power to people with knowledge of what society ought to do.

I believe this argument captures the intuitive rationale for the knowledge and power principle. But the argument moves too quickly. For the problem of what kind of governmental system to have is itself a substantive social problem. Call it the "governmental problem." There are, of course, social problems that are logically independent of the governmental problem, including problems of justice and economic efficiency. Call them the "social problems." Now the nature of a system of government can *itself* be good or bad, or have good or bad effects, leaving aside what impact it has on the social problems. We may for this reason rightly prefer a form of government that we know will likely do less well than some other form of government at identifying the correct solution to social problems. Even if government is an instrument for dealing with social problems, it would be a mistake to evaluate systems of government *solely* on the basis of how well they would identify solutions to social problems, for this would be to fail to take into account the other properties and effects of the systems. The best solution to the governmental problem may not be to implement the form of government that would do best at identifying the solutions to social problems.

To say this is not, of course, to abandon a consequentialist evaluation of democracy. It is simply to advocate the solution to the governmental problem that would have the best consequences *overall*, which is not necessarily the form of government that has the best chance of identifying the best solutions to social problems. The favored solutions must also be *implemented*, of course. Now, it may be thought that government by the intelligentsia would be best not only at recognizing the best solutions, but also at implementing them. I do not want to debate this point, although I doubt it. But to defend government by the intelligentsia in consequentialist terms, it would have to be shown that its consequences would be best overall, with everything taken into account, including its possibly deleterious indirect effects on the nature of society.

Many who advocate democracy do so at least partly because of indirect effects, effects other than or in addition to the direct effects that are due to the quality of the choices that are likely to be made by a democratic government in dealing with social problems. Tocqueville argued, for example, that although democracy is "inferior to aristocracy viewed purely as a decision-making apparatus," it "has as a by-product a certain energy and restlessness that benefits industry and generates prosperity."[19] It has also been argued that democracy offers better protection against tyranny, better protection of the rights of citizens, even leaving aside the political rights a democrat would claim. And it has been argued that democratic procedures of the proper sort would develop civic responsibility and a sense of mutual solidarity among the citizens and promote individual autonomy by giving every citizen the duty and opportunity to develop and express his own view about what ought to be done by the society to deal with social problems.

Some would seek to justify democracy on the basis of intrinsic virtues rather than consequentialist ones. It might be argued that democratic procedures are a requirement of justice or fairness, or that only a democratic system of government could show equal respect to all citizens. Democratic participation may be viewed as intrinsically good, and democracy might seem on this count to be intrinsically desirable.

These arguments obviously do not require abandoning the epistemic view of democratic debate, as debate about what society ought to do. They do not require abandoning the idea that there are political truths at stake. But to accept them is to accept that democracy has virtues other than, and perhaps in addition to, the likelihood of its leading to correct political decisions.

Jon Elster sees arguments from the indirect effects of democracy as "self-defeating," since they purport to justify democracy on the basis of "effects that are essentially by-products," effects that are not "brought about intelligently and intentionally."[20] For example, if Tocqueville is correct, industry, prosperity, energy, and restlessness are by-products of democracy, for they are effects of democracy even if they are not aimed at. Other defenders of democracy would claim that democratic government promotes the civic responsibility, solidarity, and autonomy of citizens even if these effects are not among the goals of government. Elster objects: "Although the constitution-makers may secretly have such side effects in mind, they cannot coherently invoke them in public."[21] Unless a political system has "inherent advantages in terms of justice or efficiency, one cannot coherently and publicly advocate its introduction because of the side effects that would follow in its wake." The side effects cannot be what motivate people to participate in the system. Politics must be guided by the business of governing. If democracy "was introduced solely because of its side effects [such as its effects] on economic prosperity, and no one believed in it on any other grounds, it would not produce them."[22]

Estlund adds that the desired indirect effects of democracy on the character of citizens will arise only if people have some basis for hope that their aims will be well served by the political system. Otherwise, one will have no reason to participate, and then the "character effects will be missed."[23]

My reply to these objections depends on three distinctions. First is a distinction between justifying democracy and justifying a person's participation in democratic institutions. These are separate issues, for I might believe the democratic principle is correct but see no reason why I should participate. Our problem is to justify democracy by comparison with government by the intelligentsia, not to justify participation. Elster's argument blurs this distinction, for it depends on assuming that if democracy is defended in terms of character effects, then character effects must be what would motivate participation. Second is a distinction between justifying democracy by comparison with the absence of government and justifying it by comparison with other possible forms of government. Our problem is the latter; it is to decide what kind of government to have.[24] Elster's argument also blurs this distinction, for it assumes that if we "justify democracy" on the basis of indirect effects, we have no concern with the business of government. On the contrary, we need government to discharge the business of government. But we may advocate democracy because of its indirect effects. Third is a distinction between "the purpose of government" and the goals of those who participate in government. The purpose of government is presumably to deal with the class of problems I have been calling social problems. But the goals of those who participate in democratic institutions may be quite varied. Perhaps it is true that most individuals would do better on the whole at achieving their own goals under democratic institutions than they would under any other form of government. But to say this is not to say that democracy does better than any alternative at achieving the correct solutions to social problems.

Armed with these distinctions, we are in a position to turn back Elster's attack. Advocates of democracy are primarily concerned to justify democracy by comparison with the alternatives, not to justify participation in democratic institutions. This is true even though, of course, one would not favor democracy if it seemed there would be insufficient participation to make the system work. Democrats may coherently and publicly take into account all of the expected effects of democratic institutions, including side effects, and including the variable effects of different forms of democracy on participation. Once democracy is in place, individuals will have to decide whether to participate, and their participation may be motivated by recognition of the importance of the social problems that need to be dealt with. We need government because of what Elster calls "the business of governing"; we advocate democracy partly because of its beneficial side effects; we participate because, with democracy in place, we hope to achieve our individual ends by doing so. We may, for example, desire the effects that we think participation will have on our character. If our ends include bringing about solutions to the social problems, then we may participate partly because we think that our participation will increase the chance of an outcome with which we agree. But we may obviously participate for this reason even if we do not believe that democracy is especially good at identifying correct solutions to the social problems.

By analogy, suppose a family is looking for a competitive form of recreation, and for this reason it is trying to decide whether to purchase a game of checkers or chess. There would be nothing self-defeating or incoherent in arguing for chess on the basis of the superior "educational" effects of playing chess. Once the game is purchased, family members may participate in order to get these effects. But they would perhaps be more likely to participate for other reasons, such as a desire to prove themselves against a sibling or a parent. And they might get the educational effects from participating whether or not they are seeking them. I think this is a fair analogy, and I therefore think that Elster's objection is mistaken.[25]

The idea that democracy is the best form of government carries with it the idea that the best form of government may not be the form of government best designed to yield correct decisions about society's problems. If democratic procedures bring about correct decisions, this is because of the views of the citizens, not because of the nature of the procedures. Of course, it ought to be the case, ideally, that the output of democratic procedures is that the society chooses what society ought to choose on the merits. And it would be a cause for serious concern if democratic procedures in a certain society led repeatedly to wrong decisions. But this is not a general objection to the democratic ideal, and it is not obvious that abandoning democracy would always be the best way to deal with the concern. It may be best to wait for the citizens to recognize their own errors and decide democratically to implement the better solutions.

It may be useful to compare the ideal of democracy with the ideal of individual autonomy, understood as self-government. We value autonomy for reasons that have to do with what autonomy is, and because we think an autonomous life is best overall. We do not value it (merely) because of an expectation that autonomous individuals can be expected on the whole to do better than nonautonomous individuals at deciding to do what would be best for them on the merits. In a similar way, if we are democrats, we value democracy because we think democracy will have the best consequences for society, all things considered, and because of the kind of governance it is. We do not value it because we believe its nature is such as to lead it to correct decisions about social problems. By its nature, government by those with political expertise would obviously be more successful at identifying the correct solutions to social problems. Yet, for all that, if democracy has the best consequences overall, then government by those with expertise would not be an overall improvement.

Notes

1 I do not offer this as an adequate account of the concept of democracy but nothing in this essay turns on anything more than an intuitive idea of what democracy would be. Equal "formal" power is compatible with inequalities of power of various kinds as long as such inequalities are not due to the rules governing the procedures. "Most" members ought to have equal power; the qualification may be used to exclude criminals, the insane, or certain others, perhaps on the basis that they are not mature or not morally responsible.

2 David Estlund, "Making Truth Safe for Democracy," in this volume. Estlund presented an early version of the paper to the Conference on Democracy, University of California, Davis, May 1990, and I presented a version of the present essay in reply. The page numbers of quotations in this commentary are taken from the typescript of Estlund's paper. In support of his claim about Socrates, Estlund cites *Crito* 47c9–d2, *Laches* 184e8–9, *Gorgias* 463d1–465e1, *Republic* I 341c4–342e11. He also cites Richard Kraut, *Socrates and the State* (Princeton, N.J.: Princeton University Press, 1984), pp. 231–44.

3 Estlund says, "Socrates was no authoritarian, though, since he denies that anyone was wise in the requisite way." "Making Truth Safe," p. 3.

4 Ibid., p. 2.

5 See Jon Elster, *Sour Grapes: Studies in the Subversion of Rationality* (Cambridge: Cambridge University Press, 1983), sec. II.9.

6 See Estlund, "Making Truth Safe," p. 3.

7 Ibid., p. 4.

8 Allan Gibbard, *Wise Choices, Apt Feelings: A Theory of Normative Judgment* (Cambridge, Mass.: Harvard University Press, 1990). Consult especially pp. 86–93.

9 This point was suggested by Robert Sugden's remarks in "Justified to Whom?" in this volume.

10 Estlund, "Making Truth Safe," p. 3.

11 Ibid., p. 22.

12 Ibid., p. 17.

13 Ibid.

14 Estlund addresses the problem of empowerment, and concedes it is not as "germane" as the problem of legitimacy, in ibid., p. 19.

15 Ibid.

16 He says the reasons must rule out the possibility that "some reasonable people may fail to recognize" the claim of the knowers. The reasons must ensure that the identity of the knowers "could not be doubted by reasonable people." "Being a reasonable person" must "guarantee" that one can be brought to know the knowers. Estlund, "Making Truth Safe," p. 21.

17 I do not mean to be commenting in this paragraph on the more structured argumentative strategy used by John Rawls in *A Theory of Justice* (Cambridge, Mass.: Harvard University Press, 1971), which involves the notion of an hypothetical "original position" in which the reasonable are to choose political principles. Nor do I mean to be commenting on the argument of David Gauthier, in *Morals by Agreement* (Oxford: Oxford University Press, 1986), which depends on excluding certain kinds of considerations from the reasoning of the "economically rational" individuals whose reasoning is critical in his view to the justification of moral and political principles.

18 I assume the naive view that knowledge is justified true belief.

19 Jon Elster in *Sour Grapes*, p. 96. Elster is summarizing views of Alexis de Tocqueville, *Democracy in America* (New York: Anchor Books, 1969), pp. 243–4.

20 Elster, *Sour Grapes*, p. 92. On Elster's official definition, by-products "are states that *cannot* be brought about [both] intelligently and intentionally" (p. 56, my emphasis, also p. 43). I will not attempt to explain his meaning here. Suffice it to say that I doubt that all of the consequences Elster classifies as by-products would qualify under this strict meaning. For example, government could aim to develop the energy and restlessness of its citizens, and it could also aim to develop the civic responsibility, solidarity, and autonomy of its citizens. It seems to me that it could succeed in bringing about these effects, and not merely as a "fluke" (p. 56). Elster counts these as by-products even though they do not seem to satisfy his official definition (pp. 95–6). But this terminological point does not go to the heart of Elster's argument. His central concern is to reject attempts to justify democracy on the basis of benefits of the kind I have just listed, which, he believes, it is not the "main purpose of politics" to bring about (p. 91).

21 Elster, *Sour Grapes*, p. 92.

22 Ibid., p. 96.

23 Estlund, "Making Truth Safe," p. 16.

24 This point is made by Thomas Christiano, "Freedom, Consensus, and Equality in Collective Decision Making," *Ethics* 101 (1990): 151–81, at p. 155.

25 Stephen Holmes offers an argument similar to Elster's in "Tocqueville and Democracy" in this volume. He says, "The justification of democratic processes by invoking side effects that are unnoticed and unintended by the parties involved seems deeply unsatisfactory. We tend to believe that justifications of public institutions should themselves be 'public.'" Notice, however, that even if certain side effects are not *actually* noticed by the parties, there may be nothing that prevents them from being noticed and from being offered by the parties as part of their justification for democracy. The issue is whether a putative justification of democracy on the basis of its side effects would be cogent. Holmes points out that Tocqueville's justifications of democracy have a similar structure to justifications of religion in terms of its social utility, which, he says, also "violate the 'publicity condition' for moral legitimacy." They are, he says, "powerful justifications for admiring religion as a social institution" but they cannot possibly be reasons for an individual to accept religion as true" ("Tocqueville and Democracy"). But the issue is not the violation of a "publicity condition." The issue is that a reason to accept religion as true must be a reason to believe in the existence of God. There is a distinction between justifying religion as a social institution, in terms of its social utility, and justifying it as a system of belief by providing reasons to believe that its central claims are true. In the case of democracy, no sufficiently analogous distinction is in the offing, for the issue is simply to justify a set of social institutions.

3

Democratic rights at national and workplace levels

RICHARD J. ARNESON

Democratic rights are protective. Their primary function is to safeguard other, more fundamental rights. Democratic rights are justified in a given institutional setting just to the extent that they serve this function better than do alternative feasible arrangements. Or at any rate, so I shall claim in this essay.

By "democratic rights" I refer to rights held by each member of an association to vote and stand for office in free elections in which a majority-rule procedure determines the composition of a body that by majority-rule procedure settles the rules by which the association is governed.[1] Many phrases of this definition are variously interpretable, but for purposes of this essay the rough idea it conveys before interpretation will suffice. I am especially interested in the case of democratic rights at the level of the modern nation-state, which is not a voluntary association but nonetheless coercively enforces its rules as law across its entire territory.

The more fundamental rights that democratic rights should protect are conceived as requirements of justice. My own view is that along with substantial guarantees of freedom of speech, privacy, and individual liberty, these fundamental rights include egalitarian rights to material resources such as are implied by John Rawls's difference principle regulating the shares of primary social goods or by Ronald Dworkin's principle of equality of resources or by some other principle in this family.[2] Most of the arguments that I give in this essay should go through whatever is the reader's preferred conception of fundamental rights, but the detailed implications of these arguments will vary accordingly.

Commitment to the idea that democratic procedures are justified insofar as they protect fundamental rights does not presuppose that anyone is ever in a uniquely privileged position to judge authoritatively what fundamental rights people truly possess. We can recognize that our own epistemic access to fundamental rights is limited, that other people now might be in a position to have knowledge about rights that we misperceive, and that other people in future will almost certainly come to know more than we do now about the content of individual fundamental rights. So our judgments as to what procedural rights should be accorded are always provisional and liable to be overturned by future insights into what rights people have and by increased understanding of how best to secure them.

Given a provisional understanding of the fundamental rights that the people of a specified society are owed, we can rank proposed conceptions of political rights according to how well they would operate in that society to prevent violation of fundamental rights. These rights are weighted in importance so that with any proposed conception of political procedures we can compute its "expected justice score" provided that we can identify the possible outcomes of implementing the conception and the probability of each outcome and the justice score of each outcome that might be reached. From this *ex ante* perspective there is an obvious ambiguity in the ideal of "securing the fulfillment of fundamental individual rights." This ambiguity would be resolved by deciding what attitude toward risk is appropriate when viewing constitutional outcomes from the standpoint of justice: For example, we could select political procedures in order either to maximize or to maximin their expected justice score. I do not attempt to resolve this ambiguity in this essay.[3]

The argument of this paper is that the protective account of democratic rights provides the most natural and compelling justification of political regimes of substantive constitutional democracy under modern conditions. Here some explication of terms is needed. A *constitutional democracy* is a regime run according to principles of democratic governance qualified by a constitution asserting certain rights of individual citizens that are enforced by nonelected judges holding final powers of review. These constitutionally protected rights might or might not all increase the extent to which the regime over time maintains its democratic character. In other words, a constitution might enforce only individual rights that limit majority rule in order to preserve or enhance the genuinely majority-rule character of the political order, the fulfillment of every citizen's democratic rights. If the constitution protects some individual rights that are not democracy-enhancing in this sense but, rather, justified on some other moral grounds, I call the regime a *substantive* constitutional democracy.[4] The protective account of democratic rights plausibly explains why political democracy should be substantively constitutional. A subsidiary argument urges that the proposal that the democratic rights of citizens in constitutional democracies be expanded to encompass workplace democracy is not strongly supported by the protective considerations that strongly support democracy on its home ground, the political arena.

In the absence of a demonstration that enforcing universal rights of democratic citizenship is more likely to promote fulfillment of citizens' fundamental rights than alternative proposals for rules of governance, it is not plausible to uphold the right of each citizen to vote in elections that pick political rulers and establish the laws. The exercise of the vote is an exercise of power by the voter over the lives of other citizens. No one has rights to placement in social roles that allow one to exercise power over other human beings without first obtaining their consent unless such exercise of power best promotes fulfillment of the fundamental rights of the people over whom power is exercised together with with one's own fundamental rights.[5]

An example that I hope will illustrate this point uncontroversially is the right of parents to exercise power over the lives of their young offspring. This right accrues to parents, to the extent that it does, in virtue of the fact that assigning wide discretionary authority to them over the care and nurturance of their children proves to be a good way of bringing it about that each child's right to a decent upbringing is secured. Where there is evidence that parents are abusing their children, this parental right lapses, and society has a duty to intervene for the sake of the child. Nor is this a situation in which every dog has a right to bite once before being muzzled; if there is good evidence that a parent will be an unfit parent and an alternative feasible arrangement that is better for the child can be implemented, society has a duty to intervene before any actual misuse of authority by the biological parent. The biologically determined tendency of parents to bond with their natural children creates a strong presumption that a parent who wishes to be the primary caregiver for a natural child should be allowed and encouraged to play this role, but this presumption is rebuttable.

The presumption is rebuttable not just in a single case but across the board. Suppose that highly reliable social science research of the twenty-first century establishes that it would be better for children if they were separated from their parents at birth and raised collectively on kibbutzim, or assigned to foster parents whose parental virtue has been certified. Moreover, this same research that we are imagining establishes beyond reasonable doubt that the gains to children achievable by separating them from their natural parents are so much greater than the utility loss to natural parents and grandparents and other affected persons that on any reasonable theory of justice the gains for the children morally outweigh the losses to the others under the new arrangement. In this (improbable) scenario, society has a duty to put the new arrangement into effect and parents morally do not have the right to exercise traditional parental authority over their offspring. I say democratic rights are exactly like parental rights in this respect: The rights exist insofar as they are rightly deemed to be effective means for the achievement of morally desirable states of affairs, and once better means to the same ends are available, the rights entirely lose their moral standing.[6]

Another example illustrating this viewpoint on procedural fairness is the moral status of the various rights of individuals accused of crimes – the right to confront one's accusers, the right to a speedy trial, the right against self-incrimination, the right to counsel, the right to a jury of one's peers, and so on. From a moral perspective this panoply of rights would dissolve if it were discovered that abrogating them wholesale would produce trial verdicts that are fairer (and generate no morally undesirable outcomes of such magnitude as to outweigh the increased fairness of trial verdicts).

My position that procedural rights are merely instruments for securing morally desirable outcomes invites this objection: Suppose it turned out that permitting police to torture arrested persons to obtain confessions and allowing judges to settle cases by trial by combat proved to increase the accuracy of criminal trials in given circumstances and no feasible alternative procedures would do any better in this respect. My position then seems to entail that arrested persons have no right not to be tortured and no right not to be forced to establish their innocence through trial by combat.

The objection proceeds from misunderstanding. The idea that procedures should be chosen in order to attain morally best results does not mean that the immediate consequences of operating the procedures themselves should be excluded from the calculation. The calculation of outcomes must be inclusive. In the same way, an act-utilitarian position that judges the rightness and wrongness of each act by its consequences does not tell us to distinguish act and further consequences and count only the latter in deciding what acts are right and wrong. The position I am defending is more modest and less revisionary than the objection assumes. My position is that there are no special procedural rights determinable by examining our intuitions about inherently fair procedures (supposed to be independent of our convictions about the substantively fair outcomes that procedures work to reach).[7] This does not gainsay the fact that we adhere to general principles imputing rights to individuals (such as the right not to be tortured) and that these generally binding rights do not cease to hold when individuals are undergoing institutional procedures.

A third example illustrating the claim that procedural rights are means to the fulfillment of more fundamental rights – one more relevant to the topic of democratic procedures – is the question of the appropriate voting rules for determining the level of provision of local public goods. Assume that a nation is divided into small municipalities that control the production of local public goods. Assume also that it is determined that the procedure of straight majority rule among the members of each municipality would yield a pattern of public goods provision and an incidence of taxation to pay for these goods that is less fair than the alternative of a set tax rule for public goods provision and the use of a Clarke–Groves voting mechanism to determine what quantity and quality of which public goods should be supplied.[8] The claim made in support of constitutional entrenchment of the Clarke–Groves voting mechanism would be roughly that it yields decisions regarding public goods provision that are efficient and that in this context avoidable inefficiency is unfair. On these assumptions, I submit, the imposition of the Clarke–Groves procedure would be fair and the imposition of democratic rights in my sense would be unfair. There is no content to the issue of what procedures are intrinsically unfair, apart from examination of the outcomes they might reach.

Moral entitlement to exercise power over others accrues to a person by virtue of (1) her moral competence to exercise power in ways that will be conducive to the fulfillment of the rights of those affected by her exercise of power and (2) her disposition to use her competence so that affected persons' rights will be secured.

Moral competence is not evenly distributed across the population of modern societies. Nor is moral competence randomly distributed so that any given individual is as likely as any other to be richly endowed with it. We can identify various skills and talents that combine to produce moral competence and we can sometimes identify quite reliably individuals who have better than average moral competence. The strongest argument for political democracy is that we cannot design an undemocratic political mechanism that reliably selects just persons of very high moral competence (who are otherwise qualified) to be lawmakers and governors. Democracy emerges as a second-best solution.

Any political selection process that picks rulers for an autocratic political system would have to be operated by human beings. Given that such political power is especially attractive to persons who would misuse it, there are bound to be enormous pressures of corruption and distorting influence working on the selection process. Fans of aristocratic and communist and other forms of autocracy have not yet proposed any reliable selection process. Moreover, the task of selection would not be merely to pick out individuals who exhibit the traits needed in an ideal autocrat, but rather to pick out individuals who have these traits and who would continue to display them even under the enormous temptations to corruption that are inseparable from the exercise of autocratic power. The verdict of historically informed common sense is that this task is hopeless.

These entirely familiar considerations lead to a second-best problem for which democracy emerges as a plausible solution. To simplify, suppose that there must be an absolute sovereign in the sense of an identifiable body of persons that at any given time controls the selection of governing agents and hence the conduct of government. By the argument of the preceding paragraph, there is no constitutional device that can ensure that the absolute sovereign will exercise power wisely and fairly. The question is then whether this political power should be placed equally in all citizens through the institution of majority rule with universal suffrage or in some subset of the citizens. If majorities likely to coalesce under majority rule are presumed competent to block political policies that would violate their own rights, the danger in majority rule is rights violations inflicted on minorities and the danger in any form of minority rule is rights violations inflicted on the majority. *Ceteris paribus*, the latter is worse.

An indication that the argument just given captures the major line of thought that supports democratic rights is that where this line of thought peters out, there boundaries that limit majority rule may be acceptable. Consider constitutional democracy in the United States. For my purposes in this essay the salient feature of this system is its Bill of Rights enumerating fundamental liberties enforced by an independent federal judiciary, the members of which are appointed with lifetime tenure in office.[9] Since many crucial phrases in the wording of the Bill of Rights and subsequent constitutional amendments do little more than indicate topics to be addressed, the limits on majority rule imposed by these amendments are variable over time, set by the creative interpretations and, in effect, judicial lawmaking established by the Supreme Court in each generation. The upshot is that conceptions of individual rights defined by nonelected judges constrain the lawmaking work of duly elected legislators. The rights argument for such a system is that once the assumed requirement of absolute sovereignty is dropped, then we are free to consider divided sovereignty schemes that vest some power in an elite without turning the elite into an absolute sovereign. Also, in divided sovereignty schemes, the selection process for an elite such as the membership of a Supreme Court can be sufficiently reliable to generate a superior competence argument for vesting some political power in the elite. The search for Platonic Guardians need not be utterly in vain if the role and power of the Guardians can be limited carefully by constitutional design.

If the constitutional system could be viewed as maintaining the ongoing prerequisites of democracy, there need be no conflict between constitutional politics and majority rule. Constraints on the operation of majority rule that are needed to preserve majority rule require no justification beyond democracy itself. No doubt much judicial oversight of the conduct of elected officials falls into this category. For example, a legislative majority bent on suppressing freedom of expression on matters germane to the conduct of politics would be committed to a policy that would degrade the quality of free elections and thus drain some of the democratic character from ostensibly "democratic" politics. A Supreme Court that struck down legislative incursions on freedom of expression broadly relevant to public affairs could be interpreted as limiting majority rule just in order to preserve majority rule. But some of the fundamental individual rights upheld by the Supreme Court simply do not answer to this description.

Consider the supposed moral rights of married couples to use contraceptives, of unmarried couples to do the same, and of women to be legally free to terminate their first-trimester and second-trimester pregnancies without regard for the interests of the fetus that such abortions would destroy. Such rights are not plausibly viewed as democracy-enhancing or protective of citizens interests that are necessary if they are to be genuinely in possession of equal rights of democratic citizenship.[10] A judicial system that acts to protect such rights of privacy[11] against legislation duly enacted by democratic lawmaking bodies is substantively constitutional. If such judicial action is morally defensible, it is action justified in the teeth of democratic rights, not by any sort of appeal to them.

The most natural interpretation of these constitutional limits on majority rule enforced by an activist judiciary is that they are indeed undemocratic but none the worse for that. Assume *arguendo* that married couples have the moral right to use contraceptive methods of birth control and that a democratic state that bans contraceptive use violates the rights of its citizens. If the justification of democratic rule is that such rule protects the fundamental moral rights of its citizens, the justification fails in this case. If there is a way for an elite to overrule majority rule in this instance without seriously risking the overturning of majority rule across the board with consequent overall losses in fundamental rights protection, such overruling is morally desirable. The Supreme Court announcing the *Griswold v. Connecticut* (1965) decision is that rights-protecting elite.

I should not try to leave the impression that the only plausible justification of any form of substantive constitutional constraints on what would otherwise be a democratic regime is that the constraints would protect moral rights. For example, some constraints might *ex ante* be to the advantage of all citizens and justified on this basis. Consider the problem that any government might be tempted to impose nearly confiscatory taxation on sunk investments made by economic firms. Suppose that a firm is considering what would be a profitable investment except that once the investment is made, the firm would be vulnerable to exploitive taxation that leaves it just barely better off than it would be if it abandoned the now untransferable investment. If the government would be better off introducing such taxation, it may not be able credibly to pledge to refrain from a policy that would be in its interest. Knowing this, the rational firm would eschew the investment. In this situation, all parties might be better off if a constitutional constraint prohibited the government from engaging in predatory taxation of this sort.[12]

My claim is that democratic procedures, like all procedures, should be evaluated according to the moral value of the outcomes they would be reasonably expected to produce. The preceding paragraph illustrates the truth that outcomes can be appraised according to criteria other than protection of moral rights. I believe that protection of rights is the primary standard for judging constitutional procedures, simply because I believe that protection of rights is of primary moral importance. But to pursue this issue one would have to discuss what rights we have and which ones are fundamental.[13]

Dworkin on majoritarianism and judicial review

The view I take of constitutional limits on majority rule is (in all essentials) included within an argument that Ronald Dworkin has advanced. In the course of defending judicial activism against the suggestion that on issues of constitutionality judges should defer to the deliverances of elected legislators unless the law under review is plainly inconsistent with the constitutional text, he examines two possible props to the policy of deference.[14] One argument is that judges should defer to legislators because officials accountable to an electorate are more likely to reach decisions that protect citizens' fundamental rights than nonaccountable nonelected judges. This argument, in other words, holds that majority-will decision making will usually produce better outcomes than judicial overrides. The second argument is an appeal to procedural fairness that maintains that it is intrinsically fairer for important political decisions affecting a group of people to be made by those people or their representatives in democratic fashion rather than by a small elite flouting majority will. "What concerns all should be decided by all," in the words of a medieval maxim.

Against the first argument Dworkin merely asserts his political judgment that in recent years across a broad range of issues the legal rights established by the Supreme Court exercising its power of constitutional review correspond more closely to the set of legal rights supported by correct morality than the legal rights that elected legislators deferring to majority sentiment would have established in the absence of effective judicial review. Against the second argument Dworkin appears to produce a procedural argument, but I think he is better interpreted as denying the force of purely procedural considerations in this context.

Dworkin appeals to the maxim that one should not be judge in one's own cause in order to suggest that it is procedurally anomalous for a majority to have the authority to make binding political decisions when the issue is whether or not a minority claim of right against the majority should stand. An intrinsically fairer procedure would be to place the authority to make such decisions in the hands of a third party that is neither the majority nor the minority, and according to Dworkin constitutionally mandated judicial review effects just that morally desirable distribution of authority.

Notice that nothing in the setup of judicial review guarantees that a constitutional issue that pits the interests of a majority of whites against a minority of blacks will not be decided ultimately by an all-white Supreme Court. If we assume that the maxim that one should not be judge in one's own cause is not violated in these circumstances, this must be in virtue of the capacity for impartial and fair decision making that we naturally impute to the members of the Supreme Court. We do not think of the Supreme Court justices as representing the interests of their race. This is a presumption that rests on the track record of the Court on divisive racial issues. I do not intend by this remark to challenge Dworkin's position, which I fully endorse – rather, to note its character.

It might be thought that Dworkin's appeal to the maxim that one should not be judge in one's own cause is strained in this context, for the maxim concerns proper enforcement of law, not the making of it. I believe that Dworkin's argument has some force, but I shall not try to argue the issue here. The point I wish to make is that the procedural maxim to which Dworkin appeals is straightforwardly an appeal to intuitions about how to bring about morally desirable results. The idea is not that there is something inherent in the procedure of being judge at a trial at which one is also plaintiff that offends against moral principle. The idea is, rather, that this setting for decision making is extremely unpropitious for the goal of reaching an impartial and fair decision. Perhaps a saint could play this double role properly, but most humans would find their judgment clouded by the temptation to be partial. The maxim condenses commonsense thought about what decision procedures are likely to yield best results. So both of the arguments Dworkin gives for activist judicial review presuppose his opinion – which I share – that the fundamental standard for assessing governmental procedures is the quality of the outcomes they would tend to produce.

What Dworkin is contending and what I am claiming are not exactly the same. Dworkin is wondering how Supreme Court judges who effectively have power to restrain majority rule in certain ways should exercise this power. In answer to this question he argues for activism over deference. I am wondering whether it is morally acceptable that Supreme Court judges should have the effective power to restrain majority rule in these ways – by striking down duly enacted legislation as unconstitutional, for instance. But the answer that Dworkin gives to his question, if it is acceptable, also serves to answer my question, because if it is morally desirable that Supreme Court justices should have the power to restrain majority rule and that they should exercise this power vigorously in defense of fundamental individual rights, then *a fortiori* it is morally desirable that they should have the power to restrain majority rule.

It remains to indicate that my view of the appropriate reach of majority rule and the limits of that reach are borrowed from Dworkin. He writes, "Legislators who have been elected, and must be reelected, by a political majority are more likely to take that majority's side in any serious argument about the rights of a minority against it; if they oppose the majority's wishes too firmly, it will replace them with those who do not." So other things equal, public officials who are not subject to majority control in this way are more likely to reason impartially and reach correct decisions when minority rights are in conflict with majority desires.

It is worth inquiring why this argument does not create a presumption against any form of majority-will governance altogether and in favor of any form of elite rule insulated effectively from majority control. One consideration is that public officials who form such an elite, insulated from partiality toward the majority or control by the majority, will likely be partial toward some minority section of the citizenry, with which they are affiliated. The argument just given now reapplies. Public officials controlled by a minority segment of the population or affiliated with it are more likely to take that minority's side when its political desires are in conflict with the rights of the majority. So other things equal, such officials are less likely to reason impartially and reach correct decisions when political issues put majority rights at stake.

These two parallel arguments would roughly cancel each other out unless a further assumption is made. If the moral value of the fulfillment of different sorts of rights held by different people were deemed incommensurable, then the prospect of nonfulfillment of the rights of a minority would balance the prospect of nonfulfillment of the rights of a majority, however large the majority in comparison to the size of the minority. The thought that in the worst case, if lawmakers are bent on violating rights, the violation of the rights of a smaller number of people is, other things equal, morally preferable, assumes commensurability among rights violations, at least in the sense that more rights violations are worse than fewer violations if all are the same in gravity taken one by one.

Pure procedural justice

The position I am defending is that what constitutes fair procedures depends entirely on which of the available sets of procedures would produce morally best outcomes. Furthermore, the standards for determining what outcomes are morally best do not include any standards that rank procedures as intrinsically more or less fair independently of the outcomes of establishing and operating the procedures. This has been called a "best results" theory.[15] It entails that there is no such thing as pure procedural justice. I am using the term "pure procedural justice" in the sense given it by John Rawls, who contrasts this notion with the ideas of perfect and imperfect procedural justice.[16] Where the latter notions are in play, we have a standard for assessing the justice of outcomes that is defined independently of any procedure that might be deployed to produce the outcome. A perfect procedure is one that if followed correctly is guaranteed to produce the just outcome; imperfect procedural justice applies in situations where the best procedure we can devise is not certain to produce the just outcome. In contrast, pure procedural justice is exhibited when there is no standard independent of following fair procedures for judging the justice of outcomes. When the procedure in use is determined to be fair by a standard that does not look to the outcomes that might be produced by the procedure, and any outcome that might result from the procedure inherits the fairness of the procedure itself, we are dealing with pure procedural justice.

Are there any standards of pure procedural justice or situations in which these standards apply? Rawls cites the example of a series of fair gambles. The distribution of money that results from fair bets is fair whatever it happens to be, for we have no standards for assessing the outcomes of gambles apart from standards that apply to the gambling procedures themselves.

One way of putting the doubt that nothing corresponds to this ideal of pure procedural justice is that any gambling arrangement, "fair" or "unfair," that individuals freely and voluntarily enter into will yield outcomes that are not unfair.[17] In this example all the weight is carried by the idea of free and voluntary consent, none by the idea of pure procedural fairness. If individuals freely and voluntarily agree to gambles that are actuarially unfair, or far out of line with the objective likelihoods that the events that are the objects of the gambles will occur, so long as the parties have access to the relevant information no unfairness or injustice is done. For that matter, if individuals freely and voluntarily agree to gamble using marked decks of cards, crooked roulette wheels, and the like, no unfairness or injustice is done to anyone who knowingly participates.

A possible response to these doubts is to assert that free and voluntary consent to outcomes by those affected by them is a fair procedure and that the relationship between free and voluntary consent and the outcomes reached through this process is a signal instance of pure procedural justice. The procedure of free and voluntary consent confers moral legitimacy on whatever is thus consented to. I have my doubts about whether it is perspicuous to characterize free and voluntary consent as a "fair procedure," but I shall not press that vague sense of unease. A more important source of doubt is the idea that it is better to regard free and voluntary consent as fitting within the category of imperfect procedural justice. When individuals voluntarily cooperate or associate, it is appropriate to be concerned that the interests of each voluntary cooperator or associate are adequately catered to. The procedure that no one is to be co-opted into a wide range of associations and cooperative practices except on terms that elicit everyone's free and voluntary consent is a powerful means for ensuring that each consenting party's interests are served by the arrangement. Where grave doubts arise as to whether the individual's free and voluntary consent is a good means to ensure reasonably equitable outcomes, paternalistic restriction of liberty overriding the authority of free and voluntary consent is in order. Of course, this last point does not uncontroversially settle the issue. It indicates that the claim that the concept of pure procedural justice is instantiated relies on a background deontological view of a contestable sort. The idea that individuals have serious rights to be treated in ways that accord with certain procedures quite independently of the consequences of their being so treated can be associated with views in the Lockean moral tradition interpreted in a Nozickian way.

Marx on democracy

The contextual nature of the justification of activist judicial review is dramatically illustrated by Karl Marx's writings on the Paris Commune. The insurrection of Parisian patriotism against the national government installed in the wake of the victory of Prussia in the Franco-Prussian War impressed Marx and his collaborator Friedrich Engels as fraught with constitutional lessons for the working-class communist movement. The main lesson to be drawn from the Paris Commune experience is that the machinery of government of whatever form established under capitalism is not suitable for working-class rule. Even a democratic republic that takes shape under capitalist auspices will be a tool of minority rule – either the rule of a minority section of society that controls the state or the rule of state officials themselves or a mixture of the two. In Marx's account of events the people of Paris instinctively shy away from political forms that would constrain majority rule in setting the ground rules of Commune governance. Hence in the lineaments of the Commune, Marx believes he can discern "the positive form of that Republic" that was "not only to supersede the monarchical form of class-rule, but class-rule itself."[18]

The main features of Commune governance that favorably impress Marx all tend to place the conduct of government agencies and public officials tightly under the control of majority vote of the citizens. He singles out in particular six features of Paris Commune democracy: (1) Commune members are to be elected for short terms by universal (manhood) suffrage; (2) no separation of powers – the Commune is to be legislative and executive body combined; (3) no independent judiciary – all judges are to be elected and recallable by citizen initiative; (4) public officials are to be paid workmen's wages; (5) the standing army is to be replaced with a citizens' militia; and (6) there is to be no established state religion.

The democratic reform proposals that Marx identifies with Commune democracy suggest a Marxian diagnosis of what is wrong with ordinary capitalist democracy: It tends to fetter the will of the majority. This understanding manifestly informs most of the proposals. The rejection of the norm of separation of powers indicates that the aim is not to limit the power of government backed by majority will. One possible justification of separation of powers is that it is dangerous for any one branch of government to hold all the strings in its hands. Power must be divided lest the officials who happen to possess concentrated power should use it to subvert the constitution and steamroller over all opposition to their aggrandizement. This is not the concern that worries Marx. He is concerned that if legislative and executive power is divided, majority will might be thwarted, because both executive and legislative branches will claim that the other branch is responsible if the will of the people is not implemented. Holding one branch responsible for both making law and administering it is thought to make it easier for voters to hold elected officials accountable for the good and bad outcomes of the public policies they initiate.

Paris Commune democracy seeks to render representative institutions maximally responsive to the majority will of the electorate consistent with the constraints on majority will that are necessarily bound up with a representative system. Since members of the legislature are elected for terms that are extended in time, even if short in duration, it can happen that majority sentiment swings suddenly on some issue that is of paramount concern to elected representatives, so that the policy decision the lawmakers will take is in conflict with the decision that meshes with the majority will of the moment. Or the sentiments of elected representatives might swing suddenly while the will of the electorate stays stable, yielding the same conflict. Presumably Marx holds that under modern conditions a workable parliamentary body must be a representative assembly, so some ineliminable residue of possible divergence between the will of the assembly and the will of the majority of citizen voters must be tolerated. But the aim of the ground rules that Marx singles out for praise is to reduce this residue to a minimum.

To modern readers educated on Madison and De Tocqueville, Marx's constitutional thinking might seem naive and simplistic. Marx altogether ignores the dangers of majority tyranny that are part and parcel of the unbridled majoritarianism he favors. Under Paris Commune democracy, there are no constitutional impediments that would block a majority of white citizens intent on maintaining privileges of racism from voting for legislators who would enact laws oppressive to racial minorities. Under Paris Commune democracy, judges committed to impartial enforcement of the laws on the books could be threatened with removal from office by a majority of citizens insistent on partial enforcement that would work in their favor. In these respects Paris Commune democracy could turn out to be little better than mob rule.

Accordingly, it might be held that from Marx's unqualified enthusiasm for Paris Commune democracy we can infer either that Marx simply does not care about the many morally important individual rights that such democracy would threaten or that he is massively ignorant of the threat that majority rule can pose for individual rights and of the means that constitutional theorists have devised to reduce this threat.

I would not wish to insist that Marx was a connoisseur of constitutional argument, but the interpretation of his Paris Commune writings just posed is unsympathetic. In the terms in which I have framed this discussion, Marx's position is better regarded as based on a priority judgment about individual rights and the conditions for their fulfillment than as based on a breezy dismissal of the notion of individual rights against a majority. Marx's espousal of Paris Commune democracy is not tantamount to an unqualified endorsement of this form of government for all time. Rather, he has in mind a specific set of impediments to the formation of (what he might not be entirely happy calling)[19] a just society and a strategy for overcoming these impediments. In brief, he thinks that private ownership rights that pervasively conflict with genuine individual rights of property are deeply entrenched in the constitutional and political order of capitalist societies. He foresees that a working-class majority of citizens wishing to encroach on private ownership rights would be hamstrung by constitutional provisions and institutions of long standing. So in Marx's analysis of society the best strategy for bringing about progress in the fulfillment of individual rights is to streamline the machinery of government so that it offers minimal resistance to majority will of the citizenry. It is not that Marx is oblivious of majority tyranny; rather, he sees as more menacing the minority tyranny that is protective of private property ownership.[20] On the interpretation I am suggesting, Marx's recommendation of Paris Commune–style democracy is historically conditioned and time-limited. Marx is proposing a constitutional agenda designed to solve one particular set of problems. This analysis leaves it entirely an open question what sort of protections of individual rights might be beneficial under a socialist society that has rooted out the private ownership rights that Marx identifies as the proximate enemy of moral progress. Marx is a majoritarian for the design of the dictatorship of the proletariat, not for any democratic order under any historical conditions.

To assert that Marx need not be read as blind to dangers of majority tyranny is not to argue that he treated the topic in a satisfactory way. Even if we entirely accept Marx's views on the illegitimacy of private property ownership, and on the imperative of sweeping aside constitutional impediments to democratic legislation that would expropriate private property, none of this would gainsay the need for constitutional protection of a wide range of other individual freedoms, such as freedom of speech, that would constrain majority rule from the outset of a postcapitalist political regime.[21]

Mill on plural votes

John Stuart Mill is infamous for proposing an elitist alternative to universal democratic suffrage. Instead of one-person-one-vote, Mill urges that superior mental qualifications as established by educational and career attainments or direct testing should entitle the citizens who are deemed superior in qualifications to cast extra votes.[22]

Actually, the plural vote scheme is just one of several recommendations by Mill that fly in the face of what I have been calling "democratic rights" at the level of the nation-state. Mill proposes that only citizens who can pass a literacy and arithmetical competence test should be entitled to vote. In theory Mill wishes that the individual citizen's right to vote could be made contingent on a demonstration of her sufficient general knowledge of geography, world history, and the history and institutions of her own country, although as a practical matter he doubts that a workable test of such political literacy could be devised and administered. Citizens who are not self-supporting but depend on state aid or private charity for their subsistence should be denied the right to vote, according to Mill, as should citizens who fail to pay taxes. Mill countenances the idea that there should be two chambers of the national legislative, with only the members of one chamber selected by democratic vote (Mill thinks this idea inferior to a plural vote scheme but is not opposed to it on fundamental principles). In short, Mill's commitment to democratic rights is thoroughly hedged.[23]

Mill's advocacy of all these limits on majority rule is based on the argument that such limits will better promote morally desirable outcomes than would unencumbered majority rule. Writing at a time when England limited the franchise to a minority of its citizens consisting of the propertied males, Mill supposes that under modern industrial conditions the chief reason to fear the consequences of the introduction of democracy is the danger of class legislation. If we think of a class as a group of people likely to be motivated by the same sinister interest contrary to the common good, the salient classes in modern society in Mill's judgment are laborers and employers of labor. The chief danger posed by the introduction of democratic political procedures is then the possibility that a majority of laborers would vote for legislation that favors their class but is contrary to principles of justice. (It is obvious that Mill and Marx substantially agree in their estimation of the likely upshot of introducing genuine majority rule in a capitalist society but

evaluate this prospect differently because they are committed to conflicting principles of distributive justice.) The object of constitutional
design should be to establish political institutions that do not permit any
class to carry its will against other classes in opposition to the common
good. Mill favors plural votes to the educated on the ground that a
properly weighted plural vote scheme would set the votes of propertied
individuals roughly equal to the combined votes of the propertyless, so
that the self-interested votes of the business class (augmented by plural
votes) and the laboring class should roughly cancel each other. Those
citizens who cast their votes in a public-spirited way should then be able
to tip the balance in favor of good and just legislation.

Examining Mill's plural vote scheme, Charles Beitz argues that its
defects show it is wrong to assess political procedures solely by their
outcomes, even if "outcome" is construed broadly to include any consequences of operating the procedure, not just the political decisions it
influences or determines. On the contrary, procedures should be evaluated by their intrinsic fairness as well as by the fairness of the outcomes
they produce.[24] Since the general position that Beitz attacks is the
position I wish to defend, it will be useful to see if his argument against
Mill can withstand scrutiny.

The argument that Beitz gives is oddly structured. He notes correctly
that Mill's standard for evaluating consequences is utilitarian, so a plural
vote scheme might be devised that is justified by Mill's standard, because it maximizes aggregate utility, but is nonetheless objectionable to
those who would have low-value votes under the scheme, because
aggregate utility is maximized at their expense. Suppose that plural
votes are assigned mainly to propertied individuals, who use them to
carry pro-property legislation that maximizes overall utility but reduces
the prospects of the propertyless. In this scenario it would not be
unreasonable for the propertyless to object to the plural vote scheme,
Beitz asserts. Furthermore, if the response to this objection on Mill's
behalf is to argue that all affected persons including those disadvantaged
procedurally by plural votes would benefit from the long-run operation
of the scheme, then we have in effect shifted ground from a "best
results" to a contractualist theory of fair procedures.

On the face of it, Beitz's objection against a utilitarian standard for
assessing the outcomes of procedures does not in any way undercut the
viability of a consequentialist best results approach to the justification of
procedures. The contractualist approach that is advanced looks to be a
rival best results standard. According to Beitz, "contractualism regards
moral principles as principles that 'no one could reasonably reject as a
basis for informed, unforced general agreement,' provided they were

moved by a desire to reach such an agreement."[25] If enough weight is put on the significant qualifier "reasonably" in this formulation, contractualism becomes equivalent to the view that the moral principles that are legitimately binding on individuals are those that would pass an ideal coherence or reflective equilibrium test. These will be the principles that reasonable persons would accept. So construed, contractualism states a meta-ethical position rather than a substantive ethical norm.[26] Beitz is apparently convinced that the principles that are satisfactory according to this contractualist criterion will give independent moral weight to the intrinsic fairness of procedures and to the fairness of the outcomes the procedures generate. Hence contractualism will lead one to reject not just utilitarianism but any best results position. But appealing to such a particular claim about the content of contractualism in this context seems to me just to beg the question at issue between Beitz and Mill.

Although one might diagnose errors in Mill's analysis of how a plural vote scheme would operate, whose interests it would serve, and why those interests should be thought to correspond to genuine moral rights, for present purposes these objections count as nit-picking. The issue Beitz raises is whether the kind of argument that Mill offers is sound in principle, details of execution aside. I suggest that anyone who disagrees with Mill on principle on the ground that any plural vote arrangement conflicts with a fundamental norm of democratic rights of equal citizenship should also be a principled opponent of judicial supremacy in a substantive constitutional order. After all, Mill understands that the plural vote scheme he recommends is just a gimmick. It is one possible device for protecting certain individual rights (which for Mill are determined by utilitarian calculation). Mill is not dogmatic on the issue of which constitutional gimmick that might be imagined would work best for this purpose; the answer will surely be different for different societies and for a single society at different times. Indeed, the only principle Mill associates with plural voting is the doctrine that no one has a right to an equal share of political power when other persons can be reliably identified and installed in power who are more competent to exercise political power and stably disposed to competent exercise.[27] I appealed to this same principle in order to urge that judicial supremacy is morally acceptable despite its conflict with democratic rights. Judicial supremacy is just plural votes by other means. The puzzle then is why anyone who accepts judicial supremacy should be a principled opponent of the plural vote proposal. The principles underlying judicial supremacy and plural votes are the same.

In reply to a conjectured defense of plural voting, Beitz writes, "But this does not dissolve the impression of unfairness associated with procedures that embed in public political practice the belief that some people's opinions are worthy of less attention or respect than those of others."[28] Beitz's expression of suspicion raises the question whether or not a best results approach contains adequate resources to explain and justify this impression of unfairness, which somehow does ring true. Accepting the premise that Mill's plural votes scheme appears unfair, we must conclude that rejection of the best results approach is warranted unless it can plausibly explain why this is so.

The unfairness of plural votes must be subtle. It will not do simply to say that an attractive ideal of free deliberation among equal citizens is straightforwardly violated by plural votes, for at least two reasons: (1) In deliberation, it is not the case that all opinions are equally rational, hence it is not the case that all opinions do deserve equal attention and respect. Time is always short, so a citizen does not violate any fundamental norm of respect for persons if she ruthlessly follows search strategies that confine her attention to opinions most likely to be productive in the search for truth. (2) At any rate the procedure of voting is a political decision-making process, not per se a deliberative process.[29] Hence the institution of a weighted vote scheme in order to secure fair outcomes does not necessarily imply a public judgment that the opinions of those whose votes are weighted less are less worthy than the opinions of those citizens whose votes are given extra weight. Plural votes to the educated could be justified by the expectation (if reasonable) that such weighting will create an approximate balance of power between the educated and the uneducated. The presumption here would be that if one of these groups could easily outvote the other, it would trample on the legitimate rights of the individuals who belong to the outvoted group. Comparative judgments of the expected worth of any citizens' opinions need not enter the argument at all.

A close modern analogue of Mill's plural vote scheme regarded in this way would be a scheme of vote-weighting designed to protect fundamental rights or balance approximately the political power of ethnic, religious, or racial groups troubled by a history of conflict. Consider what we might call "ultraconsociational democracy" arrangements.[30] These might include what amount to plural vote arrangements (for example, a guaranteed number of seats in the legislature set aside for each of the two major religious or ethnic groups) designed to reduce the danger that majority rule would lead to tyranny of the majority in the form of ethnic or religious domination. The ethnic or religious group that is less numerous might be assigned plural votes or the like in order to ease the fear of majority rule operating on a jurisdiction that includes a more numerous group. If fairness-of-outcome considerations and not quality-of-voter-opinion considerations motivate the creation of consociational arrangements, no citizen assigned a vote that is weighted less than the average vote should feel that the institutional rules convey a judgment that disparages his voting competence.

Someone who was prepared to support ultraconsociational democracy or plural vote arrangements on the grounds just sketched, if the empirical premises needed to back up these grounds were well confirmed, might hold that such restrictions of some citizens' democratic rights can at most be justifiable as a necessary evil, a second-best arrangement in which procedural unfairness is tolerated in order to avert worse evils. A best results approach takes a different line. According to this approach, the procedures that work to produce the fairest outcomes are by definition the fairest procedures, so no trade-off between fair procedures and fair outcomes enters into the picture. On a best results approach, if plural votes are less than ideally fair, this is so because we can envisage circumstances in which equally weighted votes for all would produce fairer outcomes than any plural vote scheme, and in these circumstances the outcomes obtained are fairer than the outcomes obtainable in the circumstances in which plural votes produce the fairest outcomes. This might be the case if we think that plural votes guard against certain big rights violations but simultaneously promote certain little rights violations, and that if a tolerant civic culture removes the danger of the big rights violations and hence the need for plural votes, then a scheme of equal votes for all does better on the score of guarding against little rights violations.

None of this quite resolves the puzzle stated four paragraphs back. There does seem to be something inherently unfair about the plural vote scheme in the form proposed by Mill, and the question is whether the best results approach can accommodate this strong impression of unfairness. My suggestion is that the bad smell of Mill's plural vote scheme arises from the circumstance that it bestows a procedural advantage on a large fraction of the adult population to the procedural disadvantage of the complementary fraction. The mechanical rule that determines who gets extra votes is bound to use at best a very rough proxy for the qualities of superior competence and public-spiritedness that are supposed to justify the procedural benefits conferred. (If it were attempted to avoid this problem by allowing the authority that issues plural votes wide discretion in the use of its authority, this would guarantee arbitrary and inconsistent determinations.) In this setting those denied plural votes would be very likely to perceive the denial as an official insult issued by public authority. "Why them and not me?" is a question bound to rankle in the mind of the nonplural voter. In contrast, a countermajoritarian institution like the Supreme Court involves the vesting of power in a small number of persons whose credentials can be carefully checked in a public procedure that commands respect.

Mill argues that a public's perception of large-scale insult in a plural vote arrangement should be discounted on the ground that such sensitivity would be rooted in popular belief in the false principle that both the competent and the foolish are entitled to equal power as citizens.[31] I suggest that the principle associating plural votes with gratuitously inflicted insult could be that when no reliable procedure is available to distinguish more competent from less competent citizens for the purpose of tailoring one's power to one's competence, no unreliable procedure should be instituted to this end.

None of the above demonstrates that a plural vote scheme is really intrinsically unfair. There could not be such a demonstration on my view. My claim is that in calculating the consequences of instituting a plural vote scheme one should give appropriate weight to the reasonable and widespread feelings of arbitrary stigma that the scheme would predictably generate.[32]

The extension of democratic rights to the workplace

Recently a number of writers have argued on various grounds that the same reasons that justify the ascription of universal rights of democratic citizenship in modern society also justify the extension of democratic citizenship rights to the workplace.[33] The approach to thinking about democratic rights proposed in this essay helps to reveal the weakness of this "parallel case" argument. Here attention is confined to what I take to be the strongest argument for the claim that the right of the worker to democratic citizenship in the firm that employs her stands on the same footing as the right of the individual to democratic citizenship in the nation in which she is a member.

The parallel case argument holds that whenever individuals cooperate together in a rule-governed common enterprise that should work to their common advantage, they all have the right to participate by way of majority-rule procedure in making the association rules, provided all have the capacity to do so.[34] The political order and the economic firm are both common enterprises in the relevant respects, so the right to democratic citizenship applies equally in both arenas.

Notice that, as stated, the parallel case argument abstracts from the question of whether the individual's membership in the common enterprise is voluntarily chosen or not.[35] So far as the argument goes, the factor of voluntariness is irrelevant. But the most significant disanalogy between the relationship of the individual to the state on whose territory she lives and her relationship to the firm that employs her is that the latter is far closer to voluntary than is the former. In the normal case the individual is born into a state, grows up forming close ties to its culture and to particular individuals within it, and would face severe dislocation and loss of life-prospects if she had to emigrate. By the time the individual becomes a young adult she needs to continue to reside in the society in which she has grown up, whereas at that time the individual is just on the verge of making occupational and career choices and can choose from a wide array of diverse possibilities, many of which are likely to hold some attraction for her. Even after the individual has committed herself to a particular line of work, there are normally many choices of jobs within that line of work, and individuals often manage to switch lines of work if the career they first selected proves not to their liking. Of course, there are great variations among persons in the initial job opportunity range they face and in the range of jobs available to choose within the line of work that attracts them. But the stylized description just given is reasonably accurate on the whole. This means that membership in one's political society is pretty nearly a nonvoluntary matter and placement in a line of work and a job is to a large extent a matter of free and voluntary choice.

The differential voluntariness of the individual's relationship to politics and to work strongly conditions the force of the individual's claim to a democratic say in each area. Rights of democratic citizenship in the nation are needed to safeguard people's fundamental interests since political decisions will affect their lives powerfully and continuously in ways that they cannot avoid save by the drastic measure of moving to another land. In contrast, the freedom of the individual on a modern labor market willy-nilly confers on each person a considerable degree of control in the form of exit rights. If the management of one's firm (or department within a firm) opts for policies one finds intolerable, one can generally escape the reach of the unwanted policies by quitting one's job and taking another (or switching to another department). The contrast here is a matter of degree: If one's nation upholds the freedom to emigrate, then one has the right to exit from one's land just as one has the right to exit from one's economic firm. But the difference of degree amounts to a morally consequential difference. The right to emigrate for the vast majority of citizens is entirely a pro forma right that never enters into their practical deliberation about how to live their lives, whereas the right to quit one's job is for almost all people a live option, even if left unexercised, and for the majority an option that is taken several times in the course of one's working life.

The argument so far is that for all practical purposes the individual cannot avoid suffering large consequences for his life brought about by state policies. The right to a democratic say in the domain of politics is meant to ensure that these consequences one cannot avoid will be tolerable overall and in the long run. In contrast, the diversity of options in a modern labor market gives the individual an effective means to avoid suffering intolerable consequences from the policies of one's firm even without any effective right to a democratic say.

The contrast drawn so far between the nonvoluntary political order and the voluntary economic order is no doubt somewhat overdrawn. The contrast shines most clearly between (1) politics at the national level in a large nation-state that is culturally distinct from neighboring nation-states and (2) economic life in an urban setting in which the market offers a wide array of genuinely diverse career and job options, some sizable portion of the array remaining available to individuals even after initial choices have foreclosed some options. This way of drawing the contrast, though stylized, is nonspurious. In special cases where the contrast becomes muted, either the case for democracy in the political realm becomes attenuated or else the case for workplace democracy becomes stronger.

Suppose there are two tiny adjacent nations in Europe. The two lands are culturally and linguistically unified, so that an individual in one nation can migrate to the other as easily as people usually can move from one side of town to the other. The laws of the two lands are substantially the same except that their political constitutions differ. For the citizens of these two lands the costs of emigrating from the one to the other are very small. If one land is an autocracy and the other is a democracy, the fact that citizens in the autocracy have the low-cost option of moving to the democratic sister nation substantially lessens the argument that the citizens of both lands have democratic citizenship rights that the autocratic order systematically violates.

Consider next the plight of coal miners in an isolated region, culturally very different from the rest of the nation. There is virtually no employment in the region except the job of coal miner. Migrating away from the region to other areas of the nation in search of alternate livelihood opportunities is rarely done and is in fact extremely difficult and costly for the coal mine region inhabitants. To move away from the coal mine region to the nearest big city would be as psychologically wrenching for almost any of its inhabitants as picking up stakes and moving to such distant foreign lands as Japan, Iraq, or Kenya. Here again, in these hypothetical circumstances the parallel case argument for workplace democracy is quite compelling.

It might be objected that in an economy in which the option of workplace democracy is virtually nonexistent, the fact that an individual who is employed by one hierarchically managed firm could secure alternate employment in some other equally hierarchically organized firm does not establish that her presumably voluntary acceptance of her current employment can plausibly be regarded as voluntary acceptance of its nondemocratic character. Along the pertinent dimension of assessment the options are so many versions of Tweedledum and Tweedledee. The mere existence of many options, it might accordingly be urged, does not undercut the parallel case argument.

The objection partly misconstrues the structure of the argument under consideration. We are taking the presence of significant options as evidence that the situation of someone who declines to exercise one of these exit options is tolerable, where the degree to which the status quo is experienced as tolerable largely hinges on whether it imposes violation of one's important rights. Having significant options is a means to achieve a tolerable level of fulfillment of one's rights, just as having democratic citizenship rights is a means to the same end. In this respect having options and enjoying democratic rights may be substitutes for one another. So the presence of significant exit options can weaken the parallel case argument for workplace democracy even though none of the significant options happens to involve a more democratic workplace arrangement.

For the sake of the argument let us ignore the point just made and assume having available a variety of work and career options that are attractive in significantly different ways does not lessen the case for democratic rights in one's current employment unless the options include jobs with democratic rights in labor-managed firms. Even if we concede as much as could possibly be proven by this argument, it does not establish a right to workers' control, a democratic political constitution in every economic enterprise. At most the argument just sketched would show that among the work and career options available to the individual, some fraction of these options must include the opportunity to carry out one's work in a labor-managed firm.[36]

Whether or not there is a compelling argument to the conclusion that each individual should be entitled to the option of employment in an economic enterprise in which all employees are accorded democratic rights, there is a compelling consideration against moving beyond this point in order to guarantee all individuals the inalienable and nonwaivable right to workplace democratic rights, on all fours with inalienable and nonwaivable rights of democratic citizenship at the national level. Mandating democratic rights in all economic enterprises would be welcomed by some individuals and greeted with sorrow or consternation by others. Workplace democracy entails costs and benefits that will be differently evaluated by individuals who see the world through different conceptions of the good. In a market setting, whether the market is composed of private or state-owned firms, some individuals would prefer to work for a firm that is hierarchically managed rather than run by elected managers. Just to mention one possibility, one might fear that majority rule in economic enterprises in one's line of industry will produce worse managerial decisions or constraints on managers that worsen the quality of managerial decision making compared to nondemocratic alternatives. Some individuals might find that in their scheme of values this risk is offset by the predictable benefits of democratic accountability whereby each individual has some "voice" in the setting of enterprise policy. Others, with different values, would find that the costs of mandated economic democracy exceed its expected benefits for them. Why should the state act to confer a special windfall on those who happen to have a taste for workplace democracy?

An example may help. Imagine that we have been persuaded by a McPherson-type argument[37] to extend to all citizens in society the option of working in a firm that offers democratic rights to all employees. If the economy is small, this goal is achieved by offering a tax subsidy that just suffices to induce one firm to institute workers' control. The question is now raised, Would it not be more just to extend the rights of democratic citizenship to all economic enterprises? The effects of instituting workers' control would be qualitatively similar in any enterprise: Output and wages would fall, and job satisfaction would rise for all employees. No detectable public goods or bads would flow from extending workers' control to all firms by law. Since this is a diverse society, individuals diversely evaluate the net effect on their welfare of being a member of a democratic firm. Some care a lot about extra income, others care less. Some care enormously about the shop floor atmospheric benefits of workers' control, others are all but indifferent to this effect. In moving from a policy of guaranteeing everyone the option of workers' control to guaranteeing everyone workers' control, the state would be helping some individuals and hurting others. We have no good reason to suppose there would be any plausible distributional reason for imposing this pattern of benefits and burdens: The gainers from the scheme are not disproportionately among the poorest or worst-off members of society, nor are they among the most deserving according to agreed criteria of deservingness, and so on. And there is no way to subsidize losers from the change from the gains of gainers without dissipating all net benefits (if indeed there are any net benefits).

In such circumstances a powerful neutrality constraint on political arrangements forbids the enforced extension of democratic rights to economic enterprises. In a diverse democracy the state is rightly expected to be strictly neutral in its dealings with citizens committed to fundamentally different conceptions of value and the good life. Neutrality here forbids the use of state power to confer special benefits on some citizens merely because they have tastes of a sort that are favored or deemed more admirable than the tastes of others. From the perspective of state neutrality, the proposal of mandated workplace democracy appears sectarian and hence unjustifiable. But to clarify the ideal of neutrality to which rhetorical appeal is being made here is the task for another essay.

Notes

1 This definition identifies democratic rights with procedures of indirect as opposed to direct democracy. I don't have in mind any theoretical rationale for this idiosyncratic feature of the definition; I simply think that in modern society the only practically viable democratic option will be representative or indirect democracy for the range of associations I mean to consider.

2 See John Rawls, *A Theory of Justice* (Cambridge, Mass.: Harvard University Press, 1971); Ronald Dworkin, "What Is Equality? Part 2: Equality of Resources," *Philosophy and Public Affairs* 10 (1981): 283–345; Amartya Sen, "Equality of What?", in his *Choice, Welfare and Measurement* (Oxford: Basil Blackwell, 1982), pp. 353–69; and Sen, "Well-being, Agency and Freedom: The Dewey Lectures 1984," *Journal of Philosophy* 82 (1985): 169–221, esp. pp. 185–203. I defend a preference satisfaction standard of equality in "Equality and Equal Opportunity for Welfare," *Philosophical Studies* 56 (1989): 77–93; "Paternalism, Utility, and Fairness," *Revue Internationale de Philosophie* 170 (1989): 409–37; "Liberalism, Distributive Subjectivism, and Equal Opportunity for Welfare," *Philosophy and Public Affairs* 19 (1990): 158–94; "Primary Goods Reconsidered," *Nous* 24 (1990): 429–54; "Neutrality and Utility," *Canadian Journal of Philosophy* 20 (1990): 215–40; and "A Defense of Equal Opportunity for Welfare," *Philosophical Studies* 62 (1991): 187–95.

3 It should also be noted that my formulation of democratic rights abstracts from the jurisdictional problem of how to determine which persons it is morally appropriate to consider as belonging to a common association that perhaps should be democratically governed. On this question, see Brian Barry, "Is Democracy Special?", reprinted in his *Democracy, Power and Justice: Essays in Political Theory* (Oxford: Oxford University Press, 1989), pp. 24–60.

4 John Hart Ely argues that the American constitutional system is (despite initial appearances) nonsubstantive, in *Democracy and Distrust: A Theory of*

Judicial Review (Cambridge, Mass.: Harvard University Press, 1980).

5 On this point, see John Stuart Mill, *Considerations on Representative Government*, in *Collected Works* 19, ed. J. M. Robson (Toronto and Buffalo: University of Toronto Press, 1977), p. 488.

6 The view stated in the text also has implications regarding what package of rights of control of children it is best to bestow on parents. For example, consider the claimed right of parents (under American constitutional law) to secure their children's release from public school work assignments that would expose the children to values contrary to the family's religious tenets. But if exposing children to alternative values and morals in the public school setting is plausibly thought to encourage a disposition to tolerance that promotes rights fulfillment in a diverse democracy, then the parent's right to control his child's access to the public school curriculum is a nonstarter.

7 One might hold that our intuitions about procedural rights always incorporate both judgments about the intrinsic fairness of the procedures under review and judgments about the fairness of the outcomes the procedures would likely generate. My suggestion is that proposed instances of the former component of our intuitions would always collapse under examination into instances of the latter component.

8 See T. Nicholas Tideman and Gordon Tullock, "A New and Superior Process for Making Social Choices," *Journal of Political Economy* 84 (1976): 1145–59; T. Groves and J. Ledyard, "Optimal Allocation of Public Goods: A Solution to the Free Rider Problem," *Econometrica* 45 (1977): 783–810; and the references cited in these articles.

9 In this system the key features of judicial freedom from majority-rule control are (a) that the top judges have lifetime tenure in office and (b) that once appointed they are not accountable to any electorate. The appointment process is indirectly democratic, however. A president elected on a national basis makes top judicial appointments subject to the approval of an elected Senate. This gives rise to the possibility that these elected officials and particularly the president might use the power of appointment to entrench in power a particular constitutional doctrine that expresses the majority will of the time and is embodied in the individual nominated for top judicial office. On this problem, see Bruce Ackerman, "Transformative Appointments," *Harvard Law Review* 101 (1988): 1164–84. The facts that occasion this concern strike me as underscoring the countermajoritarian power of the high courts.

10 For an interesting hint that such privacy rights can be shoehorned under the rights of democratic citizenship, see Joshua Cohen, "Deliberation and Democratic Legitimacy," in Alan Hamlin and Philip Pettit, eds., *The Good Polity* (Oxford: Basil Blackwell, 1989), p. 34, fn. 22.

11 For a philosopher's analysis of the American constitutional law of privacy and suggestions as to how it could be rendered coherent, see Joel Feinberg, "Autonomy, Sovereignty, and Privacy: Moral Ideals in the Constitution?", *Notre Dame Law Review* 58 (1983): 445–92.

12 John Ferejohn pointed out the relevance of the line of thought in this paragraph to my argument.

13 Notice that if one held that people's fundamental rights are few and that many decisions by government are made in contexts where fundamental rights are not at stake, there is room to hold that in these contexts policies are fair if they have been reached through fair (i.e., democratic) procedures. A view that is a bit like this is defended by Peter De Marneffe in "Liberalism, Liberty, and Neutrality," *Philosophy and Public Affairs* 19 (1990): 253–74.

14 Ronald Dworkin, "Constitutional Cases," in his *Taking Rights Seriously* (Cambridge, Mass.: Harvard University Press, 1977), pp. 131–49. In his more recent *Law's Empire* (Cambridge, Mass.: Harvard University Press, 1986), pp. 369–79, Dworkin finds reasons to consider "judicial activism" a misleading label for the judicial disposition that he favors, but for my purposes the position defended is substantially the same in the two works.

15 For this usage see Charles Beitz, *Political Equality: An Essay in Democratic Theory* (Princeton, N.J.: Princeton University Press, 1989), p. 20. A best results theory makes a stronger claim than the generic consequentialist claim that the morally right acts and policies are those that maximize some function of their consequences, weighted by their moral desirability. A consequentialist theory might permit trade-offs between the intrinsic fairness of instituting alternative procedures and the fairness of the outcomes that instituting one or another procedure would bring about. A best results theory denies that such intrinsic fairness judgments should be given any weight in decision making and policy making at all.

16 John Rawls, *A Theory of Justice*, pp. 85–6.

17 The point I mean to make is not that it is beyond dispute that whatever distribution of money results from gambles freely agreed to is fair. For example, one might object on grounds of fairness to the outcomes when poor people gamble with resources they need in order to satisfy basic needs, and lose the gambles. My point is that any inclination one might have to think that the quality of the procedure here renders any outcome morally legitimate is due entirely to the fact that the procedure is freely and voluntarily embraced and not at all to the supposed intrinsic fairness of the procedure itself.

18 Karl Marx, *The Civil War in France*, in *The Marx–Engels Reader*, ed. Robert Tucker (New York: Norton, 1978), pp. 618–52; see p. 631. See also Karl Marx and Friedrich Engels, *Writings on the Paris Commune*, ed. Hal Draper (New York: Monthly Review Press, 1971).

19 That this parenthetical hedge vastly understates the extent of Marx's revulsion from talk of rights and justice is vigorously argued by Allen Wood, *Karl Marx* (London: Routledge & Kegan Paul, 1981), pp. 125–56. See also Wood, "A Marxian Approach to 'The Problem of Justice,'" *Philosophica* 33 (1984): 9–32; and Wood, "Marx's Immoralism," in Bernard Chavance, ed., *Marx en Perspective* (Paris: Editions de l'Ecole des Hautes Etudes en Sciences Sociales, 1985), pp. 681–98. For an opposed view, see my "What Is Wrong with Exploitation?", *Ethics* 91 (1981): 202–27; and Norman Geras, "The Controversy about Marx and Justice," *New Left Review* 150 (1985): 47–85.

20 But see Jon Elster's judgment, "Nowhere does [Marx] show any awareness

of the problems involved in such direct democracy [as is exemplified in Marx's description of the Paris Commune]," in his *Making Sense of Marx* (Cambridge: Cambridge University Press, 1985), p. 448. A possible exception is a passage in the "Critique of the Gotha Program" in which Marx states that the monitoring of schools by the state to ensure that minimum standards are met "is a very different thing from appointing the state as the educator of the people! Government and Church should rather be equally excluded from any influence on the school. Particularly, indeed, in the Prusso-German Empire . . . the state has need, on the contrary, of a very stern education by the people." I concede that the passage is tangential to Elster's judgment. But Marx appears to be concerned that centralized control of schools by government or established church would threaten the imposition of one curriculum on all, eliminating desirable diversity. The word "particularly" indicates that the concern does not cease to be pertinent in a democratic state. There are some jobs that no government – not even a direct democracy – should be trusted to perform.

21 Here I express agreement with Allen Buchanan's reservations concerning the strands in Marx's thought that identify a movement toward communism with a liberating movement away from institutions that aim to secure individual rights of any sort. See Buchanan, *Marx and Justice: The Radical Critique of Liberalism* (Totowa, N.J.: Rowman & Allenheld, 1982), pp. 162–79.

22 In *Considerations on Representative Government*, chap. 8.

23 Ibid.

24 Beitz, *Political Equality*, pp. 31–48.

25 Beitz, p. 101. The material in single quotes is from T. Scanlon, "Contractualism and Utilitarianism," in Amartya Sen and Bernard Williams, eds., *Utilitarianism and Beyond* (Cambridge: Cambridge University Press, 1982), p. 110.

26 For a different understanding of contractualism, see Thomas Nagel, "Moral Conflict and Political Legitimacy," *Philosophy and Public Affairs* 16 (1987): 215–40; esp. p. 221.

27 It should be acknowledged that Mill denies the principle that it is intrinsically fair that all should have equal power regardless of competence but does embrace the principle that every citizen (above some threshold level of competence?) should have some political power. No one should be officially rendered a political nonentity; everyone should have the vote, though not necessarily an equal vote. See Mill, *Considerations on Representative Government*, pp. 473, 474, and 478. My hunch, however, is that this does not represent any retreat on Mill's part from a purely consequence-regarding position but, rather, expresses his firm conviction that entire exclusion of a citizen (of normal competence) from influence on political affairs can never be conducive to overall maximal fulfillment of individual rights or utility in the largest sense.

28 Beitz, p. 43.

29 Of course, majority-rule voting might be conceived as one element in a

comprehensive ideal of democratic deliberation. See Jürgen Habermas, *Legitimation Crisis* (Boston: Beacon Press, 1975), Jon Elster, "The Market and the Forum: Three Varieties of Political Theory," in Elster and Aanund Hylland, eds., *Foundations of Social Choice Theory* (Cambridge: Cambridge University Press, 1986), pp. 103–32; and Joshua Cohen, "Deliberation and Democratic Legitimacy," pp. 17–34. But it is an open question whether instituting reforms that move a political order closer to this ideal would also be the best way to maximize fulfillment of individuals' fundamental rights, and I hold that the latter should have priority. See also Thomas Christiano's survey article on democratic theory, "Freedom, Consensus, and Equality in Collective Decision Making," *Ethics* 101 (1990): 151–81.

30 See Arend Lijphart, *The Politics of Accommodation: Pluralism and Democracy in the Netherlands* (Berkeley and Los Angeles: University of California Press, 1968); Lijphart, "Consociational Democracy," *World Politics* 21 (1969): 207–25; Lijphart, *Democracies: Patterns of Majoritarian and Consensus Government in Twenty-One Countries* (New Haven and London: Yale University Press, 1984); also Brian Barry, "Political Accommodation" and "The Consociational Model and its Dangers," both reprinted in his *Democracy, Power and Justice: Essays in Political Theory*, pp. 100–55. For the most part the term "consociational" describes political practices that facilitate accommodation among ethnic, linguistic, and religious communities within a democratic order; consociational democracies are not any less democracies than nonconsociational democracies. An instance of what I call ultraconsociational arrangements is the precoup Fiji political constitution as described by Joseph Carens, unpublished manuscript.

31 Mill, *Considerations on Representative Government*, pp. 473–4.

32 The position in the text finesses an issue that should be faced: If the stigma is a public mark of inferiority, wouldn't the stigma grow worse as the selection process that assigned plural votes was improved so as to be less arbitrary and more carefully discriminating?

33 See Robert Dahl, *A Preface to Economic Democracy* (Berkeley and Los Angeles: University of California Press, 1985); Michael Walzer, *Spheres of Justice: A Defense of Pluralism and Equality* (New York: Basic Books, 1983), pp. 291–303; and Joshua Cohen, "The Economic Basis of Deliberative Democracy," *Social Philosophy and Policy* 6 (1989): 25–50. I discuss Walzer's views on this topic in "Is There a Right to Workers' Control?", forthcoming in *Economics and Philosophy*. For Dahl's most recent views on the justification of democracy in general, see his *Democracy and Its Critics* (New Haven and London: Yale University Press, 1989). For an argument that criticizes Rawls for failing to insist that the basic liberties of citizenship should be upheld in the economic as well as in the political realm, see Gerald Doppelt, "Rawls' System of Justice: A Critique from the Left," *Nous* 15 (1981): 259–308.

34 This statement of the argument follows Cohen's helpful formulation in "The Economic Basis of Deliberative Democracy," p. 27.

35 Walzer is especially careful to stress the parallel between the argument for

democracy in economic firms and the argument for democracy at the township or municipality level. My response is that the argument for democracy at the township level just is weaker than the argument for democracy at the level of the nation-state. A related but different point: If a national democratic assembly institutes a program of centralized top-down municipal government, with local mayors appointed by the national government, such a scheme might be objectionable on various grounds but not on the ground that it is undemocratic. The same point would hold of a scheme in which a democratic assembly at the national level controls the economic agency that appoints the managers of public firms – this top-down management being an alternative to workers' control.

36 A nuanced statement of a view of this sort is found in Richard Krouse and Michael McPherson, "A 'Mixed' Property Regime: Equality and Liberty in a Market Economy," *Ethics* 97 (1986): 119–28.

37 See note 35.

Justified to whom?

ROBERT SUGDEN

Is there a right to democracy? Richard Arneson argues that there is not. Democracy, he argues, has only instrumental value: It is good only to the extent that it promotes good outcomes. More generally, the supposed right to democracy is an example of a "procedural right," and "procedural rights are merely instruments for securing morally desirable outcomes." Similarly: "There is no content to the issue of what procedures are intrinsically unfair, apart from examination of the outcomes they might reach." There may well be cases in which democracy does *not* secure morally desirable outcomes, and in these cases it may be right for democracy to be constrained.

Arneson sees this line of argument as a justification for constitutional constraints on majority rule, and in particular for the role of the judiciary in the American Constitution. He claims that this role allows judges to *make* law, and not merely to interpret it. If this is right, we have to explain how an otherwise democratic constitution can allow such unelected lawmakers. For Arneson, the Supreme Court judges are Platonic Guardians, chosen for their superior "moral competence." This justification for giving lawmaking power to judges is essentially the same as John Stuart Mill's argument for giving additional votes to better-educated people. Although Arneson does not endorse Mill's specific proposal for plural voting, he sees nothing fundamentally objectionable in it. If plural voting could be relied on to produce better outcomes than simple majority voting, then plural voting would be justified.

These claims might well have come from a Benthamite utilitarian, taking the robustly consistent position that any talk about rights is sentimental nonsense. And at times, we find the authentic voice of Benthamite utilitarianism in Arneson's essay – most notably in the chilling passage on the upbringing of children, where we are told that it is uncontroversial that natural parents' having custody of their children is of merely instrumental value. If the utilitarian calculus could be shown to require children to be separated at birth from their natural parents and assigned to superior foster parents, then (according to Arneson) society would have a duty to intervene in this way.

This case is significant as an illustration of the extent of Arneson's commitment to egalitarianism. It is unfair – in the same sense that life is unfair – that some of us are born to wealthy parents and others to poor ones, and that some of us are born to exceptionally caring parents while others are born to merely adequately caring ones. From an egalitarian perspective, it would be comforting to believe that this unfairness was an unavoidable by-product of a set of social arrangements that tended to maximize social welfare, and thus to be able to conclude that compulsory fostering was not required. This is what Arneson thinks is the case. (Natural parents, he says, tend to be so much better than foster parents that, on balance, compulsory fostering would do more harm than good.) But suppose we could come up with a scheme of compulsory fostering that would do more good than harm. Does the government really have a duty to set it in motion? Perhaps there are forms of unfairness that it is not the government's business to try to correct. More generally, perhaps the government does not have a duty to maximize the social good in all possible circumstances.

Arneson, however, is not a classical utilitarian. Outcomes, he says, must be judged (at least in part) in terms of rights-fulfillment. Democracy has instrumental value because it tends to protect "fundamental," nondemocratic rights. Among these fundamental rights are freedom of speech, privacy, and individual liberty, and "egalitarian rights to material resources." Similarly, in evaluating procedures for the upbringing of children, we should take account of a child's "right to a decent upbringing." Thus, Arneson has to maintain a distinction between those rights which are "fundamental" and those which are merely "procedural": The extent to which fundamental rights are respected enters into the assessment of outcomes, whereas procedural rights have merely instrumental value. Or to put the same point another way, Arneson has to maintain a distinction between procedures and outcomes, while allowing rights-fulfillment to count as part of the description of an outcome.

This distinction is not easy to maintain. It is not obvious, for example, that the right to freedom of speech is fundamental while the right to participate in democratic decision making is not. An obvious argument for the right to free speech is that being free to speak one's own thoughts, and having access (by mutual consent) to the ideas of others, is a crucial part of being autonomous, of being able to live *one's own* life. But then, being able to participate in collective decisions which will affect one's life (whether in the nation or in the workplace) seems to be an aspect of autonomy too. Similarly, we may wonder why privacy is a fundamental right, but involvement in the upbringing of one's children is not.

Part of the difficulty is that many rights seem to be most naturally described as requirements about the procedures that must be used in order to arrive at social outcomes. For example, we would normally say that every individual has a right to be free of sexual contact with others, if he or she chooses, but also that adults have the right to sexual relations by mutual consent. This may be construed as a procedure for determining which sexual contacts take place (that is, those that are chosen by consenting adults). Similarly, the rights to free association and to free speech are procedures for determining who meets whom, and who says what to whom. I can see no qualitative difference between these rights and the right to democratic participation.

It must be conceded that some of the rights invoked by Arneson cannot be construed as procedures. In particular, consider the egalitarian rights to material resources which Arneson particularly values. The idea, I take it, is that the government has a duty to ensure that each individual has a certain endowment of material resources. This need not imply the existence of any procedure by which the individual can bring about the state of affairs in which the government acts on its duty; this may be a right that cannot be *used* by the individual who is its beneficiary. But if the concept of a right is interpreted as widely as this, even classical utilitarianism can be described in terms of rights-fulfillment. A classical utilitarian would say that the government has a duty to maximize total utility, with each person counting for one and no one for more than one. This could be restated as the principle that each person has a right to be treated in the way that maximizes total utility. There is nothing incoherent in saying this; but the concept of a right seems to be doing no work.

I suspect that Arneson's conclusions would not be much affected if all talk of fundamental rights was eliminated from the argument, and if *all* rights were viewed as instrumental for the maximization of the overall good. This would make Arneson's position much closer to that of Mill. If the criterion for evaluating outcomes is, as it is for Mill (1859, chap. 1), "utility in the largest sense, grounded in the permanent interests of a man as a progressive being," then it would not be difficult to generate instrumental arguments for most of the rights which Arneson invokes.

Having located Arneson firmly in Mill's camp, I want to look at Mill's argument for plural voting. Recall that on this issue, Arneson's disagreements with Mill are over matters of detail. For Arneson, "judicial supremacy is just plural votes by another name," and judicial supremacy *is* justified. If this is right, there is a puzzle to be solved. Why does the principle of judicial supremacy command widespread support, at least in the United States, while Mill's argument for plural votes offends modern democratic sensibilities?

Arneson speaks of *justifying* constitutional constraints on democratic decision making. But *to whom* are these constraints being justified? This question becomes important when it is being claimed that some people are more competent than others, and the more competent are to be given a greater role in collective decision making. Is this inequality of influence being justified to everyone, including the less competent? And is the form of justification one that the less competent can accept?

According to Mill, the answer to each of these questions is "Yes"; but I am not convinced. Mill (1861, chap. 8) tries to protect the argument of *On Liberty* by drawing a distinction between private and public affairs. In matters that are private to an individual, the foolish have the same rights as the wise: "In an affair which concerns only one of two persons, that one is entitled to follow his own opinion, however much wiser the other may be than himself." Presumably, the argument extends to associations of individuals, insofar as the issue is between insiders and outsiders. (Marriage partners, for example, are entitled to organize their joint affairs how they see fit, without interference from more competent outsiders.) But when an issue is of joint concern to a number of individuals, the more competent of those individuals are entitled to claim greater influence in decision making:

. . . if the more ignorant does not yield his share of the matter to the guidance of the wiser man, the wiser man must resign his to that of the more ignorant. Which of these modes of getting over the difficulty is most for the interest of both, and most conformable to the general fitness of things? If it be deemed unjust that either should have to give way, which injustice is greatest? that the better judgment should give way to the worse, or the worse to the better?

Mill argues that this solution ought to be acceptable to the ignorant as well as to the wise:

No one but a fool, and only a fool of a particular description, feels offended by the acknowledgement that there are others whose opinion, and even whose wish, is entitled to a greater amount of consideration than his. To have no voice in what are partly his own concerns is a thing which nobody willingly submits to; but when what is partly his concern is also partly another's, and he feels the other to understand the subject better than himself, that the other's opinion should be counted for more than his own accords with his expectations, and with the course of things which in all other affairs of life he is accustomed to acquiesce in.

I do not see how this argument can work. Of course, only a fool would deny that others had greater competence than himself on many matters requiring technical judgment, or special experience. My opinions on the design of dams are not equal in weight to those of a civil engineer. My opinions on foreign policy are not equal in weight to those of career diplomats. Perhaps there is moral competence too, so that my opinions on moral questions are not equal in weight to those of a Supreme Court judge. I need feel no sense of stigma in admitting all of this. But no democratic decision-making procedure prevents citizens from deferring to the judgments of those whom they believe to be more competent than themselves.

Before voting in an election, I may talk with friends and relatives, read newspaper columnists, and listen to television pundits and pressure-group leaders. If, for example, I believe that the Catholic Church has special competence on moral questions, I may accept guidance from it in deciding how to vote on the issue of abortion, even though I do not understand the theological arguments involved. If I am concerned about the preservation of wilderness areas, I may endorse the judgments of the Sierra Club about the policies that will best promote this end, even though I cannot explain why those policies are best. In deciding which candidate to vote for, I can take account of their education and experience. If there is such a thing as moral competence, I can take account of any visible signs of it in the candidates.

In most democracies, elected representatives are far from being a random sample of the population. In Britain, for example, after more than a hundred years of a wide franchise, Members of Parliament are still overwhelmingly drawn from the traditional elites and from the ranks of the university-educated. Men and the middle-aged are also vastly overrepresented. There are many explanations for this, but deference has surely played a part: Working-class people, women, the young and the old, have seen middle-aged professional men as particularly fitted to act as legislators. Perhaps all these groups have been wrong to be so deferential, but that is not what is at issue. My point is that if one group of people *perceive* another group as more competent than themselves, a democratic system allows the one to defer to the other.

Thus, if we are to justify giving extra votes to an elite group of citizens, or if we are to justify giving lawmaking powers to unelected Platonic Guardians, we must do more than argue that the members of these elites are especially competent at taking political or moral decisions. We must also argue that ordinary citizens lack the ability to recognize the required elite qualities. From one point of view, of course, this extra step is a small one. If political decision making is a specialized skill, isn't the ability to recognize this skill also a skill? And aren't these skills quite similar, so that people who lack one are likely to lack the other? (Compare some other fields of human activity: We expect scientists to be the best judges of scientists, doctors of doctors, artists of artists . . .) But from another point of view, the extra step marks a fundamental change in the nature of the argument. It marks the move from a justification that might be endorsed by everyone to one that cannot be endorsed by the "ignorant" or "incompetent" citizens who are in some degree to be disenfranchised.

For a utilitarian, a proposition about the overall good can be true even if a majority of people do not recognize its truth; and its moral force is undiminished by this. If, taking everything into account, we (the more competent) can establish that the best consequences for society can be achieved only if the more competent are given special weight in decision making, then the more competent *ought* to be given special weight. That the less competent cannot recognize this truth does not make it any less true. If the more competent have the power to give themselves special weight in decision making, then they are morally justified in using this power, even though the justification is not recognized by others.

But is this how we should conceive of justification in the realm of political institutions? There is an alternative view, according to which political institutions must be justified *to everyone* in terms each person can accept. Legitimate institutions are seen as if they were the product of some kind of agreement, by which each person has freely consented to be bound by their rules. This tradition of thought – the contractarian tradition of Hobbes and Locke, represented today by Rawls – is deeply embedded in Western, and particularly in American, political thinking. To the extent that we are influenced by these ideas, we find it difficult to accept Mill's argument for plural voting. Even if we could agree with Mill that plural voting would bring about the best consequences, we may still say that this does not *justify* plural voting in the required sense, since the justification is, by its very nature, one that not everyone can accept. For the same reasons, we may say that Arneson's argument does not justify the special role of the judiciary in the American Constitution.

References

John Stuart Mill, *On Liberty*, London, 1859.
John Stuart Mill, *Considerations on Representative Government*, London, 1861.

The text I have used for both is: *Utilitarianism, On Liberty, and Considerations on Representative Government*, edited by H. B. Acton (London: J. M. Dent & Sons, 1972).

Part II

Democracy and preferences

4

Public choice
versus democracy

RUSSELL HARDIN

Public-choice theory offers two main classes of findings. First, aggregation from individual to collective preferences may not be well defined. Even though every individual may have a clear preference ranking of all alternatives before us, we may not be able to convert these individual rankings into a collective ranking. Second, individual motives for action may not fit collective preferences for outcomes even when the latter are well defined. We may all agree, for example, that we would all be better off if we would all pay extra for better pollution control equipment on our cars, but no individual has an interest in making the extra expenditure. Not only are we damned if we don't agree on what to do, we may also be damned if we do.

The first class of findings casts doubt on the conceptual coherence of majoritarian democracy. The second class has commonly been thought to yield a consensual justification for the coercive power of the state if, of course, the state is democratic. Just because our individual motivations work against our collective interests, we should choose to coerce ourselves to act in our collective interests. This consensual argument for coercion is, however, as logically flawed as the notion of majoritarian democracy. All that we may rightly conclude from the misfit of individual and collective interests is that we would benefit from having some central determination of our actions. We cannot conclude which of several possible determinations we should make.

The disconcerting implication of public-choice theory is that majoritarian democracy is both conceptually and motivationally flawed. Perhaps the actual practice of democracy may sensibly be viewed as a compromise to live within the constraints of these perverse conclusions. That practice is not an altogether happy compromise because it is not particularly majoritarian.

This essay has benefited from critical commentaries by John W. Chapman, Thomas Christiano, Robert E. Lane, and Alan Wertheimer. It was originally published in *Nomos* XXXII (1990): 184–203.

After a brief historical account of the recognition of the discoveries of public-choice theory, I address their bearing on democratic theory and practice. I then examine one possible empirical escape from the negative implications by way of the communitarian claim that we do not face the assumptions or conclusions of the theory's account of democracy. Finally, I consider an alternative solution to the difficulties of democratic theory, namely, that institutional devices can achieve what democratic choice may not. Throughout, my concern is majoritarian democracy, that is, procedures based on majority rule. This is the form in which we face the following problems because we have come to accept merely majority rule rather than to require broad consensus to make democracy workable. In modern political thought, the core of the notion of democracy is its etymological core – rule by the people – which translates most naturally as majority rule if there are divisions of opinion.

1. Two problems

Public-choice theory's first class of results is associated with Condorcet's problem of cyclic majorities and Kenneth Arrow's General Possibility Theorem, which is more aptly known as Arrow's Impossibility Theorem.[1] According to this theorem, there is no general rule for aggregating to a social choice from individual preferences that can meet certain apparently acceptable criteria. This theorem is essentially normative and conceptual. It says that collective preference cannot be defined as a logical analog of individual preference as that is commonly understood in economics. I will refer to this as the problem of social choice or, in its specific variants, as Condorcet's or Arrow's problem.

The second class of results is associated with Anthony Downs's analysis of voting, Mancur Olson's account of the logic of collective action, and the game theorist's Prisoner's Dilemma.[2] I will refer to this as the collective action or prisoner's dilemma problem. It is essentially an explanatory problem of motivation. It arises in contexts in which a common goal can be achieved only through individual contributions of effort or resources. For example, we may reduce pollution if each of us contributes by driving more expensively equipped cars. It may be in my interest not to cooperate in achieving our common purpose if I can get away with it even though it is in my interest for all of us to cooperate. How then do we get ourselves to cooperate? If we face no contrary sanction or inducement, we may all choose not to cooperate and so fail to achieve our goal.

Both of these problems are relevant to the general issues of organizing political societies. And they are a perverse and demoralizing pair. Arrow's theorem says we cannot generally stipulate a rule for acceptably aggregating to a collective preference from individual preferences. The conclusion of the standard prisoner's dilemma analysis is that, even where we find an acceptable rule for aggregating, we may still have motivational difficulties in implementing the collective preference.

The two problems are not only a perverse but a natural pair. Arrow's theorem is strictly about what state of affairs we want to attain. It does not deal with how to get there once we know what we want. Arrow never reaches the motivational concerns of how to implement a collective or aggregate preference once it is defined. In a sense, he need not reach such concerns for the simple reason that he shows we cannot in general define a determinate aggregate preference merely as a function of individual preferences. His proof involves logical assumptions that are far more complete in their possibilities than our real world may be. Although no general aggregation rule would fit all possible worlds, there might be one that fits ours. In that case, we would want to know how to implement our collective preference. The logic of collective action says that, for an important class of seemingly quite consensual issues, implementation may be fouled by narrow self-interest. Arrow's theorem is not concerned with how to enforce a collective preference. The usual prisoner's dilemma analysis and Olson's theory are fundamentally about enforcement.

2. Historical background

Public-choice theory is an extension of neoclassical economics in that it is based, both normatively and explanatorily, on the assumptions of individual choice or preference. In early efforts to understand productivity, these assumptions worked wonders by replacing notions of intrinsic value with an understanding of relations of supply and demand. When the simple theory of incentives was systematically applied to economic life, the results were generally counterintuitive and sanguine. The main result was expressed in Mandeville's law that private vices beget public virtues. Or, more explicitly, narrowly self-interested behavior in production and exchange leads to collective benefits in the form of a general increase in wealth. According to a contemporary variant on Mandeville, greed makes America strong and prosperous.

Not everything can be handled by incentives for personal benefit in free exchange. Public-choice theory arose mainly to deal with what remains for the public to do, to deal with what cannot be or is not done through the market.[3] This residual is large and important. Hence, the problem of public choice is also large and important, as is the scope of government. The results of economic analysis of this residual are often counterintuitive but not at all sanguine.

The problem of gaining compliance with government policies has been recognized in political philosophy from Plato forward. It is, of course, central for Hobbes. With slightly tendentious or generous reading one can presume that many have seen the logic of collective action or the prisoner's dilemma. For example, Glaucon (in Plato's *Republic*) and Hobbes think social order depends on threatening individuals to get them not to transgress against others. This sanctioning is mutually beneficial if it means that virtually none of us transgresses or can transgress.[4] Ideally, for any one of us, it might be best if all others are intimidated into orderliness while we free ride on the general order and the wealth that it generates.

Most of the earlier treatments of motivating beneficial collective action focused on the negative issue that provoked Glaucon and Hobbes: to prevent harm by securing mutual abstinence. The more common modern focus, exemplified by Hume and Rousseau, has been on the possibility of securing cooperation for creative purposes.[5] This may owe some inspiration to economic thought, culminating in Adam Smith, and some to the development of contract law and doctrine, both of which treat cooperation and exchange as productive. In this sanguine variant of government's intervention to resolve a collective action problem, we might agree on mutual coercion to get all to contribute to a state of affairs that we all prefer to the status quo. Alas, although we might successfully use the state to prod us into mutually beneficial collective action, we might not agree on what collective actions to prod ourselves into.

The other class of issues in public-choice theory, the impossibility of finding a rule for aggregating diverse preferences into a single collective preference, has been noticed in limited ways in many contexts. Its general importance has only recently been widely recognized. The special problem is that, when we face a choice among three or more mutually exclusive policies, we may form a majority in favor of policy A over B, another majority for B over C, and yet another majority for C over A. No policy is preferred by majorities over all others. Condorcet saw cyclic majorities as an aspect of complex choices. C. L. Dodgson (Lewis Carroll), with his wonderful sense of the perversities of daily life, saw it in elections at his Christ Church College.[6] Generalization of the problem and appreciation of its potentially pervasive importance begins with the work of Duncan Black and Kenneth Arrow. Black saw the problem as inherent in committee choice and Arrow proved quite generally that there can be no acceptable universal rule to convert any collection of individual preferences into a collective preference ordering.

On his own account of his theorem, Arrow writes that he hit upon the general impossibility in the course of trying to show how individual preference orderings could be aggregated into a national ordering so that, in the analysis of international relations, one could treat nations as though they were individuals with standard game-theoretic utility functions.[7] In essence, Arrow was asking whether a state can be conceived as a unitary actor with its preferences derived in an acceptable way from those of its citizens. His answer was "no."

The history of our two issues has some irony. The first clear recognition of the trouble with aggregating individual into collective preferences came from Condorcet soon after sanguine views of the creative possibilities of the state in such thinkers as Hume and Smith[8] and of Rousseau's vision of a general will. As though in proof of the implications of his discovery, Condorcet died in the sanguinary aftermath of the French Revolution.

3. Social-choice problems

Although Condorcet's cyclic majorities are commonly associated with Arrow's theorem, as though the latter were merely a generalization of the former, the two are in fact quite different problems. The possibility of cyclic majorities arises when we vote on a specific issue that has three or more resolutions. This is a kind of choice that we may often face in political life at any level on which we decide by majority vote. Indeed, we can face this quandary no matter what our majority must be. For example, if we need a super-majority of 99 percent in favor to select a winner, we can have a cyclic majority with a hundred voters and a hundred possible positions on our issue.

Arrow's theorem is far more general in a powerful way that makes it unrealistic in direct application to our daily lives. Arrow supposes that we face a choice over whole states of affairs that are fully determined in every way that matters to us. We do not merely choose a president or decide on a law. We choose a total world in which everything is settled: all presidents, all laws. Once we have made this single social choice, nothing remains for us to choose collectively. Arrow was forced to conceive of the matter in this way because he wished to assume nothing more than purely ordinal preferences on the part of all individuals and in our final collective choice.

Why does this ambition push us into considering choices over whole states of affairs, states that are fully determined? Take any ordinary claim that I prefer A to *not-A*. There are few, if any, As of which we can believe that anyone would prefer A to *not-A* no matter what. In principle, we can almost always conceive a package, say of $A + B$, such that I would prefer (*not-A* + *not-B*) to $(A + B)$. If so, then it is not true that I prefer A to *not-A tout court*. Hence, in principle I cannot make ordinal choices over mere aspects of my state of affairs. I can make ordinal choices only over whole states of affairs.[9]

A certain lunacy lurks in thinking of our social-choice problem as a once-and-for-all choice over whole states of affairs. But for the moment, the only escape from that lunacy seems to be an alternative that almost all social theorists reject outright or one that any democratic theorist must reject. One alternative that might be compelling if it were conceptually sensible is to suppose we can make cardinal, interpersonally comparable evaluations of aspects of states of affairs. Then we could make a social choice by simply adding the evaluations of each of us together for all possible choices and selecting the choice that produces the largest sum. Of course, to say that I can make a cardinal evaluation of a particular aspect of my state of affairs is to assert that my evaluation of that aspect is not affected by other aspects. But that violates the principle stated above. This alternative is not cogent.

Another alternative is to suppose that we, or I, or someone simply knows a principle by which to evaluate aspects of our state of affairs that is not directly derivative from the preferences or interests of all of us. Candidate principles include various religious dogmas, naturalistic claims from what happens to be the apparent preference in a given community, and various intuited principles that one or another theorist approves. With the possible exception of the communitarian alternative, none of these is consistent with democratic principles. I will therefore not consider noncommunitarian principles further. I will leave the communitarian alternative for later.

In his theorem, Arrow supposes that our choice rule must meet several apparently appealing conditions. If our concern with the theorem is its relevance to our understanding of the possibilities of democracy, two assumptions in the theorem are in clear tension. First, our choice rule must be general in the very strong sense that it must apply successfully to any set of individual preferences. For example, it must be able to handle even a case in which the set of individual preferences is a cyclic majority. This is the condition of universal domain, or U. Second, the rule must be subject to the following Pareto principle: if no one prefers state of affairs x to state y and at least one of us prefers y to x, then the social choice must rank y above x. In particular, of course, if all of us prefer y to x, then our social choice must rank y above x. Suppose all of us prefer y to every other state of affairs. Then, as is true of any specific set of preferences, our set of individual preferences clearly violates condition *U*. But it does so in such a way that our society may have no difficulty at all in making a social choice that no one could object to on democratic principles.

Hence, Arrow's Impossibility Theorem does not rule out the possibility that we could reach a democratic social choice. It merely rules out the logical possibility that every society, no matter how lacking in agreement, can follow one single aggregation rule for the social ordering of all its alternative whole states of affairs. This is a logically strong conclusion, but it may fail to be empirically relevant. In this respect, it is like the Condorcet analysis of cyclic majorities: that analysis can be troubling, but it may not always be, because sometimes we may not have cyclic majority preferences.

What are we finally to make of Arrow's Impossibility Theorem? It is mitigated by other impossibilities. We cannot even get to Arrow's problem in general because we cannot know enough to give rank orderings over all whole states of affairs. The individual preference information that must be fed into an Arrovian social-choice mechanism or procedure is impossible. We might even suppose that the description of whole states of affairs in the real world, in which there are births and deaths that continually change the society of those choosing, makes little sense. And we may realistically suppose of many aspects of our social order that all or almost all prefer *A* to *not-A* in any plausible circumstances. And we typically need to make only a first choice without concern for the further ranking of all other alternatives. For these reasons, and perhaps others, we might actively prefer, and think it better, to make our social choices piecemeal. At most we decide a few things at one time and then decide other things later. And at that later time we might reconsider some of what seemingly has already been decided.

Unfortunately, this pragmatic response to Arrow's Impossibility Theorem is only a negative, not a positive, answer. It does not suggest how we may normatively determine what would be a best or a most democratic procedure for deciding what to decide now and what later, what to reconsider and what to leave decided, whom to include in the decision procedure and whom to leave out. Arrow's initial concern was to find a social-choice procedure that would meet a particular kind of normative justification, namely that the procedure was a rule for aggregating to a social choice from nothing but individual preferences subject to several constraints that, prima facie, seemed likely to be generally acceptable. His discovery is that there can be no such rule. We may rightly claim that his conditions and the general form of what he counted as a social choice (a complete ordering over all states of affairs) are unrealistic and therefore not compelling for our actual social choices. But we cannot thereby normatively rescue any social choice rule or mechanism. We need positive arguments in defense of a particular rule.

We have positive arguments for many social-choice procedures, but none is as tight and complete as the considerations Arrow raises. And no social-choice procedure seems fully acceptable even for a particular one of many contemporary complex national societies. Indeed, most social choice procedures that are analyzed by philosophers and others are not even sufficiently well defined for us to know how they work or whether they would work in plausible circumstances. We know that some societies seem to struggle through from one social choice to another. But success seems to turn on nondemocratic, coercive, and deceptive moves too much of the time for us to feel normatively at ease with it. Not only may minorities get trampled, but so may majorities. Within a democratic shell even the seemingly most democratic of modern governments may often be undemocratic.

Hence, although the conditions and form of Arrow's theorem are not ideally suitable for evaluation of social-choice procedures and possibilities, we must still be troubled by the negative implications of that theorem. More realistic assumptions will not block the conclusion that public-choice procedures are normatively incoherent if they are to translate individual into collective choices, as majoritarian democracy is supposed to do.

4. Collective-action problems

If many of us would benefit from completion of a project that no one of us could afford to undertake alone, we may confront the perversities of the logic of collective action. If we depend on voluntary contributions to our collective interest in this project, I may wish to take a free ride on the efforts of others. My own contribution, whether an equal share or otherwise, might benefit me less than it would cost me, even though, if all of us contribute, all of us benefit more than our own contributions. Alas, we may all try to free ride and may therefore all fail to benefit from the project.

One resolution of this problem is to vote to have our government force us to contribute, usually through taxes. As Hume stated,

Political society easily remedies [such] inconveniences. Magistrates find an immediate interest in the interest of any considerable part of their subjects. They need consult no body but themselves to form any scheme for the promoting of that interest. . . . Thus bridges are built; harbours open'd; ramparts rais'd; canals form'd; fleets equip'd; and armies disciplin'd; every where, by the care of government, . . . one of the finest and most subtle inventions imaginable.[10]

Hume's is a lovely vision. Once we have government, we can resolve our collective-action problems. Moreover, we can move from this vision to a justification for coercion, in the collection of taxes and other ways, to provide collective benefits. Mild coercion might well be sanctioned by our own democratic preferences. Is this conclusion compelling? Unfortunately, it is far too quick. It faces at least two obstacles. First, few instances of collective provision are likely to be uniquely preferred, so that we may wonder about the justice of coercing those whose preferences are overridden. Second, despite the fineness and subtlety of the invention of government for the provision of collective benefits, our control of government is subject to problems of the logic of collective action even when there is strong popular agreement on particular collective provisions.

With reference to the first obstacle, suppose we have before us two mutually exclusive collective provisions. They could be mutually exclusive for various reasons. For example, either of them may be in essence an opportunity cost of the other. When provision q has been arranged, the additional marginal benefits of providing p may no longer outweigh p's costs. We may collectively benefit from dredging a harbor somewhere, but if we dredge the one in your community, dredging the one in mine will no longer be an attractive option. Or one collective provision may logically preclude another, as one system of property rights, s, might preclude another, t, or as the constitutional arrangements that promote the interests of Federalists might undermine those of Antifederalists.

Unfortunately for Hume, some of us may strongly prefer p and t to q and s and may consider ourselves losers when q and s are provided. Government may indeed overcome a collective-action problem, but it may overcome the wrong one for many of us. Is it now justified in its coercion of those of us who lost? Perhaps, but it is not justified by a simple claim that we mutually benefit, because we could also have mutually benefited from the alternative resolutions.[11] We can often get a utilitarian justification for sticking to a policy choice once it has been in place awhile.[12] But we cannot always get a prior democratic or consensual justification for the choice when it is made from a menu of variously preferred alternatives.

As to the second obstacle, recall Downs's analysis of voting in major elections. His most widely cited proposition is that two-party elections tend to produce candidates whose positions mirror those of the median voter. It may be stodgy to say so, but that would not be a bad or undemocratic result. The more discouraging result of Downs's analysis is the analog of the logic of collective action that is faced by ordinary citizens. Most of us much of the time, perhaps most of the time, cannot justify any special effort to understand the value of electing one candidate rather than another. Egregious failure of leadership on a major policy issue may lead to rejection at re-election time, as Herbert Hoover learned in 1932, because it will take us no effort to relate failure to the candidate. But most voters cannot be expected to know enough to cast votes in ways that would properly constrain most elected officials. To some extent this is merely a reflection of the difficulty of making good causal predictions no matter how well informed one might be. For example, many Americans who voted for peace in 1964 got Lyndon Johnson's Vietnam War; many who voted for a balanced budget in 1980 got Ronald Reagan's record deficits. But many voters would misstate even the clearly predictable policies of their candidates.

We have a tremendous body of empirical work on what voters know and what motivates their choices in elections. Some of that work is reassuring for our concern with democratic control of government. But some is demoralizing. Early views that voters are virtually stupid have given way over the past couple of decades to more complex views that voters, in deciding on candidates, do what sensible people do when making any decisions that affect their interests: given the costs of acquiring information, they take short cuts and use proxy measures of many things. Even on the most favorable accounts of voter sophistication and the quality of voter decisions, however, one cannot make strong claims that the outcome of democratic voting procedures is a coherent mapping of citizen preferences onto policies. This conclusion is not theoretically surprising because, in at least broad outline, it seems clearly to follow from the Downsian analysis of the incentives voters face.

5. The communitarian alternative

Consider a political community in which Arrow's condition of universal domain is violated by widespread agreement on major issues. By Arrow's general principles, we may suppose the community can succeed in following the simple choice procedure of majority rule. We can do so because we will typically have overwhelming majorities in favor of one choice over any other that we may face. Suppose also that we do not face perverse interactive effects. If we think we prefer A to not-A and B to not-B, then we will not find ourselves also preferring (not-A + not-B) to (A + B). Hence, we can make our social choices piecemeal without needing to make a single choice over all possible whole states of affairs, and we can make then consensually.

Under these suppositions it would seem that we escape at least the conceptual flaws of democracy. Wouldn't majoritarian democracy therefore work perfectly well for us? Surely the answer could be yes. With such agreement on our major political issues, we should even be able to overcome some of the motivational problem of the logic of collective action by creating political devices for the mild coercion necessary to get us to abide by our collective decisions. Recent communitarian moral and political theory seems to be based on these assumptions and, hence, to meet the objections of public-choice theory. I think this conclusion is correct as a matter of pure possibility. This is to say that, by sufficiently balking the implications of Arrow's condition of universal domain and by not falling to the inherent logic of the interaction of the value of every aspect of our state of affairs with the value of every other aspect, we may be fortunate enough to make majority rule at least conceptually coherent. Moreover, it seems plausible that societies have existed in which these problems of public-choice theory have not dominated social choice. For example, many small societies studied by anthropologists may meet these conditions.

It is hard to read the communitarian literature without thinking that much more is being assumed than merely the possibility of such a factual state of consensus. In particular, many communitarians seem to be driven by a more profound and determinate notion of the sources of consensus. The presumed fact of consensus is put as a constitutive point: individuals in a society get their values from the society. Unfortunately, despite a "common" source for our values in a given society, general consensus on major issues does not follow, as must be obvious for anyone living in a modern society. Alasdair MacIntyre seems to take conflict over values in our society as a criticism of the society, although he rather perversely supposes that the Athens that has given us a rich record of deep and occasionally violent conflict over values was exempt from this criticism.[13]

Irrespective of whether our dissensus is ground for moral criticism, it is ground for doubting the conceptual coherence of democracy in our condition. The communitarian alternative is not one we can simply adopt. We either do or do not find ourselves in it. If we had found ourselves in communitarian consensus, neither public choice theory nor much of historical political theory might ever have arisen. Jane Mansbridge notes that in "the early seventeenth century, both citizens and their representatives believed that a nation-state could make most decisions on the basis of a common good." That belief has since been so thoroughly shattered that, she says, "majority rule, once an incomplete substitute for full consensus, is now almost synonymous with democracy itself."[14] It seems likely that it is not our era but rather the era of belief in a common good that is the odd exception in the long history of the effort to understand politics. In any sense that would serve the analyses of the communitarians, we are not a community.

6. The compromises of democracy

There is a third, emerging body of work in public choice in addition to work on the problems of social choice and collective action. This attends to the way institutions work. It is almost exclusively positive rather than normative. But it may have normative implications. Its central problem is how things manage to get publicly decided and implemented despite the impossibilities of Arrow and Condorcet and the motivational conundrums of Downs and Olson. For example, how does a legislative body such as Congress regularly succeed in adopting policies by apparently majority votes despite the supposed frequency of Condorcet cycles? Institutional public choice theorists argue that it may do so through the use of devices that mask cyclic majorities or that give someone or some group authority or power to force majority votes.

Well-recognized antimajoritarian devices include deference to the status quo and giving some person or group power to manipulate the order of voting on issues. Votes in legislative bodies may be restricted to simple yes or no votes on particular issues, so that each measure is compared to the status quo rather than to alternative measures. If there is a cyclic majority over two alternatives and the status quo, the cycle can only show up in a future year when a measure that lost to the status quo this year defeats one that has since become the new status quo. In the meantime, we seem to be quite decisive. Alas, any historical bias in who benefits from the status quo may be further maintained by this device for handling cyclic majorities.[15]

We can break the status quo by giving decisive control over legislative voting to specific individuals or groups to contrive determinate outcomes. In the United States Congress, small committees often have extraordinary control over the content of legislation. Almost no congressional committee bill could be safe from amendments that would make it inferior to the status quo in the view of the committee members. Committees get the last word when legislation goes to conference committee to work out House and Senate differences. In conference, committee members have an ex post veto that guarantees that they do no worse than the status quo.[16] Committee control of legislation introduces strong bias if special interests tend to dominate committees that oversee their issues, as they commonly do. Hence, instead of a bias for the status quo, we have biased change. Moreover, this device may not only overcome the status quo domination of cyclic majorities, it may also overcome clear majority preferences that are not cyclic.

The bent here is not unlike part of the bent in the communitarian literature. It simply asserts facts of the matter that run against the demands of democratic theory and that allow us to make political choices. Unlike the communitarians, however, institutional public-choice theorists seek to show how we make choices in nonmajoritarian, even antimajoritarian ways. This is not a happy ploy for the democratic theorist. Recognition of the problems of public choice theory, however, should alert us to look for points in the system at which nonmajoritarian resolutions may be inherently biased. We may sometimes suppose such resolutions are unobjectionable, but we cannot easily reach this conclusion from merely democratic principles.

If there is a first constitutional lesson to be drawn from public choice theory, it is that there is no universally workable way for aggregating individual interests, preferences, or values into collective decisions. A positive implication of this finding is that no government of a complex society is likely to be coherently democratic. If we wish to explain political outcomes in such a society, we will require more than merely a rule for converting individual into collective views.

A normative implication of this lesson is that political theory cannot be grounded exclusively in democratic procedural values. If we wish to justify particular practices for adopting and implementing policies, we must have recourse to extra-democratic values. For example, we often call on such values as the protection of individuals in various respects and on such utilitarian values as the value of stable expectations or the value of making decisive choices so that we may get on with life. Or we call on psychological values not directly related to particular outcomes, such as the sense of satisfaction citizens may get from apparently fair procedures. Even though we might discover general consensus on any of these values in the abstract, they would not evoke general consensus in application in particular policy choices when, for example, we still must choose one or another policy before getting on with life.

We finally still face something vaguely like Arrow's problem. The terms and conditions of Arrow's theorem may not seem properly to fit the problems of political choice in actual societies. But they clearly challenge any effort to reach a sound conception of majoritarian democracy, without which we may not be able to make normative assessments of democratic procedures and institutions, and without which we have no coherent argument for justifying our social order in democratic terms. Moreover, in the face of the motivational problems of the logic of collective action we cannot give democratic justification of state coercion in our common political enterprise.

Where does public-choice theory leave us? Against the trend of results in the early incentive analysis of markets and production, it leaves us understanding less than what we might earlier have thought we knew. It does so by clarifying issues to reveal their apparent intractability. In the end, lack of agreement is the modal problem of democracy. Because of it we must have some kind of aggregation principle. But, after four decades of public choice theory, we have little ground to expect to justify any particular principle. Indeed, the more we understand the nature of the task, the more we seem to find it incoherent.

This is not to say that the democratic, majoritarian urge is wrong. At base it seems to have genuine appeal, both moral and practical. But it is nevertheless conceptually incoherent and, when defined in simple terms, practically infeasible. The application of economic reasoning and the assumption of self-interested economic motivation has done wonders for explicating many aspects of production and the wealth of nations. But, in keeping with the seemingly destructive tenor of findings in many areas of inquiry in this century, their recent application to democratic theory has largely helped to expose flaws – grievous foundational flaws – in democratic thought and practice.

Against the conceptual and motivational flaws of majoritarian democracy, one might argue, as Churchill did, that democracy is the worst form of government, except for all the other forms. This cannot be a comfortable a priori claim, however, if the very notion of majority rule is conceptually incoherent. If government is inherently nonmajoritarian, how are we to assess the degree to which it is democratic? If Churchill's judgment is merely an empirical assertion about the good that various forms of government do for us, it is clouded by still other conceptual problems. We might easily judge some actual governments worse than others and even some general forms of government worse than certain others. But we cannot easily present coherent principles to ground our judgments and our vision.

Notes

1 Kenneth J. Arrow, *Social Change and Individual Values*, 2d ed. (New York: Wiley, 1963). See also relevant readings in Brian Barry and Russell Hardin, *Rational Man and Irrational Society?* (Beverly Hills: Sage, 1982). Despite voluminous work over the past two decades, the best textbook treatment is

still Amartya K. Sen, *Collective Choice and Social Welfare* (San Francisco: Holden-Day, 1970; reprinted, Amsterdam: North-Holland, 1979).

2 Anthony Downs, *An Economic Theory of Democracy* (New York: Harper, 1957); Mancur Olson Jr., *The Logic of Collective Action* (Cambridge: Harvard University Press, 1965); Anatol Rapoport and Albert M. Chammah, *Prisoner's Dilemma* (Ann Arbor: University of Michigan Press, 1965); Russell Hardin, *Collective Action* (Baltimore: Johns Hopkins University Press, 1982). See also the readings in Barry and Hardin, *Rational Man* for more general information.

3 Geoffrey Brennan and James M. Buchanan write that, before the rise of public choice theory, economists ignored the difficulties of institutional implementation of policies and were satisfied merely to determine what was, in the abstract, the normatively best policy (*The Reason of Rules: Constitutional Political Economy* [Cambridge: Cambridge University Press, 1985], 83).

4 Hobbes was also concerned with the origins of the state – indeed, one may say this is the principal focus of his *Leviathan*. This problem is often related in contemporary writing to the prisoner's dilemma. I think this analogy is mistaken, that the rational creation of a state is more nearly a problem of coordination. For example, on Hobbes's account the state arises by coordination on a particular ruler.

5 Even before Hobbes, this was a sometime focus, as in Robert Bellarmine, *De Laicis* (New York: Fordham University Press, 1928, trans. Kathleen E. Murphy; Latin original from 1586–1593), 48.

6 For an account of Condorcet and Dodgson, see Duncan Black, *The Theory of Committees and Elections*, 2d ed. (Cambridge: Cambridge University Press, 1963), 156–238. Pliny the Younger saw a hint of the difficulties of social choice when there are more than two possible choices in a vote of the Roman Senate over three possible verdicts for freedmen accused of murdering their master. The freedmen could be acquitted and released, convicted and banished, or convicted and executed. Social-choice theorists might readily suppose that the result would be the median of these positions, or conviction and banishment. Pliny's discussion of the case is reprinted in Robin Farquharson, *Theory of Voting* (New Haven: Yale University Press, 1969), 57–60; see also William H. Riker, *The Art of Political Manipulation* (New Haven: Yale University Press, 1986), 78–88.

7 Kenneth J. Arrow, *Social Choice and Justice*, vol. 1, *Collected Papers* (Cambridge, Mass.: Harvard University Press, 1983), 3–4.

8 Smith is commonly supposed to represent the view that the state is destructive in its interventions, as when it grants monopolies and other favors that stand in the way of greater productivity. Those hostile to the growth of the state in our time have successfully captured Smith as their predecessor. But it was also Smith's view that the state can work miracles of collective action that are beyond the reach of individuals. Proponents of many state initiatives can therefore persuasively claim support from his writings.

9 See further, Russell Hardin, "Rational Choice Theories," *Idioms of Inquiry:*

Critique and Renewal in Political Science, ed. Terence Ball (Albany: State University of New York Press, 1987), 67–91, esp. 78–80; and Barry and Hardin, *Rational Man*, 224.

10 David Hume, *A Treatise of Human Nature*, ed. L. A. Selby-Bigge and P. H. Nidditch, 2d ed. (Oxford: Clarendon Press, 1978: originally published 1739–1740), book 3, pt 2, sec. 7, 538–39.

11 Russell Hardin, "Political Obligation," *The Good Polity: Normative Analysis of the State*, ed. Alan Hamlin and Philip Pettit (Oxford: Basil Blackwell, 1989), 103–19.

12 Russell Hardin, "Does Might Make Right?" *Authority Revisited*, ed. J. Roland Pennock and John W. Chapman, NOMOS 29 (New York: N.Y. University Press, 1987), 201–17.

13 Alasdair MacIntyre, *After Virtue* (Notre Dame: University of Notre Dame Press, 1981).

14 Jane J. Mansbridge, "Living with Conflict: Representation in the Theory of Adversary Democracy," *Ethics* 91 (April 1981): 466–76. For evidence of the adversarial temper of democratic thought, see other articles in the "Symposium on the Theory and Practice of Representation" in that issue of *Ethics*. See also Mark Kishlansky, "The Emergence of Adversary Politics in the Long Parliament," *Journal of Modern History* 49 (1977): 617–40.

15 Despite the status quo rule, we might see cyclic majorities working their way through the legislative amendment process. The late Senator James B. Allen of Alabama was reputedly able to use cyclic majorities to wreck many legislative measures that seemed otherwise sure to defeat the status quo. Through his sophisticated reading of fellow senators he contrived amendments, each of which was favored by a majority, to produce a newly amended bill that would be voted down, leaving the status quo intact.

16 For an example of such an effort, see Kenneth A. Shepsle and Barry R. Weingast, "Institutional Foundations of Committee Power," *American Political Science Review* 81 (March 1987): 85–104. Shepsle and Weingast explain how committees in the House of Representatives succeed in controlling the content of their bills against amendments on the floor of the House. This is hardly a democratic result, but it may be quite stabilizing.

Social choice and democracy

THOMAS CHRISTIANO

It is often argued that the results of social choice theory in general and Kenneth Arrow's impossibility theorem in particular constitute an insuperable barrier to the moral justification of democracy.[1] I shall explore the basis of this claim and undermine it. I argue that democracy has firm foundations in an egalitarian principle of justice. In my estimation the impossibility results of social choice theory have much less significant implications for normative democratic theory than is usually claimed. The social choice theoretic conception of democratic procedure is misconceived. Social choice theory, as it has been practiced, does not address problems connected with the justification of democratic procedure; rather, it is concerned with elaborating principles with which one can evaluate states of affairs on the basis of individual preferences. And I argue that it does not fare very well in this pursuit either. I shall show that democracy rests on firm foundations. A more defensible conception of majority rule and the democratic process is that they provide for equal distributions of resources over collective decision making. A moral justification of democracy so conceived can be derived from defensible principles of justice.

Arrow's theorem and the coherence of democracy

In Russell Hardin's words, Arrow's theorem states that "there is no general rule for aggregating to a social choice from individual preferences that can meet certain acceptable criteria."[2] The criteria are: A rule must select one and only one alternative, given a set of individual preferences; a rule must not permit anyone's preferences to be the social choice regardless of what anyone else prefers; from among two alternatives a rule must choose the alternative that is unanimously preferred; a rule must produce a transitive preference ordering as its result; with respect to any two alternatives, a rule must select an outcome on the basis of the individuals' preferences between those two alternatives alone; a rule must satisfy these requirements for any possible array of preferences.

A moral justification of democracy is a justification of the democratic process of decision making in terms of moral principles. A democratic process of decision making is one where everyone in the relevant group has an opportunity to participate equally in an essential stage of decision making by means of voting. Such a process can be evaluated morally in two different ways. We can ask whether the process, when used, produces outcomes such as legislation or character traits for those who participate or any other outcomes that accord with defensible moral principles. We might call this an instrumentalist moral evaluation of democracy. The principles used in such an evaluation may be but need not be consequentialist; they may be nonconsequentialist principles for evaluating legislation. An argument for democracy along instrumentalist lines will be concerned with the fit between the moral principles and the outcomes of the use of the procedure. Morally, such arguments will be comparative. We may say that though democracy does not produce the best conceivable results, it is better than other processes in that they produce worse outcomes. Of course, such evaluation could also be used to criticize democratic decision making. The second kind of moral evaluation may involve properties inherent in the procedure itself. We may say that the procedure is intrinsically fair or reasonable regardless of the results of using it. And there is a suggestion of the intrinsic fairness of democracy in the fact that democracy requires some kind of equal opportunity to effect outcomes. Of course, whether there is any such justification of democracy will depend on the moral principles. These two forms of moral assessment may also be combined in various ways. One may evaluate all decisions in terms of both the way the decision came about and of the worth of the outcomes. Or one might evaluate the process in terms of its intrinsic fairness with regard to some kinds of issues and in terms of the worth of the outcomes for other kinds.

Given these brief remarks about democratic decision making and the two forms of moral evaluation of a process, we can see how the impossibility theorem might be thought to bear on the moral justification of democracy. Hardin states that a "positive implication of this finding is that no government of a complex society is likely to be coherently democratic," and a "normative implication . . . is that political theory cannot be grounded exclusively in democratic procedural values."[3] His argument for this position is based on the following premises: (1) Democratic government is based on a majority-rule procedure;[4] (2) majority-rule procedures are general rules for the aggregation of individual preferences into a social preference; (3) from Arrow's theorem, no majoritarian rule can aggregate individual preferences into a social preference in the wide variety of circumstances of disagreement and conflict of preference that obtains in democratic societies. Therefore, political questions cannot be solved by majority rule and no society can be coherently democratic.

I shall contest the first two premises of this argument and make some remarks about the proper interpretation of the results of social choice theory. I shall discuss some of the difficulties of majority rule and then give a different account of the problems of majority rule. I shall then argue that the problems I identify do not undermine democracy if we construe it in a certain way. Finally, I shall sketch a moral argument for democracy that will undergird my conception of the democratic process and show how democracy can be justified.

Majority rule and manipulation

In this section, I shall show, first, why we ought not to think of the majority-rule procedure as a function from individual preferences to a social preference; that argument will be generalized in the next section. Also, I shall lay the basis for my own distributive conception of democratic procedures and processes.

Under circumstances of widespread disagreement and conflict of preferences a majority-rule function such as the Condorcet rule may well produce cycles.[5] See Figures 1 and 2 later in the section for examples of this situation. In these cases there is no basis in the majoritarian principle for a decision. Majority rule will be indeterminate. And this result is a special case of the difficulties Arrow's theorem points to. But we should be clear about what this means. Strictly speaking, whether there is a Condorcet winner or a cycle tells us only about the relation between preferences, as the example shows. In actual uses of the majority-rule procedure, some decision will be made if only to delay making a decision. More often, decisions are made in these circumstances because of the strategic manipulation of the agenda or the voting procedure by some or all of the members of the group.

Most voting procedures encourage strategic manipulation.[6] Indeed, this is in part an implication of the failure to satisfy the criteria that Arrow says cannot be simultaneously satisfied by voting procedures. If one votes in a way that does not put one's first preference among alternatives first, second preference second, and so on, one can achieve an outcome that is better than if one votes in a way that does. For example, a plurality voting rule where each person casts a vote for a single alternative among three will encourage one to vote for one's second preference if one's first preference does not have many supporters. If one's first preference is not likely to win and one's last choice

	A	B	C	D	E
1	x	x	w	z	z
2	y	y	y	x	w
3	z	z	z	w	x
4	w	w	x	y	y

Figure 1.

will win if one does not vote for one's second choice, then one will have an incentive to vote for one's second choice. The vote is cast in order to determine the outcome, and in order to do that one must assess the alternatives in accordance with one's preferences and one must determine how others are voting. This is called strategic voting. In many cases of voting, one will vote for one's first preference because that will be the best way of making it the outcome of the procedure. But if one is voting strategically, it is the outcome of the procedure that one is most concerned with and not whether one's vote is for one's first preference. When one votes for one's first preference over outcomes, this is usually called "sincere" voting. I shall call it "straightforward" voting so as to avoid the suggestion of insincerity in the notion of strategic voting.[7]

For an example of manipulation, suppose that, given the preferences described in Figure 1, C was aware that the distribution of the preferences would lead to an indeterminate outcome with x and z as the main contenders (since they each defeat two of the three alternatives, while w and y will both probably lose since they each defeat only one alternative). C might choose to switch her chosen vote for one in which z is placed ahead of y. In this way, she could assure that z would win and since she prefers z to x, it might well be reasonable for her to vote for z over y rather than risk a victory for x, which is last on her preference ordering. If A and B had been aware of C's preferences and strategy, they might have joined in a coalition to defeat z by both placing w in front of z, thus producing another cycle. And this process could go much further than this.

The crucial elements that are affecting the outcomes here are information and the ability to manipulate individually as well as collectively. The amount of information required for the participants in this simple example includes information on everyone's preference orderings, on who is willing to vote strategically, and on what competence they have at this, as well as on what coalitions are likely to form. Furthermore, each person must be able to manipulate and form coalitions. Virtually any contested alternative can be defeated depending on the level and distribution of this information and these abilities.

	A	B	C	D	E
1	*wz*	*wz*	*xy*	*xy*	*xz*
2	*wy*	*xz*	*wy*	*xz*	*wz*
3	*xz*	*wy*	*xz*	*wy*	*xy*
4	*xy*	*xy*	*wz*	*wz*	*wy*

Figure 2. Vote trading

That the nature of the voting procedure may not matter as much as other considerations as long as certain constraints are imposed becomes more evident when we consider that voting procedures are not used just once. We have been discussing voting procedures as if they were used to decide all relevant conflicts in one single event. But this way of thinking of voting procedures is extremely unrealistic. The information required of participants to determine what issues would be relevant over a long period of time as well as what their views on these issues will be is far greater than any person could acquire. In general, procedures are used to make piecemeal decisions about marginal aspects of social life. The decisions can also be revised over time given new information. And the collection of such partial procedures may not produce the same outcome as a procedure that decided all the relevant issues at once.

But this feature of the use of procedures introduces the possibility of vote trading. Insofar as voting procedures are concerned with piecemeal changes in the society and those piecemeal changes are most of the time complementary in value for individuals, or at least some issues are more important than other issues, individuals will attempt to trade votes on issues for other votes. Hence, an individual's vote on an issue will not be independent of his or her preferences over other alternatives when the procedures are concerned with piecemeal changes. As Hardin notes, this is not true for the social choice function that is the subject of Arrow's theorem.[8] Such a rule would not give any incentive to individuals to compromise and make trades since all issues would be combined into the one global choice. With partial procedures we get vote trading and with a global procedure, no vote-trading. Of course there can still be strategic manipulation in a global procedure both of an individual and a collective kind.

The extent to which people can successfully trade votes so as to get outcomes that they desire also depends on their ability to form coalitions as well as on their information about others' preferences and voting strategies. People with more information will be in a better position to get the outcomes they want. This is illustrated by the example in Figure 2.

These are the preference schedules over the combination of issues w-x and y-z. As we can see, if the issues were to be decided separately and everyone voted according to their preferences, C, D, and E would ensure the victory of x and A, B, and E would make up a majority for z. If there were a combined procedure, xz would also be the Condorcet winner. To return to the separate procedures, let us suppose that A and C were aware of the preference orders of the others and knew that they would vote straightforwardly. A and C would then have an incentive to trade votes on the issue. Since w-x is a more significant issue for A and y-z is more important to C, A could give up voting for z and vote for y in return for C's voting for w over x. They together would then be able to get the outcomes w and y.[9]

Obviously, however, these outcomes could be upset as well. The point here is the same as for manipulation in individual procedures. The importance of information and coalition-building abilities is highlighted. Outcomes will depend heavily on their distribution of these resources. Hence, majority-rule procedures may well permit decisions to be made even when the relation between preferences is that of a cycle; those decisions will depend on the resources individuals have to manipulate the procedure.

The problem with the social choice conception of procedures

In this section I discuss two prominent ways of interpreting the results of social choice theory. The first understands collective decision-making procedures as kinds of social choice functions. The second understands social choice functions as principles for evaluating states of affairs in terms of the preferences of individuals and social preferences in this theory are understood as the common good or as a maximum of welfare. I reject both interpretations in turn.

Let us turn now to the very idea of a procedure as a method by means of which outcomes are derived from *preferences*. This is a common way of thinking about democratic procedure.[10] At this point, however, we need to reconsider this approach because, as we have already seen, it is impossible to have a method that can derive decisions directly from the unadulterated preferences of the participants. This is demonstrated by the virtually universal manipulability of voting procedures, which not only permit but encourage individuals to vote in a way that does not reveal their real preferences. I shall show now that first, it is incorrect to say that a mapping from individual preferences to a social preference describes any actual procedure. Second, such a "procedure" need not be democratic at all. It is more reasonable to think of a social choice function as a principle that tells us how to evaluate outcomes of any collective decision-making procedure. Third, it is not clear that the notion of a social choice function can give us anything like the kind of principle we need to evaluate the outcomes of democratic procedures.

The first point is that collective decision procedures do not take us from the preferences of members of the collective to outcomes. One has to participate in a collective decision procedure to have any influence on the outcome. The fact that not everyone participates does not imply there was no procedure. Further, even with an incentive compatible procedure, it is possible for someone to make a mistake when they vote. The procedure will still produce an outcome even if the vote did not express the person's preference. The fact that a procedure is manipulable also shows that it is a rule that goes not from preferences to outcomes but from *actions* to outcomes. Many times those actions do not reveal the real preferences of the voter and sometimes they do. This is a choice of the voter that is left open by the procedure.

Second, it is not clear whether any procedure that goes directly from the preferences of the members of a collective to an outcome is democratic. If we were to suppose there were a benevolent dictator who was required to implement the preferences of the members and who had perfect information regarding those preferences, then, on the standard account of democratic procedure, a society governed by the benevolent dictator would be democratic. This would, in Brian Barry's definition, be a democratic procedure because it established a "formal connection between the preferences of the voters and the social decisions."[11] But the society ruled by a benevolent dictator is the paradigm case of a nondemocratic society. One of the central contrasts that determines our notion of democracy, vague as it is, is the contrast with benevolent dictatorship.

These points suggest that social choice theory cannot be directly applied to democratic procedures but is suited to define what a good state of affairs is. As a consequence it may be more reasonable to think of social choice functions in terms of principles for evaluating outcomes of democratic procedures or any collective choice procedure. Then we may look at the impossibility result as saying something about the possibility of discovering principles for evaluating states of affairs. The results would not figure in as a criticism of "democratic procedural values" and hence would not constitute a criticism of attributions of intrinsic worth to democratic procedures. The criticism might rather be directed at the possibility of an instrumentalist evaluation of democratic procedure or any kind of collective decision-making procedure (including, the rule by which a benevolent, all-knowing dictator might determine what is a good policy).

There is another reason for thinking that social choice theory is in fact concerned with principles for evaluating states of affairs. The usual reason for developing a social choice function is belief in an aggregative conception of procedures. This conception states that the purpose of a collective decision procedure is to take a set of individual preferences and transform them into a social preference. The use of the procedure must guarantee that we have an outcome of a certain sort. This is because the aim of the procedure will be to produce an outcome that reflects either the common will of the individual participants or a maximum of welfare for those individuals. These are the two standard interpretations of the idea of a social preference. This is the justification on such an account of using such a procedure. And one necessary condition for a procedure to produce such outcomes is that it be incentive compatible. That is, only if the procedure aggregates over the true preferences of individuals can the procedure guarantee that the outcome reflects the common will or a utilitarian solution. If individuals misrepresent their preferences by voting strategically, the outcome will not be an aggregation from their preferences and, social choice theorists argue, the outcome will have no meaning and will be simply arbitrary.[12] That is, the results will not necessarily be the common will or greatest good. Much of social choice theory seems to be concerned with finding a social welfare function that will always produce one of these. It seems clear however, that the concern for discovering the common will or some notion of aggregate welfare described above which motivates efforts at defining a social choice function are more correctly described as concerns relating to the instrumentalist evaluation of political institutions. Therefore, social choice theory is more suitable as an attempt to find a general principle that will tell us what the common good or the maximum good is, given a domain (possibly unlimited) of preferences. On this view, Arrow's theorem suggests that no such general principle can be elaborated if we accept the restrictions listed above. I would like briefly to explore this possible interpretation of the critical role of social choice theory.

I think there are reasons for doubting whether the axioms of social choice will permit us to develop principles describing the common will or aggregate welfare on the basis of individual preferences. I shall discuss each of these possible interpretations.

That the social preference should necessarily reflect the common will seems misconceived from the start. The basis for the idea of a common will is that everyone should benefit from the decision or that the decision should in some way proceed from, or at least accord with, the will of each and every person. To achieve this, one must find out what is in common between the desires that all individuals have, and this will be the common will.[13] It is not a procedural principle; it is the idea that there are, if there is to be any society at all, areas of mutual advantage among the individuals in the society. The questions for those who adopt such a principle will always be, What is the best method for discovering this area of mutual advantage?[14] and, What are the best circumstances under which reasonable agreement on this area can be had? Clearly, this approach is inimical to that of social choice theorists because they are concerned with defining a function that satisfies certain properties among which is that the function can operate on a relatively large if not unlimited domain of preferences. Social choice theory starts from the assumption of a high degree of irresolvable disagreement among participants. And it assumes that it makes sense to attempt to define a social preference on all issues, no matter how great the disagreements are. The idea of a common will is quite different. It is simply that in a society the preferences of individuals bear a certain relation of similarity to each other or can come to bear such a relation as a result of reasoned discussion, and that the point of a procedure is to *discover* these areas of similarity. To say that there is a common good on some issue is just to say that a certain profile of preferences obtains (everyone has the same preference) with regard to that issue.[15] The idea behind social choice theory is that it is reasonable to try to determine what the social preference is no matter how much difference there is. Hence, in many cases where the social choice theorist will be attempting to determine what the social preference is among a group of individuals, the common-good theorist can legitimately say that there is no common good. Therefore, the common-will interpretation of the notion of social preference will not work.

A more plausible interpretation is that the social preference is a kind of maximum of welfare. There are two important reasons why at least some social choice theories cannot be interpreted this way. First, the domain of preferences over which the social choice function is defined does not and cannot distinguish between self-regarding and other-regarding preferences, which distinction is crucial for any utilitarian notion of maximum welfare. It is not to my benefit to have my desire satisfied that another be treated fairly, at least certainly not in the way that it is to my benefit that my desire for ice cream be fulfilled. Satisfying the former preference will not contribute in itself to my welfare. Second, even were we to restrict the domain of preferences to self-regarding preferences, the social choice function would not take into account intensity of preference. This is the consequence of requiring the social preference to be a function of preference orderings only and not allowing intensity measures in. No conception of social preference that ignores these two points can guarantee or define utilitarian outcomes. This difficulty, of course, is limited to those theories such as Arrow's which eschew interpersonal comparisons of utility.

Hence, the idea that there is some normative significance to Arrovian social choice functions is to be rejected if the two interpretations I have discussed are the only possible ones.[16] And these seem to be the only plausible interpretations. Note that acceptance of the preceding remarks does not call the results of Arrow's social choice theory into question. The issue addressed above is, What is the proper interpretation of this theory? I have rejected what I take to be the main interpretations, and I am not sure what other possible interpretation can work. In my view, this branch of theorizing has been useful mainly as an impetus to the game theoretic analysis of social institutions, but I am not sure we understand what it itself is about.

A distributive conception of procedures

In this section I give an alternative analysis of voting procedures that I call a distributive conception. Furthermore, I elaborate on one kind of standard, an egalitarian standard, by which such procedures might be evaluated and show how our conception of democratic procedure must be modified if we adopt this standard. The next section provides a moral argument for the adoption of such a standard. That argument will not be subject to the difficulties that social choice theorists have discussed.

What, then, is a collective decision procedure? It is a set of rules that operates (like a function) on a domain of *actions* (usually called "voting for x") and produces an outcome that is a decision that is binding on the collectivity.[17] The purpose of the procedure is to permit various members of the group to play a part in determining what decisions are to be made regarding some issue.

I shall call this the distributive conception of procedures. What the procedure does is assign the participants resources for determining the outcome. The general name for these resources is "voting power." Each individual may use the voting power they are assigned by the procedure to try to affect the outcome. These uses of voting power are what the procedure operates on to produce the outcomes. The distribution of voting power is defined by the particular properties of the procedure. This is what makes voting power a procedural resource; it is a resource the distribution of which is defined by the properties of the procedure.

On this account, procedures can have various distributional properties and we can define an egalitarian decision procedure. It is a procedure wherein the distribution of procedural resources is equal. Majority rule is an egalitarian procedure because the distribution of voting power is determined by the principles of one person–one vote, anonymity, and neutrality.[18] These properties of majority rule ensure an equal distribution of voting power. Inegalitarian methods of decision making such as monarchy and oligarchy can be described as methods that do not satisfy the anonymity property. If the king votes for x, then x is chosen regardless of what anyone else wants. Or if a majority of oligarchs vote for x, then that is the choice. All the resources for decision making are given to one or a few.

Social choice theory puts us in a position to see what is missing in majority rule from an egalitarian standpoint. The trouble is that even when we have distributed the procedural resources equally as in a majority-rule procedure, we will frequently get indeterminate outcomes if we simply assume that individuals vote straightforwardly. We now have two choices for resolving this issue. Either we relax the egalitarian features of the procedure, as with the amendment procedure, or we think of individuals as voting strategically. Let us suppose that we wish to preserve political equality. From the preceding section we can see that knowing the situation they are in, individuals will vote strategically to produce an outcome more to their liking. They will do this on the basis of information they have. This information is a crucial resource for individuals in determining outcomes. Furthermore, this resource can be distributed in certain ways and the outcome may well depend on how it is distributed. Finally, this is not a procedural resource. Its distribution is not defined by the properties of any procedure. Indeed, this resource can be distributed unequally even while procedural resources are equally distributed.

Let us say that when a person votes he is participating in a collective decision-making *procedure*. This action takes place in a larger context. People are trying to get information about alternatives, others' preferences and strategies, as well as building coalitions to trade votes. Let us call all of these activities, as well as the procedure, the collective decision-making *process*. Let us say furthermore that a collective decision-making process is egalitarian when all the resources relevant to determining the outcome are equally distributed. It is this collective decision-making process that must be egalitarian and not merely the collective decision-making procedure that is a part of it.

Why is this so? First of all, collective decisions that are brought about as a result of a procedurally equal but inegalitarian process are no more nor less subject to criticisms from an egalitarian standpoint than a procedurally unequal method of making decisions. They simply involve different resources. Why should an inequality in the distribution of the nonprocedural resources be any less arbitrary for an egalitarian than an inequality in procedural resources?

Second, if we were, on a systematic basis, to allot fewer votes to one person or group of persons than others but give them much more information and means for building coalitions than the others so that they were effectively able to secure the outcomes they desired, would they have reason to complain? Certainly it should be possible to compensate a person for his lack of procedural resources with nonprocedural resources.

The implications of the distributive conception of procedures for another important issue of democratic theory is clear. Consider the following argument: "Vote bargaining undermines the ideal of equal control that animates the insistence on democratic control over allocation and distribution, because it is equivalent to giving some individuals more votes than others on a given issue by giving them fewer votes on other issues."[19] The critic assumes here what ought not to be assumed, that is, that equality of control over a decision-making process entails equality of control over each and every decision. This is a simple mistake. It is of the same order as a view of economic equality requiring that for individuals to be economically equal overall, they must have the same quantity of resources as everyone else has for each possible object of consumption. That is, if objects of economic value such as money, land, and capital had to be distributed equally overall it would be a mistake to think that each item had to be distributed equally, in other words, that everyone had to get an equal quantity of each of the items. This distribution may be compatible with overall equality, but it is not required by it. All that is required is that each person's total bundle be equal, which equality may be defined as an envy-free distribution of resources. Hence, it is no violation of the principle of political equality that individuals have more power regarding some decisions and others have more power regarding other decisions as long as these differences are compatible with an overall equality. From this it should be clear that vote bargaining is quite consistent with political equality.[20]

But political equality is not only consistent with vote bargaining. It requires it. A collection of partial procedures will not adequately implement equality over complete life prospects.[21] We come much closer to an egalitarian conception of the collective decision process if we permit individuals to trade on the resources they have between procedures. This is because vote trading makes it possible for them to use their procedural resources in ways that reflect the complementarity of their preferences and the varying importance that different issues have for them. And any distribution of political resources that neglects the complementarity of preferences and differences of intensity, especially to the point that it will defeat Condorcet choices, is unable to guarantee equality of resources for determining total life prospects. Hence, insofar as a society must use partial procedures for collective decision making, it must also allow vote trading to take place.[22]

This endorsement of vote trading introduces another difficulty with the purely procedural approach to political equality. For as I show in the section on manipulation, one's success or failure at vote trading in achieving the ends one wants to achieve will depend greatly on the distribution of nonprocedural resources such as information and resources for building coalitions. The examples I considered illustrate that a maldistribution of these resources could enable some to achieve their ends at the expense of others just as much as a maldistribution of procedural resources might help those who have the procedural resources to achieve their ends at the expense of others. This is a result not of the indeterminacy of egalitarian procedures but of political equality's being a relation between individuals who are using many procedures. Again our notion of a collective decision process will come in handy. It can be used to describe the use of procedural and nonprocedural resources on one issue; it also differs from a collective decision procedure in that a process will encompass the application of procedures to many issues.

A collective decision process will be inegalitarian while the procedures used are egalitarian when the resources used for vote bargaining are unequally distributed. Now it is amply clear that equality of resources in the collective decision-making process is what the ideal of political equality amounts to rather than a mere equality in procedural resources.

Hence, our conception of political equality is not procedural. That is, political equality cannot be defined as a method or set of rules for deciding outcomes on the basis of choices over these outcomes. Nonprocedural resources are an important part of the process and must on an egalitarian conception be part of the bundle of resources that are equally distributed. On the other hand, this conception of political equality is not outcome-oriented. It does not require equal satisfaction of desires for individuals with respect to states of the society as a whole. Nor does it impose any particular standard on the outcomes of democratic decision making.

The argument for political equality

Here I would like to sketch a defense of the underlying normative conception of democracy that animates my concern with democratic procedures and process. I defend an egalitarian theory of democracy. The basic principle is: Political equality in the central decision-making process is a requirement of the principles of justice when we are concerned with aspects of the society that are marked by a high degree of interdependence of interests among the members. These aspects I call collective properties. Hence, there is an intrinsic justification for democratic decision making in a society or any group for the collective properties of the society or the group.

There are three steps in the argument that democracy is defensible in terms of a principle of justice: (1) Justice requires that individuals be equally treated; (2) the principle of equality requires that the resources individuals use for achieving their ends be distributed equally; (3) the principle of equality of resources requires democratic decision making for objects of a certain sort, called collective properties of society. The same principle of equality will have different implications for other kinds of objects, for example the objects desired in personal projects. Here, the principle will require an egalitarian distribution of economic resources.

First I shall develop the idea of collective properties. After that I shall say why they should be subject to principles of justice, then I shall say why political equality is required by the principles of justice in these circumstances.

Collective properties

Some examples of collective properties are: (1) the arrangement of public symbols and spaces, (2) environmental protection, (3) the geographical disposition of various elements of the community by means of zoning laws, (4) defense, (5) some aspects of public education. These and other unlisted concerns relating to the arrangement of public institutions must not only be decided on in themselves; their relative importance will also be in contention. For any set of aims that a society has, it has only a finite budget of resources with which to pursue those aims. Hence, choices will have to be made as to what aims are more important than others. Individuals will have to make decisions about the whole package of items. And there will be conflicts concerning what is the best complete package.

I define "collective property of the society" in the following way:

A property of individuals' lives in a society is a collective property iff in order to change one person's welfare with regard to this property one must change all or almost all of the other members' welfare with regard to this property.

This definition imposes four conditions on collective properties. First, they must satisfy a condition of *nonexclusivity*. It cannot be possible to affect one person's life without affecting the lives of the others. Collective goods and bads such as pollution control are the most obvious example of this. But it is not necessary that everyone be affected in the same way by the change; some may be benefited and some harmed. What is important is that everyone is somehow affected by the change in this property. Zoning, or the lack of zoning, is a property of the whole community in which it is done. When one zones a community, one arranges the various parts of it in a certain way. It is the whole community that one is interested in arranging. The same is true for public monuments and institutions as well as limitations on publicly displayed behavior. These sorts of concerns are cultural in their nature. They are collective properties, but there is conflict over the goods themselves.

The second condition is *publicity*. The point of talking about welfare rather than preference satisfaction *simpliciter* is that it rules out the possibility that the property satisfies purely nosy preferences. For example, it might be thought that homosexuality is a collective property when some members of the society desire that others participate in or abstain from this activity. But insofar as I can participate in, or abstain from, homosexual activities without affecting other people's self-regarding preferences, I do not affect others' welfare with regard to this property. Hence, collective properties must be experienced as public objects.

Note that the publicity condition does not require that a private realm be protected from paternalistic or other intrusions. It merely implies that there is no intrinsic justification for democratic decision making concerning this realm. The fact that someone does something that I do not like does not, of itself, give me a reason to complain of injustice. There may be grounds for criticism of private actions but not that I or others have been unjustly treated.

Another condition is that of *nondivisibility*. This condition requires that the benefit of the property not be divisible into shares of resources, which can then be used to satisfy purely self-regarding preferences in a way that does not affect others' welfare. An example of a divisible feature is a decision regarding whether to introduce a new piece of technology in a factory whose effect is *merely* to increase the productivity of the factory. The factory will produce more wealth and hence affect all the members of the firm, but the wealth itself is a divisible object, the shares of which can be divided up in accordance with a principle of just distribution and can be used in any way that the possessors of those shares wish without affecting others. I take this condition to follow from the condition of publicity, since the real effect of the property on each person's welfare is independent of the effect on the others.

An important feature of these properties is that even if there is no way of deciding what collective properties a society is to have, that society will have some such properties. For example, every society has a public environment. That public environment is characterized by its collective properties. The public environment can have different properties attached to it in the same way that a surface can be different colors. And it will have some properties whether anyone wants them or not. The same is true of the geographical structuring of communities. They can be zoned in one way or another or they can be left to develop without planning, but the society will have some collective properties or others. We can say the same thing concerning public goods or bads. In the case of pollution control, we have no choice as to whether there is air or water, but we may have some choice about what properties this air or water has. In any case, the object will have certain collective properties whether we decide on them or not.

These four conditions describe a high level of social interdependence with regard to individuals' interests. Collective properties are not all collective goods in the economists' sense, some collective properties affect some citizens in a positive way while affecting others in a negative way. All collective goods are, however, collective properties.

One choice for a community is between making some kind of centrally coordinated decision and not making a decision, thus leaving the determination of what collective properties there are up to the play of social forces. In the case of collective goods, this may be unpalatable because many of them will simply not be provided at all even if everyone wants them or almost everyone wants *some* level of provision.[23] In this instance, not making any decision would likely be making a bad decision. Such is also the case, I think, with the more cultural collective properties I have identified. If it is true that most individuals have interests (albeit, conflicting) in living in one kind of public environment or another and it is unlikely that such an environment would come about without some planning, then, in many cases, making no decision at all would be tantamount to making a kind of decision of which no one would approve.

Justice and collective properties

Now the question is, Is there an intrinsic argument for democratic control over these collective properties? Principles of economic justice provide the solution to the problem of the division of benefits and burdens in society when there is a scarcity of goods. The way such scarcity comes about is when the interests of individuals are such that they conflict as a result of there not being enough resources to satisfy them all. Without abundance, some principle for dividing the social wealth fairly must be found.

I claim that for collective properties there is an analogy to the problem of economic scarcity. There may be considerable disagreement among individuals over all these things. In the case of collective goods, there will be conflict over the level of provision insofar as different levels of provision have different costs. In the case of the cultural goods, there will be conflict over the very goods to be provided as well as the level of provision. All that is necessary is that these concerns determine the whole nature of the community. That is, individuals have common areas of concerns in which there are conflicts. Insofar as there is a reasonable diversity of opinion among the citizens on the issues of which collective properties to implement, few will get their way on any particular issue. Hence, there is a high demand (relative to what can be supplied) for having one's preferred possible collective property implemented.

These last claims provide reasons for thinking that collective properties ought to be subject to principles of just distribution. What does justice require in these circumstances? And why are properties that are not collective to be treated differently?

As I noted above, collective properties are *not divisible* into units. We cannot give some proportion to one individual and another proportion to another. But we can vote on what they are to be and the collective properties of a society can be the object of a compromise. That is, individuals may decide to agree to bring about a compromise that only partially satisfies the previously competing collective concerns. Naturally, the outcomes of such compromises will depend on the relative power of the concerned groups. The idea of political equality is to distribute power so as to have a just resolution to the conflict over collective properties.

Although I do not argue for it here, justice requires that individuals' lives in a society be equally well provided for. But one question is, What is it that is to be distributed equally? The two most common answers are: happiness or welfare, and the means to happiness. I argue that egalitarian justice is best understood as equality of resources. The basic idea is that equality of welfare is an unacceptable ideal insofar as it requires that welfare is something that can be summed up over a lifetime in some unambiguously valuable way. But individuals do not value the unrestricted maximization of desire satisfaction any more than pleasure or some other specifiable mental state. Nor is it possible to come up with any notion of value and its aggregation that accords equally with every reasonable individual's conception of the good life. There is an irreducible pluralism of ends that individuals pursue that undermines the idea of a unique metric for measuring and comparing amounts of well-being across individuals and the coherence of equality of well-being.[24]

These arguments, along with the relatively universal quality of individuals' interests in resources (admittedly as instrumentally valuable), combine to suggest that an equal distribution of resources is the only acceptable ideal connected with equality. Well-being may be intrinsically valuable for each individual; the equal distribution of resources is what justice requires. Hence, an egalitarian will be concerned to determine collective properties in accordance with an equality-of-resources scheme.

Therefore, the principles of justice require that resources, or the means to the ends that people have, be divided equally. In the case of collective properties, we need a collective decision procedure to determine these objects since these objects are indivisible and must be subject to a principle of justice. The resources to be divided are the resources to be used in determining the outcomes of the collective decision-making procedure. The way to solve the problem of just distribution in the case of collective properties is to give individuals equal political resources for determining what these collective properties are to be. Hence, I conclude that equality of political resources is required by the principles of justice when choices must be made about collective properties. That completes the intrinsic argument for democracy.

Four points should be made in connection with this argument. The first is that such a notion of democracy is not purely formal in that it requires the equal distribution of all resources that go into collective decision making. Hence, information, and resources for coalition building, must be distributed equally along with votes and other formal devices.[25] I have said a few things about this in previous sections. Nevertheless, there is a broad sense in which this grounds democracy in "procedural values" because it is in terms of the way in which the decision is made and not the outcome of the decision that democracy is defended.

The second point is that this foundation for democracy is not challenged by any of the results of social choice theory. Riker's worry that the outcomes of democratic processes may be meaningless does not apply, since the point of democracy is not to express a common will or a conception of the greatest good but merely to have decisions made in such a way that everyone has a fair opportunity to have an effect on the outcome.

The third point is that the basic principle of equality will require that the equality be complex in the following sense: There will be an equal distribution of economic resources, which are the means for pursuing interests that are not fundamentally interdependent. And there will be an equal distribution of political resources, which are the means for pursuing ends that are fundamentally interdependent.

The fourth point is that this theory of democracy is a mixed one. Decision-making processes will be defensible inasmuch as they *embody* an equal distribution of political resources and also insofar as they *preserve* political and economic equality. With regard to the distribution of economic resources, democratic decision making will be defensible only insofar as it produces just legislation, that is, legislation in accordance with the two principles of equality. With regard to decision making concerning distributions of political resources, we can evaluate it in terms of whether it produces just legislation. These aspects of decision-making institutions will be evaluated on an instrumentalist basis. On the other hand, for the collective properties of society, democratic decision making will be intrinsically defensible as embodying the ideal of equality.

In my view, the egalitarian conception of democracy I have argued for helps us understand the special relation between democracy and justice. Insofar as the right to an equal say is deduced from a more general conception of equality of resources, such equality, in both the political and the economic realms, must be preserved. That is, no outcome of a democratic procedure may violate the principle of equality in either of its forms. The argument for this is based on a kind of principle of universality. If *A* claims the moral right to participate equally in the determination of collective properties, then any other member *B* of the same community must be recognized as having the same right. But this right is derived from the more basic right to an equal share of resources. Hence, if anyone has this more general right, then all others do as well and thereby have those rights (both political and economic) that are derivative from this more general right. Therefore, it cannot be justified for anyone to exercise his moral right to equal political resources in such a way as to restrict others' moral right to equal resources.

A partial example of this dual attitude can be found in American politics. Although legislation on many issues is required to be determined by some species of democratic rule, there are also issues we prefer to have resolved by means of a more complex mechanism, including the Supreme Court. In matters concerning basic issues of justice, including the fairness of the electoral system as well as the fairness of the economic system in the cases of civil rights and education, we evaluate the decisions in terms of the fairness of the outcome of the decision and not in terms of how it was made. Here, we see the value of the decision-making procedure as something to be determined instrumentally.

It is here that the game theoretic analysis of social institutions can have an important role to play. Although the intrinsic value of the democratic process does not face any challenge from social choice or game theory, the latter can tell us about the consequences of instituting the democratic process under certain circumstances. In some circumstances, for example, Pareto inferior outcomes may be the result of using democratic institutions.[26] Hence, the use of these institutions may produce inefficient outcomes. This does not undermine the intrinsic fairness of the institution, but if the inefficiency is sufficiently great, we may wish to give up some fairness so as to avoid it.

Conclusion

A number of difficult problems remain, such as the difficulty of completely spelling out the implications of the notion of political equality and determining the proper relations between the instrumentalist and intrinsic arguments for democracy. But I have argued that Arrow's social choice theory is not devastating to an intrinsic justification of democracy. Democratic procedural values are not called into question by this approach. And its implications regarding an instrumentalist evaluation of democracy are deeply unclear at best. The proper role of social choice theory as well as game theory is to tell us about the consequences in certain conditions of having certain political institutions.[27]

Notes

1 See William Riker, *Liberalism Against Populism: A Confrontation Between the Theory of Democracy and the Theory of Social Choice* (San Francisco: W. H. Freeman, 1982), for a compelling argument for this position.
2 Russell Hardin, "Public Choice Versus Democracy," in this volume (p. 185 in *Nomos* XXXII, all page citations refer to *Nomos*).
3 Hardin, p. 199.

4 Ibid., p. 185.
5 The Condorcet rule is a kind of majoritarian procedure for more than two alternatives. Each alternative is compared separately with every other alternative given the votes of the individuals, and the Condocet winner is the alternative that defeats all the others by simple majority in pairwise comparisons.
6 Allan Gibbard, "Manipulation of Voting Schemes: A General Result," *Rational Man and Irrational Society?* pp. 355–66. Gibbard's result is that all nonchance, nondictatorial voting schemes that apply to more than two alternatives and do not admit of ties are manipulable.
7 See Robin Farquharson, *Theory of Voting* (New Haven: Yale University Press, 1969), and Gibbard, "Manipulation of Voting Schemes," for this. In most discussions, the words "strategic" and "sincere" do not refer at all to attitudes but only to the actions. One may determine how one ought to vote by seeing how others are voting and vote straightforwardly because this is the best way of ensuring the best outcome.
8 Hardin, p. 190.
9 This example is adapted from Riker, *Liberalism Against Populism*, p. 159.
10 For this kind of definition of democratic procedures, see Brian Barry, "Is Democracy Special?," *Philosophy, Politics and Society*, 5th Series, ed. James Fishkin and Peter Laslett (New Haven: Yale University Press, 1979), p. 156, as well as Robert Dahl's essay in the same volume, "Procedural Democracy," pp. 97–133. This sort of conception of democratic procedures is standard among those social choice theorists who think that social choice theory is directly applicable to democracy; see Riker, *Liberalism Against Populism*, p. 22, as well as critics of his, Jules Coleman and John Ferejohn, "Democracy and Social Choice," *Ethics* (October 1986): 7. See also Robert Dahl, *A Preface to Democratic Theory* (Chicago: University of Chicago Press, 1956), ch. 3, and Jane Mansbridge, *Beyond Adversary Democracy* (Chicago: University of Chicago Press, 1983); Peter Jones, "Political Equality and Majority Rule," in *The Nature of Political Theory* (Oxford: Oxford University Press, 1983), pp. 155–82. See also Peter Singer, *Democracy and Disobedience* (Oxford: Oxford University Press, 1973), for a view that appears to entail this.
11 Barry, "Is Democracy Special?," p. 156.
12 This is the conclusion of William Riker in his *Liberalism Against Populism*.
13 See J.-J. Rousseau, *The Social Contract and Discourses*, trans. G. D. H. Cole (London: J. M. Dent & Sons, 1973), p. 200; and Brian Barry, "The Public Interest," *Proceedings of the Aristotelian Society* 38 (1964): 9–14.
14 See Rousseau, *The Social Contract*, pp. 276–9; and Joshua Cohen, "An Epistemic Conception of Democracy," *Ethics* (October 1986): 34.
15 I don't think that the idea of the common good can be understood in terms of preferences at all since the notion of a person's good cannot be so understood, but this point can only bolster my argument.
16 These arguments suggest that even if one could develop "incentive compatible"

methods of voting that had the effect of tricking individuals into revealing their preferences, this may not be much to look forward to.

17 This is more in accord with the game theoretic account of procedures; see Gibbard, "Manipulation of Voting Schemes." David Estlund expresses a similar idea when he argues that the idea of agency is a necessary element in the interpretation of voting in "Democracy Without Preferences," *Philosophical Review* 49, no. 3: 397–423.

18 See Kenneth O. May, "A Set of Independent, Necessary, and Sufficient Conditions for Simple Majority Decision," in *Rational Man and Irrational Society?*, ed. Brian Barry and Russell Hardin (Beverly Hills: Sage, 1982), pp. 297–304, for the proof that majority rule satisfies the properties of anonymity and neutrality. Also, see my "Political Equality," *Majorities and Minorities: Nomos XXXII*, ed. John Chapman and Alan Wertheimer (New York: New York University Press, 1990), pp. 151–83; pp. 154–7 for the argument that these are egalitarian requirements.

19 This argument is given by Allen Buchanan in his *Ethics, Efficiency and the Market* (Totowa, N.J.: Rowman & Allanheld, 1985), p. 31.

20 Of course, it may be necessary to restrict trades in some ways so as to preserve equality from the cumulative effects of many persons acting in an uncoordinated way. For an egalitarian justification of these restrictions in the economic sphere, see G. A. Cohen, "Robert Nozick and Wilt Chamberlain: How Patterns Preserve Liberty," *Erkenntnis* 11 (1979): 5–23.

21 See my "Political Equality," pp. 159–63, for a fuller discussion of this topic.

22 Unfortunately, even these tentative solutions cannot give us a complete answer to the problem of global versus marginal political equality. This is because the information requirements that exist for adequately making decisions that take whole lives into consideration are too great for any person to meet. But from the point of view of equality, it is clearly an improvement to extend equality past the restrictions imposed by a decision-making procedure that insulates every decision from every other.

23 See Mancur Olsen, *The Logic of Collective Action* (Cambridge, Mass.: Harvard University Press, 1965), as well as Russell Hardin, *Collective Action* (Baltimore: Johns Hopkins University Press, 1982), for detailed discussions of the nature of these sorts of objects.

24 See Ronald Dworkin, "What is Equality? Part I: Equality of Welfare," *Philosophy and Public Affairs*, Summer 1981, for a version of this kind of argument. See Gerald Cohen, "On the Currency of Egalitarian Justice," *Ethics* (July 1989), for a critical discussion of many of the theories on this subject. I have criticized a nonwelfarist view, similar to the one Cohen outlines, in my "Difficulties with the Principle of Equal Opportunity for Welfare," in *Philosophical Studies* (May 1991): 179–86. I should note here that we are a long way from understanding even the idea of equality of resources. Work on this idea is essential to a full elaboration of an intrinsic defense of democracy. For lack of space I cannot provide that here, although I believe that the preponderance of arguments strongly favor it.

John Roemer has argued in his essay "Equality of Talent," *Economics and Philosophy* 1 (1985): 151–87, that equality of resources implies equality of welfare. His argument relies on the idea that there are shared fundamental preferences among human beings such that any difference in actual desires and values among persons can be explained by differences in the resources with which individuals are endowed. Thus, any equalization of resources will entail equality of welfare. This view implicitly denies the irreducible plurality of ends that I have asserted, on the grounds that in fact everyone shares the fundamental preferences. I do not think that such a view is cogent except as a purely representational device. Thus, I do not think it provides an argument against the irreducible plurality of ends. If we accept the irreducible plurality of ends, we imply a distinction between a person's ends and that person's resources and thus reject Roemer's attempted reduction. Much more ought to be said about this matter, but it cannot be said here.

25 The term "information" is ambiguous. What I have in mind is the sense of information as an external resource. An example of an attempt at increasing, if not equalizing, information in this sense is the voter's information pamphlets handed out to citizens of various states during election periods.

26 See Riker, *Liberalism Against Populism*, for some illustrations of these difficulties.

27 I thank John Christman, David Estlund, Jean Hampton, and Russell Hardin for their helpful comments.

5

Democracy and shifting preferences

CASS R. SUNSTEIN

The drafting of the United States Constitution, it is often said, signaled a rejection of conceptions of politics founded on classical ideals in favor of a quite different modern view.[1] The precise terms of the alleged shift are not altogether clear, but it is possible to identify the most prominent strands. The classical conception assumes a relatively homogeneous people and prizes active participation by the polity's citizenry. In the classical conception, the polity is self-consciously concerned with the character of the citizens; it seeks to inculcate in them and to profit from a commitment to the public good. Plato said that politics is the "art whose business it is to care for souls";[2] and under the classical conception, civic virtue, not private interest, is the wellspring of political behavior. Whether or not the state imposes a "comprehensive view"[3] on the nation, it relies relatively little on private rights to constrain government. The underlying vision of "republican" politics is one of frequent participation and deliberation in the service of decision, by the citizenry, about the sorts of values according to which the nation will operate.

In the modern account, by contrast, government is above all respectful of the divergent conceptions of the good held by its many constituents. People are taken as they are, not as they might be. Modern democracy has no concern with souls. Although electoral processes are ensured, no special premium is placed on citizen participation. Self-interest, not virtue, is understood to be the usual motivating force of political behavior. Politics is typically, if not always, an effort to aggregate private interests. It is surrounded by checks, in the form of rights, protecting private liberty and private property from public intrusion.

I am grateful to Jon Elster for many valuable discussions of these issues; to Elizabeth Anderson, Joshua Cohen, George Loewenstein, Jon Macey, Jane Mansbridge, Frederick Schauer, and Elisabeth Wood for helpful comments on an earlier draft; and, for their lively responses, to participants in the University of Toronto Legal Theory Workshop and the University of Chicago seminar led by Gary Becker and James Coleman on rational models in the social sciences. This essay appeared in somewhat different form under the title "Preferences and Politics" in *Philosophy and Public Affairs*, pp. 3–34, and is reprinted by permission.

In this system, the goal of the polity is quite modest: the creation of the basic ground rules under which people can satisfy their desires and go about their private affairs. Much of this is famously captured in *The Federalist* No. 10, in which Madison redescribed the so-called republican problem of the corruption of virtue as the so-called liberal problem of the control of factions, which, as Madison had it, were inevitable if freedom was to be preserved.

In fact, the conventional division between the American founders and their classical predecessors is far too crude. The founders attempted to create a deliberative democracy, one in which the institutions of representation, checks and balances, and federalism would ensure a deliberative process among political equals rather than an aggregation of interests.[4] But respect for private preferences, rather than collective deliberation about public values or the good life, does seem to be a distinguishing feature of American constitutionalism. Indeed, the view that government should refuse to evaluate privately held beliefs about individual welfare, which are said to be irreducibly "subjective," links a wide range of views about both governmental structure and individual rights.

In this essay I explore the question whether a contemporary democracy might not sometimes override the private preferences and beliefs of its citizens, not in spite of its salutary liberalism but because of it. It is one thing to affirm competing conceptions of the good; it is quite another to suggest that political outcomes must generally be justified by, or even should always respect, private preferences. A large part of my focus here is on the phenomenon of endogenous preferences. By this term I mean to indicate that preferences are not fixed and stable but are instead adaptive to a wide range of factors – including the context in which the preference is expressed, the existing legal rules, past consumption choices, and culture in general. The phenomenon of endogenous preferences casts doubt on the notion that a democratic government ought to respect private desires and beliefs in all or almost all contexts.[5] It bears on a number of particular problems as well, including the rationale for and extent of the constitutional protection accorded to speech; proportional representation and checks and balances; and the reasons for and limits of governmental regulation of the arts, broadcasting, and the environment. I take up these issues at several points in this article.

The argument proceeds in several stages. Section I sets forth some fairly conventional ideas about welfare and autonomy, in conjunction with the endogeneity of desires, in order to argue against the idea that government ought never or rarely to override private preferences. In

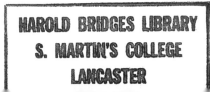

Section II, I contend that in three categories of cases, private preferences, as expressed in consumption choices, should be overridden. The
first category involves what I call collective judgments, including considered beliefs, aspirations for social justice, and altruistic goals; the
second involves preferences that have adapted to undue limitations in
available opportunities or to unjust background conditions; the third
points to intrapersonal collective action problems that, over a lifetime,
impair personal welfare. In all of these cases, I suggest, a democracy
should be free and is perhaps obliged to override private preferences. In
Section III, I make some remarks about the relevance of these claims to
several current issues of constitutional controversy. These include proportional representation in politics and governmental regulation of the
speech "market," including rights of access to the media, democratic
controls on the electoral process, hate speech, and pornography.

I. Against subjective welfarism

Should a constitutional democracy take preferences as the basis for
political choice? In contemporary politics, law, and economics, the
usual answer is affirmative. Modern economics, for example, is dominated by a conception of welfare based on the satisfaction of existing
preferences, as measured by willingness to pay; in politics and law,
something called "paternalism" is disfavored in both the public and
private realms.[6] But the idea that government ought to take preferences
as the basis for political decisions is a quite modern one. This is not to
say that the idea is without foundations. Partly a function of the perceived (though greatly overstated) difficulty of making interpersonal
comparisons of utility, the idea is also a product of the epistemological
difficulties of assessing preferences in terms of their true connection with
individual welfare, and, perhaps most of all, the genuine political dangers of allowing government to engage in such inquiries.
    The constellation of ideas that emerges from these considerations has
been exceptionally influential. It embodies a conception of political
justification that might be described as "subjective welfarism."[7] On this
view, the government, even or perhaps especially in a democracy,
should attend exclusively to conceptions of welfare as subjectively held
by its citizens. Many prominent approaches to politics turn out to be
versions of subjective welfarism. These include, for example, certain
forms of utilitarianism; the view that some version of Paretian efficiency
ought to be treated as the foundational norm for political life; opposition to paternalism in public and private life; approaches to politics
modeled on bargaining theory (rational or otherwise); and conceptions

of politics that see the democratic process as an effort to aggregate individual preferences.

It is important to understand that subjective welfarism, thus defined, may or may not be accompanied by a broader notion that ethical and moral questions should generally be treated in welfarist or subjectivist terms. It is as a political conception, rather than an ethical one, that subjective welfarism underlies a wide range of approaches to public life, including ideas about institutional arrangements and individual or collective rights. What I want to argue here is that subjective welfarism, even as a political conception, is unsupportable by reference to principles of autonomy or welfare, the very ideas that are said to give rise to it.

A. *The inevitability of preference shaping*

The initial objection to the view that government should take preferences "as they are," or as the basis for political choice, is one of impossibility. The basic problem is that governmental neutrality among preferences cannot be achieved, at least if the neutrality is intended to be global. The reason is that whether people have a preference for a commodity, a right, or anything else is in part a function of whether the government has allocated it to them in the first instance. There is simply no way to avoid the task of initially allocating an entitlement, and the decision to grant an entitlement to one person frequently makes that person value that entitlement more than he would if the right had been allocated to someone else. (It also makes other people value it less than they otherwise would.) The initial allocation serves to reflect, to legitimate, and to reinforce social understandings about presumptive rights of ownership. That allocation has an important causal connection to individual perceptions about the good or right in question.

The point is simply a factual one, and it has received considerable empirical confirmation. The effect on preferences of the initial allocation of a commodity or an entitlement is commonly described as the "endowment effect."[8] The endowment effect has immense importance. It suggests that any initial allocation of an entitlement – and government cannot refuse to make an initial allocation – may well have effects on preferences.

Economists and psychologists have found this effect in many places, including both real exchange experiments and surveys. For example, a recent study showed that people who were allocated certain consumption objects – pens, coffee mugs, and binoculars – placed a much higher valuation on those objects than did those who were required to purchase them.[9]

A similar study gave some participants a mug and others a chocolate bar, and told them they could exchange one for the other. Participants in a third group, not given a prior entitlement, were told they could select one or the other; 56 percent of these selected the candy bar. By contrast, 89 percent of those initially given the mug refused to trade it for the candy bar, and only 10 percent of those initially given the candy were willing to trade it for the mug.[10] The different evaluations could not be explained by reference to anything other than the initial endowment.

Studies based on survey research have made similar findings. One such study found differences between payment and compensation valuations of trees in a park of about five to one.[11] When hunters were questioned about the potential destruction of a duck habitat, they said they would be willing to pay an average of $247 to prevent the loss – but would demand no less than $1,044 to accept it.[12] In another study, participants required payments to accept degradation of visibility ranging from five to more than sixteen times higher than their valuations based on their willingness to pay.[13] According to yet another study, the compensation demanded for accepting a new risk of immediate death of .001 percent was one or two orders of magnitude higher than the amount of willingness to pay to eliminate an existing risk of the same magnitude.[14]

A related survey showed similarly large status quo biases in willingness to pay for changes in risks. Thus only 39 percent of respondents would accept $700 to have their chance of a serious accident increased by 0.5 percent (from 0.5 percent to 1.0 percent); the substantial majority of 61 percent would refuse the trade. By contrast, only 27 percent would trade an identical decrease in accident risk (from 1 percent to 0.5 percent) for $700; here an even larger majority of 73 percent would refuse to do so.[15] In another study, people were willing to pay $3.78 on average to decrease the risk from an insecticide, but 77 percent refused to buy the product at any price, however reduced, if the risk level would increase by an equivalent amount.[16] A powerful status quo bias appears to affect reactions to risks or losses.

In many settings, then, it has been shown that people place a higher value on rights or goods that they currently hold than they place on the same goods when in the hands of others. Endowment effects often reflect a genuine preference-shaping consequence from the initial assignment. Some studies suggest that that assignment creates the basic "reference state" from which judgments of fairness are subsequently made, and those judgments affect preferences and private willingness to pay.[17] An especially influential account of the endowment effect stresses "loss aversion," which refers to the fact that a negative change from the status quo is usually seen as more harmful than a positive change is seen as beneficial. The problem with this account[18] is that it sets out a new description of the phenomenon without describing the mechanism by which the phenomenon occurs.

But perhaps people prefer received income to opportunity income because of psychological attachments. Endowment effects may reflect an effort to reduce cognitive dissonance: High valuation of what one owns, and low valuation of what one does not, is a means of reducing dissonance, which is in some respects highly adaptive. Perhaps, too, the initial allocation has an important legitimating effect, suggesting that the entitlement "naturally" belongs where it has been placed, and putting a social burden on even voluntary changes. In some cases the divergence between willingness to pay and willingness to accept is probably a product of the change in social norms brought about by the change in the allocation of the entitlement.

For present purposes, it is not necessary to explain the mechanism behind endowment effects. It is enough to say that the initial allocation has preference-shaping effects and that when this is so, there is no acontextual "preference" with which to do legal or political work.

If all this is correct, large consequences follow. One would expect that a decision to give employees a right to organize, farmers a right to be free from water pollution, or women a right not to be subject to sexual harassment will have an impact on social attitudes toward labor organization, clean water, and sexual harassment. The allocation will affect the valuation of the rights by both current owners and would-be purchasers.

More generally, much of democratic behavior – the acts of government and of those who seek to influence it – might well be a product of endowment effects. For example, one would expect both private and public reactions to risks to reflect a status quo bias. The point has a range of positive implications; indeed, it helps to explain a wide range of political outcomes and political behavior. Thus, government regulation of new risks will probably be more stringent than government regulation of (equivalent) old risks, and precisely because the public demand for regulation will be a product of the endowment effect. This is in fact what we observe: Old risks are regulated far more stringently than new ones, even though this strategy sometimes creates extremely perverse results.[19]

Another example is the effort to describe a proposal as a "restoration" of the status quo ante, rather than a new departure. Thus the various civil rights proposals of the late 1980s and the early 1990s are described as "restoration" acts, when in fact they were no such thing; thus the attack on the nomination of Robert Bork to the United States Supreme Court emphasized above all that Bork would "turn back the clock" on civil rights. When political actors can identify the problem in these terms, there are important strategic benefits.

The dramatic public outcry over the Supreme Court's partial repudiation of *Roe v. Wade* may well have been fueled by the fact that the right to an abortion had come to be seen as part of existing endowments; we might doubt whether a similar reaction would be produced by the Court's failure to recognize an otherwise analogous but not yet established right. The inability of the political process to restrict social security benefits is undoubtedly in part a product of the endowment effect brought about by social security system itself.

The most general point is that if the rules of allocation have preference-shaping effects, it is hard to see how a government might even attempt to take preferences "as given" in any global sense, or as the basis of social choice. When preferences are a function of legal rules, the rules cannot be justified by reference to the preferences.[20] Often there is no such thing as a prelegal or prepolitical "preference" that can be used as the baseline for decision. And the endowment effect is not relevant only for normative purposes; it might also be used to create a range of predictions about the nature and consequences of different legal regimes, and about the processes of preference formation in various areas of law and politics.

B. *On liberty and welfare*

To some degree this concern might be put to one side. Surely there is a difference between a government that concerns itself self-consciously and on an ongoing basis with private preferences and a government that sets up the basic rules of property, contract, and tort and then lets things turn out however they may. To say that no legal system can avoid some preference-shaping effects is not to deny that in making particular decisions, a system can respect preferences once they have been formed by existing institutions (including, in part, legal ones). The fact that the initial allocation often affects preferences does not establish that a state can never respect preferences after they are in place. In this sense, there is a fully workable distinction between a system that respects preferences – at least in individual cases – and one that does not. The frustration, resentment, and misallocations that are bred by governmental rejection of existing desires are quite familiar phenomena; of course, they can be minimized and perhaps even avoided.

Moreover, a legal system that provides an initial allocation of entitlements – that is, any system – should not be confused with one that attempts to ensure that citizens adhere to a particular or unitary conception of the good. The former system might well allow a large diversity in the stock of available conceptions, and that diversity can promote individual liberty and freedom of choice. And perhaps endowment effects are in many cases small or nonexistent. Perhaps across a fairly large territory, preferences and desires, within a culture, are constant and impervious to dramatic change through different legal rules. Nothing in the empirical literature yet proves that this hypothesis is false.

If one can put endowment effects to one side in this way, disagreements about the relationship between politics and preferences turn on competing notions about autonomy or freedom on the one hand and welfare on the other. Subjective welfarism is founded on the claim that an approach that treats preferences as sovereign is most likely to promote both individual freedom, rightly conceived, and individual or social welfare.

It will be useful to begin with welfare. Even if one accepted a purely welfarist view, one might think that the process of promoting welfare should take place not by satisfying current preferences but by promoting those preferences and satisfying them to such an extent as is consonant with the best or highest conception of human happiness. This view is connected with older (and some current) forms of utilitarianism; it also has roots in Aristotle.[21] Here one does not take existing preferences as given, and one does not put all preferences on the same plane. A criterion of welfare remains the ultimate one, but the system is not focused solely on preference satisfaction, since it insists that welfare and preference satisfaction are entirely different things.[22]

A central point here is that preferences are shifting and endogenous rather than exogenous, and as a result are a function of current information, consumption patterns, legal rules, and general social pressures. An effort to identify welfare with preference satisfaction would be easier to understand if preferences were rigidly fixed at some early age, or if learning were impossible; if this were so, democratic efforts to reflect on change, or select preferences would breed only frustration. But because preferences are shifting and endogenous, and because the satisfaction of existing preferences might lead to unhappy or deprived lives, a democracy that treats all preferences as fixed will lose important opportunities for welfare gains.

With respect to welfare, then, the problem posed by the endogeneity of preferences is not the origin of desires but their malleability. At least if the relevant cases can be confidently identified in advance, and if collective action can be justified by reference to particular good reasons, the argument for democratic interference will be quite powerful. Respect for preferences that have resulted from unjust background conditions and that will lead to human deprivation or misery hardly appears the proper course for a liberal democracy.[23]

For example, legal rules prohibiting or discouraging addictive behavior may have significant advantages in terms of welfare. Regulation of heroin or cigarettes (at least if the regulation can be made effective) might well increase aggregate social welfare, by decreasing harmful behavior, removing the secondary effects of those harms, and producing more healthful and satisfying lives. Similarly, governmental action relating to the environment, broadcasting, or culture – encouraging or requiring, for example, protection of beautiful areas, broadcasting about public issues, high-quality programs, or public support of artistic achievement – may in the end generate (or, better, prevent obstacles to the generation of) new preferences, providing increased satisfaction and in the end producing considerable welfare gains. The same may well be true of antidiscrimination measures, which affect the desires and attitudes of discriminators and victims alike. A system that takes existing private preferences as the basis for political choice will sacrifice important opportunities for social improvement on welfarist criteria. This point was a crucial one in the early stages of utilitarian thought; it has been lost more recently with the shift from older forms of welfarism to the idea of "revealed preferences."

Moreover, the satisfaction of private preferences, whatever their content and origins, does not respond to a persuasive conception of liberty or autonomy. The notion of autonomy should refer instead to decisions reached with a full and vivid awareness of available opportunities, with reference to all relevant information, and without illegitimate or excessive constraints on the process of preference formation. For those who think this idea foreign to the liberal tradition in America, it might be worthwhile to recall Dewey's words: "Liberalism knows that social conditions may restrict, distort, and almost prevent the development of individuality. It therefore takes an active interest in the working of social institutions that have a bearing, positive or negative, upon the growth of individuals. . . . It is as much interested in the positive construction of favorable institutions, legal, political, and economic, as it is in the work of removing abuses and overt oppressions."[24] And elsewhere, in an essay on freedom, Dewey suggested that "choice signifies a capacity for deliberately changing preferences."[25]

When there are inadequate information or opportunities, decisions should be described as unfree or nonautonomous; for this reason it is most difficult to identify autonomy with preference satisfaction. If preferences are a product of available information, existing consumption patterns, social pressures, and governmental rules, it seems odd to suggest that individual freedom lies exclusively or by definition in preference satisfaction, or that current preferences should, on grounds of autonomy, be treated as the basis for settling political issues. It seems even odder to suggest that all preferences should be treated equally, independently of their basis and consequences, or of the reasons offered in their support.

For purposes of autonomy, then, governmental interference with existing desires may be justified because of problems in the origins of those desires. Welfare-based arguments that invoke endogeneity tend to emphasize the malleability of preferences after they are formed; arguments based on autonomy stress what happens before the preferences have been created, that is, the conditions that gave rise to them. Because of this difference, the two arguments will operate along different tracks; and in some cases autonomy-based arguments will lead to conclusions different from those that would emerge from arguments based on welfare. In many cases, however, considerations of autonomy will argue powerfully against taking preferences as the basis for social choice.

Consider, for example, a decision to purchase dangerous foods, consumer products, or cigarettes by someone unaware of the (serious) health risks; an employer's decision not to hire blacks because of a background of public and private segregation or racial hostility in his community; a person who disparages or has no interest in art and literature because the culture in which he has been reared centers mainly around television; a decision of a woman to adopt a traditional gender role because of the social stigma attached to refusing to do so; a decision not to purchase cars equipped with seat belts or not to wear a motorcycle helmet produced by the social pressures imposed by one's peer group; a lack of interest in environmental diversity resulting from limitation of one's personal experiences to industrialized urban areas; a decision not to employ blacks at a restaurant because of fear of violence from whites.

These examples are different from one another. The source of the problem varies in each. But in all of them, the interest in liberty or autonomy does not call for governmental inaction, even if that were an intelligible category. Indeed, in many or perhaps all of these cases, regulation removes a kind of coercion.

One goal of a democracy, in short, is to ensure autonomy not merely in the satisfaction of preferences, but also, and more fundamentally, in the processes of preference formation. John Stuart Mill himself was emphatic on this point, going so far as to suggest that government should be evaluated in large measure by its effects on the character of the citizenry.[26] The view that freedom requires an opportunity to choose among alternatives finds a natural supplement in the view that people should not face unjustifiable constraints on the free development of their preferences and beliefs. It is not altogether clear what such a view would require – a point to which I will return. At the very least, however, it would see a failure of autonomy, and a reason for collective response, in beliefs and preferences based on insufficient information or opportunities.

Governmental action might also be justified on grounds of autonomy when the public seeks to implement, through democratic processes culminating in law, widely held social aspirations or collective desires. Individual consumption choices often diverge from collective considered judgments: people may seek, through law, to implement a democratic decision about what courses to pursue. If so, it is ordinarily no violation of autonomy to allow those considered judgments to be vindicated by governmental action. Collective aspirations or considered judgments, produced by a process of deliberation on which competing perspectives are brought to bear, reflect a conception of political freedom having deep roots in the American constitutional tradition. On this view, political autonomy can be found in collective self-determination, as citizens decide, not what they "want," but instead who they are, what their values are, and what those values require. What they "want" must be supported by reasons.

To summarize: On the thinnest version of the account offered thus far, the mere fact that preferences are what they are is at least sometimes and perhaps generally an insufficient justification for political action. Government decisions need not be and in some cases should not be justified by reference to preferences alone. More broadly, a democratic government should sometimes take private preferences as an object of regulation and control – an inevitable task in light of the need to define initial entitlements – and precisely in the interest of welfare and autonomy. Of course, there are serious risks of overreaching here, and there must be some constraints (usually denominated "rights") on this process. Checks laid down in advance are an indispensable part of constitutional government. Those checks will include, at a minimum, basic guarantees of political liberty and personal security, and such guarantees may not comprise processes of collective self-determination. I return to this point below.

II. Democratic rejection of revealed preferences: a catalogue

In this section I attempt to particularize the claims made thus far by cataloguing cases in which considerations of autonomy and welfare justify governmental action that subjective welfarism would condemn. In all of these cases, I claim that participants in a liberal government ought to be concerned with whether its citizens are experiencing satisfying lives and that the salutary liberal commitment to divergent conceptions of the good ought not to be taken to disable government from expressing that concern through law. The cases fall into three basic categories.

A. Collective judgments and aspirations

Citizens in a democratic polity might act to embody in law not the preferences that they hold as private consumers, but instead what might be described as collective judgments, including aspirations or considered reflections. Measures of this sort are a product of deliberative processes on the part of citizens and representatives. In that process, people do not simply determine what they "want." The resulting measures cannot be understood as an attempt to aggregate or trade off private preferences.

1. Politics, markets, and the dependence of preferences on context. Frequently political choices cannot easily be understood as a process of aggregating prepolitical desires. Some people may, for example, support nonentertainment broadcasting on television, even though their own consumption patterns favor situation comedies; they may seek stringent laws protecting the environment or endangered species, even though they do not use the public parks or derive material benefits from protection of such species; they may approve of laws calling for social security and welfare even though they do not save or give to the poor; they may support antidiscrimination laws even though their own behavior is hardly race- or gender-neutral. The choices people make as political participants are different from those they make as consumers. Democracy thus calls for an intrusion on markets.

The widespread disjunction between political and consumption choices presents something of a puzzle. Indeed, it sometimes leads to the view that market ordering is undemocratic and that choices made through the political process are a preferable basis for social ordering.

A generalization of this sort is far too broad in light of the multiple breakdowns of the political process and the advantages of market ordering in many arenas. Respect for private markets is an important way of respecting divergent conceptions of the good and is thus properly associated with individual liberty. Respect for markets is also an engine of economic productivity, an important individual and collective goal. But it would be a mistake to suggest, as some do, that markets always reflect individual choice more reliably than politics; or that democratic choices differ from consumption outcomes only because of confusion, as voters fail to realize that they must ultimately bear the costs of the programs they favor; or that voting patterns merely reflect a willingness to seek certain goods so long as other people are footing the bill.

Undoubtedly, consumer behavior is sometimes a better or more realistic reflection of actual preferences than is political behavior. But in light of the fact that preferences depend on context, the very notion of a "better reflection" of "actual" preferences is a confusing one; there is no such thing as an "actual" (in the sense of unitary or acontextual) preference in these settings. Moreover, the difference might be explained by the fact that political behavior reflects a variety of influences that are distinctive to the context of politics, and that justify according additional weight to what emerges through the political setting.

These influences include four closely related phenomena. First, citizens may seek to implement individual and collective aspirations in political behavior but not in private consumption. As citizens, people may seek the aid of the law to bring about a social state that they consider to be in some sense higher than what emerges from market ordering. Second, people may, in their capacity as political actors, attempt to satisfy altruistic or other-regarding desires, which diverge from the self-interested preferences sometimes characteristic of markets.[27] Third, political decisions might vindicate what might be called metapreferences or second-order preferences. People have wishes about their wishes, and sometimes they try to vindicate those second-order wishes, including considered judgments about what is best, through law. Fourth, people may precommit themselves, in democratic processes, to a course of action that they consider to be in the general interest. The adoption of a constitution is itself an example of a precommitment strategy.

Three qualifications are necessary here. First, some of these objections might be translated into the terms of subjective welfarism. Some preferences, after all, are most effectively expressed in democratic arenas, and that expression can be supported precisely on the grounds that they are subjectively held and connected to a certain form of individual and collective welfare. My broader point, however, is that political choices will reflect a kind of deliberation and reasoning, transforming values and perceptions of interests, that is often inadequately captured in the marketplace. It is this point that amounts to a rejection or at least a renovation of subjective welfarism as a political conception. It is here that democracy becomes something other than an aggregative mechanism, that politics is seen to be irreducible to bargaining, and that prepolitical "preferences" are not taken as the bedrock of political justification.

Second, to point to these various possibilities is not at all to deny that market or private frequently reflects considered judgments, altruism, aspirations, or far more complex attitudes toward diverse goods than are captured in conventional accounts of preference structures. There are countless counterexamples to any such claim. All I mean to suggest is that divergences between market and political behavior will sometimes be attributable to phenomena of the sort I have described.

Third, a democratic system must be built on various safeguards to ensure that its decisions are in fact a reflection of deliberative processes of the sort described here. Often, of course, such processes are distorted by the fact that some groups are more organized than others, by disparities in wealth and influence, and by public and private coercion of various kinds. I am assuming here that these problems have been sufficiently overcome to allow for a favorable characterization of the process.

2. Explanations. Thus far I have suggested that people may seek, through law, to implement collective desires that diverge from market choices. Is it possible to come up with concrete explanations for the differences? There are a number of possibilities.

First, the collective character of politics, which permits a response to collective action problems, is critical here. People may not want to implement their considered judgments, or to be altruistic, unless there is assurance that others will be bound to do so as well. More simply, people may prefer not to contribute to a collective benefit if donations are made individually, with no guarantee that others will participate; but their most favored system, obtainable only or best through democratic forms, might be one in which they contribute if (but only if) there is assurance that others will do so as well. Perhaps people feel ashamed if others are contributing and they are not. Perhaps they feel victimized if they are contributing and others are not. In any case, the satisfaction of aspirations or altruistic goals will sometimes have the characteristics of the provision of public goods or the solution of a prisoner's dilemma.

Second, the collective character of politics might overcome the problem, discussed below, of preferences and beliefs that have adapted, at least to some extent, to an unjust status quo or to limits in available opportunities.[28] Without the possibility of collective action, the status quo may seem intractable, and private behavior, and even desires, will adapt accordingly. But if people can act in concert, preferences might take on a quite different form. Consider social movements involving the environment, labor, and race and sex discrimination. The collective action problem thus interacts with aspirations, altruistic desires, second-order preferences, and precommitment strategies. All of these are most likely to be enacted into law if an apparatus such as democratic rule is available to overcome collective action problems.

Third, social and cultural norms might incline people to express aspirational or altruistic goals more often in political behavior than in markets. Such norms may press people, in their capacity as citizens, in the direction of a concern for others or for the public interest.

Fourth, the deliberative aspects of politics, bringing additional information and perspectives to bear, may affect preferences as expressed through governmental processes. A principal function of a democratic system is to ensure that through representative or participatory processes, new or submerged voices, or novel depictions of where interests lie and what they in fact are, are heard and understood. If representatives or citizens are able to participate in a collective discussion of (for example) broadcasting or levels of risk in the workplace, they might well generate a far fuller and richer picture of diverse social goods, and of how they might be served, than can be provided through individual decisions as registered in the market. It should hardly be surprising if preferences, values, and perceptions of both individual and collective welfare are changed as a result of that process.

Fifth, and finally, consumption decisions are a product of the criterion of private willingness to pay. which creates distortions of its own. Willingness to pay is a function of ability to pay, and it is an extremely crude proxy for utility or welfare. Political behavior removes this distortion – which is not to say that it does not introduce distortions of new kinds.

3. Qualifications. Arguments from collective desires are irresistible if the measure at issue is adopted unanimously. But more serious difficulties are produced if (as is usual) the law imposes on a minority what it regards as a burden rather than a benefit. Suppose, for example, that a majority wants to require high-quality television and to ban violent and dehumanizing shows, but that a significant minority wants to see the latter. (I put the First Amendment questions to one side.) It might be thought that those who perceive a need to bind themselves, or to express an aspiration, should not be permitted to do so if the consequence is to deprive others of an opportunity to satisfy their preferences.

The foreclosure of the preferences of the minority is unfortunate, but in general it is difficult to see what argument there might be for an across-the-board rule against collective action of this sort. If the majority is prohibited from vindicating its considered judgments through legislation, an important arena for democratic self-government will be eliminated. The choice is between the considered judgments of the majority and the preferences (and perhaps judgments as well) of the minority. On the other hand, the foreclosure of the minority should probably be permitted only when less restrictive alternatives, including private arrangements, are unavailable to serve the same end.

Of course, the argument for democratic outcomes embodying collective judgments is not always decisive. It is easy to imagine cases in which that argument is weak. Consider a law forbidding atheism or agnosticism, or barring the expression of unpatriotic political displays. And while I cannot provide in this space a full discussion of the contexts in which the case for democratic outcomes is overcome, it might be useful to describe, in a preliminary way, three categories of cases in which constraints on collective judgments seem especially appropriate.

First, if the particular choice foreclosed has some special character, and especially if it is a part of deliberative democracy itself, it is appropriately considered a right, and the majority has no authority to intervene. Political expression and participation are prime examples. The equal political rights of members of the minority, as citizens, should be respected even if a general aspiration, held by the majority, argues for selective exclusions. So, too, other rights fundamental to autonomy or welfare – consider consensual sexual activity – ought generally to be off-limits to government.

Second, some collective desires might be objectionable or a product of unjust background conditions. A collective judgment that racial intermarriage is intolerable could not plausibly be justified even if it is said to reflect a collective social aspiration. To explain why, it is of course necessary to offer an argument challenging that judgment and invoking principles of justice. Such an argument might itself involve notions of autonomy or welfare. However that may be, the example suggests that the collective judgment must not be objectionable on moral grounds.

Third, some collective desires might reflect a special weakness on the part of the majority: consider a curfew law, or perhaps prohibition. In such circumstances, a legal remedy might remove desirable incentives for private self-control, have unintended side effects resulting from the "bottling-up" of desires, or prove unnecessary in light of the existence of alternative remedies. When any one of these three concerns arises, the case for protection of collective judgments is implausible. But in many contexts, these concerns are absent, and democratic controls initiated on such grounds are justified.

B. Excessive limitations in opportunities or unjust background conditions

Citizens in a democracy might override existing preferences in order to foster and promote diverse experiences, with a view to providing broad opportunities for the formation of preferences and beliefs and for distance on and critical scrutiny of current desires. This goal usually supports private ordering and freedom of contract as well. But it calls for collective safeguards when those forces push toward homogeneity and uniformity, as they often do in industrialized nations. Here the argument for governmental controls finds a perhaps ironic origin in Mill. Such controls are necessary to cultivate divergent conceptions of the good and to ensure a degree of reflection on those conceptions.

A system that took this goal seriously could start from a range of different foundations. It might find its roots in the principles that underlie a deliberative democracy itself.[29] Here the notions of autonomy and welfare would be defined by reference to the idea of free and equal persons acting as citizens in setting up the terms of democratic life. That idea will impose constraints on the sorts of preferences and beliefs that a political system would be permitted to inculcate. Perhaps more controversially, the system could be regarded as embodying a mild form of liberal perfectionism. Such a system would see the inculcation of critical and disparate attitudes toward prevailing conceptions of the good as part of the framework of a liberal democracy. Liberal education is, of course, the principal locus of this concern, but the principles embodied in liberal education need not be confined to the school system. Still another foundation would be Aristotelian. Here the governing goal would be to ensure that individual functionings and capabilities are promoted and not thwarted by governmental arrangements.[30] And this set of ideas, a different kind of perfectionism, is not so dramatically different from Mill's version of utilitarianism.

If government can properly respond to preferences that are based on limitations in available opportunities, it might well undertake aggressive initiatives with respect to the arts and broadcasting: subsidizing public broadcasting, ensuring a range of disparate programming, or calling for high-quality programming not sufficiently provided by the marketplace. Indeed, the need to provide diverse opportunities for preference formation suggests reasons to be quite skeptical of unrestricted markets in

communication and broadcasting. There is a firm theoretical justification for governmental regulation here, including the much criticized,
and now largely abandoned, "fairness doctrine," which required broadcasters to cover controversial issues and to give equal time to competing
views. In view of the inevitable effects of programming on character,
beliefs, and even conduct, it is hardly clear that governmental "inaction" is always appropriate in a constitutional democracy. Indeed, the
contrary seems true. I take up this issue in more detail below.

Market behavior is sometimes based on an effort to reduce cognitive
dissonance by adjusting to undue limitations in current practices and
opportunities. When this is so, respect for preferences seems unjustified
on grounds of autonomy and under certain conditions welfare as well.
Preferences might be regarded as nonautonomous insofar as they are
reflexively adaptive to unjust background conditions, and collective
responses to such preferences might yield welfare gains.[31] The point has
significant implications. For example, workers appear to underestimate
the risks of hazardous activity partly in order to reduce the dissonance
that would be produced by an accurate understanding of the dangers of
the workplace.[32] Democratic controls might produce gains in terms of
both welfare and autonomy.

Similar ideas help account for principles of antidiscrimination. In
general, the beliefs of both beneficiaries and victims of existing injustice
are affected by dissonance-reducing strategies.[33] The phenomenon of
blaming the victim has distinct cognitive and motivational foundations.
The strategy of blaming the victim, or assuming that an injury or an
inequality was deserved or inevitable, permits nonvictims or members
of advantaged groups to reduce dissonance by enabling them to maintain that the world is just – a pervasively, insistently, and sometimes
irrationally held belief.[34] The reduction of cognitive dissonance is a
powerful motivational force, and it operates as a significant obstacle to
the recognition of social injustice or irrationality.

Victims also participate in dissonance-reducing strategies, including
the lowering of their own self-esteem to accommodate both the fact of
victimization and the belief that the world is essentially just. Sometimes
it is easier to assume that one's suffering is warranted than that it has
been imposed cruelly or by chance. Consider here the astonishing fact
that after a draft lottery, participants decided that the results of the
purely random process, whether favorable or not, were deserved.[35] The
phenomenon of blaming the victim also reflects the "hindsight effect,"
through which people unjustifiably perceive events as having been more
predictable than they in fact were, and therefore suggest that victims or
disadvantaged groups should have been able to prevent the negative

outcome. All of these phenomena make reliance on existing or revealed preferences highly problematic in certain contexts.

There is suggestive evidence to this effect in the psychological literature in this area. Some work here reveals that people who engage in cruel behavior begin to devalue the objects of their cruelty; observers tend to do the same.[36] Such evidence bears on antidiscrimination law in general. Certain aspects of American labor and race discrimination law can be understood as a response to the basic problem of distorted beliefs and preferences. For example, the Supreme Court has emphatically rejected freedom-of-choice plans as a remedy for school segregation.[37] Such plans would simply permit whites and blacks to send their children to whichever school they wished. The Court's rejection of such plans might well be puzzling to proponents of subjective welfarism, but the outcome becomes more reasonable if it is seen as based in part on the fact that, in this area, preferences and beliefs have conspicuously grown up around and adapted to the segregative status quo. Under these circumstances, freedom of choice is no solution at all; indeed, in view of the background and context the term seems an oxymoron.

In labor law as well, American law rejects freedom of contract and freedom of choice in order to protect collective bargaining. Some of this legislation must stand on a belief that private preferences have been adaptive to a status quo skewed against unionization. Special steps are therefore necessary in order to encourage collective bargaining, which also, of course, overcomes the prisoner's dilemma faced by individual workers, and thus facilitates collective deliberation on the conditions of the workplace.

Poverty itself is perhaps the most severe obstacle to the free development of preferences and beliefs. Programs that attempt to respond to the deprivations faced by poor people – most obviously by eliminating poverty, but also through broad public education and regulatory efforts designed to make cultural resources generally available regardless of wealth – are fully justified in this light. They should hardly be seen as objectionable paternalism or as unsupportable redistribution. Indeed, antipoverty efforts are tightly linked with republican efforts to promote security and independence in the interest of creating the conditions for full and equal citizenship.

Sometimes, of course, preferences are only imperfectly adapted. At some level there is a perception of injury, but a fear of social sanctions or a belief that the cause is intractable prevents people from seeking redress. Here the collective character of politics, permitting the organization of numerous people, can be exceedingly helpful.

Standing by itself, the fact that preferences are shifting and endogenous is hardly a sufficient reason for the imposition of democratic controls. All preferences are to some degree dependent on existing law and current opportunities, and that fact cannot be a reason for governmental action without creating a license for tyranny. The argument for democratic controls in the face of endogenous preferences must rely on a belief that welfare or autonomy will thereby be promoted. Usually governmental interference should be avoided. But far too often, the salutary belief in respect for divergent conceptions of the good is transformed into an unwillingness to protect people from either unjust background conditions or a sheer lack of options.

The actual content of democratic controls here will of course be controversial, and it probably should begin and usually end with efforts to provide information and to increase opportunities. Thus, for example, governmentally required disclosure of risks in the workplace is a highly laudable strategy. In a few cases, however, these milder initiatives are inadequate, and other measures are necessary. A moderately intrusive strategy could involve economic incentives, which might take the form of tax advantages or cash payments. For example, the government might give financial inducements to day-care centers as a way of relieving child-care burdens. Such a system might well be preferable to direct transfers of money to families, a policy that will predictably lead many more women to stay at home. In view of the sources and consequences of the differential distribution of child-care burdens, it is fully legitimate for the government to take steps in the direction of equalization. The most intrusive option, to be used rarely, is direct coercion, as in the case of governmentally mandated use of safety equipment.

The category of democratic responses to endogenous preferences of this sort overlaps with that of measures that attempt to protect collective aspirations. Frequently, aspirations form the basis for laws that attempt to influence processes of preference formation.

C. Intrapersonal collective action problems

There is also a case for democratic controls on existing preferences when such preferences are a function of past acts of consumption and when such acts alter desires or beliefs in such a way as to cause long-term harm. In such cases, the two key facts are that preferences are endogenous to past consumption decisions and that the effect of those decisions on current preferences is pernicious. For government to act in this context, it is important that it be confident of its conclusions; in the face of uncertainty, freedom of choice is appropriate here. An absence of information on the part of the private actors is usually a necessary condition for collective controls.

Regulations of addictive substances, myopic behavior, and habits are familiar examples. In the case of an addiction, the problem is that the costs of nonconsumption increase dramatically over time as the benefits of consumption remain constant or fall sharply. The result is that the aggregate costs, over time or over a life, of consumption exceed the aggregate benefits, even though the initial consumption choice provides benefits that exceed costs. Individual behavior that is rational for each individual consumption choice ultimately leads people into severely inferior social states. In such cases, people, if fully informed, would in all likelihood not want to choose the good in the first place. Governmental action is a possible response.

Menahem Yaari offers the example of a group of traders attempting to induce alcoholism in an Indian tribe.[38] At the outset, alcoholic beverages are not extremely valuable to consumers. The consumers are willing to buy only for a low price, which the traders accept. But as a result of consumption, the value of the beverages to the consumers steadily increases to the point where they are willing to pay enormous sums to obtain them. Thus the traders are able "to manoeuvre the Indian into a position where rationality conflicts with Pareto-efficiency, i.e., into a position where to be efficient is to be irrational and to be rational is to be inefficient. . . . [T]he disadvantage, for an economic unit, of having endogenously changing tastes is that, even with perfect information and perfect foresight, the unit may find itself forced to follow an action which, by the unit's own standards, is Pareto-dominated."

Because of the effect over time of consumption on preferences, someone who is addicted to heroin is much worse off than he would have been had he never started, even though the original decision to consume was not irrational in terms of immediate costs and benefits. Statutes that regulate addictive substances respond to a social belief, grounded on this consideration, that the relevant preferences should not be formed in the first place.

We might describe this situation as involving an intrapersonal collective action problem, in which the costs and benefits, for a particular person, of engaging in an activity change dramatically over time.[39] A central point here is that consumption patterns induce a significant change in preferences, and in a way that makes people worse off in the long run.[40] In the case of addictions, there will also be interconnections between intrapersonal collective action problems and preferences and beliefs that are adaptive to unjust background conditions, at least as a general rule. (Yaari's own example, involving whites trading alcohol with native Americans, is a prime example.) The problem of drug addiction is hardly distributed evenly throughout the population, and the process of addiction is in large part a response to social institutions that severely limit and condition the range of options.

While addiction is the most obvious case, it is part of a far broader category. Consider, for example, myopic behavior, defined as a refusal, because the short-term costs exceed the short-term benefits, to engage in activity having long-term benefits that dwarf long-term costs. Another kind of intrapersonal collective action problem is produced by habits, in which people engage in behavior because of the subjectively high short-term costs of changing their behavior, regardless of the fact that the long-term benefits exceed the long-term costs. *Akrasia*, or weakness of the will, has a related structure, and some laws respond to its individual or collective forms.

For the most part, problems of this sort are best addressed at the individual level or through private associations, which minimize coercion; but social regulation is a possible response. Statutes that subsidize the arts or public broadcasting, or that discourage the formation of some habits and encourage the formation of others, are illustrations. There are similar arguments for compulsory recycling programs (the costs of participation in which decrease substantially over time, and often turn into benefits) and for democratic restrictions on smoking cigarettes.[41]

The problem with collective controls in this context is that they are unlikely to be fine-tuned. They will often sweep up so many people and circumstances as to create serious risks of abuse. In some settings, however, citizens will be able to say with confidence that the effect of consumption on preferences will lead to severe welfare or autonomy losses. In such cases democratic controls are justified.

III. Examples

A. The frontiers of free speech law: the fairness doctrine, campaign regulation, hate speech, and pornography

The most important issues in the contemporary law of free expression have produced cleavages between groups and ideas that were previously closely allied. Thus the First Amendment has been invoked, with considerable vigor and passion, on behalf of cigarette companies seeking to advertise their products; corporations attempting to influence electoral outcomes; people engaged in racial hate speech; pornographers; and large networks objecting to a private right of access to broadcasting or to other efforts to promote quality and diversity in the media. The effort

to invoke the First Amendment is increasingly resisted – often, ironically, on the theory that it runs counter to the goals of deliberative
democracy and free expression itself – by individuals and groups formerly associated with an absolutist or near-absolutist position against governmental regulation of speech.

These debates raise exceedingly complex issues, and I can only touch
on them briefly here. The complexities are increased by the fact that a
system dedicated to freedom of expression ought to be highly sensitive
to the idea that speech alters preferences and beliefs. It should also find
that process to be one to which a democracy is generally quite receptive.
As Justice Louis D. Brandeis wrote in what is probably the most
distinguished judicial opinion in the entire history of free expression,
"the fitting remedy for evil counsels is good ones. . . . If there be time
to expose through discussion the falsehood and fallacies, to avert the
evil by the processes of education, the remedy to be applied is more
speech, not enforced silence."[42]

Justice Brandeis's statement notwithstanding, I want to suggest that
attention to the endogenous character of preferences and to the considerations traced thus far provides some basis for receptivity to democratic controls in this context.

1. The fairness doctrine. There is a growing consensus that the government should not concern itself with the airwaves and that total
reliance on private markets and consumer preferences is the appropriate
strategy for government. On this view, broadcasting should be treated
like soap, cereal, or any other commodity. Indeed, there is a growing
consensus that this result is ordained by the First Amendment. But if the
claims made here are persuasive, the consensus is misguided. The
meaning of the First Amendment is a function of competing views about
what sort of relation between government and markets will best promote democratic deliberation. Lawyers (and not a few nonlawyers)
have an unfortunate habit of thinking that the meaning of the First
Amendment precedes rather than postdates that inquiry.

The consequence of market-based strategies in broadcasting is a
system in which most viewers see shows that rarely deal with serious
problems; are frequently sensationalistic, prurient, dehumanizing, or
banal; reflect and perpetuate a bland, watered-down version of the most
conventional views about politics and morality; are influenced excessively by the concerns of advertisers; produce an accelerating "race to
the bottom" in terms of the quality and quantity of attention that they
require and encourage; and are often riddled with violence, sexism, and

racism. It simply defies belief to suggest that such shows do not affect the preferences and even the character of the citizenry. Is it so clear that a constitutional democracy ought to consider itself unable to respond to this situation? Is it so clear that a First Amendment enacted in order to ensure democratic self-determination bars a democratic corrective here?

In my view, the considerations marshaled thus far suggest that citizens in a constitutional democracy ought to be conceded, and ought to exercise, the power to engage in a wide range of controls. If welfare and autonomy provide the governing criteria, large gains might be expected from such controls. All three of the categories I have described argue in favor of some form of regulation. Democratic controls would probably reflect collective desires, which deserve respect. They would respond to the fact that in spite of the large number of channels, the current regulatory regime diminishes genuine options, to the detriment of both welfare and autonomy; they would also counteract a kind of intrapersonal collective action problem faced by many of those habituated to the broadcasting status quo.

Such controls might permit the government to regulate advertising on television, certainly for children, but for others as well; to require broadcasters to pay attention to public affairs; to limit gratuitous or prurient violence on television, especially when it is sexualized; to require, as a condition for licensing, a subsidy to public television; to provide financial incentives and to give licensing preferences for high-quality programming; and to impose a broad fairness doctrine, in the form not only of an obligation of attention to important issues but also a chance to speak for divergent sides. The evident dangers notwithstanding, there would be a wide range of collective and external benefits from such controls, which would thus carry forward a strand of the liberal tradition that calls for governmental action in such cases.[43]

At least in principle, rights of private access to the media for differing positions and associated kinds of controls ought to be considered congenial to the free speech guarantee. Surely this is so if that guarantee is understood as a protection of a deliberative process centered on public values rather than of a "marketplace." The First Amendment need not be seen as an obstacle to such efforts. If anything, the existing system might be thought to raise serious constitutional questions. A system in which access to the media, with its inevitable consequences for the shaping of preferences and beliefs, is made dependent on private willingness to pay raises genuine problems for free expression.[44]

2. Campaign regulation. It would not be difficult to argue that a variety of regulations on the electoral process are necessary both to promote a deliberative process among political equals and to ensure that the deliberative process is a genuine one. Properly conceived, such efforts would be highly congenial to the purposes of the free speech guarantee. Both restrictions on campaign contributions – to eliminate the distorting effects of wealth[45] – and qualitative measures to reduce the "soundbite" phenomenon and to promote more in the way of reflective discussion hold considerable promise.

Currently, however, there is a large if ironic obstacle to such efforts: the First Amendment. The Supreme Court has generally been unreceptive to governmental efforts to regulate electoral campaigns.[46] In the key passage in *Buckley* v. *Valeo*, the Court said that "the concept that government may restrict the speech of some elements of our society in order to enhance the relative voice of others is wholly foreign to the first amendment."[47] It is crucial to note here that the Court did not say that the effort to promote deliberation among political equals was insufficiently weighty or inadequately promoted by the legislation at hand. Instead the Court said, far more broadly, that the effort was constitutionally illegitimate.

Under the approach suggested here, campaign regulation would be treated more hospitably. In view of the effects of wealth on the formation of political beliefs, and the corrosive consequences of some forms of electioneering, democratic controls on the process might be welcomed. The First Amendment might be understood not as a guarantor of unrestricted speech "markets," and much less as a vehicle for the translation of economic inequalities into political ones, but instead as an effort to ensure a process of deliberation that would, under current conditions, be promoted rather than undermined through regulatory measures. This is so especially if citizens in a democratic polity support regulation of the electoral process in order to pursue their desire for a well-functioning deliberative process.

Of course, there are great risks here, and any regulatory efforts must be carefully monitored to ensure that they do not act as incumbent protection bills or as serious constraints on speech that should instead be encouraged. But the issue is far more complex, from the standpoint of the First Amendment itself, than existing law allows.

3. Violent pornography and hate speech. Many Western democracies, including those firmly committed to freedom of speech, regulate speech that casts contempt on identifiable social groups (hate speech). Some such democracies also control sexually explicit speech, especially when it associates sex and violence. These controls have been justified on mixed grounds of human dignity, community morality, and sexual equality. In the United States, the precise status of such restrictions remains unclear. Probably the best account of current law is that with the possible exception of simple epithets amounting to "fighting words," hate speech is protected, as is most speech that associates sex and violence, even if that speech is not conceivably part of a serious exchange of ideas but instead qualifies as pornography.[48]

The cases of hate speech and pornography raise somewhat different problems. Hate speech is self-consciously directed toward an issue of public concern; it is conspicuously and intentionally political in nature. Violent pornography is, of course, political too, in the sense that it has political origins and consequences. But it cannot be thought to be a self-conscious contribution to democratic deliberation about public issues. In this way it differs from misogynist speech of a more straightforward sort, where the political content is explicit. In terms of its connection to the First Amendment, pornography should probably be thought to fall in the same category as commercial speech, libel of private persons, bribes, and conspiracies. The reason is that most pornography does not amount to an effort to contribute to deliberation on matters of public interest, even if that category is broadly conceived, as it should be. Expression that is not central to the free speech principle counts as speech, but it is entitled to a lesser degree of protection. It may be regulated, not on a whim, but on a basis of demonstration of harm that is weaker than that required for political speech.

Should the First Amendment be taken to disable government from regulating hate speech and pornography? The affirmative answer of current law may well be unsound. Both of these forms of speech have serious and corrosive effects on beliefs and desires. Both have the additional and unusual characteristic of denying victimized groups the right to participate in the community as free and equal persons. With respect to certain kinds of violent pornography, there are especially severe consequences in terms of how men and women perceive sexuality, how men perceive women, and how women perceive themselves. One need not believe that the regulation of violent pornography would eliminate sexual violence or even do a great deal to produce sexual equality in order to recognize that the pervasiveness of material that associates sex with violence has a variety of harmful social consequences.

The case for regulation of these forms of speech is strongest when the relevant speech is pervasive, when it causes tangible harm, and when it falls outside the category of speech that is guaranteed First Amendment protection unless there is a demonstration of unavoidable, imminent, and serious danger. The considerations marshaled here suggest that at least certain forms of violent pornography ought to be regulated, and that perhaps in certain restricted settings, hate speech may be an appropriate subject of democratic controls.

B. Proportional representation

In recent years, there has been a revival of interest in systems of proportional or group representation, both for disadvantaged groups and perhaps generally as well. There is a solid constitutional pedigree for such systems, notwithstanding the constant and emphatic rejections, by the Supreme Court, of constitutionally based arguments for representation of members of racial minority groups. Despite the rigidity of the one-person-one-vote formula, with its majoritarian and individualistic overtones, group representation has always been a feature of American constitutionalism.[49]

Moreover, the basic constitutional institutions of federalism, bicameralism, and checks and balances share some of the appeal of proportional representation, and owe their origins in part to notions of group representation. These institutions proliferate the points of access to government, increasing the ability of diverse groups to influence policy, multiplying perspectives in government, and improving deliberative capacities. In this respect, they ensure something in the way of group representation, at least when compared with unitary systems. Of course, both the separation of powers and bicameralism grew in part out of efforts to promote representation of diverse groups. Bicameralism allowed representation of both the wealthy and the masses, while the notion of separation derived from (though it also repudiated) notions of mixed government, which was designed to ensure a measure of representation of groups defined in social and economic terms.

Proportional representation might be designed, as in its Western European forms, to ensure representation in the legislature of all those groups that are able to attain more than a minimal share of the vote. In another form, the system might be an effort to ensure that members of disadvantaged groups are given the power to exert influence on political outcomes. In America, the Voting Rights Act goes far in this direction for blacks.

There are serious problems with both of these efforts, and I do not mean to evaluate them in detail here. I do suggest that efforts to ensure proportional representation become much more acceptable if they are justified on grounds that do not take existing preferences as the basis for governmental decisions and if they emphasize the preference-shaping effects of discussion and disagreement in politics.[50] The argument here is that deliberative processes will be improved, not undermined, if mechanisms are instituted to ensure that multiple groups have access to the process and are actually present when decisions are made. Proportional or group representation, precisely by having this effect, would ensure that diverse views are expressed on an ongoing basis in the representative process, where they might otherwise be excluded.

In this respect, proportional or group representation could be regarded as a kind of second-best solution for the real-world failures of Madisonian deliberation. And the primary purpose of access is not to allow each group to have its "piece of the action" – though that is not entirely irrelevant – but instead to ensure that the process of deliberation is not distorted by the mistaken appearance of a common set of interests on the part of all concerned. In this incarnation, proportional representation is designed to increase the likelihood that political outcomes will incorporate some understanding of all perspectives. That process should facilitate the healthy expression of collective values or aspirations and the scrutiny of preferences adaptive to unjust background conditions or limited opportunities.

For this reason, proportional representation may be the functional analogue of the institutions of checks and balances and federalism, recognizing the creative functions of disagreement and multiple perspectives for the governmental process. In this sense there is continuity between recent proposals for proportional representation and some of the attractive features of the original constitutional regime. Indeed, Hamilton himself emphasized that in a system of checks and balances, the "jarring of parties . . . will promote deliberation."[51] If this is so, proportional representation is most understandable in a democracy that does not take existing preferences as the basis for social choice but instead sees the broadest form of deliberation, covering ends as well as means, as a central ingredient in democratic politics.

IV. Conclusion

A constitutional democracy should not be self-consciously concerned, in a general and comprehensive way, with the souls of its citizens. Under modern conditions, liberal constraints on the operation of the public sphere and a general respect for divergent conceptions of the good are indispensable. At the same time, it would be a grave mistake to characterize liberal democracy as a system that requires existing preferences to be taken as the basis for governmental decisions. Citizens should not be prohibited from enacting their considered judgments into law, or from counteracting, through the provision of opportunities and information, preferences and beliefs that have adjusted to an unjust status quo. Ironically, a system that forecloses these routes – and that claims to do so in the name of liberalism or democracy – will defeat many of the aspirations that gave both liberalism and democracy their original appeal, and that continue to fuel them in so many parts of the world.

Notes

1 See Gordon Wood, *The Creation of the American Republic, 1776–1787* (New York: W. W. Norton, 1972); Thomas Pangle, *The Spirit of Modern Republicanism: The Moral Vision of the American Founders and the Philosophy of Locke* (Chicago: University of Chicago Press, 1988); and Martin Diamond, "Ethics and Politics: The American Way," in *The Moral Foundations of the American Republic*, ed. Robert Horwitz (Charlottesville: University Press of Virginia, 1986), pp. 75–106.

2 *The Laws* 650b.

3 See John Rawls, "The Idea of an Overlapping Consensus," *Oxford Journal of Legal Studies* 7 (1987): 1–25.

4 Indeed, participants in the liberal tradition, in its classical forms, emphasized the need for deliberation in government and placed a high value on political virtue. Many liberals do not take private preferences as the basis for social choice, without regard to their sources and consequences, or to the reasons that might be offered in their support. See my "Beyond the Republican Revival," *Yale Law Journal* 97 (1988): 1539–89.

5 On the limits of preference-based theories, see Amartya Sen, "Rational Fools: A Critique of the Behavioral Foundations of Economic Theory," *Philosophy & Public Affairs* 6, no. 4 (Summer 1977): 317–44; Jon Elster, *Sour Grapes* (New York: Cambridge University Press, 1983); and John Roemer, "'Rational Choice' Marxism," in *Analytical Marxism*, ed. John Roemer (New York: Cambridge University Press, 1986), pp. 191–201. Of course, the satisfaction of private preferences in markets or elsewhere may create prisoners' dilemmas or collective action problems, and here governmental controls (or social norms) are a natural solution. I will not, however, deal with this narrower problem here.

It might well be that literature, in addition to economics and political theory, is a fruitful place to explore this subject. See Martha Nussbaum, *Love's Knowledge* (New York: Oxford University Press, 1990), and "Shame, Separateness, and Political Unity: Aristotle's Criticism of Plato," in *Essays on Aristotle's Ethics*, ed. Amelie Rorty (Berkeley: University of California Press, 1980), pp. 395–435. It is thus no accident that writers in politics and economics sometimes draw on literature. See, e.g., Elster, *Sour Grapes*.

6 David Gauthier, *Morals by Agreement* (New York: Oxford University Press, 1986), contains arguments in this direction; for a representative example at the intersection of economics and law, see Richard Posner, *Economics of Justice* (Cambridge, Mass.: Harvard University Press, 1983), p. 53. There are,

of course, criticisms within all of these fields. In economics, see Sen, "Rational Fools"; in politics, see Elster, *Sour Grapes*.

It is notable that the great expositors of liberalism in the nineteenth and twentieth centuries are emphatic in their rejection of the view that satisfaction of existing preferences is adequate for purposes of ethics or politics. See John Stuart Mill, *Considerations on Representative Government*, ed. C. V. Shields (1861; New York: Liberal Arts Press, 1958), and *The Subjection of Women*, ed. Susan Moller Okin (1869; Indianapolis: Hackett, 1988); and John Rawls, *A Theory of Justice* (Cambridge, Mass.: Harvard University Press, 1971). Mill's rejection of that view is especially emphatic in his essay on Bentham, where he criticizes Bentham for the view that "[t]o say either that man should, or that he should not, take pleasure in one thing, displeasure in another, appeared to him as much an act of despotism in the moralist as in the political ruler." Mill, by contrast, emphasized the need to explore the influences "on the regulation of . . . affections and desires," and pointed to "the deficiencies of a system of ethics which does not pretend to aid individuals in the formation of their own character" (*Mill on Bentham and Coleridge*, ed. F. R. Leavis [London: Chatto & Windus, 1950], pp. 68, 71, 70). Of course, there is a difference between what a system of ethics and what a system of politics should say about that question, as Mill clearly believed.

Dewey spoke in similar terms, invoking the need for critical reflection on the "conditions under which objects are enjoyed" and "the consequences of esteeming and liking them," and arguing that "*judgments about values are judgments about that which should regulate the formation of our desires, affections and enjoyments*" (John Dewey, *The Quest for Certainty: A Study of the Relation of Knowledge and Action* [New York: Putnam, 1960], pp. 259, 265, 272–3; emphasis in original).

7 I am grateful to Joshua Cohen for this formulation. I will not explore the complexities of the notion of "preference" here. I mean to refer simply to choices, mostly as these are observed in market behavior. This understanding of course captures the economic notion of "revealed preference" and also is a foundational part of subjective welfarism as I understand it. For a recent and interestingly offhand example, see Ingemar Hansson and Charles Stuart, "Malthusian Selection of Preferences," *American Economic Review* 90 (1990): 529, 542: "We use natural selection to explain behavior, or equivalently, preferences." I do not explore the view, much broader than the claims defended here, that the existence of even widely held preferences, thus defined, furnishes no argument at all for governmental action.

If the notion of preference is intended to refer to an internal psychological force, or to a supposed wellspring of action, difficulties of course abound: people have first-, second-, and nth-order preferences, and their desires can be organized into many different categories, ranging from whimsy to considered judgments.

8 It was first so called in Richard Thaler, "Toward a Positive Theory of Consumer Choice," *Journal of Economic Behavior & Organization* 1 (1980): 39.

9 D. Kahneman, J. Knetsch, and R. Thaler, "Experimental Tests of the Endowment Effect and the Coase Theorem," *Journal of Political Economics* 98 (1990): 1325. See also Knetsch, "The Endowment Effect and Evidence of Nonreversible Indifference Curves," *American Economic Review* (1989): 1277; Knetsch and J. A. Sinden, "Willingness to Pay and Compensation Demanded: Experimental Evidence of an Unexpected Disparity in Measures of Value," *Quarterly Journal of Economics* (1984): 507.

10 Knetsch, "The Endowment Effect."

11 David Brookshire and Don Coursey, "Measuring the Value of a Public Good: An Empirical Comparison of Elicitation Procedures," *American Economic Review* 77 (1987): 554.

12 John Hammock and George Brown, *Waterfowl and Wetlands: Toward Bioeconomic Analysis* (1974).

13 Robert Rowe, Ralph d'Arge, and David Brookshire, "An Experiment on the Economic Value of Visibility," *Journal of Environmental Economics and Management* 7 (1980): 1.

14 Thaler, "Toward a Positive Theory of Consumer Choice," p. 39.

15 Knetsch, "The Endowment Effect."

16 W. Kip Viscusi, Wesley Magat, and Peter Huber, "An Investigation of the Rationality of Consumer Valuations of Multiple Health Risks," *RAND Journal of Economics* 18 (1987): 465.

17 See Kahneman, Knetsch, and Thaler, "Fairness and the Assumptions of Economics," in *Rational Choice: The Contrast Between Economics and Psychology*, ed. R. Hogarth and M. Reder (Chicago: University of Chicago Press, 1987), p. 101, esp. at pp. 113–14.

18 See Kahneman, Knetsch, and Thaler, ibid.

19 See C. Sunstein, *After the Rights Revolution* (1990).

20 See Elster, *Sour Grapes*; Rawls, *A Theory of Justice*. The problem here is not the simple fact of endogeneity, but that social rules and practices cannot be justified by reference to preferences that they have produced.

21 For a modern utilitarian account along these lines, see Richard Brandt, *A Theory of the Good and the Right* (New York: Oxford University Press, 1979). For Aristotelian accounts, see Nussbaum, "Aristotelian Social Democracy," and Amartya Sen, "Well-Being, Agency, and Freedom," *Journal of Philosophy* 82 (1985): 169–221.

22 See Amartya Sen, *The Standard of Living*, The Tanner Lectures on Human Values, ed. Geoffrey Hawthorne (Cambridge: Cambridge University Press, 1987). On various conceptions of welfare, see James Griffin, *Well-Being: Its Meaning, Measurement and Moral Significance* (Oxford: Clarendon Press, 1986).

23 The objection here is not solely that preferences are endogenous to state action of some sort. As discussed in more detail below, the fact of endogeneity is not in itself an argument for democratic control of preferences. The argument is instead that misery that is a product of unjust background conditions calls for collective change. A subjectively satisfactory status quo

produced by unjust background conditions will also call for change in some settings, for reasons taken up below. I do not deal with the possibility that subjective unhappiness that is a product of just background conditions also calls for governmental action, except insofar as an intrapersonal collective action problem is involved.

Moreover, to say that a preference is endogenous is not to say that it is a mere whim or fancy, or highly malleable. Some preferences are in fact relatively stable, even if they are a function of legal rules, social pressures, or existing institutions. A high degree of stability, and great resistance to change, will counsel against efforts at changing preferences, certainly on welfare grounds, and perhaps on grounds of autonomy as well (though even stable preferences may be nonautonomous, as in the case of rigid adaptations to an unjust status quo). In the face of extremely stable preferences, democratic efforts at change will merely breed resentment and frustration on the part of the objects of those efforts.

24 John Dewey, "The Future of Liberalism," in *Dewey and His Critics*, ed. S. Morgenbesser (1977), pp. 695, 697. This theme appears throughout Dewey's work. J. Dewey, *Freedom and Culture* (1989) p. 108: "The assumption that desires are rigidly fixed is not one on its face consistent with the history of man's progress from savagery through barbarism to even the present defective state of civilization"; ibid. at 22: "A certain complex culture stimulates, promotes, and consolidates native tendencies so as to produce a certain pattern of desires and purposes."

25 "Philosophies of Freedom," in *Freedom in the Modern World*, ed. H. Kallen (1936), p. 243: "We may say that a stone has its preferential selections set by a relatively fixed, a rigidly set, structure. . . . The reverse is true of human action. In so far as a variable life history and intelligent insight and foresight enter into it, choice signifies a capacity for deliberately changing preferences." See also John Dewey, *The Quest for Certainty* (1929), pp. 258–9, stating that his "objection is that the theory in question holds down value to objects *antecedently* enjoyed, apart from reference to the method by which they come into existence; it takes enjoyments which are causal because unregulated by intelligent operations to be values in and of themselves. . . . Without the intervention of thought, enjoyments are not values but problematic goods, becoming values when they re-issue in a changed form from intelligent behavior. The fundamental problem with the current empirical theory of values is that it merely formulates and justifies the socially prevailing habit of regarding enjoyments as they are actually experienced as values in and of themselves. It completely side-steps the question of regulation of these enjoyments. This issue involves nothing less than the problem of the directed reconstruction of economic, political and religious institutions."

26 See Mill, *Considerations on Representative Government*.

27 See Howard Margolis, *Selfishness, Altruism, and Rationality: A Theory of Social Choice* (Cambridge: Cambridge University Press, 1982). Of course,

the work by Kenneth Arrow and his followers in social choice theory creates
serious problems for all preference-based theories of politics.

28 Cf. Mill's discussion of the ability of regimes to create active or passive
characters, in *Considerations on Representative Government.*

29 See Joshua Cohen, "Deliberation and Democratic Legitimacy," in *The
Good Polity: Normative Analysis of the State*, ed. Alan Hamlin and Philip
Pettit (Oxford: Basil Blackwell, 1989), pp. 17–34.

30 See Amartya Sen, *Inequality Reexamined* (Cambridge, Mass.: Harvard University Press, 1992), and Nussbaum, "Aristotelian Social Democracy."
Here, as above, I do not attempt to choose among foundations but instead
suggest that those adopting a wide range of starting points should reject
subjective welfarism. To say this is not, of course, to deny the need to rely
ultimately on some conception of the good. For these purposes a wide
variety of possibilities should do, including a form of liberal perfectionism, or
a thin but relatively precise conception, as in Rawls' *A Theory of Justice*, or a
thick but vague one, as in "Aristotelian Social Democracy."

31 There is a difference between self-conscious adaptation to an intractable
status quo and the sorts of processes I am describing. If a person without
musical talent decides to counteract and revise a desire to be a world-famous
pianist, it would be odd to find that (healthy) decision to be inconsistent with
personal autonomy. The cases under discussion involve a reflexive process
based on a socially produced absence of sufficient opportunities. Of course,
the notion of sufficient opportunities itself requires a baseline; every system
contains limited opportunities.

32 See George Akerlof and William Dickens, "The Economic Consequences of
Cognitive Dissonance," *American Economic Review* 72 (1982): 307–18.

33 On cognitive dissonance, see Leon Festinger, *A Theory of Cognitive Dissonance* (Stanford, Calif.: Stanford University Press, 1957); on some of its
implications for social theory, welfare, and autonomy, see Elster, *Sour
Grapes.* See also the preceding discussion of endowment effects and reference states.

   Consider also Mary Wollstonecraft, *A Vindication of the Rights of Women*,
ed. Carol Poston (1792; New York: W. W. Norton, 1975), which can be seen
as an extended discussion of the social formation of preferences and the
phenomenon of the adaptation of preferences, beliefs, and desires to an
unjust status quo. Thus Wollstonecraft writes, "I will venture to affirm, that
a girl, whose spirits have not been damped by inactivity, or innocence tainted
by false shame, will always be a romp, and the doll will never excite attention
unless confinement allows her no alternative" (p. 43). Similar points are
made in Mill, *The Subjection of Women*, as against the claim that the existing
desires of women are a product of consent.

   Consider finally the discussion of women's illiteracy in Bangladesh in
Nussbaum, "Aristotelian Social Democracy." Drawing on Martha Chen, *A
Quiet Revolution: Women in Transition in Rural Bangladesh* (Cambridge,
Mass.: Schenkman, 1983), Nussbaum explores the fact that many women in

Bangladesh did not demand or even want greater education or literacy, and indeed expressed satisfaction with their current educational status. Of course, desires of this sort were a product of a lack of available opportunities and of social and cultural pressures.

34 See Melvin Lerner, *The Belief in a Just World: A Fundamental Delusion* (New York: Plenum Press, 1980).

35 Zick Rubin and Anne Peplau, "Belief in a Just World and Reaction to Another's Lot," *Journal of Social Issues* 29 (1973): 73–93.

36 See Lerner, *The Belief in a Just World*.

37 See *Green v. County School Bd.*, 391 U.S. 430 (1968), and Paul Gewirtz, "Choice in the Transition," *Columbia Law Review* 86 (1986): 728–98.

38 Menahem Yaari, "Endogenous Changes in Tastes: A Philosophical Discussion," in *Decision Theory and Social Ethics: Issues in Social Choice*, ed. Hans Gottinger and Werner Leinfellner (Boston: D. Reidel, 1978), pp. 59–98.

39 Thomas Schelling, "Egonomics, or the Art of Self-Management," *American Economic Review* 68 (1978): 290–94; Jon Elster, "Weakness of Will and the Free-Rider Problem," *Economics and Philosophy* 1 (1985): 231–65.

40 Of course, all consumption has an effect on preferences. For example, exposure to classical music usually increases appreciation. But the pattern under discussion is a rare one: It is that pattern, producing miserable lives, to which a democracy might respond. To be sure, in practice the response might make things worse rather than better.

41 See Robert Goodin, *No Smoking: The Ethical Issues* (Chicago: University of Chicago Press, 1989).

42 *Whitney v. California*, 274 U.S. 357, 377 (1927).

43 See, e.g., John Stuart Mill, *Principles of Political Economy*, ed. W. J. Ashley (1871; London and New York: Longmans, Green, 1929). See also Owen Fiss, "Free Speech and Social Structure," *Iowa Law Review* 71 (1986): 1405–25; this essay carries the argument considerably further than I do here.

44 The Supreme Court seemed to recognize this point in *Red Lion Broadcasting Co. v. FCC*, 395 U.S. 367 (1969), but the point has dropped out of the current debate. If this analysis is correct, moreover, it is by no means clear that the print media should be more immunized from regulation than broadcasting, especially now that the original scarcity rationale seems weak.

45 See John Rawls, "The Basic Liberties and Their Priority," in *The Tanner Lectures on Human Values*, ed. Sterling McMurrin (Salt Lake City: University of Utah Press, 1982), 3:76.

46 See *Buckley v. Valeo*, 424 U.S. 1 (1976), and *First National Bank of Boston v. Bellotti*, 435 U.S. 765 (1978).

47 424 U.S. at pp. 48–9.

48 I collapse some complex issues here. See *Miller v. California*, 413 U.S. 15 (1973), and my "Pornography and the First Amendment," *Duke Law Journal* (September 1986): 589–627.

49 At the time of the framing, for example, geography was thought to define

distinct communities with distinct interests; representation of the states as such seemed only natural. It would not be impossible to argue that racial and ethnic groups (among others) are the contemporary analogues to groups that were defined in geographical terms during the founding period.

50 In part this is Mill's defense of such efforts. See *Considerations on Representative Government*. For valuable discussions, see Charles Beitz, *Political Equality: An Essay in Democratic Theory* (Princeton, N.J.: Princeton University Press, 1989), pp. 123–40; and Iris Young, "Polity and Group Difference: A Critique of the Ideal of Universal Citizenship," *Ethics* 99 (1989): 250–84. Beitz's argument that proportional representation is not a requirement of political fairness is not inconsistent with the more prudential considerations invoked here: Young's claims about the need for discussion among the differently situated are highly compatible with my account.

51 *The Federalist* No. 70.

Must preferences be respected in a democracy?

JOHN FEREJOHN

I. Introduction

In "Democracy and Shifting Preferences," Cass Sunstein argues that democratic government must not take privately held preferences as the sole basis for its decisions – a view he criticizes as subjective welfarism – and that sometimes it is permissible or even obligatory for a democratic government to intervene in the formation of the preferences of its citizens. Thus, Sunstein seeks to cast doubt on the ideas that private desires and beliefs ought to be respected in all contexts and that they could be the unique source of legitimation for public action. In particular he argues that

> in three categories of cases, private preferences as expressed in consumption choices, should be overridden. The first category involves . . . collective judgments, including considered beliefs, aspirations for social justice, and altruistic goals; the second involves preferences that have adapted to undue limitations . . . or to unjust background conditions; the third points to intrapersonal collective action problems that, over a lifetime, impair personal welfare.

Once we accept this claim, Sunstein suggests that we are committed to accepting a theory of democracy that is significantly different than the subjective welfarist view, which locates the authority for public action purely in its relation to privately held preferences. He means to criticize an economic conception of government that sees justifiable public action as aimed at remediating market failure and "is dominated by a conception of welfare based on the satisfaction of existing preferences, as measured by willingness to pay; in politics and law, something called 'paternalism' is disfavored in both the public and private realms." A more serviceable democratic conception would recognize the central place of deliberation in promoting both individual autonomy and a richer conception of welfare.

Sunstein introduces some specific examples in which the case for public action aimed at affecting preferences appears intuitively to be more or less persuasive. These cases include addictive behavior, preferences that are formed in miserable social conditions, broadcasting of high-quality programs, and the like. That the case for intervention is persuasive in each of these cases seems to require that we adopt an understanding of the relationship between the preferences of citizens and democratic rule that can account for these intuitions. Second, he claims that a republican conception of government can explain why it is that public intervention in preference formation is justified in these cases and that a subjective welfarist conception cannot.

I begin by formulating two views that are characteristically suspicious of public intervention in the preferences of citizens. In the subjective welfarist view, individuals are supposed to be prefabricated independent moral entities who exist complete with well-formed preferences in some sense prior to and independently of society and the state. On the surface, in this case, state intervention in preference formation seems at best inefficacious and in any case of doubtful ethical status since the only source of authority in this view is individual agreement. I shall claim later on that, depending on how "preferences" are to be understood in this view, this (neoclassical or Hobbesian) theory need not generally resist state intervention in preference formation.

What I call the Burkean view holds that while individual preferences are formed in social, economic, and institutional settings and might be, therefore, subject to alteration as a result (deliberate or not) of governmental actions, it is hard both to know what these effects are and, even if the effects were known, to believe that political actors will generally either wish or be able to make appropriate choices.

The Burkean view does not take a foundational stand against political intervention in preference formation but, instead, is practically skeptical about such policies having good effects and is concerned about licensing a coercive agency in these circumstances. A conservative Burkean may argue that it is wrong for government to take actions aimed at altering preferences because government will tend as a matter of "fact" to get things wrong. But Burkeans are not committed to regard government with any greater suspicion than they do social or economic processes. In general, whether or not government intervention or nonintervention in preference formation is defensible depends on having a satisfactory theory that allows one to predict the likely results of such actions. In this sense the Burkean view hardly seems to provide a basis for rejecting government intervention in preference formation in favor of letting other processes work.

Sunstein gives a number of examples in which he believes that government intervention aimed at influencing preferences might be justified. These include cases of addiction, in which individuals come to have preferences based on their consumption histories and which they themselves might see as preferences that are somehow harmful to them; the distribution of wealth or opportunity, which Sunstein argues might affect the sorts of things that individuals come to want by unduly constraining their views of what is possible for them to do or want in their lives; and the allocation of cultural political information that, he suggests, would not be provided at sufficient levels in the private economy.

I cannot discuss each of these cases in detail, but both subjective welfarists and Burkeans could agree that, depending on how the argument actually went, there might be reasons in each case for public action aimed at influencing preferences. For the subjective welfarist, the crucial thing about Sunstein's examples is that they all seem to involve what we might call cognitive aspects of preferences: Addicts might behave as they do because they fail to foresee fully the consequences of their behavior. The poor might have self-limiting preferences because they fail to foresee what it is truly possible for them to have or to be. The public might choose mediocre television programming because it fails to grasp just how pleasurable culturally rarefied television can be. In each case, privately formed individual preferences are partly based on false beliefs. If only these beliefs could be corrected, individuals might be counted on to have and to act on appropriate preferences: preferences that would be better for their well-being as they see it.

In any of these cases, the subjective welfarist can understand public deliberation about the cognitive aspects of preferences and the public provision of information aimed at correcting misconceptions. Subjective welfarists in any of these cases could agree *ex ante* to public action based on expectations that they will, sometimes, be inadequately informed as to the consequences of their actions.

For the Burkean, the central problem in these examples is the hypothesis that the state can be counted on to correct the defective vision of its citizens. Without a plausible social theory explaining just why it is that we should expect governmental intervention to improve things, the Burkean would remain skeptical about public intervention in preference formation. But if such theory is available, the Burkean could agree to public action. To illustrate this argument in a concrete case, I shall consider Sunstein's example of the fairness doctrine. I claim, therefore, that the Burkean can understand and account for public deliberation about preferences; such deliberation would be over the social and political theories that could underpin and justify state action.

In summary, my argument is this. First, subjective welfarists are not generally committed to opposing governmental intervention in preference formation. Everything depends on how "preferences" are to be understood and what the effects of government action are. Government intervention in preference formation might very well be justifiable on either of the foundational pluralist theories. Subjective welfarists may choose to employ the coercive apparatus of the state to limit the availability of addictive substances or to provide information as a public good. Such choices would be aimed not at changing what I will call fundamental preferences but, instead, at changing the opportunity sets faced by individuals, or their beliefs, and therefore their "induced" preferences.

Sunstein's stronger claim is that it is best to see democratic practices and institutions as aimed at developing and fostering values of citizenship and participation and not merely as devices to aggregate previously formed preferences. He argues:

> The phenomenon of endogenous preferences casts doubt on the notion that a democratic government ought to respect private desires in all or almost all contexts. It bears on . . . the rationale for and extent of the constitutional protection accorded to speech; proportional representation and checks and balances; and the reasons for and limits of governmental regulation of the arts, broadcasting, and the environment.

I doubt that Burkeans would have much trouble understanding deliberative phenomena and their importance in government, but subjective welfarists seem, on the face of things, less able to account for the deliberative aspects of democratic practices. But, again, I suggest that the specific version of subjective welfarism that Sunstein considers is not the strongest version and the source of this weakness is a failure to specify adequately how preferences are to be understood. When an adequate (but still neoclassical) theory of preferences is introduced, at least some deliberative practices – those aimed at changing beliefs – can be fully accommodated.

II. Starting points: republicanism and pluralism

Sunstein enunciates two different views of the nature of human agents and government. On the classical or republican view, one envisions a coherent or singular conception of what would constitute the good or virtuous life, and government institutions are to be arranged in such a way as to facilitate and encourage the leading of good lives by its citizens. Generally speaking, this entails providing (institutional and cultural) conditions under which publicly oriented virtues will tend to take precedence over private consumption. Indeed the classical view recognizes private economic activity – production and consumption – as a principal and undesirable source of diversity. It encourages participation in a public life and deliberation aimed at providing individuals with ways to surmount such temptations.

The modern liberal conception, by contrast, recognizes the diversity of individual goals and preferences – the multiplicity of the good – as fundamental and chooses its institutions to protect a private sphere in which individuals may pursue their separate concepts of the good. Public intervention is to be limited in this case, not only because state action can be tyrannical but also and principally because there is no shared acceptance of public values to be encouraged. Public action in this model might best be seen as legal ratification of private bargains among contending groups, each seeking to improve the private lives of its members.

Sunstein argues that the framers drew from the republican conception as much as they did from the modern one and that they are best seen as republican liberals who valued political virtue and sought to design institutions to make a virtuous public life possible. Indeed, while he doesn't make the claim in this paper, I suspect that he would argue that the framers' attachment to liberal institutions was primarily practical. The protection of the private sphere is defended on grounds of political prudence – the avoidance of majority tyranny – and not on grounds of the intrinsic value of diverse conceptions of the good. In this sense, the attachment of the framers to republican values might be seen as more fundamental than their endorsement of liberal ones. Liberal institutions are "second best" solutions in an imperfect world.

The question I have is this: So what? I am willing to grant that the framers, like their classical predecessors, believed citizens would have diverse goals and that a principal source of preference diversity was the appetites, and that these can hardly be avoided in a nation engaged in commerce. Preference diversity might be seen, in this sense, as an endemic disease that we cannot hope to cure but whose effects or symptoms might be treated or controlled. Thus, when Madison talks of the evils of faction or of "putting ambition against ambition" by suitably arranging institutions, it seems to me that he is speaking as a practical physician hoping to make a chronically ill patient as comfortable as possible.

This is not our view of diversity. We don't think that the only source or even the main source of desirable diversity is material temptation, and we certainly don't believe that deep down we all agree on what a good way to live would be. I am not saying that we know what it is that produces diverse preferences, or even that we care. I think the question has really lost its pertinence. Even if everyone actually had identical preferences, we can easily imagine that other preferences might be just as defensible as the ones we currently hold. In any case, we wish to protect a large private sphere on the grounds that we value private flourishing directly and for its own sake and not only on the grounds that we are suspicious of government action.

This suggests that the framers' classical diagnosis of the situation of a small, geographically insulated republic in the eighteenth century might actually be irrelevant to a diagnosis of our situation today. But this doesn't mean that their institutional prescriptions aren't pertinent anyway. Liberal institutions do seem to be appropriate ways to preserve our rather more elaborated views of diversity, though maybe not exactly the institutions the framers defended. Indeed it's always good to remember that they weren't so enthusiastic about instituting "rights" in the Constitution in the first place.

III. Preferences

Thus, it seems to me that as preference diversity has become both inescapable and directly valued, the "place to stand" from which to recommend government intervention in preference formation has gotten smaller and shakier. There are some places left to be sure. I argue that subjective welfarists can defend collective intervention in preference formation in some circumstances if preferences are understood in an appropriate way.

One has to specify what it is that real preferences – the things subjective welfarists take as fixed – are defined on. Here the range of options is from such things as brand-labeled breakfast cereals all the way down to "primary goods." Clearly, unless we stop at the surface, there is plenty of room for maneuver. And within neoclassical theory there is ample theoretical precedent for regarding superficial preferences with some skepticism, and instead making a distinction between fundamental things over which genuine preferences are defined and constructed entities over which induced preferences are defined. Several considerations arise once this view is taken.

First, preferences over some entities embody beliefs about the world. One reason we might prefer one thing rather than another is that we believe thing one has better consequences than thing two. Change those beliefs, and preference between things one and two will also shift. There seems to be no problem here for subjective welfarists. Thus, in some circumstances the public provision of information that will bear on induced preferences in this sense might be rationally agreed to in a neoclassical society.

Second, among the constructed entities over which preferences might be defined are laws or coercive practices. My induced preference for charitable contributions ordinarily would depend on institutions or laws linking my contributions to those of others and so would everyone else's. Thus, I have induced preferences over alternative institutional arrangements that would be expected to induce different aggregate levels of contributions to worthy causes. But the actual content of my preferences over institutions depends not only on my beliefs about the way others would respond to institutions but also on who these others are. Preferences of this sort would surely be subject to deliberation and debate even in a subjective welfarist society.

Third, that humans are situated in time implies that preferences in many cases may evolve over time and sometimes this evolution may be anticipated. This produces the classical problems of dynamic choice in which an agent foresees that one effect of his current action is to induce a shift in his tastes. This is, of course, a common way to think about addiction, but similar issues arise in many other areas as well. Political and legal institutions might, in such cases, make it possible for individuals to employ commitment strategies that would otherwise be unavailable to permit themselves to undertake courses of action that would otherwise be unachievable. Again, neoclassical agents might rationally have induced preferences over coercive instruments.

In any of these cases we can understand deliberation and persuasion as aimed at influencing or changing induced rather than fundamental preferences by shifting beliefs as to the consequences of various courses of action or by changing the domain of alternatives under consideration. In either case, subjective welfarists could advocate public intervention in the formation of induced preferences, if only it was possible to believe that such intervention would be effective. We turn now to the two principal problems in this connection: information and control.

IV. Knowing and acting

The customary defense of consumer sovereignty is the presumption that individuals know better than others what they themselves really want or what is really in their best interest. If we wish to override this presumption, we need some reason to believe both that individuals are likely to be mistaken about what is best for them and that the government is less likely to be mistaken. I would think that the most plausible way to argue these claims is to suggest that individuals might, in some circumstances, confuse what they want with what is best for them and that government is not subject to such confusions. Obviously, these arguments need a theory that permits the differentiation of individuals' wants with what is best for them. I don't have such a theory, and I must say I'm skeptical about the availability of such a theory in most cases.

In any case, arguments of this sort do seem common in instances of addiction and seem to be present as well in arguments for public broadcasting of cultural and political information. It is doubtful that such claims have much scope, however, and even in these cases, such arguments are controversial. Is it actually true, for example, that people become addicted to drugs or alcohol because they cannot foresee the consequences of their behaviour, or that people underfund cultural programming because they cannot envision the pleasures of watching opera on television? It is easy to see that public policy based on the theory that individuals are systematically unable to evaluate the consequences of their actions can be both dangerous and welfare decreasing.

In the interest of advancing the argument, however, I shall simply accept the hypothesis that there are areas in which these tests are both met. But even in such instances it's not clear that government intervention would be a good thing. Even if people would be better off with public intervention, and even if public officials knew perfectly well how to intervene to achieve this end, we must still ask whether we could count on them actually to do so.

V. The problem of political control

We come back now to Burkean theory: the theory that based its skepticism about government action on doubts that government officials would be likely to intervene in an efficacious manner. This problem was as real to the framers as it is to many of those currently concerned with constitutional issues. A problem with constituting public authority is that officials (as officials) have their own interests, which are generally distinct from those of the governed. Thus, central to democratic government is the problem of the control of officials. Sometimes this problem is identified with the problem of agency – how is it that as private citizens we can get specialists (doctors, mechanics) to do what we wish them to do, when we do not have access to the information they have? But the problem is more difficult in political life because "we" are not of one mind about what we want government officials to do.

A simple way to see the issue is this: Suppose there is an official who is delegated the authority to take an action on behalf of a democratic polity and that he holds office at the sufferance of a majority of the citizens. Assume also that the issue has a distributional component so that in addition to whatever other aspects it has, the official can shift the incidence of benefits and costs across citizens (including himself). Thus, the incumbent official is faced with the problem of enacting a policy sufficiently favorable to a majority that he will be reelected. The problem faced by citizens is how to decide when a policy is sufficiently favorable to warrant voting to return the incumbent.

Suppose that citizens use the following principle: Set a "reservation" utility level and vote for the incumbent just in case he gives you at least that much utility. What system of reservation utilities may be sustained as an equilibrium? Assuming that the incumbent has some claim on residual resources, for any such system of reservation utilities, an incumbent will find it rational to satisfy those of a bare majority. But that means that if some individual is not in that bare majority, she has an incentive to lower her reservation utility in order to bid her way in. But this is true for any set of reservation utilities above the minimum attainable utility levels. Thus, the only sustainable set of reservation utilities are the minimal ones and the incumbent is ensured of reelection no matter what policy is followed. In this sense, in any democratic system, incumbents have both the opportunity and the incentive to take advantage of competition among citizens to become essentially uncontrollable.

Now, I'm not saying there's no way out of this problem for a democratic citizenry. I introduce it only to underscore the problem of control of officials and to emphasize that insofar as problems of control are unresolved, there is reason to be skeptical about the efficacy and purpose of public intervention in preference formation. Justifying such intervention seems to require, minimally, a positive theory of government that affords reason to believe that the result of public intervention is likely to be better than available alternatives.

I don't suggest there are no strong reasons also to be skeptical about decentralized or market choices in many contexts, and I believe we need positive theories of private as well as public ordering. The decision as to what sorts of institutions are best rests (at minimum) on a comparative evaluation of what these different institutions would do in settings that are likely to arise. Specifically in the case of preference formation, I think Sunstein is right to claim there ought to be no general prohibition on public intervention in preferences. The reasons against undertaking such actions turn on a specific comparison of consequences of public action and inaction. Frequently, a reason to avoid governmental action will turn out to be that such action entails a high level of public monitoring of private lives and of relationships of command and hierarchy that risk the violation of other values. Sometimes this is acceptable to us; sometimes it isn't. To illustrate this claim I turn to the case of the fairness doctrine.

VI. An example: the fairness doctrine

Sunstein argues that "there is a firm theoretical justification for the much criticized, and now largely abandoned, 'fairness doctrine,' which required broadcasters to cover controversial issues and to ensure competing views." I am not sure just how firm this theoretical basis is. Let me grant the point that competing information on public issues is probably underprovided, but I must also ask whether there is reason to believe that the fairness doctrine would have the effect of increasing the level of information provision.

The fairness doctrine worked by requiring two things: that broadcasters air controversial topics and that they provide time for competing views. In practice this policy requires that someone determine what a controversial issue is and what a genuinely competing view would be. Obviously, given the announced policy, broadcasters will wish to minimize their airing of political views altogether because after airing any one point of view, they will be required to air others as well for free. Moreover, they also have incentives to shape the definitions of controversiality and of "competing" views in order to limit their obligation to provide free airtime.

Clearly, then, the conduct of this policy requires some kind of monitoring and regulatory apparatus to combat these tendencies, and whether or not the imposition of the fairness doctrine leads either to more coverage of politics or to more genuine political discussion depends wholly on how this regulatory regime actually works. I don't claim to know how it did or would in the future, and I suggest, instead, that the answers to this question are neither obvious nor available a priori.

VII. Conclusion

Both subjective welfarists and Burkeans can sometimes recommend public intervention in preference formation, and therefore there are versions of their theories that can make sense of the deliberative aspects of democratic practices. I don't believe the argument for governmental intervention in preference formation, as opposed to some version of liberal neutrality with respect to preferences, is likely to be settled by noting the importance of deliberative aspects of democracy or by pointing to instances in which individual preferences seem not to deserve respect.

The argument for or against intervention in preference formation must be made on some other terrain. There seem to be two alternative grounds for this discussion: foundational and practical. A foundational argument for state intervention in preferences would have to endorse a conception of human nature and capacity that emphasizes both our fundamental similarities and our ability to learn from one another in democratically conducted public discourse about what a good life would be. The public or the state might be justified in intervening in private lives if the purpose of such intervention was aimed at enhancing our chances to live good lives whether the affected individuals would agree or not.

A foundational argument for liberal neutrality with respect to preferences, by contrast, would emphasize ways in which humans are or can be fundamentally different from one another and would point to the centrality of maintaining a private moral sphere in which diverse concepts of the good can be pursued. In any case, such a view would deny to both the public and the state any morally separate stance from which to intervene in genuinely private conceptions of good lives. But liberal neutrality is not committed to arguing that public action in providing information, or the coercive services of the state, would always be unjustified. We have been arguing these foundational views for more than two hundred years and I suspect we are not much closer to resolution now than we were at the beginning. Indeed, as I suggested earlier, I think we are farther away.

It seems more likely that progress can be made at the practical level – the level at which I believe the framers largely focused and the level at which we as citizens must operate. Here the argument is between those who emphasize the risks of the practices of liberal neutrality – its permissive public and private morality and its lack of a conception of a shared public life – and those who point to the risks of a republican conception, with its broader endorsement of state authority and of the concomitant possibilities of either official or majoritarian tyranny. In a world that is becoming increasingly diverse and in which the instruments of state power are steadily growing, there is little doubt in my mind as to what the appropriate practical stance would be.

Part III

Democracy and public reason

6

The domain of the political and overlapping consensus

JOHN RAWLS

Introduction

In this article, I shall examine the idea of an overlapping consensus[1] and its role in a political conception of justice for a constitutional regime. A political conception, I shall suppose, views the political as a special domain with distinctive features that call for the articulation within the conception of the characteristic values that apply to that domain. Justice as fairness, the conception presented in my book *A Theory of Justice* [*Theory*][2] is an example of a political conception and I refer to it to fix ideas. By going over these matters I hope to allay misgivings about the idea of an overlapping consensus, especially the misgiving that it makes political philosophy political in the wrong way.[3] That is, this idea may suggest to some the view that consensus politics is to be taken as regulative and that the content of first principles of justice should be adjusted to the claims of the dominant political and social interests.

This misgiving may have resulted from my having used the idea of an overlapping consensus without distinguishing between two stages in the exposition of justice as fairness and without stressing that the idea of an overlapping consensus is used only in the second. To explain: in the first stage justice as fairness should be presented as a free-standing political conception that articulates the very great values applicable to the special domain of the political, as marked out by the basic structure of society. The second stage consists of an account of the stability of justice as fairness, that is, its capacity to generate its own support,[4] in view of the content of its principles and ideals as formulated in the first stage. In this second stage the idea of an overlapping consensus is introduced to explain how, given the plurality of conflicting comprehensive religious, philosophical, and moral doctrines always found in a democratic society

An earlier version of this article was the John Dewey Lecture in Jurisprudence, given at New York University School of Law, November 15, 1988. The present version is reprinted from 64 *N.Y.U. L. Rev.* 2 (May 1989), pp. 233–55, with permission.

– the kind of society that justice as fairness itself enjoins – free institutions may gain the allegiance needed to endure over time.

I. Four general facts

I begin with some background. Any political conception of justice presupposes a view of the political and social world, and recognizes certain general facts of political sociology and human psychology. Four general facts are especially important.

The first fact is that the diversity of comprehensive religious, philosophical, and moral doctrines found in modern democratic societies is not a mere historical condition that may soon pass away; it is a permanent feature of the public culture of democracy. Under the political and social conditions that the basic rights and liberties of free institutions secure, a diversity of conflicting and irreconcilable comprehensive doctrines will emerge, if such diversity does not already exist. Moreover, it will persist and may increase. The fact about free institutions is the fact of pluralism.

A second and related general fact is that only the oppressive use of state power can maintain a continuing common affirmation of one comprehensive religious, philosophical, or moral doctrine. If we think of political society as a community when it is united in affirming one and the same comprehensive doctrine, then the oppressive use of state power is necessary to maintain a political community. In the society of the Middle Ages, more or less united in affirming the Catholic faith, the Inquisition was not an accident; preservation of a shared religious belief demanded the suppression of heresy. The same holds, I believe, for any comprehensive philosophical and moral doctrine, even for secular ones. A society united on a form of utilitarianism, or on the liberalism of Kant or Mill, would likewise require the sanctions of state power to remain so.

A third general fact is that an enduring and secure democratic regime, one not divided into contending doctrinal confessions and hostile social classes, must be willingly and freely supported by at least a substantial majority of its politically active citizens. Together with the first general fact, this means that for a conception of justice to serve as the public basis of justification for a constitutional regime, it must be one that widely different and even irreconcilable comprehensive doctrines can endorse. Otherwise the regime will not be enduring and secure. As we shall see later, this suggests the need for what I have referred to as a political conception of justice.[5]

A fourth fact is that the political culture of a reasonably stable democratic society normally contains, at least implicitly, certain fundamental intuitive ideas from which it is possible to work up a political conception of justice suitable for a constitutional regime. This fact is important when we come to specify the general features of a political conception of justice and to elaborate justice as fairness as such a view.

II. The burdens of reason

These facts, especially the first two – namely, the fact that a diversity of comprehensive doctrines is a permanent feature of a society with free institutions, and that this diversity can be overcome only by the oppressive use of state power – call for explanation. For why should free institutions with their basic rights and liberties lead to diversity, and why should state power be required to suppress it? Why does our sincere and conscientious attempt to reason with one another fail to lead us to agreement? It seems to lead to agreement in science, or if disagreement in social theory and economics often seems intractable, at least   in the long run – in natural science.

There are, of course, several possible explanations. We might suppose that most people hold views that advance their own more narrow interests; and since their interests are different, so are their views. Or perhaps people are often irrational and not very bright, and this mixed with logical errors leads to conflicting opinions.

But such explanations are too easy, and not the kind we want. We want to know how reasonable disagreement is possible, for we always work at first within ideal theory. Thus we ask: how might reasonable disagreement come about?

One explanation is this. We say that reasonable disagreement is disagreement between reasonable persons, that is, between persons who have realized their two moral powers[6] to a degree sufficient to be free and equal citizens in a democratic regime, and who have an enduring desire to be fully cooperating members of society over a complete life. We assume such persons share a common human reason, similar powers of thought and judgment, a capacity to draw inferences and to weigh evidence and to balance competing considerations, and the like.

Now the idea of reasonable disagreement involves an account of the sources, or causes, of disagreement between reasonable persons. These sources I shall refer to as the "burdens of reason." The account of these burdens must be such that it is fully compatible with, and so does not impugn, the reasonableness of those who disagree among themselves.

What, then, goes wrong? If we say it is the presence of prejudice and bias, of self- and group-interest, of blindness and willfulness – not to mention irrationality and stupidity (often main causes of the decline and fall of nations) – we impugn the reasonableness of at least some of those who disagree. We must discover another explanation.

An explanation of the right kind is that the burdens of reason, the sources of reasonable disagreement among reasonable persons, are the many hazards involved in the correct (and conscientious) exercise of our powers of reason and judgment in the ordinary course of political life. Except for the last two sources below, the ones I mention now are not peculiar to reasoning about values; nor is the list I give complete. It covers only the more obvious sources of reasonable disagreement:

(a) The evidence – empirical and scientific – bearing on the case may be conflicting and complex, and hence hard to assess and evaluate.

(b) Even where we agree fully about the kinds of considerations that are relevant, we may disagree about their weight, and so arrive at different judgments.

(c) To some extent all of our concepts, not only our moral and political concepts, are vague and subject to hard cases; this indeterminacy means that we must rely on judgment and interpretation (and on judgments about interpretations) within some range (not itself sharply specificable) wherein reasonable persons may differ.

(d) To some unknown extent, our total experience, our whole course of life up to now, shapes the way we assess evidence and weigh moral and political values, and our total experiences surely differ. Thus, in a modern society with its numerous offices and positions, its various divisions of labor, its many social groups and often their ethnic variety, the total experiences of citizens are disparate enough for their judgments to diverge, at least to some degree, on many if not most cases of any significant complexity.

(e) Often there are different kinds of normative considerations of different force on both sides of a question and it is difficult to make an overall assessment.[7]

(f) Finally, since any system of social institutions can admit only a limited range of values, some selection must be made from the full range of moral and political values that might be realized. This is because any system of institutions has, as it were, but a limited social space. In being forced to select among cherished values, we face great difficulties in setting priorities, and other hard decisions that may seem to have no clear answer.[8]

These are some sources of the difficulties in arriving at agreement in judgment, sources that are compatible with the full reasonableness of those judging. In noting these sources – these burdens of reason – we do not, of course, deny that prejudice and bias, self- and group-interest, blindness and willfulness, play an all-too-familiar part in political life. But these sources of unreasonable disagreement stand in marked contrast to sources of disagreement compatible with everyone's being fully reasonable.

I conclude by stating a fifth general fact: we make many of our most important judgments subject to conditions which render it extremely unlikely that conscientious and fully reasonable persons, even after free discussion, can exercise their powers of reason so that all arrive at the same conclusion.

III. Precepts of reasonable discussion

Next I consider how, if we are reasonable, we should conduct ourselves in view of the plain facts about the burdens of reason. I suppose that, as reasonable persons, we are fully aware of these burdens, and try to take them into account. On this basis we recognize certain precepts to govern deliberation and discussion. A few of these follow.

First, the political discussion aims to reach reasonable agreement, and hence so far as possible it should be conducted to serve that aim. We should not readily accuse one another of self- or group-interest, prejudice or bias, and of such deeply entrenched errors as ideological blindness and delusion. Such accusations arouse resentment and hostility, and block the way to reasonable agreement. The disposition to make such accusations without compelling grounds is plainly unreasonable, and often a declaration of intellectual war.

Second, when we are reasonable we are prepared to find substantive and even intractable disagreements on basic questions. The first general fact means that the basic institutions and public culture of a democratic society specify a social world within which opposing general beliefs and conflicting comprehensive doctrines are likely to flourish and may increase in number. It is unreasonable, then, not to recognize the likelihood – indeed the practical certainty – of irreconcilable reasonable disagreements on matters of the first significance. Even when it seems that agreement should in principle be possible, it may be unattainable in the present case, at least in the foreseeable future.[9]

Third, when we are reasonable, we are ready to enter discussion crediting others with a certain good faith. We expect deep differences of opinion, and accept this diversity as the normal state of the public culture of a democratic society. To hate that fact is to hate human nature, for it is to hate the many not unreasonable expressions of human nature that develop under free institutions.[10]

I have suggested that the burdens of reason sufficiently explain the first two general facts – the facts of pluralism, given free institutions, and the necessity of the oppressive use of state power to maintain a political community (a political society united on a comprehensive doctrine) – whatever further causes those facts might have. Those facts are not, then, mere historical contingencies. Rather, they are rooted in the difficulties of exercising our reason under the normal conditions of human life.

IV. Features of a political conception of justice

Recall that the third general fact was that an enduring and stable democratic regime is one that at least a substantial majority of its politically active citizens freely support. Given this fact, what are the more general features of a political doctrine underlying a regime able to gain such allegiance? Plainly, it must be a doctrine that a diversity of comprehensive religious, philosophical, and moral doctrines can endorse, each from its own point of view.[11] This follows not only from the third general fact but also from the first, the fact of pluralism: for a democratic regime will eventually, if not from the outset, lead to a pluralism of comprehensive doctrines.

Let us say that a political conception of justice (in contrast to a political regime) is stable if it meets the following condition: those who grow up in a society well-ordered by it – a society whose institutions are publicly recognized to be just, as specified by that conception itself – develop a sufficient allegiance to those institutions, that is, a sufficiently strong sense of justice guided by appropriate principles and ideals, so that they normally act as justice requires, provided they are assured that others will act likewise.[12]

Now what more general features of a political conception of justice does this definition of stability suggest? The idea of a political conception of justice includes three such features:[13]

First, while a political conception of justice is, of course, a moral conception, it is worked out for a specific subject, namely, the basic structure of a constitutional democratic regime. This structure consists in society's main political, social, and economic institutions, and how they fit together into one unified system of social cooperation.

Second, accepting a political conception of justice does not presuppose accepting any particular comprehensive doctrine. The conception presents itself as a reasonable conception for the basic structure alone.[14]

Third, a political conception of justice is formulated so far as possible solely in terms of certain fundamental intuitive ideas viewed as implicit in the public political culture of a democratic society. Two examples are the idea of society as a fair system of social cooperation over time from one generation to the next, and the idea of citizens as free and equal persons fully capable of engaging in social cooperation over a complete life. (That there are such ideas is the fourth general fact.) Such ideas of society and citizen are normative and political ideas; they belong to a normative political conception, and not to metaphysics or psychology.[15]

Thus the distinction between political conceptions of justice and other moral conceptions is a matter of scope, that is, of the range of subjects to which a conception applies, and of the wider content which a wider range requires. A conception is said to be general when it applies to a wide range of subjects (in the limit, to all subjects); it is comprehensive when it includes conceptions of what is of value in human life, ideals of personal virtue and character, and the like, that inform much of our nonpolitical conduct (in the limit, our life as a whole).

Religious and philosophical conceptions tend to be general and fully comprehensive; indeed, their being so is sometimes regarded as a philosophical ideal to be attained. A doctrine is fully comprehensive when it covers all recognized values and virtues within one rather precisely articulated scheme of thought; whereas a doctrine is partially comprehensive when it comprises certain, but not all, nonpolitical values and virtues and is rather loosely articulated. By definition, then, for a conception to be even partially comprehensive it must extend beyond the political and include nonpolitical values and virtues.

Keeping these points in mind, political liberalism tries to articulate a workable political conception of justice. The conception consists in a view of politics and of the kind of political institutions which would be most just and appropriate when we take into account the five general facts. From these facts rises the need to found social unity on a political conception that can gain the support of a diversity of comprehensive doctrines. Political liberalism is not, then, a view of the whole of life: it is not a (fully or partially) comprehensive doctrine.

Of course, as a liberalism, it has the kind of content we historically associate with liberalism. It affirms certain basic political and civil rights and liberties, assigns them a certain priority, and so on. Justice as fairness begins with the fundamental intuitive idea of a well-ordered society as a fair system of cooperation between citizens regarded as free and equal. This idea together with the five general facts shows the need for a political conception of justice, and such a conception in turn leads to the idea of "constitutional essentials," as we may refer to them.

A specification of the basic rights and liberties of citizens – rights and liberties they are to have in their status as free and equal – falls under those essentials. For such rights and liberties concern the fundamental principles that determine the structure of the political process – the powers of the legislative, executive and the judiciary, the limits and scope of majority rule, as well as the basic political and civil rights and liberties legislative majorities must respect, such as the right to vote and to participate in politics, freedom of thought and liberty of conscience, and also the protections of the rule of law.

These matters are a long story; I merely mention them here. The point is that a political understanding of the constitutional essentials is of utmost urgency in securing a workable basis of fair political and social cooperation between citizens viewed as free and equal. If a political conception of justice provides a reasonable framework of principles and values for resolving questions concerning these essentials – and this must be its minimum objective – then a diversity of comprehensive doctrines may endorse it. In this case a political conception of justice is already of great significance, even though it may have little specific to say about innumerable economic and social issues that legislative bodies must regularly consider.

V. The special domain of the political

The three features of a political conception[16] make clear that justice as fairness is not applied moral philosophy. That is, its content – its principles, standards, and values – is not presented as an application of an already elaborated moral doctrine, comprehensive in scope and general in range. Rather, it is a formulation of a family of highly significant (moral) values that properly apply to basic political institutions; it gives a specification of those values which takes account of certain special features of the political relationship, as distinct from other relationships.

The political relationship has at least two significant features:

First, it is a relationship of persons within the basic structure of society, a structure of basic institutions we enter only by birth and exit only by death (or so we may appropriately assume).[17] Political society is closed, as it were; and we do not, and indeed cannot, enter or leave it voluntarily.

Second, the political power exercised within the political relationship is always coercive power backed by the state's machinery for enforcing its laws. In a constitutional regime political power is also the power of equal citizens as a collective body. It is regularly imposed on citizens as individuals, some of whom may not accept the reasons widely thought to justify the general structure of political authority (the constitution), some of whom accept that structure, but do not regard as well grounded many of the statutes and other laws to which they are subject.

Political liberalism holds, then, that there is a special domain of the political identified by at least these features. So understood, the political is distinct from the associational, which is voluntary in ways that the political is not; it is also distinct from the personal and the familial, which are affectional domains, again in ways the political is not.[18]

Taking the political as a special domain, let us say that a political conception formulating its basic values is a "free-standing" view. It is a view for the basic structure that formulates its values independent of non-political values and of any specific relationship to them. Thus a political conception does not deny that there are other values that apply to the associational, the personal, and the familial; nor does it say that the political is entirely separate from those values. But our aim is to specify the special domain of the political in such a way that its main institutions can gain the support of an overlapping consensus.

As a form of political liberalism, then, justice as fairness holds that, with regard to the constitutional essentials, and given the existence of a reasonably well-ordered constitutional regime, the family of very great political values expressed by its principles and ideals normally will have sufficient weight to override all other values that may come into conflict with them. Justice as fairness also holds, again with respect to constitutional essentials, that so far as possible, questions about those essentials should be settled by appeal to those political values alone. For it is on those questions that agreement among citizens who affirm opposing comprehensive doctrines is most urgent.

Now, in holding these convictions we clearly imply some relation between political and non-political values. Thus, if it is said that outside the church there is no salvation,[19] and that hence a constitutional regime, with its guarantees of freedom of religion, cannot be accepted unless it is unavoidable, we must make some reply. From the point of view of political liberalism, the appropriate reply is to say that the conclusion is unreasonable:[20] it proposes to use the public's political power – a power in which citizens have an equal share – to enforce a view affecting constitutional essentials about which citizens as reasonable persons, given the burdens of reason, are bound to differ uncompromisingly in judgment.

It is important to stress that this reply does not say that a doctrine *Extra ecclesiam nulla salus* is not true. Rather, it says that it is unreasonable to use the public's political power to enforce it. A reply from within an alternative comprehensive view – the kind of reply we should like to avoid in political discussion – would say that the doctrine in question is incorrect and rests on a misapprehension of the divine nature. If we do reject the enforcement by the state of a doctrine as unreasonable we may of course also regard that doctrine itself as untrue. And there may be no way entirely to avoid implying its lack of truth, even when considering constitutional essentials.[21]

Note, however, that in saying it is unreasonable to enforce a doctrine, we do not necessarily reject it as incorrect, though we may do so. Indeed, it is vital to the idea of political liberalism that we may with perfect consistency hold that it would be unreasonable to use political power to enforce our own comprehensive religious, philosophical or moral views – views which we must, of course, affirm as true or reasonable (or at least as not unreasonable).

VI. How is political liberalism possible?

The question now arises, how, as I have characterized it, is political liberalism possible? That is, how can the values of the special domain of the political – the values of a sub-domain of the realm of all values – normally outweigh any values that may conflict with them? Or put another way: how can we affirm our comprehensive doctrines as true or reasonable and yet hold that it would not be reasonable to use the state's power to gain the allegiance of others to them?[22]

The answer to this question has two complementary parts. The first part says that values of the political are very great values indeed and hence not easily overridden. These values govern the basic framework of social life, "the very groundwork of our existence,"[23] and specify the fundamental terms of political and social cooperation. In justice as fairness some of these great values are expressed by the principles of justice for the basic structure: the values of equal political and civil liberty, of fair equality of opportunity, of economic reciprocity, the social bases of mutual respect among citizens, and so on.

Other great values fall under the idea of free public reason, and are expressed in the guidelines for public inquiry and in the steps taken to secure that such inquiry is free and public, as well as informed and reasonable. These values include not only the appropriate use of the fundamental concepts of judgment, inference, and evidence, but also the virtues of reasonableness and fair-mindedness as shown in the adherence to the criteria and procedures of common sense knowledge, and to the methods and conclusion of science when not controversial, as well as respect for the precepts governing reasonable political discussion.[24]

Together these values give expression to the liberal political ideal that since political power is the coercive power of free and equal citizens as a corporate body, this power should be exercised, when constitutional essentials are at stake, only in ways that all citizens can reasonably be expected to endorse publicly in the light of their own common, human reason.[25]

So far as possible, political liberalism tries to present a free-standing account of these values as those of a special domain – the political. It is left to citizens individually, as part of their liberty of conscience, to settle how they think the great values of the political domain relate to other values within their comprehensive doctrine. We hope that by doing this we can, in working political practice, firmly ground the constitutional essentials in those political values alone, and that these values will provide a satisfactory shared basis of public justification.

The second part of the answer as to how political liberalism is possible complements the first. This part says that the history of religion and philosophy shows that there are many reasonable ways in which the wider realm of values can be understood so as to be either congruent with, or supportive of, or else not in conflict with, the values appropriate to the special domain of the political as specified by a political conception of justice for a democratic regime. History tells of a plurality of not unreasonable comprehensive doctrines. That these comprehensive doctrines are divergent makes an overlapping consensus necessary. That they are not unreasonable makes it possible. A model case of an overlapping consensus of the kind I have considered elsewhere shows how this is so.[26] Many other such cases could make the same point.

VII. The question of stability

Justice as fairness, as I have said, is best presented in two stages.[27] In the first stage it is worked out as a free-standing political (but of course moral) conception for the basic structure of society. Only when this is done and its content – its principles of justice and ideals – is provisionally on hand do we take up, in the second stage, the problem of stability and introduce the idea of an overlapping consensus: a consensus in which a diversity of conflicting comprehensive doctrines endorse the same political conception, in this case, justice as fairness.

In describing the second stage, let us agree that a political conception must be practicable, that is, must fall under the art of the possible. This contrasts with a moral conception that is not political; a moral conception may condemn the world and human nature as too corrupt to be moved by its precepts and ideals.

There are, however, two ways in which a political conception may be concerned with stability.[28] In one way, we suppose that stability is a purely practical matter: if a conception fails to be stable, it is futile to try to base a political structure upon it. Perhaps we think there are two separate tasks: one is to work out a political conception that seems sound, or reasonable, at least to us; the other is to find ways to bring others who reject the conception to share it in due course, or failing that, to act in accordance with it, prompted if need be by penalties enforced by state power. As long as the means of persuasion or enforcement can be found, the conception is viewed as stable; it is not utopian in the pejorative sense.

But as a liberal conception, justice as fairness is concerned with stability in a second, very different way. Finding a stable conception is not simply a matter of avoiding futility. Rather, what counts is the kind of stability and the nature of the forces that secure it. The idea is that, given certain assumptions specifying a reasonable human psychology[29] and the normal conditions of human life, those who grow up under basic institutions that are just – institutions that justice as fairness itself enjoins – acquire a reasoned and informed allegiance to those institutions sufficient to render the institutions stable. Put another way, the sense of justice of citizens, in view of their traits of character and interests as formed by living under a just basic structure, is strong enough to resist the normal tendencies to injustice. Citizens act willingly so as to give one another justice over time. Stability is secured by sufficient motivation of the appropriate kind acquired under just institutions.[30]

The kind of stability required of justice as fairness is based, then, on its being a liberal political view, one that aims at being acceptable to citizens as reasonable and rational, as well as free and equal, and so addressed to their free public reason. Earlier we saw how this feature of liberalism connects with the feature of political power in a constitutional regime, namely, that it is the power of equal citizens as a collective body. It follows that if justice as fairness were not expressly designed to gain the reasoned support of citizens who affirm reasonable although conflicting comprehensive doctrines – the existence of such conflicting doctrines being a feature of the kind of public culture which that conception itself encourages – it would not be liberal.[31]

The point, then, is that, as a liberal conception, justice as fairness must not merely avoid futility; the explanation of why it is practicable must be of a special kind. The problem of stability is not the problem of bringing others who reject a conception to share it, or to act in accordance with it, by workable sanctions if necessary – as if the task were to find ways to impose that conception on others once we are ourselves convinced it is sound. Rather, as a liberal political conception, justice as fairness relies for its reasonableness in the first place upon generating its own support in a suitable way by addressing each citizen's reason, as explained within its own framework.[32]

Only in this manner is justice as fairness an account of political legitimacy. Only so does it escape being a mere account of how those who hold political power can satisfy themselves, in the light of their own convictions, whether political or fully comprehensive, that they are acting properly – satisfy themselves, that is, and not citizens generally.[33] A conception of political legitimacy aims for a public basis of justification and appeals to free public reason, and hence to all citizens viewed as reasonable and rational.

VIII. Comparison with *A Theory of Justice*

It may seem that the idea of an overlapping consensus and related topics are a significant departure from Theory. They are some departure certainly; but how much? Theory never discusses whether justice as fairness is meant as a comprehensive moral doctrine or as a political conception of justice. In one place it says that if justice as fairness succeeds reasonably well, a next step would be to study the more general view suggested by the name "rightness as fairness."[34]

But Theory holds that even this view would not be fully comprehensive: it would not cover, for example, our relations to other living things and to the natural order itself.[35] Theory emphasizes the limited scope of justice as fairness, and the limited scope of the kind of view it exemplifies; the book leaves open the question of how far its conclusions might need revision once these other matters are taken into account. There is, however, no mention of the distinction between a political conception of justice and a comprehensive doctrine. The reader might reasonably conclude, then, that justice as fairness is set out as part of a comprehensive view that may be developed later were success to invite.

This conclusion is supported by the discussion of the well-ordered society of justice as fairness in Part III of Theory.[36] There it is assumed that the members of any well-ordered society, whether it be a society of justice as fairness or of some other view, accept the same conception of justice and also, it seems, the same comprehensive doctrine of which that conception is a part, or from which it can be derived. Thus, for example, all the members of a well-ordered society associated with utilitarianism (classical or average), are assumed to affirm the utilitarian view, which is by its nature (unless expressly restricted) a comprehensive doctrine.

Although the term was introduced in another context,[37] the idea of an overlapping consensus was first introduced to think of the well-ordered society of justice as fairness in a different and more realistic way.[38] Given the free institutions which that conception itself enjoins, we can no longer assume that citizens generally, even if they accept justice as fairness, also accept the particular comprehensive view in which it might seem to be embedded in Theory. We now assume citizens hold two distinct views; or perhaps better, we assume their overall view has two parts. One part can be seen to be, or to coincide with, a political conception of justice; the other part is a (fully or partially) comprehensive doctrine to which the political conception is in some manner related.[39]

The political conception may be simply a part of, or an adjunct to, a partially comprehensive view; or it may be endorsed because it can be derived within a fully articulated comprehensive doctrine. It is left to citizens individually to decide for themselves in what way their shared political conception is related to their wider and more comprehensive views. A society is well-ordered by justice as fairness so long as, first, citizens who affirm reasonable comprehensive doctrines generally endorse justice as fairness as giving the content of their political judgments; and second, unreasonable comprehensive doctrines do not gain enough currency to compromise the essential justice of basic institutions.

This is a better and no longer utopian way of thinking of the well-ordered society of justice as fairness. It corrects the view in Theory, which fails to take into account the condition of pluralism to which its own principles lead.

Moreover, because justice as fairness is now seen as a free-standing political conception that articulates fundamental political and constitutional values, endorsing it involves far less than is contained in a comprehensive doctrine. Taking such a well-ordered society as the aim of reform and change does not seem altogether impracticable; under the reasonably favorable conditions that make a constitutional regime possible, that aim is a reasonable guide and may be in good part realized. By contrast, a free democratic society well ordered by any comprehensive doctrine, religious or secular, is surely utopian in a pejorative sense. Achieving it would, in any case, require the oppressive use of state power. This is as true of the liberalism of rightness as fairness, as it is of the Christianity of Aquinas or Luther.

IX. In what sense political?

To trace our steps, I put before you this brief summary.[40] I have suggested that once we recognize the five general facts[41] and the inevitable burdens of reason even under favorable conditions,[42] and once we reject the oppressive use of state power to impose a single comprehensive doctrine as the way to achieve social unity, then we are led to democratic principles and must accept the fact of pluralism as a permanent feature of political life. Hence, to achieve social unity for a well-ordered democratic regime, what I have called political liberalism introduces the idea of an overlapping consensus and along with it the further idea of the political as a special domain. Political liberalism does this not only because its content includes the basic rights and liberties the securing of which leads to pluralism, but also because of the liberal ideal of political legitimacy, namely, that social cooperation, at least as it concerns the constitutional essentials, is to be conducted so far as possible on terms both intelligible and acceptable to all citizens as reasonable and rational. Those terms are best stated by reference to the fundamental political and constitutional values (expressed by a political conception of justice) that, given the diversity of comprehensive doctrines, all citizens may still be reasonably expected to endorse.

We must, however, be careful that a political conception is not political in the wrong way. It should aim to formulate a coherent view of the very great (moral) values applying to the political relationship and to set out a public basis of justification for free institutions in a manner accessible to free public reason. It must not be political in the sense of merely specifying a workable compromise between known and existing interests, nor political in looking to the particular comprehensive doctrines known to exist in society and in then being tailored to gain their allegiance.

In this connection let us ensure that the assumptions about pluralism do not make justice as fairness political in the wrong way. Consider first the five general facts reviewed in Parts I and II. These we suppose are accepted from the point of view of you and me as we try to develop justice as fairness. When the original position is viewed as a device of representation, these facts are made available to the parties in that position as they decide which principles of justice to select. So if principles that require free democratic institutions are accepted in the first stage, then the account of the stability in the second stage must show how justice as fairness can be endorsed by an overlapping consensus. As we have seen, this follows because free institutions themselves lead to pluralism.

The crucial question, then, is whether the five general facts, along with other premises allowed by the constraints of the original position in the first stage, suffice to lead the parties to select the two principles of justice;[43] or whether certain further assumptions related to pluralism are also needed, assumptions that make justice as fairness political in the wrong way. I cannot settle this matter here; it would require a survey of the argument from the original position.

I believe we need only suppose in the first stage that the parties assume the fact of pluralism to obtain, that is, that a plurality of comprehensive doctrines exists in society.[44] The parties must then protect against the possibility that the person each party represents may be a member of a religious, ethnic, or other minority. This suffices for the argument for the equal basic liberties to get going. In the second stage, when stability is considered, the parties again assume that pluralism obtains. They confirm principles leading to a social world that allows free play to human nature and thus, we hope, encourages a diversity of reasonable rather than unreasonable comprehensive doctrines, given the burdens of reason.[45] This makes stability possible.

Now it is often said that the politician looks to the next election, the statesman to the next generation. To this we add that the student of philosophy looks to the standing conditions of human life, and how these affect the burdens of reason. Political philosophy must take into account the five general facts we noted, among them the fact that free institutions encourage a diversity of comprehensive doctrines. But in doing this we abstract from the particular content of these doctrines, whatever it may be, and from the many contingencies under which the doctrines exist. A political conception so arrived at is not political in the wrong way but suitably adapted to the public political culture that its own principles shape and sustain. And although such a conception may not apply to all societies at all times and places, this does not make it historicist, or relativist; rather, it is universal in virtue of its extending appropriately to specify a reasonable conception of justice among all nations.[46]

X. Concluding remarks

The foregoing shows, I think, that the freedoms discussed have a dual role. On the one hand, they are the result of the working out, at the most basic level (in what I called the first stage of justice as fairness), of the fundamental ideas of a democratic society as a fair system of cooperation between citizens as free and equal. On the other hand, in the second stage, we know on the basis of general facts and the historical condition of the age that a conception of political justice leading to free institutions must be acceptable to a plurality of opposing comprehensive doctrines. That conception must, therefore, present itself as independent of any particular comprehensive view and must firmly guarantee for all citizens the basic rights and liberties as a condition of their sense of security and their peaceful, mutual recognition.

As the first role is perhaps clearer than the second, I comment on the latter. We know from the burdens of reason that even in a well-ordered society, where the basic freedoms are secure, sharp political disagreement will persist on their more particular interpretation. For instance, where exactly should the line be drawn between church and state? Or, granting there is no such crime as seditious libel, who precisely belongs to the class of public persons in regard to whom the law of libel is relaxed? Or, what are the limits of protected speech? So the question arises: if disagreements on such constitutional essentials always remain, what is gained by a publicly recognized political conception? Isn't the aim – to underwrite the basic rights and liberties of citizens by achieving an overlapping consensus, thereby giving everyone the sense that their rights are indeed secure – still unresolved?

There are two replies to this. First, by securing the basic rights and liberties, and assigning them a due priority, the most divisive questions are taken off the political agenda. This means that they are publicly recognized as politically settled, once and for all, and so contrary views on those questions are emphatically rejected by all political parties.[47] Though disagreements remain, as they must, they occur in areas of less central significance, where reasonable citizens equally attached to the political conception may reasonably be expected to differ. If liberty of conscience is guaranteed and separation of church and state is enjoined, we still expect there to be differences about what more exactly these provisions mean. Differences in judgment on the details in matters of any complexity even among reasonable persons are a condition of human life. But with the most divisive questions off the political agenda, it should be possible to reach a peaceful settlement within the framework of democratic institutions.

A second reply, complementing the first, is that the political conception, when properly formulated, should guide reflective judgment both to an agreed enumeration of the basic rights and liberties and to an agreement about their central range of significance. This it can do by its fundamental intuitive idea of society as a fair system of cooperation between citizens as free and equal persons, and by its idea of such persons as having the two moral powers, one a capacity for a sense of justice and the other a capacity for a conception of the good, that is, a conception of what is worthy of their devoted pursuit over a complete life.[48] Basic rights and liberties secure the conditions for the adequate development and exercise of those powers by citizens viewed as fully cooperating members of society. Citizens are thought to have and to want to exercise these powers whatever their more comprehensive religious, philosophical, or moral doctrine may be. Thus, the equal political liberties and freedom of speech and thought enable us to develop and exercise these powers by participating in society's political life and by assessing the justice and effectiveness of its laws and social policies; and liberty of conscience and freedom of association enable us to develop and exercise our moral powers in forming, revising, and rationally pursuing our conceptions of the good that belong to our comprehensive doctrines, and affirming them as such.[49]

But in view of the truism that no conception, whether in law, morals, or science, interprets and applies itself, we should expect various interpretations of even the constitutional essentials to gain currency. Does this jeopardize the rule of law? Not necessarily. The idea of the rule of law has numerous elements and it can be specified in a variety of ways. But however this is done, it cannot depend on the idea of a clear, unambiguous directive that informs citizens, or legislators, or judges what the constitution enjoins in all cases. There can be no such thing. The rule of law is not put in jeopardy by the circumstance that citizens, and even legislators and judges, may often hold conflicting views on questions of interpretation.

Rather, the rule of law means the regulative role of certain institutions and their associated legal and judicial practices. It may mean, among other things, that all officers of the government, including the executive, are under the law and that their acts are subject to judicial scrutiny, that the judiciary is suitably independent, and that civilian authority is supreme over the military. Moreover, it may mean that judges' decisions rest on interpreting existing law and relevant precedents, that judges must justify their verdicts by reference thereto and adhere to a consistent reading from case to case, or else find a reasonable basis for distinguishing them, and so on. Similar constraints do not bind legislators; while they may not defy basic law and can try politically to change it only in ways the constitution permits, they need not explain or justify their vote, though their constituents may call them to account. The rule of law exists so long as such legal institutions and their associated practices (variously specified) are conducted in a reasonable way in accordance with the political values that apply to them: impartiality and consistency, adherence to law and respect for precedent, all in the light of a coherent understanding of recognized constitutional norms viewed as controlling the conduct of all government officers.[50]

Two conditions underwrite the rule of law so understood: first, the recognition by politically engaged citizens of the dual role of the basic rights and liberties; and second, its being the case that the main interpretations of those constitutional essentials take the most divisive matters off the political agenda and specify the central range of significance of the basic liberties in roughly the same way. The ideas of the domain of the political and of an overlapping consensus indicate how these conditions strengthen the stability of a political conception.

It is important for the viability of a just democratic regime over time for politically active citizens to understand those ideas. For in the long run, the leading interpretations of constitutional essentials are settled politically. A persistent majority, or an enduring alliance of strong enough interests, can make of the Constitution what it wants.[51] This fact is simply a corollary to the third general fact – that an enduring democratic regime must be freely supported by a substantial majority of its politically active citizens. As a fact, we must live with it and see it as specifying further one of the conditions of achieving a well-ordered constitutional state.

Notes

1 An overlapping consensus exists in a society when the political conception of justice that regulates its basic institutions is endorsed by each of the main religious, philosophical, and moral doctrines likely to endure in that society from one generation to the next. I have used this idea mainly in Rawls, Justice as Fairness: Political not Metaphysical, 14 Phil. & Pub. Aff. 223 (1985) [hereinafter Justice as Fairness] and Rawls, The Idea of an Overlapping Consensus, 7 Oxford J. Legal Stud. 1 (1987) [hereinafter Overlapping Consensus]. The idea is introduced in J. Rawls, A Theory of Justice 387–88 (1971) [hereinafter Theory].

2 Theory, supra note 1.

3 For an awareness of these misgivings I am indebted to the comments of G. A. Cohen and Paul Seabright (soon after the lecture "Overlapping Consensus" was given at Oxford in May 1986), see Overlapping Consensus, supra note 1, and to discussions with Jürgen Habermas (at Harvard the following October). For a better understanding of and suggestions for how to deal with the misgivings, I am greatly indebted to Ronald Dworkin, Thomas Nagel, and T. M. Scanlon. I also have gained much from Wilfried Hinsch, to whom I owe the important idea of a reasonable comprehensive doctrine, which I have simply elaborated a bit. This idea, when joined with suitable companion ideas such as the burdens of reason, see Part II infra, and the precepts of

reasonable discussion, see Part III infra, imposes an appropriate limit on the comprehensive doctrines we may reasonably expect to be included in an overlapping consensus.

4 See Part VIII infra.

5 See Part VII infra.

6 These powers are those of a capacity for a sense of justice and a capacity for a conception of the good. Theory, supra note 1, at 505; Justice as Fairness, supra note 1, at 232–34.

7 This source of disagreement I have expressed in a somewhat flat way. It could be put more strongly by saying, as Thomas Nagel does, that there are basic conflicts of value in which there seem to be decisive and sufficient (normative) reasons for two or more incompatible courses of action; and yet some decision must be made. See T. Nagel, Mortal Questions 128–41 (1979). Moreover, these normative reasons are not evenly balanced, and so it matters greatly what decision is made. The lack of even balance holds because in such cases the values are incomparable. They are each specified by one of the several irreducibly different perspectives within which values arise, in particular, the perspectives that specify obligations, rights, utility, perfectionist ends, and personal commitments. Put another way, these values have different bases which their different formal features reflect. These basic conflicts reveal what Nagel thinks of as the fragmentation of value. See id. I find much in Nagel's discussion very plausible, and I might endorse it were I stating my own (partially) comprehensive moral doctrine; since I am not doing that, but rather trying so far as possible to avoid controversial philosophical theses and to give an account of the difficulties of reason that rest on the plain facts open to all, I refrain from any statement stronger than (e).

8 This point has often been stressed by Sir Isaiah Berlin, most recently in his article, On the Pursuit of the Ideal, N.Y. Rev. Books, Mar. 17, 1988, at 11.

9 For instance, consider the questions of the causes of unemployment and the more effective ways to reduce it.

10 I have adapted this idea from Pliny the Younger's remark, "He who hates vice, hates mankind," quoted in J. Shklar, Ordinary Vices 192 (1984).

11 Here I assume that any substantial majority will include citizens who hold conflicting comprehensive doctrines.

12 Note that this is a definition of stability for a political conception of justice. It is not to be mistaken for a definition of stability, or of what I call the security, of a political regime (as a system of institutions).

13 The features of a political conception of justice are discussed in more detail in Justice as Fairness, supra note 1, at 224–34.

14 A political conception for the basic structure must also generalize to, or else fit in with, a political conception for an international society of constitutionally democratic states; but here I put this important matter aside. See note 46 infra.

15 See Justice as Fairness, supra note 1, at 239–40 & n. 22 (discussing a "political conception of the person").

16 See Part IV supra.

17 The appropriateness of this assumption rests in part on a point I shall only mention here, namely, that the right of emigration does not make the acceptance of political authority voluntary in the way that freedom of thought and liberty of conscience make the acceptance of ecclesiastical authority voluntary. This brings out a further feature of the domain of the political, one that distinguishes it from the associational.

18 The associational, the personal, and the familial are only three examples of the non-political; there are others.

19 The common medieval maxim *Extra ecclesiam nulla salus* ("Outside the church there is no salvation") was used, for example, in the famous bull "Unam sanctam" of Nov. 18, 1302, by Pope Boniface VIII, reprinted in Enchiridion symbolorum definitionum et declarationum de rebus fidei et morum 870 at 279 (33d ed. H. Denzinger & A. Schönmetzer eds. 1965).

20 For clarity on this point I owe thanks to Wilfried Hinsch and Peter de Marneffe.

21 See Rawls, Overlapping Consensus, supra note 1, at 14.

22 Recall here the formulation of political liberalism a few lines back, namely, given the existence of a well-ordered constitutional democratic regime, the family of great values expressed by its principles and ideals, and realized in its basic institutions, normally has sufficient weight to override whatever other values may come into conflict with them. See Part IV supra.

23 J. S. Mill, Utilitarianism, ch.5, ¶ 25 (3rd ed. 1867), reprinted in John Stuart Mill: A Selection of His Works 216 (J. Robson ed. 1982).

24 See Part III supra.

25 On this point see the instructive discussion by Jeremy Waldron, Theoretical Foundations of Liberalism, 37 Phil. Q. 127 (1987).

26 See Justice as Fairness, supra note 1, at 250. The model case of an overlapping consensus is one in which the political conception is endorsed by three comprehensive doctrines: the first endorses justice as fairness, say, because its religious beliefs and understanding of faith lead to the principle of toleration and support the basic equal liberties; the second doctrine affirms justice as fairness as a consequence of a comprehensive liberal conception such as that of Kant or Mill; while the third affirms justice as fairness as a political conception, that is, not as a consequence of a wider doctrine but as in itself sufficient to express very great values that normally outweigh whatever other values might oppose them, at least under reasonably favorable conditions. Id. See also Overlapping Consensus, supra note 1, § III, at 9–12 (more fully discussing this model case).

27 These two stages correspond to the two parts of the argument from the original position for the two principles of justice contained in Theory, supra note 1. In the first part the parties select principles without taking the effects of the special psychologies into account. Id. at 118–93. In the second part they ask whether a society well ordered by the principles selected in the first part would be stable, that is, would generate in its members a sufficiently strong sense of justice to counteract tendencies to injustice. Id. at 395–587.

The argument for the principles of justice is not complete until the principles selected in the first part are shown in the second part to be sufficiently stable. So in Theory the argument is not complete until the next to last section, section 86. Id. at 567–77. For these two parts, see id. at 144, 530–31.

28 In this and the next several paragraphs I am indebted to a very helpful discussion with T. M. Scanlon.

29 The assumptions of such a psychology are noted briefly in Overlapping Consensus, supra note 1, at 22–23. In Section VI of the same essay I also consider the way in which a political conception can gain an allegiance to itself that may to some degree shape comprehensive doctrines to conform to its requirements. Id. at 18–22. This is plainly an important aspect of stability and strengthens the second part of the answer as to how political liberalism is possible. See Part VI supra.

I wish to thank Francis Kamm for pointing out to me several significant complications in the relation between a political conception and the comprehensive doctrines it shapes to accord with it, and how far as a result the viability of political liberalism depends on the support of such doctrines. It seems best not to pursue these matters here but to postpone them until a more complete account of stability can be given.

30 As stated in Theory, the question is whether the just and the good are congruent. Theory, supra note 1, at 395, 567–77. In section 86 of Theory, it is argued that a person who grows up in a society well ordered by justice as fairness, and who has a rational plan of life, and who also knows, or reasonably believes, that everyone else has an effective sense of justice, has sufficient reason, founded on that person's good (and not on justice) to comply with just institutions. Id. at 567–77. These institutions are stable because the just and the good are congruent. That is, no reasonable and rational person in the well-ordered society of justice as fairness is moved by rational considerations of the good not to honor what justice requires.

31 Recall that reasonable comprehensive doctrines are ones that recognize the burdens of reason and accept the fact of pluralism as a condition of human life under free democratic institutions, and hence accept freedom of thought and liberty of conscience. See Parts II and III supra.

32 The force of the phrase "within its own framework" as used in the text emerges in the two parts of the argument from the original position in Theory, supra note 1. Both parts are carried out within the same framework and subject to the same conditions embedded in the original position as a device of representation.

33 For this distinction, see Nagel, What Makes Political Theory Utopian? 5 (unpublished paper, dated Apr. 1988, on file at New York University Law Review).

34 Theory, supra note 1, at 17.

35 Id. at 512.

36 Id. at 453–62.

37 Id. at 387–88.

38 Justice as Fairness, supra note 1, at 248–51.

39 For example, in the well-ordered society of justice as fairness, some may hold a form of utilitarianism as their comprehensive doctrine, provided they understand that doctrine, as I believe J. S. Mill did, so as to coincide in its requirements with justice as fairness, at least for the most part. See J. S. Mill, supra note 23, ch.3, ¶ 10.

40 I am grateful to Erin Kelley for valuable discussion about how to put this summary.

41 See Parts I & II supra.

42 See Part II supra.

43 These two principles are:

1. Each person has an equal right to a fully adequate scheme of equal basic rights and liberties, which scheme is compatible with a similar scheme for all.

2. Social and economic inequalities are to satisfy two conditions: first, they must be attached to offices and positions open to all under conditions of fair equality of opportunity; and second, they must be to the greatest benefit of the least advantaged members of society.

Justice as Fairness, supra note 1, at 227.

44 I should like to thank David Chow for very helpful comments on this point.

45 The reasons for thinking reasonable rather than unreasonable doctrines are encouraged are sketched briefly in Overlapping Consensus, supra note 1, at 18–23.

46 Perhaps I should explain briefly that the political conception so arrived at may not apply to some societies because the general facts we have assumed may not appropriately obtain in their case. Nevertheless, those facts do obtain widely in the modern world, and hence the political conception applies. Its not applying in some cases, however, does not make that conception relativist or historicist so long as it provides grounds for judging the basic institutions of different societies and their social policies. Thus, the appropriate test of a conception's universality is whether it can be extended to, or developed into, a reasonable political conception of justice for an international society of nation-states. In Theory, supra note 1, at 377–79, I noted briefly how, after the principles of justice have been adopted for the basic structure of society (viewed as a closed scheme of cooperation), the idea of the original position can be used once more at the higher level. The parties are now seen as representatives of states. We start with (closed) societies and build up to the international society of states. Doing this locates us where we are and follows the historical tendencies of democratic societies. Others may want to begin with an original position in which the parties are seen as representatives of citizens of the world society. I supposed that in any case the outcome would be something like the familiar principles of international justice governing a society of states rather than a world state, for example, a principle of equality among peoples as organized into states, although states who recognize certain duties towards other states. For I think that Kant is right that a world state would likely be either highly oppressive if not autocratic, or else torn by civil strife as separate peoples and cultures tried to win their autonomy. I. Kant, Perpetual Peace: A Philosophical Sketch (1795;

L. Beck trans. 1949). If so, the principles of international justice will include a principle of equality among peoples as organized into states; and there will also be, I think, principles for forming and regulating loose confederations of states, and standards of fairness for various cooperative arrangements between them, and so on. In such a confederation or arrangement, one role of the state, however arbitrary its boundaries may appear from a historical point of view, is to be the representative of a people as they take responsibility for their territory and the numbers they put on it, and especially for maintaining its environmental integrity and its capacity to sustain them in perpetuity.

Theory does not pursue these larger matters but only mentions the extension to the international system as background for discussing conscientious refusal in section 58. Theory, supra note 1, at 377–82. But given this extension, as briefly indicated, we can see that justice as fairness as a political conception is universal in at least two ways. First, its principles extend to the international society and bind all its members, the nation-states; and second, insofar as certain of a society's domestic institutions and policies are likely to lead to war or to expansionist aims, or to render a people unreliable and untrustworthy as partners in a confederation of states or in a cooperative arrangement, those institutions and policies are open to censure and sanctions of varying degrees of severity by the principles of international justice. Here violations of what are recognized as human rights may be particularly serious. Thus, the requirements of a just international society may reflect back and impose constraints downwards on the domestic institutions of states generally. But these constraints will already be met, I assume, by a just constitutional regime.

I cannot pursue these matters further here, and have appended this footnote only to indicate why I think the political conception of justice as fairness is in a suitable way universal, and not relativist or historicist, even though it may not apply to all societies at all times and places. Thomas Pogge's work forthcoming from Cornell University Press includes an account of international justice from within a conception much like justice as fairness, but very importantly revised and extended in a different way to the global sphere. His much fuller discussion will sustain, I believe, the same general point about the universality of such a conception, although his approach to international justice is very different.

47 For example, it is not on the political agenda whether certain groups are to have the vote, or whether certain religious or philosophical views have the protections of liberty of conscience and freedom of thought.

48 This conception of the person, which characterizes citizens, is also a political conception. Justice as Fairness, supra note 1, at 239–44. I add that persons understand their own conceptions of the good against the background of their own comprehensive doctrines.

49 For further discussion of the basic rights and liberties, see Rawls, Basic Liberties and Their Priority, in 3 Tanner Lectures on Human Values 1 (S. McMurrin ed. 1982).

50 I owe thanks to T. M. Scanlon for helpful discussion of the rule of law as summarized in the last two paragraphs.
51 On this point, see A. Bickel, The Least Dangerous Branch 244–72 (1962), discussing politics of Dred Scott v. Sanford, 60 U.S. (19 Haw.) 393 (1857), and the school segregation cases, notably Brown v. Board of Educ., 347 U.S. 483 (1954).

Moral pluralism and political consensus

JOSHUA COHEN

The idea of normative consensus plays a central role in John Rawls's theory of justice.[1] In a well-ordered society, he says, "everyone has a similar sense of justice and in this respect a well-ordered society is homogeneous."[2] But is a consensus on fundamental norms of justice a realistic and attractive prospect for a morally pluralistic society?[3]

Rawls says little about this question in *A Theory of Justice*. Although he is closely attentive there to the diversity of interests and of conceptions of good among citizens in a well-ordered society, he is generally inattentive to the pluralism of moral conceptions that can be expected when expressive and associative liberties are protected. As a consequence, he does not consider the possibility that this pluralism might either exclude consensus on justice altogether or throw its value into question by turning it into mere compromise. Moreover, since the argument in *A Theory of Justice* that justice as fairness is a realistic conception – in particular, the case for the stability of a just society – depends on the idea that a just society features a consensus on principles of justice, the inattention to moral pluralism renders the force of that argument uncertain. So justice as fairness may be, after all, unrealistic and utopian.[4]

To address these concerns and show that the case for justice as fairness can be restated under more realistic assumptions, Rawls recently introduced the idea of an *overlapping consensus* and, corresponding to this idea, a condition on the acceptability of a conception of justice that I refer to as the "pluralistic consensus test." A society features an *overlapping consensus* on norms of justice if and only if it is a morally pluralistic society with a consensus on norms of justice in which citizens holding the different moralities that win adherents and persist over time in the society each support the consensual norms as the correct account of justice. Norms of justice satisfy the *pluralistic consensus test* if and only if those norms could provide the focus of an overlapping consensus in a society regulated by those norms and operating under favorable conditions.[5] A conception of justice that would not be so supported by at least some of the moral doctrines that persist within a society reg-ulated by it, and so could not be the focus of an overlapping consen-sus, fails to meet the pluralistic consensus test and is, to this extent, unreasonable.[6]

Why unreasonable? Why (if at all) should requirements of justice be realistic? "Because ought implies can" will not do as an answer, because the question concerns justice, not what ought to be done, all things considered. Judgments about what ought to be done, all things consi-dered, must, of course, be sensitive to all sorts of practical matters, since issues of practicality plainly are among the things to be considered. The question is what sorts of constraints on realizability are constitutive of ideal justice. And in matters of justice, realism is an uncertain good. By accepting the "demands" of realism, we may be led to build an accom-modation to unhappy, grim, and even hideous facts of political life into the foundations of political justification and into fundamental principles of justice themselves.

Focusing this general concern about the demands of realism on the pluralistic consensus test, one might say that in aiming for a conception of justice that could realistically be supported by a pluralistic consensus one in fact undercuts the attraction of the conception that results. Consider the following elaboration of this objection:

The pluralistic consensus test asks us to evaluate a conception of justice in part by asking whether we can realistically expect the conception to be supported as the correct account of justice by the diverse moralities in a well-ordered society. But why should we be concerned with such support? In fact, requiring it forces an accommodation to power at the foundations of a theory of justice – to the power of those who believe the false and spurn the good. Accommodation to power is commonly prudent and often recommended by our all-things-considered judgments about the application of moral ideals to the facts of life. We give money to the thief who threatens our life; we let the rich get richer if that is what's needed to get them to invest; we pay the lion's share of the surplus to the greedy if that is necessary to motivate them to use their talents for the common good (at least in the first case we don't call it "justice"). And we often frame our political arguments and proposals to win broad acceptance, if that is what we must do to keep those who don't believe the true and love the good from making life worse for those of us who do. But adjustments designed to build support do not define ideal justice. To suppose otherwise would be to permit the facts of power to fix the content of the fundamental requirements of justice, thus undercutting their attraction as basic requirements. Philosophers, above all, should resist the confusion of justice with accommodation and a moral ideal with a consensus on principles that accommodate the power of thieves, pirates, and benighted souls. Because if philosophers are not good for that, then just what are they good for?[7]

Responding to this objection, Rawls argues that consensus on justice is both a realistic and an attractive prospect for a morally pluralistic society, and that subjecting conceptions of justice to the pluralistic consensus test is not tantamount to substituting mere compromise for genuine moral consensus and through that substitution advancing an account of justice that is "political in the wrong way" (p. 234).[8]

I agree with Rawls's main contentions, and my aim here is to explore the problem itself, to discuss some surrounding issues, and to clarify the grounds of agreement. After some initial points of clarification, I offer a generic statement of the problem of moral consensus and pluralism. Then I discuss some historical background, linking the problem of pluralism, realism, and moral consensus to a line of argument extending from Rousseau through Hegel to Marx. Next I discuss and criticize one source of concern about imposing constraints of realism and in particular the pluralistic consensus test on a conception of justice – that the constraint of realism undermines a substantively egalitarian conception of justice. Although this discussion does not address the concern about pluralism and realism in its most generic form, I include it because I suspect that the energy surrounding the debate about pluralism and political consensus derives importantly from alleged implications of the debate for matters of equality. Finally, I argue in more general terms that the pluralistic consensus condition does not fall prey to the objection I have sketched here. The argument turns on understanding what Rawls calls "the fact of pluralism" (p. 235) in a certain way. In particular, I distinguish the fact of pluralism from the fact of reasonable pluralism and, drawing on this distinction, I suggest that in aiming to find a conception of justice that meets the pluralistic consensus test, we are not simply adjusting ideals to the facts of life and to moral pluralism as one such fact. Instead we are acknowledging the scope of practical reason. Put otherwise, in aiming to find a conception of justice that meets the pluralistic consensus test we are not accommodating justice to an unfavorable condition of human life, since, as the idea of reasonable pluralism shows, we ought not to count moral pluralism itself among the unfavorable conditions.

The place of consensus

Before getting to these issues, I need to clarify one remark I made earlier. I said that a conception of justice that fails to meet the pluralistic consensus test is, *to this extent*, unreasonable. The phrase "to this extent" is meant to indicate the place of the pluralistic consensus test in an account of justice and in particular its role in the two-stage strategy of argument that Rawls sketches in "The Domain of the Political."

Rawls emphasizes that the idea of an overlapping consensus and the pluralistic consensus test come into play at the second stage of a two-part argument for a conception of justice. The aim of the first stage is, roughly, to show that the content of a conception is attractive – that it organizes a set of fundamental political values in a plausible way. The aim of the second stage is to determine whether a conception of justice that is in other respects attractive is also realistic – in particular, that it is stable. Showing that it is stable consists in part in showing that it satisfies the pluralistic consensus test: that different people, brought up within and attracted to different traditions of moral thought might each affirm the conception as the correct account of justice.

But how, more precisely, are we to understand the relationship between the results of the first stage and the argument at the second? What would follow if there were problems at the second stage? Three possibilities suggest themselves: (1) It is *necessary* that the correct account of justice satisfy the pluralistic consensus test; (2) satisfying the test is not necessary though it does provide *some support* for a conception of justice; or (3) satisfying the test is a *desideratum* that has *no bearing on the correctness* of an account of justice. In case (3), the pluralistic consensus test might be interpreted as a condition on the all-things-considered reasonableness of a conception of justice or perhaps as a test of the *legitimacy* of the exercise of state power, not as a condition on the justice of the institutions through which that power is exercised. On this interpretation if the best understanding of justice failed to satisfy the pluralistic consensus test even under favorable conditions, we ought to conclude that there is an unhappy divergence between justice and legitimacy – that even under the best conditions we can realistically hope for it will be illegitimate to secure justice – but not that we should revise our conception of justice.

Interpretation (3) may be suggested by Rawls's emphasis (p. 234) on the importance of separating the two stages of argument, and so distinguishing questions of justice from issues about the course of the world. But it is, in fact, ruled out by the description of the conclusions of the first stage as "provisionally on hand" (p. 246) and the remark that the argument is "not complete" until the case for stability has been presented (p. 245, n. 27). I am not sure which of the other two views Rawls means to endorse. But for the purposes of this essay, I will assume that (2) is right, that satisfying the pluralistic consensus condition does count in favor of the correctness of a conception of justice, and that while failure to meet it is not a sufficient reason for rejecting a conception, it would provide some reason to modify a view to bring it into conformity with that test.

Consensus and moral pluralism

Pluralism takes a variety of forms, and so there are correspondingly a variety of ways that it might raise troubles for consensus and social unity. To state the specific problem of pluralism and consensus that I will be considering here, I first need to fix some terminology. Following Rawls, then, I will say that a "well-ordered society" is a society in which it is common knowledge that the members share an understanding of justice and a willingness to act on that understanding. A well-ordered society, that is, features a restricted but important moral consensus. The moral consensus is restricted in that it extends only to certain basic constitutional values and principles and norms of distributive justice, and not to all aspects of the conduct of life. Despite this limitation, the consensus that defines a well-ordered society is a genuinely *moral* consensus. For the norms and ideals on which there is consensus play a reason-giving and authoritative role in the deliberation and choices of individual citizens.[9]

At the same time, a well-ordered society may be morally pluralistic in that members may have conflicting views about the fundamental norms and ideals that ought to guide conduct in life more generally. In a morally pluralistic society, the members hold different theories about what is valuable and worth doing. Thus understood, moral pluralism is to be distinguished both from cultural pluralism – the existence of groups of people within a single society who share distinct histories and ways of life, and a common identity as members of a group – and from organizational pluralism – the existence of a plurality of organized groups pursuing distinctive interests or ideals. These forms of pluralism are distinct phenomena, and less plausibly understood as a matter of people holding different theories. So the discussion here of moral pluralism and consensus is limited and does not naturally translate into an account of consensus and either cultural or organizational pluralism.

Moving now from terminology to substance: a moral consensus on political fundamentals is a fundamental good for at least three reasons. First, for any conception of justice, the likelihood that social order will stably conform to the conception is increased by the existence of a moral consensus on it.[10]

Second, the existence of a moral consensus supports a variety of specific values of considerable importance. It increases social trust and harmony, supports social peace, reduces the complexity of decision making, encourages a willingness to cooperate and so reduces the costs of monitoring and enforcement, and – assuming the consensus is reflected in public debate and decisions – reduces alienation from public choices because citizens embrace the norms and ideals that guide those choices.

Third, a consensus on norms of justice provides a way to reconcile the ideal of an association whose members are self-governing with an acknowledgment of the central role of social and political arrangements in shaping the self-conceptions of citizens, constraining their actions, channeling their choices, and determining the outcomes of those choices.[11] For when a consensus on norms and values underlies and explains collective decisions, citizens whose lives are governed by those decisions might nonetheless be said to be self-governing because each endorses the considerations that produce the decisions as genuinely moral reasons and affirms their implementation.[12]

But not just any consensus is attractive, as is indicated by reflection on these reasons themselves. If, for example, a moral consensus is attractive because it provides a way to make the ideal of free association consistent with the unavoidable chains of political connection, then the consensus must be a free moral consensus and not simply a form of enforced homogeneity. A free consensus is a consensus arrived at under conditions that ensure the possibility of individual reflection and public deliberation – conditions in which, for instance, expressive and associative liberties are protected.

It is at just this point that a minimal condition of realism appears to undermine either the possibility of consensus or at least its attractions as an ideal. For the assurance of expressive and associative liberties – an assurance that is necessary if the consensus is to be free and attractive – will also produce moral, religious, and philosophical pluralism.[13] But can a genuine moral consensus survive this "fact of pluralism" (p. 235)? Or does an insistence on consensus under conditions of pluralism in effect turn political philosophy into a search for a political compromise among people who disagree?

Historical excursus

These concerns about the pluralistic consensus condition ought to have a familiar ring. Earlier I mentioned the problem of reconciling self-government with the chains of political connection. Rousseau identified this problem, and thought it could be solved if social order were regulated by a consensual understanding of the common good – a "general will." Rousseau's solution is commonly rejected on the ground that it is inattentive to differences among people and to the diversity of human interests and ideals. In the face of that diversity, according to the objection, consensus on the common good can only be achieved through the unattractive combination of a sectarian conception of virtue and, for those who do not share that conception, enforced subordination and homogeneity in the name of freedom.

Hegel's response to Rousseau was more complex. He agreed that freedom could be reconciled with the chains of political connection, and applauded the notion of a general will as the way to achieve that reconciliation.[14] But he also appreciated the force of the critique of Rousseau that I just sketched. His conclusion was that it was necessary to reformulate the classical ideal of a political community organized around a moral consensus in light of the modern distinction between the unity of political society and the diversity of civil society. This distinction shapes Hegel's own political conception in three important ways:

1. He endorsed a fundamental distinction between civic diversity and political unity, associating that distinction with the differentiation between two spheres of social life. While the civil sphere would feature a diversity of aims and ideals and a range of individual and group activities organized around those aims and ideals, the political sphere would be organized around a set of values that both claim authority over individual concerns and are alleged to lie within the diverse aspirations of civil life and to provide their common ground.[15]

2. His distinction between political unity and civic diversity is associated with an acceptance of substantially inegalitarian forms of civic diversity,[16] as though an acceptance of that distinction and of a social sphere in which people pursue diverse aims itself brings inegalitarian implications in its wake.

3. Concerned to affirm the unity of the state in the face of the tendencies to social fragmentation that might follow from civic diversity, he defended a strong, highly centralized, executive-dominated constitutional monarchy, featuring a corporatist form of representation and special political rights for the landed class.

At least since Marx, critics of Hegel have objected that some or all of these gestures at reinterpreting the ideal of political unity in the face of civic diversity represent unwanted accommodations to de facto power in the formulation of basic political ideals. Marx, for example, objected to all three.[17] Putting Hegel's favored form of state to the side, these allegations of "accommodation" raise two questions that are relevant for our purposes here.

First, does the reformulation of the ideal of consensual political unity with an eye to respecting the diversity of civil society itself represent an objectionable accommodation? Do we find unacceptable accommodation in Hegel's reformulation of the ideal of political society to accommodate the diversity of aspirations characteristic of civil society or in Rawls's broadly parallel idea that a reasonable conception of justice should be supportable by an overlapping consensus?

Second, does the affirmation of moral diversity lead to an accommodation of social and economic privilege? *A Theory of Justice* defended an egalitarian liberalism that departed from Hegel's accommodation to inegalitarian forms of civic diversity. Does this egalitarianism survive the gesture at realism reflected in the pluralistic consensus condition? Put otherwise: The pluralistic consensus condition presumably restricts the content of norms of justice in some way. More demanding norms are less plausibly the object of agreement than less demanding norms. So does the importance of accommodating moral diversity lead to a thinner conception of justice that lacks the critical egalitarian dimension of Rawls's earlier position?

Because an affirmative answer to the second question would fuel an affirmative answer to the first, I will begin with diversity and equality.

The case of equality

A number of commentators on Rawls's recent work have noted that the many reformulations of his views about political justification have not yet been matched by similar revisions in the substance of the theory. My impression[18] is that lots of people now think that Rawls's recent discussions of political justification – with their emphasis on the importance of realism, on the practical nature of political philosophy, and on the associated idea of an overlapping consensus – do require a shift in the substance of his theory of justice, and in particular a shift in an inegalitarian direction.[19]

The reasoning goes something like this: "Rawls recognizes the utopianism of his earlier conception of a well-ordered society. So he now recommends that political justification proceed by identifying the common ground among the diverse moralities and conceptions of justice in our own society. But if we follow that recommendation, we will certainly not find support for the specifically egalitarian aspects of *Theory of Justice*, since there is (to put it mildly) considerable contemporary controversy about egalitarian political views."

This account of the idea of an overlapping consensus, with its emphasis on locating common ground among current political views, is mis-

278 JOSHUA COHEN

taken in several ways. Once we see where it goes wrong we shall see as well that the concern for realism expressed in the pluralistic consensus test has none of the alleged implications. To make this case, I will begin with a sketch of the egalitarian content of the theory and the strategy of argument for it, and then proceed to a discussion of the objection.

The egalitarian content of *A Theory of Justice* is encapsulated in three requirements: the fair value of political liberty, fair equality of opportunity, and the maximin criterion of distributive equity. These three conditions, which are meant to sever the distribution of advantage from social background and natural difference, represent substantively egalitarian interpretations of more formal and less controversial norms of equal liberty, equal opportunity, and the common good.[20] A contention common to egalitarian liberal political conceptions generally, and advanced in *A Theory of Justice* in particular, is that we are led to these substantively egalitarian interpretations by considering the justification of the more formal and less controversial political norms.

The basic strategy of argument for this contention is familiar, and proceeds by *bootstrapping*. Thus, associated with the more formal requirements of equal liberties and assurances of opportunity is a conception of the properties of human beings that are important for the purposes of political justification. That conception of persons supposes that the relevant features are not race, color, cultural creed, sex, religion, and the like. The relevant features are certain potentialities (moral powers) – for example, the capacity to govern one's conduct and to revise one's aspirations – rather than the determinate form in which those potentialities are realized. The rationale for the protection of liberties and formal opportunity, for example, lies in part in the importance of assuring favorable conditions for the realization of the basic potentialities. But – and here is the where the bootstrapping comes in – once we acknowledge the need for favorable conditions for realizing the basic potentialities, we are naturally led from the more formal to the more substantively egalitarian requirements since the latter more fully elaborate the range of favorable conditions.

With this quick sketch as background, I can now state more precisely the concern already noted about the idea of an overlapping consensus. The intuitive objection was that the need to confine fundamental political justification to considerations that lie on common ground would undercut the egalitarian components and result in an unacceptable accommodation to power in the formulation of principles. Is this right? Does the requirement of proceeding on common ground deprive us of the argumentative resources necessary for the bootstrapping argument for an egalitarian form of liberalism?

Common ground

To see why the answer is no, it is important to note first that the bootstrap argument for the egalitarian view is itself meant to proceed on common ground shared by different moral conceptions in a well-ordered society governed by it. That may seem puzzling, since the conception of potentialities as morally fundamental may strike some as peculiarly Kantian. But the contention of the argument (which I am not evaluating here) is that those ideas will seem attractive for the purposes of political argument to anyone who considers how best to defend the liberties, formal norms of equal opportunity, and the requirement that public powers be exercised for the common good.[21]

Noting this draws attention to a first feature of the notion of an overlapping consensus that is important in assessing the objection. What lies in the intersection of different moral conceptions is not simply a set of policies or a system of norms within which political conflict and competition proceed.[22] Nor is it simply a determinate set of moral principles. Instead, the consensus extends to a view of persons, of the importance of fairness and other political values, of what counts as an advantage, and of which practices are paradigmatically evil (e.g., slavery, religious intolerance, and racial discrimination). In short, what lies at the intersection of different views is a (restricted) terrain on which moral and political argument can be conducted, and not simply a fixed and determinate set of substantive points of political agreement.

To show, then, that an egalitarian conception of justice meets the pluralistic consensus test, one needs to show that the bootstrap argument succeeds and that the terrain on which that argument proceeds could itself be the focus of an overlapping consensus in a society governed by it. One need not deny the obvious fact of disagreement on egalitarian political ideals or the only slightly less obvious fact that such disagreement is likely to persist even under favorable conditions.

Contemporary support

When the case for an egalitarian conception of justice is understood as a bootstrap argument and the common ground is understood in the way that I just sketched, it is not so obvious that an appeal to a wide range of *contemporary* political views will fail to support the substantively egalitarian aspects of the conception. For we do not require de facto agreement on substantively egalitarian norms, but only that the reasoning supporting those norms proceed on common ground. That is, we require that the egalitarian features represent a reasonable extension of what people do agree to – that they "extend the range of some existing consensus" by bringing the best justification of certain fundamental points of agreement to bear on unsettled and controversial matters.[23] That contention is not so implausible, because – as I noted earlier – the bootstrap argument for the egalitarian ideals proceeds principally by reference to points of agreement about the value of the liberties and certain formal requirements of equality.

Role of overlapping consensus

While the contention that the resources for defending an egalitarian political conception are implicit in current understandings may not, then, be entirely implausible, it should *not* be *identified* with the thesis that an egalitarian liberal political conception can meet the pluralistic consensus test. That test does not require that we rummage through the political culture searching for underlying points of agreement among the views featured in it.[24] Rummaging may serve an important function, and I will say a word about it below. But the pluralistic consensus test does not itself command a search for de facto points of agreement at all, and so the failure to find any would not undercut the force of an egalitarian conception of justice.

Instead it formulates a test on the reasonableness of a political conception that is in other respects attractive. The test is this: Consider a proposed conception of justice in operation, and then consider whether the principles, ideals, and terms of argument that figure in it provide moral reasons within the views that could be expected to arise among those who live in a society governed by it. Bringing this to bear on the issue of egalitarian liberalism, then, we are to imagine a society regulated by such a conception and existing across several generations. In such a society, we can reasonably expect moral diversity. We also can expect widespread agreement on the fundamental value of the liberties and on at least formal understandings of equality. But then, if there is such agreement and if the bootstrap argument has any force, the diverse moral understandings would each still have the resources necessary for supporting the substantively egalitarian conception as the correct conception of justice.

I have, of course, not tried to defend the bootstrap argument here. Instead, I have only argued that the pluralistic consensus test does not undercut the force (whatever its magnitude may be) of that argument. The *acknowledgment of diversity* underscored by the notion of an overlapping consensus does not undercut the *critique of privilege* contained in the egalitarian aspects of egalitarian liberalism.

Contemporary support, again

I have been emphasizing that the pluralistic consensus test does not itself require a search for implicit points of agreement in current moral views. Nonetheless the existence of such points might have a certain indirect relevance to justification. For, given that the deliberative liberties now receive some protection, it seems implausible to suppose that the full range of existing moral views simply represent accommodations to current and historical injustices, and would not continue to have some hold under just conditions. So it would be surprising if we could not already find the resources available in current moral understandings for defending a view of justice that we would also be able to defend under more favorable conditions. And if the pluralistic consensus test is acceptable, then there is also some rationale for taking current points of agreement seriously.

But it must be emphasized that when we understand the rationale for an examination of current points of agreement this way, we are not letting anything about justification turn on the mere fact of current consensus. In fact, it is never the case – not in the gesture to current understandings of value, and not in the requirement of overlapping consensus – that de facto agreement itself plays a role in justification.

With this last point I have begun to tread on the issues of the next section and so shall move directly to them.

Realism and reason

Now we come to the first of the issues about accommodation that I noted earlier: Does the pluralistic consensus test represent an unwanted accommodation to power? I begin my discussion of this question with some distinctions that will play an essential role in my (negative) answer.

Reasonable pluralism

Rawls refers to the fact that the deliberative liberties produce diversity as "the fact of pluralism." I think that this terminology may be misleading because "fact" puts the emphasis in the wrong place.[25] To explain why, I need first to introduce the idea of reasonable pluralism.[26]

The idea of reasonable pluralism is that there are distinct understandings of value, each of which is fully reasonable (pp. 235–8). An understanding of value is fully reasonable just in case its adherents are stably disposed to affirm it as they acquire new information and subject it to critical reflection.[27] The contention that there are a plurality of such understandings is suggested by the absence of convergence in reflection on issues of value, which leaves disagreements, for example, about the value of choice, welfare, and self-actualization; about the value of contemplative and practical lives; about the value of devotions to friends and lovers as distinct from more diffuse concerns about abstract others; and about the values of poetic expression and political engagement.

What we ought to suppose about the truth of our beliefs about any subject matter, evaluative or otherwise, in the face of such an apparently "irresoluble rivalry" of reasonable alternative views is an open philosophical question.[28] But among the rationally acceptable answers to that question is that it is permissible, even with full awareness of the fact of reflective divergence, to take the *sectarian* route of affirming one's own view, that is, believing it as a matter of faith. And since believing is believing true, a rationally permissible (though not mandatory) response to an apparently irresoluble rivalry of evaluative conceptions is to affirm that one's own view contains the whole truth, while the truths in other views are simply the subsets of those views that intersect with one's own. This being one of the options, and the option that creates the most trouble for the pluralistic consensus test, I will frame the rest of my discussion so that it is consistent with it.

These remarks about reasonable pluralism suggest two different ways to understand the fact of pluralism:

> *The simple fact of pluralism*: The protection of the deliberative liberties will result in moral pluralism.

> *The fact of reasonable pluralism*: The protection of the deliberative liberties will result in moral pluralism, and some of the moral conceptions will fall within the set of fully reasonable conceptions.

The reasonable pluralism interpretation does make a factual claim. The asserted fact, however, is not simply that the protection of deliberative liberties will result in a plurality of conceptions of value but, further, that a number of those conceptions will be reasonable, and permissibly taken by their adherents to be true.

The reasonable pluralism explanation

Consider now a conception of justice that we wish to subject to the pluralistic consensus test. We imagine a society regulated by that conception and in which the condition of reasonable pluralism obtains. The pluralistic consensus test requires that the values and principles used to authorize the exercise of power by the state must be restricted to those that are compelling to the different reasonable moral views adhered to in the society. Consider some people – call them "us" (or "we") – who hold one such view, and think that others believe what is false about the domain of value. Should we think that the pluralistic consensus test, which prevents us from relying on the whole truth in authorizing the use of power, is simply an accommodation to the de facto power of those others? It depends, and what it depends on is clarified by the distinction between simple and reasonable pluralism.

Suppose that we are impressed by the lack of reflective convergence in understandings of value, that we acknowledge the idea of reasonable pluralism, and at the same time embrace (not unreasonably) the sectarian view that our moral views are true. Because these are consistent positions, our sectarianism does not require that we condemn as unreasonable everyone who believes what we take to be false. And this provides a rationale for formulating a conception of justice that is confined to considerations that they take to be moral reasons as well.

In particular, when we restrict ourselves in political argument to the subset of moral considerations that others who have reasonable views accept as well, we are doing three things. First, we are advancing considerations that we take to be genuine moral reasons; the adherents of each of the views that supports the overlapping consensus hold that *nothing but the truth* lies in the overlapping consensus.

Second, in restricting ourselves to a subset of the true moral reasons – appealing to nothing but the truth, though not to the whole truth – we are not simply acknowledging that those who believe the false and spurn the good have the power to make their voices heard, or to make our lives miserable if we fail to heed those voices. Instead, we are acknowledging that their views are not unreasonable, even if they do believe what is false. In short, we are moved not by their power, but by an acknowledgment that they are reasonable.

Third, we are taking cognizance of a peculiarity in insisting on the whole (sectarian) truth in the face of our acknowledgment of the idea of reasonable pluralism. For suppose we acknowledge it, and affirm the divergence of moralities under reflection. Then we must see that if we were to appeal to the whole truth, that appeal would be, from the standpoint of others who we take to be reasonable, indistinguishable from simply appealing to what we believe. But we already acknowledge that the mere appeal to what we believe carries no force in justification.[29]

Suppose, for example, we believe that welfare is the sole ultimate good, and we understand that view to imply that choice is not an independent final value. In the course of political argument, we affirm:

"It is true that welfare is the sole ultimate good." Now others ought not to suppose that what we *mean* is equally well captured by "We believe that welfare is the sole ultimate good." The indistinguishability at issue is not semantical. The point, rather, is that if others accept the idea of reasonable pluralism, then they notice what we also notice, namely, that what lies between our taking our views to be reasonable (about which there may be no disagreement) and our taking them to be true (about which there is disagreement) is not a further reason, but simply our (rationally permissible) belief in those views. Because there is nothing else that lies in between, an appeal to the whole truth will seem indistinguishable from an appeal to what we believe.

The simple-fact explanation

Following the reasonable pluralism interpretation, then, when we restrict ourselves to common ground in face of the fact of diversity, we are acknowledging that reason does not mandate a single moral view and then are refraining from imposing ourselves on others who are prepared to be reasonable. This account of whom we need to accommodate turns on our willingness to acknowledge that some people with whom we fundamentally disagree are not unreasonable. That is why we are not simply accommodating principles to power when we are concerned to ensure that the conception of justice is acceptable to them as well. This explanation of the pluralistic consensus test might be clarified by contrasting it with another explanation, which is suggested by some of Rawls's remarks, but which is not persuasive.

As I indicated at the outset, Rawls emphasizes the importance of realism in the formulation of reasonable ideals. And he suggests that when we confine ourselves to considerations that are reasons for others as well, we are simply adjusting to certain general facts about the social world. Here the emphasis is on the need to be realistic, to find common ground because disagreement is a basic fact of life under free conditions.

To see why this explanation of the need to accommodate diversity is not right, notice that it is a plausible general fact that there will always be people with unreasonable views. But the fact that there are some people with unreasonable views does not require that we *adjust our conception of justice* so that it can be supported by an overlapping consensus that will appeal to them. While we need to take the fact of disagreement into account in some way in deciding what to do, the pluralistic consensus condition is certainly not the only way to do that and is not mandated by the recognition that there are and will always be such people. Furthermore, if we did embrace the requirement that a conception of justice be able to bring everyone on board – that it restrict itself to reasons embraced by all understandings of value – then it is hard to see what the response would be to the objection that the requirement of an overlapping consensus simply forces an accommodation to power.

The problem with this explanation is that it makes too much of the de facto diversity highlighted in the simple-fact interpretation. The first explanation – which draws essentially on the idea of reasonable pluralism – does not deny the relevance of the fact that under conditions of deliberative liberty there will be diversity. But the response to that fact is not undiscriminating, and in particular is controlled by the distinction between reasonable and unreasonable understandings of value.

Ensuring that a conception of justice fits the fact of diversity under conditions of deliberative liberty is not, then, an unacceptable accommodation to power. But the reason that it is acceptable is not because diversity is a fact of life, as the simple-fact interpretation of pluralism states, and because adjustment to general and unalterable facts of social life is always to be distinguished from accommodation to power. Instead, that adjustment is reasonable because some forms of diversity are the natural consequence of the free exercise of practical reason. Once we agree that they are, we will not be inclined to count moral diversity among the unfavorable facts of human life, nor to confuse a concern to find a conception of justice consistent with it with a willingness to compromise justice in the face of the course of the world.

Exclusion

Answering the charge of unwarranted accommodation, then, commits us to the view that we need not accommodate the unreasonable. Indeed, given the explanation for this view, if we did accommodate the unreasonable in the formulation of fundamental principles, then we would be unacceptably adjusting principles to de facto power.

But this brings me to a different concern about power and political consensus: that the promise of consensus is associated with the practice of arbitrary exclusion. In view of the problem of securing general agreement on anything, claims to speak on behalf of all of the reasonable depend, it will be argued, on drawing arbitrary boundaries around the community of the reasonable.[30] So the charge is that any appeal to the ideal of consensus in fact rests on the power to exclude, exercised in this case through the pretense of discovering that some people are unreasonable.

In the case at hand, the exclusion is of a special kind. It does not amount to a deprivation of liberties or of what are conventionally understood to be the advantages of social cooperation. Instead, exclusion lies in the fact that the arguments used to justify the exercise of power depend on norms, values, and ideals that are rejected by some people whose views will as a consequence not belong to an overlapping consensus. Although this does not violate the ideal of consensus, which requires that justification proceed by reference to reasons located on the common ground occupied by all who are prepared to listen to reason, it is exclusion all the same. And it is of a troublesome form. Its implication is that some people will reject the values, ideals, principles, and norms that serve, at the most fundamental level, to justify the exercise of power over them.

These are extremely important and complicated matters, not least because the charge of unreasonableness is commonly a ponderous way to express simple disagreement, or, in the distinctively American political idiom, a thinly disguised signal that one's opponents are poor, or female, or black. But as important as these issues are, I must be very brief here, and intend my comments only as a way to mark out certain issues for further examination and to introduce some doubts about the alleged arbitrariness of characterizations of views as unreasonable.

Consider, then, some views that might end up being excluded in this way, in particular those that would deny the protection of liberties on the basis of the doctrine that "outside the church there is no salvation." Rawls discusses this case, and states that it is "unreasonable" to use public powers to enforce this doctrine. I agree. But it is important to distinguish two ways that such enforcement might be unreasonable. Distinguishing them will help illustrate what is involved in exclusion on the grounds of unreasonableness.

The first case is presented by a "rationalist fundamentalist." This is the person who denies the idea of reasonable pluralism, affirming instead that it lies within the competence of reason to know that salvation is the supreme value, that there is a single path to salvation, that there is no salvation among the damned, and therefore that liberty of conscience is to be condemned. This is not a common view, if only because it claims for reason territory usually reserved for faith.[31] But if someone were to advance it, then one ought to say that they are simply mistaken. Even if these views are all rationally permissible, reason surely does not mandate them, and in insisting that it does they are not acknowledging the facts.

This response will not do in the second case. These are the nonrationalist fundamentalists who accept the limited competence of reason, but deny that reason is controlling in the authorization to use power. By contrast with the rationalist fundamentalists, they agree that an appreciation of the value of salvation and of the conditions for achieving it fall outside the competence of reason, and that grasping the truth about the proper conduct of life depends on faith. But they affirm that truths accessible only through faith are sufficient to authorize the legitimate exercise of power. What is important is that they are *truths*, and not the mode of access to them available for finite human creatures. Faced with nonrationalist fundamentalists, it will not do to state the case for the idea of reasonable pluralism; they know that case, celebrate the limited competence of reason as a guide in human affairs, and lament the self-imposed disabilities of those who insist on proceeding within its narrow compass.

Still, what they are prepared to do is to impose on those who are outside the faith in a way that – so far as those others can tell – is indistinguishable from the concededly irrational practice of imposing in the name of their beliefs. To resist such imposition is not simply to affirm a disagreement with the nonrationalist fundamentalist. Instead, it is to complain about this fundamental form of unreasonableness. And finding them unreasonable in this way is sufficient to show that the exclusion is not arbitrary.

Conclusions

I noted earlier that the problems addressed in Rawls's essay – the reasonableness of the ideal of a consensual order and of the pluralistic consensus condition – echo a set of concerns familiar from Hegel's political philosophy and critical discussion of it. Returning now to these concerns, what conclusions about them can we draw from the discussion here?

First, in *A Theory of Justice* Rawls proposed a formulation of the distinction between political and civil society and a conception of justice that was meant to accommodate that distinction without carrying the inegalitarian implications that some have thought intrinsic to it. Whatever the merits of that earlier defense of egalitarian liberalism, the pluralistic consensus condition does nothing to weaken it.

Second, Hegel thought that an account of the ideal of a consensual polity suited to modern conditions needed to accommodate the diversity of values and attachments characteristic of civil society.[32] While Hegel emphasized that the universal–particular distinction and its institutionalization in the separation of civil and political spheres is a distinguishing feature of modern societies, he did not suppose it to be simply a brute fact about post-Reformation Europe. Instead, his rationalism led him to suppose that this peculiarity represented a historically situated discovery about the operation of practical reason. In accommodating the diversity institutionalized in civil society, then, political philosophy was not simply accommodating the bare fact that people differ in aims and aspirations. Instead, it was acknowledging the diverse promptings of practical reason itself, even as it sought to find within that diversity the seeds of the set of common values underlying political society.[33] In short, some form of civil–political society distinction is an unavoidable aspect of any attractive ideal, once we see the scope and competence of practical reason. In a Hegelian *Doppelsatz*: We need to accommodate the ideal to the real because the real manifests the ideal.

Rawls's talk about the fact of pluralism, the role of the Reformation in prompting acknowledgment of that fact, and the need for an overlapping consensus can be taken in this same spirit. If we accept the idea of reasonable pluralism, then moral diversity is not simply a bare fact, even a bare general fact about human nature, but, rather, indicates something about the operation and powers of practical reason. With this account of diversity, we have a response to the contention that accommodating different understandings of value in the formulation of basic moral principles for the political domain is tantamount to supposing that justice commands that we turn our money over to thieves. The response is that we are accommodating basic principles not to the reality of power but, rather, to the way that social reality reveals the powers of practical reason.[34]

Notes

1 This essay began as comments on an unpublished paper by John Rawls on "A Reasonably Realistic Idea of a Well-ordered Society." I have rewritten it to address Rawls's "The Domain of the Political and Overlapping Consensus," originally published in *New York University Law Review* 64, no. 2 (May 1989): 233–55, and reprinted in this volume.

2 John Rawls, *A Theory of Justice* (Cambridge, Mass.: Harvard University Press, 1971), p. 263.

3 Rawls is concerned with forms of diversity that extend beyond the domain of morality, for example, to religious and philosophical matters. Nothing turns on the limitation that I adopt here.

4 The ideal of consensus may, of course, be unrealistic in other ways as well.

5 I return to the issue of favorable conditions later.

6 I explain the point of the phrase "to this extent" later.

7 The objection extrapolates on some points made by Jerry Cohen in a conversation about Rawls's difference principle.

8 All references to "The Domain of the Political" are included parenthetically within the text. Page numbers refer to the *New York University Law Review* edition cited in note 1.

9 I identify moral reasons by their functional role in individual deliberation and choice, not their content. There may be content restrictions as well, but I think that the functional role characterization captures a central aspect of ordinary usage and in any case suffices for my purposes here.

10 See Rawls's "third general fact," p. 235.

11 See Jean-Jacques Rousseau, *On the Social Contract*, trans. Judith R. Masters (New York: St. Martin's, 1978), Book 1, chap. 6.

12 We also need to add that everyone believes with good reason that the decisions express the values.

13 This is what Rawls calls the "first general fact." See pp. 234–5.

14 Hegel's discussion of Rousseau in the *History of Philosophy* are more balanced than his critical remarks in the *Philosophy of Right*. Compare *Lectures on the History of Philosophy*, vol. 3, trans. Elizabeth Haldane (New York: Humanities Press, 1968) with *Philosophy of Right*, trans. T. M. Knox (Oxford: Clarendon Press, 1952), pp. 156–7.

15 See *Philosophy of Right*, paragraph 261, where Hegel says that the state is both an "external necessity" with respect to the family and civil society, and "the end immanent within them."

16 Hegel did acknowledge the need to regulate property in the name of the general welfare, and to avoid certain extreme cases of poverty (see *Philosophy of Right*, paragraphs 234–48). But his view does not appear to countenance the regulation of economic activity with an eye to ensuring that the final distribution of resources is not determined by differences of social background and natural ability.

17 See his "On the Jewish Question," in *Marx-Engels Reader*, second edition, ed. Robert Tucker (New York: Norton, 1978), pp. 26–46; *Critique of Hegel's Philosophy of Right*, trans. Joseph O'Malley (Cambridge: Cambridge University Press, 1970).

18 This impression was confirmed by conversations at the conference at which I presented the first draft of these comments. See also the concerns about the "abstraction, vagueness, and conservativism" of Rawls's later work expressed in Thomas Pogge's *Realizing Rawls* (Ithaca, N.Y.: Cornell University Press, 1989), p. 4.

19 See, for example, John Gray, "Contractarian Method, Private Property, and Market Economy," in *Markets and Justice, Nomos XXIII*, eds. John W. Chapman and J. Roland Pennock (New York: New York University Press, 1989), pp. 13–58; and William Galston, "Pluralism and Social Unity," *Ethics* (July 1989): 711.

20 See *Theory of Justice*, p. 65.

21 The attribution to Kant in particular of the idea that abstract human potentialities are morally fundamental is also off the mark historically. That idea plays a central role in Rousseau's view, and is also suggested in Locke's theory of natural law. The variations on this general theme are complex, as is the evolution of the idea; fortunately these details are not relevant here.

22 Robert Dahl, for example, emphasizes the importance of "underlying consensus on policy" and on the basic rules of political competition in *A Preface*

to Democratic Theory (Chicago: University of Chicago Press, 1956), pp. 75–84, 132.

23 See *Theory of Justice*, p. 582. For elaboration of this strategy, see my "Democratic Equality and the Difference Principle," *Ethics* (July 1989): 727–51.

24 See John Rawls, "The Priority of the Right and Ideas of the Good," *Philosophy and Public Affairs* 17, no. 4 (Fall 1988): 275–6.

25 One reason for referring to a *fact* of pluralism is to distinguish the view that we need to accommodate the diversity of values that follows on the protection of the liberties from the view that that diversity should be accommodated because it is a good thing in itself. Nothing that I say is meant to challenge the propriety of this usage.

26 My discussion of reasonable pluralism is in agreement with Rawls's account of the "burdens of reason" (pp. 235–8). The point of the discussion is largely to indicate the special importance of those burdens, as distinct from the four other general facts that Rawls discusses (pp. 234–5), in explaining the pluralistic consensus test and in responding to objections to it.

27 I take this formulation from Mark Johnston.

28 See, for example, W.V.O. Quine, *Pursuit of Truth* (Cambridge, Mass.: Harvard University Press, 1990), pp. 98–101, from whom I take the phrase "irresoluble rivalry," and the term "sectarian" as it is used in the next sentence.

29 For elaboration of this point, see Thomas Nagel, "Moral Conflict and Political Legitimacy," *Philosophy and Public Affairs* 16, no. 3 (Summer 1987): 215–40. Joseph Raz has criticized Nagel's point, suggesting that it rests on an untenable distinction between the position of the speaker who advances a justification, and the listener to whom it is addressed. See his "Facing Diversity: The Case of Epistemic Abstinence," *Philosophy and Public Affairs* 19, no. 1 (Winter 1990): 37–9. I am not persuaded by Raz's contention. He is right that the positions of speaker and listener are parallel. But taking up the point of view of the person to whom a justification is addressed is simply a heuristic for understanding the limited force of an argument that appeals to the whole truth. So far from undermining Nagel's point, the parallelism is essential to drawing the right conclusions from the use of the heuristic.

30 I am indebted to Uday Mehta for many discussions of these issues. For discussion of a variety of different strategies of exclusion, see his "Liberal Strategies of Exclusion," *Politics and Society* 18, no. 4 (December 1990): 427–54.

31 It is an analog to "creation science," operating in the domain of salvation. The proper response is the same in both cases.

32 I am not confident that Hegel held the view I attribute to him in this paragraph. It does fit with and make sense out of various pieces of his view, including his account of the relationship between civil society and the state, his conception of the role of reason in history, and his views about the

rationality of modern social arrangements. But he does not state it anywhere in the way that I put it here. If I am wrong in thinking that he held it, nothing else in the article would need to change.

33 See *Philosophy of Right*, paragraph 261.

34 I thank Michael Hardimon, John Rawls, Tim Scanlon, and Judith Thomson for very helpful comments on earlier drafts of this essay.

The moral commitments
of liberalism

JEAN HAMPTON

The latent causes of faction are thus sown in the nature of man.
James Madison, *Federalist Paper Number 10*

In "The Domain of the Political and Overlapping Consensus" (here-after DPOC), John Rawls attempts to refine and further develop his recent conception of the nature and importance of what he calls the "overlapping consensus" in a modern liberal democracy.[1] One of his primary reasons for doing so is to allay misgivings that some political philosophers have had not only about this notion but also about what Rawls has called his "political" method of theorizing about matters of justice (which, in earlier articles, he contrasted to the "metaphysical" theorizing standard in other areas of moral philosophy). These philo-sophers, myself included, have worried that Rawls's recent work consti-tutes a retreat from the moral objectivity he seemed so clearly to embrace in his earlier work.[2] In DPOC, Rawls attempts to show that no such retreat has occurred and the trajectory of his thinking in that essay will certainly be welcomed by such critics. But I want to argue here that his development of the idea of an overlapping consensus is still not complete, and that, to complete it, he must either develop it further along objectivist lines, and thereby kill off any claim that the resulting theory is 'political' rather than 'metaphysical,' or else retain that distinc-tive political methodology but make the resulting theory (to use his words) "political in the wrong sense."[3] My remarks are intended not only to show that such a choice is required for the completion of his view but also to show that to remain a liberal he must choose the first alternative. If I am right, then any theorist who has been persuaded by Rawls's recent work to attempt to develop a "theoretically neutral form of liberalism" is doomed to fail.

I. The overlapping consensus

There is a remarkable diversity of what Rawls calls "comprehensive" or "partially comprehensive" religious, philosophical, and moral views among the populations of modern constitutional democracies.[4] Yet such democracies must function to survive: Conflicts must be adjudicated, and policies formulated and instituted without provoking widespread or severe dissent among the citizenry. How can such a society be, as Rawls puts it, "well ordered" and yet continue to respect that diversity? On what common ground can political discourse proceed if the community is going to rule out (as democracies invariably do) the use of force to put an end to the diversity of views within it? Rawls's answer is that such communities must develop a consensus that includes not only substantive principles of justice but also a conception of public reason that the citizenry will use when articulating and justifying claims and proposals for resolving conflicts. Moreover, to ensure that the ground is common, Rawls insists that these societies must exclude all philosophical or religious explanations for *why* the principles being endorsed are right, or true, or justified. Only in this way, he says, can we develop a shared basis of public justification while eschewing oppression.

Joseph Raz has recently coined a nice name for one of the motivating assumptions behind this Rawlsian conception of democracy: epistemic abstinence.[5] On Rawls's view political philosophers in a democratic society are supposed to abstain from promoting particular metaphysical justifications of their society's public charter in the political arena, in order, first, to respect the diversity of metaphysical views that are part of our social culture and, second, to avoid placing unnecessary barriers in the way of those averse to the philosopher's particular metaphysics from embracing central tenets of that charter. The first is a reason of fairness; the second is a practical reason arising out of a concern that the political society remain stable. Rawls maintains that the political philosopher's job is to "provide a shared public basis of the justification of political and social institutions" that will help "ensure stability from one generation to the next."[6] The political philosopher who pursues this objective is either looking for or else striving to develop a common ground of ideas latent in the culture that can be endorsed by people no matter what their metaphysical views.

Like much of Rawls's work, the ideas in DPOC are greatly influenced by the American political experience. Although Rawls characterizes political societies as "closed" in the sense that we enter them only by birth and exit only by death,[7] historically this has not been quite true in the United States, which has had large numbers of immigrants choose as adults to leave the political culture in which they were born and enter this one. Historians are in agreement that despite calls from some quarters for "Anglo-conformity,"[8] immigrants were allowed by Americans already here to retain large amounts of their culture and even (in many contexts) their language. Nonetheless, they were only thought to become American when they repudiated antidemocratic political vestiges of the old country and took on the democratic political culture of the United States. Horace Kallen, a philosopher at the turn of the century who coined the term "cultural pluralism," argued that the democratic values implicit in American political culture that these immigrants embraced mandated the tolerance of ethnic diversity and respect for their refusal to assimilate.[9] Kallen maintained that this was an inevitable consequence of adherence to democratic ideals, which allowed individuals to choose how to fashion their own lives. So for Kallen and others who embraced the idea of cultural pluralism in the early part of this century, the political culture of this country (denoted by the word 'democratic') simultaneously unified the country into one, even while encouraging a diversity of belief and life-style.

Kallen's description of "American political culture" sounds something like Rawls's "overlapping consensus in a liberal democratic society": Both are supposed to comprise a set of beliefs that individuals embrace no matter what their other philosophical and religious views, and that mandate tolerance and respect for the diversity of views in the country. Moreover, both are understood to be the intellectual "glue" that not only holds a country together despite its pluralism, but also provides the source of both legitimacy and stability for the style of political governance in that society.

But Kallen appears to assume that his fellow citizens are justified in insisting that these democratic values be embraced by all newcomers because they are the right values for a just political society and included in the public charter by the founding fathers for that reason. I call this sort of theorist, that is, one who takes what are standardly considered "liberal" political values to be objectively correct and for that reason the appropriate foundation for political power, an" objectivist liberal." It is not at all clear that Rawls's understanding of the overlapping consensus makes him this kind of liberal. How does Rawls believe that the content of such a consensus ought to be arrived at? Does he think that the values in an overlapping consensus in a modern constitutional democracy have been (correctly) determined to be right by their citizens, and included in the consensus for that reason, or does he assume only that they are mutually agreed upon and for that reason alone serviceable as constituents of a public charter? To put the same question somewhat differently: Does he regard the beliefs it comprises to be common ground because they are taken by the citizenry to be normatively correct, or does he think they should be allowed to play a normative role in the society only because (as it happens) they are common ground?

The objectivist liberal worries that Rawls's writings commit him to the latter "political" answer.[10] For it seems that if someone were to give these ideas a standard normative defense, she would most likely make reference to conceptions of morality, personhood, or religious beliefs that would be part of a comprehensive or partially comprehensive doctrine, and thus invariably the subject of contention in a pluralist society. So instead, this sort of critic has taken Rawls to be committed to the view that the components of an overlapping consensus in a well-ordered society are just those that are implicit in and common to all the comprehensive or partially comprehensive views of the disparate groups in such societies. For example, in DPOC Rawls makes the beliefs in human freedom and equality part of the overlapping consensus of contemporary political democracies, and in at least one place he appears to do so because he takes it to be a *fact* that virtually all people in such democracies accept these beliefs.[11]

But doesn't such a defense of the content of an overlapping consensus make that consensus "political" in a bad sense, requiring that a democratic society take as its intellectual common ground whatever happens to be the intersection of their views (where, admittedly, philosophical reflection might be necessary to work out what that is)? Is Rawls saying, reminiscent of Hobbes, that what counts as "just" for a democratic society is defined not by some conception taken to be objectively correct, but solely by reference to the content of a ruling consensus created by a sovereign electorate? Such a position strikes the objectivist liberal as unacceptable: On her view, an overlapping consensus that allowed differential economic opportunities depending upon race or sex, or that tolerated severe impoverishment or certain forms of religious intolerance, would be an illegitimate charter for that society – and deserve the adjective "unjust" – no matter how much support it received from the citizenry, and no matter how well ordered the society. So why shouldn't Rawls commend to the citizenry of democratic societies the search for principles which instantiate justice itself (as he appeared to do in *A Theory of Justice*) rather than those principles which people happen to agree upon, and which may depart substantially from the requirements of justice?

In DPOC, Rawls is concerned to allay worries that he is commending a positivist approach to the nature of justice in political theorizing. For example, he says explicitly:

We must, however, be careful that a political conception is not political in the wrong way. It should aim to formulate a coherent view of the very great (moral) values applying to the political relationship and to set out a public basis for justification for free institutions in a manner accessible to free public reason. It must not be political in the sense of merely specifying a workable compromise between known and existing interests, nor political in looking to the particular comprehensive doctrines known to exist in society and in then being tailored to gain their allegiance.[12]

So Rawls does not want the content of the overlapping consensus to be merely the product of political negotiation among diverse groups, presumably because such a process could produce a fragile and highly unjust public charter. The question I shall consider in the rest of this article is, Has Rawls formulated a conception of the overlapping consensus that successfully allows him to see it as a political conception rather than as a partially comprehensive philosophical or religious view, but nonetheless not political in the wrong sense, so that it could plausibly be said to instantiate justice in a modern constitutional democracy?

II. Being reasonable

We should start by appreciating why it should be so hard for Rawls to ward off the misgivings of objectivist liberals. Consider his defense of "political" as opposed to "metaphysical" theorizing in his earlier papers. The word "metaphysical" is never explicitly defined in those papers, but he appears to use it not, as a positivist would, as "nonsense to be dismissed" but in a more Hobbesian sense, as "doctrines for which an incontrovertible demonstration is not possible."[13] And he takes it to be offensive of the state to incorporate metaphysical ideas into the public charter, because that would mean the state would be using ideas, for which it had no proof, to justify a coercive response against groups who did not endorse such ideas.

In DPOC, Rawls abandons the word 'metaphysical' but mounts a very similar argument about the limits of political power using what he calls "the burdens of reason" argument. We disagree, he points out, for many reasons, and often those reasons reflect our prejudices, bad reasoning processes, or limited intellectual capacities. But even when we are properly open-minded, well reasoning, and intelligent, we can still disagree (often intractably) because of "the many hazards involved in the correct (and conscientious) exercise of our powers of reason and judgment in the ordinary course of political life."[14] He goes on to list six sources of such reasonable disagreement, including incomplete evidence, differing backgrounds that shape our judgment differently, and conflicting normative considerations that are difficult to weigh or assess. In situations where any of these conditions hold, each of us may arrive at very different conclusions, and we may be quite unable to resolve our disagreements. To put it another way, in such situations each of us is right to take her position as reasonable, given what she can ascertain about the world, and thus each of us is reasonable to resist any claim made by those who disagree with her that she *must* be wrong.

How does a political society respond to the reasonable intractability of disagreement? Rawls argues that precisely because such disagreement is reasonable, a society would be unreasonable to use its power to resolve the disagreement in favor of one of the parties. In the course of explaining why a liberal political society could not tolerate the attempt by a religious constituency to enforce its religious views on the whole of the population, Rawls maintains:

From the point of view of political liberalism, the appropriate reply is to say that the conclusion is unreasonable: it proposes to use the public's political power – a power in which citizens have an equal share – to enforce a view affecting constitutional essentials about which citizens as reasonable persons, given the burdens of reason, are bound to differ uncompromisingly in judgment.

It is important to stress that this reply does not say that a doctrine *Extra ecclesiam nulla salus* is not true. Rather it says that it is unreasonable to use the public's political power to enforce it.[15]

This passage suggests what Rawls goes on explicitly to articulate, namely, what I call the *"reasonableness" principle of legitimate political coercion*: "Since political power is the coercive power of free and equal citizens as a corporate body, this power should be exercised, when constitutional essentials are at stake, only in ways that all citizens can reasonably be expected to endorse publicly in the light of their own common, human reason."[16] I shall only note, but postpone discussion of, the suggestion that this principle derives from the idea that citizens are "free and equal." Disregarding that rhetoric for the moment, the principle says that it is not the purported truth or falsity of a view, but rather the lack of decisive proof of its truth in the eyes of all reasonable human beings, that makes it unenforceable.

Let me use Rawls's old term 'metaphysical' to mean "any view whose truth or falsity cannot be decisively determined by fully reasonable and intelligent human beings." If a political society cannot enforce any such metaphysical view, how can it hope to govern a people in a world where proof is hard to come by?

To answer this question, we must first determine to what the principle actually applies. Consider the fact that any political society, in order to function, must resolve all sorts of contentious issues, and often it will be genuinely unclear what the correct resolution is. For example, rules about property must be developed and enforced in any society, and surely there is no set of property rules that one could argue is indisputably correct. How could a political society formulate legislation defining property rights that is consistent with Rawls's principle? I suspect Rawls would reply that although innumerable controversial issues such as property rights would have to be decided and enforced by the government, such enforcement would still be consistent with his principle as long as it was directed by a democratically elected government that sought to implement policies reflecting the common values of the citizenry. So to be fully charitable we should interpret Rawls's test not as applying to particular legislation nor even to the overarching policies directing legislation, both of which might be subject to irreconcilable conflict, but rather to the fundamental values or (more generally) the normative beliefs which the legislation of a democracy is either striving to implement or to which it is attempting to adhere. These beliefs define not only the common conception of justice, which all parties will invoke as they mount their political arguments, but also standards of reasonable discussion, to which they will adhere as they participate in the political arena.

So the intellectual unity Rawls attempts to define for democratic societies is (and must be) at a very high level. Rawls's remarks indicate he believes that as a society strives to create such unity, its members must adhere to his principle defining the legitimate uses of political power. I want to argue that this means he believes his principle generates what I will call a "reasonableness test" providing the citizens with the criterion of admission for any normative belief proposed for membership in the set of such beliefs comprising the overlapping consensus. I will state it (using Rawls's own language from his reasonableness principle) as follows:

> *The reasonableness test for admissible beliefs in the overlapping consensus*: The beliefs which comprise the overlapping consensus must be ones that all citizens can reasonably be expected to endorse publicly in the light of their own common, human reason.

Note that this test appears to allow two kinds of normative beliefs to be admitted: first, those for which there is either an incontrovertible proof or which can be taken to be self-evident; and second, those which, as it happens, everyone in the society rationally endorses given the (partial) evidence available to them, but which could be contested by anyone with differing evidence or experiences with life.

In a footnote Rawls suggests a way to rely on the test itself to derive part of the content of such a consensus.[17] If disagreement on philosophical and religious matters is, on the whole, reasonable, it should be unreasonable, not merely for the state, but for any person or institution to insist that coercion should be used to resolve the disagreement in favor of one party rather than another. Therefore, if such an unreasonable belief should be part of the comprehensive view of any religious or philosophical group in the society, then the government would be reasonable not only to disregard it but also to insist that members of such groups be prevented from acting on it. In practical terms this amounts to requiring that an overlapping consensus in a pluralist democratic society include the principle of tolerance. To the extent that any group refuses to endorse such a principle, then to that extent they are cut out of (and legitimately subject to the enforcement power of) that consensus.

What else should such a consensus include? Rawls replies that it must include special "political" values that "give expression to the liberal political ideal."[18] And in addition to the principle of toleration, he goes on to mention the idea that human beings are free and equal, although without going into very much detail about what these notoriously difficult concepts should be understood to mean.

But what justifies the inclusion of a belief in our freedom and equality in such a consensus, particularly if some members of the pluralist society do not accept them, or have substantially different interpretations than Rawls of what these concepts mean? For example, suppose there were a democratic society that recognized universal adult suffrage but that included citizens who embraced a religion that used certain criteria to divide people up into different castes that defined their status, the work for which they are supposed to be fitted, and their social responsibilities. They might even support the use of political power to structure the opportunities and powers of people, depending on their caste. Such people, in view of their religious beliefs, would reject and take to be unreasonable the use of political power to enforce Rawls's idea of equality. Where is your proof, they would ask, for our equality? And if you cannot give one, how can you insist that our public charter endorse this idea? What would Rawls say to such people?

Perhaps he might deny that he need say anything to them at all. Often in his recent work, Rawls stresses the fact that the content for the sort of overlapping consensus he is commending depends on the political society's being a modern Western democracy with certain fundamental beliefs (e.g., in freedom and equality) that are part of the intellectual culture of that society. Hence, he might claim it is beside the point to ask what kind of overlapping consensus should be created if the society changed so much that it was substantially different from the sort of society his theory assumes. If he took this position, Rawls's justification of his theory of justice is critically dependent on the fact that certain contingent features hold in the society to be governed by that theory.

Taking such a position, however, will undermine the effectiveness of his defense of his theory of justice in the eyes of many philosophers. On this view Rawls would be arguing: "If a society believes in x, y and z, then the theory of justice I commend will be shared by all the members." The force of the 'will' is interesting here: Either it means that members of the society do in fact believe that theory, or it means that were the theory explained to them, and a deduction of that theory from the fundamental beliefs performed, they would have to accept it as long as they were fully reasonable and rational. Either position, however, makes the justification of his theory of justice entirely contingent on what fundamental beliefs people happen to believe. And what is the moral status of these fundamental beliefs? "Okay," say the members of this society, "maybe you are right that we're logically required to hold this view or that we already do hold it (albeit, perhaps, unaware of our doing so) in virtue of the other ideas we embrace. But *ought* we to hold these other ideas? If they come under challenge by some of our members who begin to question them, are we required – and do we have the conceptual resources – to defend them, and if necessary use the power of the state to enforce them? Or have we little or nothing to say as a way of establishing their reasonableness in the face of this challenge? And if the latter, do we eschew the use of force, and try to work out a new overlapping consensus that takes into account the fact that some of our members embrace fundamental beliefs substantially different from our own?"

It is quite clear from his writings that Rawls would not want to answer positively to the last question, insofar as doing so would make the democratic overlapping consensus a mere modus vivendi, a product of political compromise that could not be morally defended. In the next two sections, I discuss Rawls's arguments in DPOC to determine whether or not he has the resources to argue that these ruling ideas of our democracy can and should be defended as *right* against those who would try to dethrone them. Can he take this position consistent with his aim of giving a political rather than a metaphysical defense of his theory?

III. The reasonableness of freedom and equality

The position that I believe Rawls wants to take is that no society can be politically legitimate, much less "democratic and liberal," unless it is governed by the values of freedom and equality. On this position the citizenry would be somehow justified in criticizing the caste-based religious views of the people in my example as unjust, opposing any proposals from them to use political power to enforce their views, and persisting in policies that adhere to and even enforce (using the state's coercive power) the idea of equality.

There are a number of times in DPOC where Rawls suggests ideas that fit with such a response. In his account of the values of the political, he explicitly says "some of these great values are expressed by the principles of justice for the basic structure: the values of equal political and civil liberty, of fair equality of opportunity, of economic reciprocity, the social basis of mutual respect among citizens, and so on."[19] The discussion strongly suggests that not just *any* value can count as a political value, no matter how many people embrace it. To be politically legitimate, an overlapping consensus must have the *right* values.

How can we tell which values are right? A bit later in the article, Rawls says that the political values he endorses, which are implicit in his own conception of justice, are "reasonable," suggesting these values are ones that the proper exercise of reason will uncover:

As a liberal political conception, justice as fairness relies for its reasonableness in the first place upon generating its own support in a suitable way by addressing each citizen's reason, as explained within its own framework.

Only in this manner is justice as fairness an account of political legitimacy. Only so does it escape being a mere account of how those who hold political power can satisfy themselves, in the light of their own convictions, whether political or fully comprehensive, that they are acting properly – satisfy themselves, that is, and not citizens generally. A conception of political legitimacy aims for a public basis of justification and appeals to free public reason, and hence to all citizens viewed as reasonable and rational.[20]

So Rawls appears to be saying that the values of freedom and equality are and should be part of the overlapping consensus of Western democracies not because they happen to be widely endorsed in these societies, but rather because these values would be endorsed by fully reasonable people; and it is that fact which makes them the right ones to include in such a consensus. Because belief in these values is reasonable (and, it seems, disbelief unreasonable), any political power used to enforce them is legitimate, and not an unfair exercise of coercion by a group of citizens based on their particular disputable religious or philosophical views.

I confess this is the type of reply I should like Rawls to give, and the fact that it is so strongly suggested in DPOC would mollify the misgivings of those of us who are objectivist liberals about his theory, but for the fact that, given other ideas to which Rawls has committed himself, it is not clear whether he really has the theoretical resources to make it. The reply depends on being able to call the use of political power to enforce the values of freedom and equality "reasonable." How can we do so? And when we do so, are we ruling out the "wrong" views (i.e., the intolerant, freedom-denying, equality-denying views) by covertly presupposing a particular controversial comprehensive moral view to do so?

Rawls might argue that we can answer both questions positively as long as

> (1) it is not true that the only defense of these values presupposes a particular comprehensive or partially comprehensive view that, given the burdens of reason, some people in the society could reasonably reject, and
> (2) the values of freedom and equality have a force or authority in and of themselves that is so powerful that the burdens of reason are not sufficient for us to allow that someone could reasonably dispute them.

Is it possible for Rawls to establish both of these claims?

I take it that when Rawls says these values are "free-standing"[21] he is insisting that (1) is true. It would seem that values could be free-standing so that (1) is true in one of two ways. First, such values can be embraced "on their own," without being derived from any larger philosophical or religious view. (Rawls suggests this idea when he notes: "It is left to citizens individually, as part of their liberty of conscience, to settle how they think the great values of the political domain relate to other values within their comprehensive doctrine.")[22] I would think that this way of endorsing such values is common: The terrain of our moral life is complicated, and I doubt that either philosophy or religion is always or even usually important in explaining why we hold particular moral or political beliefs, or that those beliefs are always the logical conclusion of trains of deductive reasoning. Consequently, a citizen's perception of the necessity of insisting that her society foster freedom and equality for all may be a judgment to which she is committed independently of her commitments to other philosophical and religious views, and in this sense free-standing. (Indeed it may even be at odds with some of her other views, in a way that might be hard for her to reconcile.) I suspect that one reason many of us who call ourselves political philosophers were attracted to this area of inquiry is that we wished to understand and justify our free-standing commitments to the moral values animating our democracies. But when values are free-standing, our fundamental commitments are to the values themselves, and not to the theoretical speculations we generate to explain them. ("We hold these truths to be self-evident," writes Thomas Jefferson.) Some things we come to think (no matter whether or not our speculations are conclusive) that we *know*, even if we are not sure why we know them.

Second, values can be free-standing even when individuals in a community come to develop differing comprehensive doctrines that incorporate the values, as long as their fundamental commitment is still to the values themselves, and not to the differing philosophical or religious speculations in which they have embedded those values. For example, suppose that all of them hold the belief that we are free and equal, but some of them construct a religious justification for that belief, while others develop a secular, reason-based justification. As long as all of them are agreed that the belief is true, and admit that the comprehensive view in which they had embedded the belief might be the wrong justification for it, their commitment to the belief is still free-standing in the right sense. That is, all are committed to the idea *that* the belief is true, and not similarly committed to any particular explanation of *why* it is true.

I suspect that a lot of our beliefs are free-standing, forming a bedrock of ideas which we use to approach the world. Indeed, just as epistemological theories attempt to articulate and supply warrant for bedrock beliefs such as the existence of the material world, so too can political philosophy or religious theology involve, at least in part, the attempt to articulate and supply the warrant for bedrock political and religious beliefs that are part of the public charter. Such reflection can not only deepen our appreciation of and commitment to these ideas, but can also help to correct our understanding of them. But in such cases our reflection comes *after* the endorsement of the political or the religious values; our endorsement of them does not depend on these speculations being true.[23]

So I take (1) to be often – perhaps even usually – correct. I do not see how Rawls can establish that it is true for all such values, and for all citizens in democratic societies, and if he cannot, then the existence of the right kind of overlapping consensus in such societies is still a contingent matter. But this needn't be taken as a problem for his position as long as he has a way of defending the liberal values as inescapably correct, such that reasonable people would have to accept them. This is what (2) says is possible: So can Rawls defend (2)?

To do so, he must argue that it is unreasonable *not* to believe that we are free and equal. Now I would find it easy to say such a thing, but I have a morally informed conception of reasonableness, making it, to use

Rawls's terminology, a partially comprehensive conception. In contrast, Rawls tells us that his notion of reasonableness is meant to be deliberately uninformed by nonpolitical values. So how can he use it to criticize the rejection of freedom and equality?

Might he be able to do so if the notion was invested, not with moral norms, but with epistemic ones? On this view, when Rawls called someone unreasonable, he would be saying that this person rejects a view for which other fully reasonable and rational people believe a proof exists or which is reasonably taken to be self-evident. So if he would call those who reject the liberal ideas of human freedom and equality unreasonable, he would believe that reasonable and rational people would believe these ideas to be either self-evident or decisively proved. Such a position makes the ultimate defense of Rawls's theory of justice depend not on the authority of any particular moral theory but on the authority of epistemic and logical norms. Instead of grounding his political theory on the shaky norms of morality, he would be grounding it on (what would be taken to be) the incontrovertible authority of the norms of epistemology and logic.

But are they so incontrovertible? Philosophers who are used to questioning the authority of these norms may believe that Rawls has made no great bargain trading moral norms for these norms if he wished thereby to purchase a more solid foundation for his theory. For is it plausible to suppose there is a decisive proof for these ideas, or a way of showing that they are self-evident? Many will insist there is neither: Certainly there is no universally accepted proof establishing their truth, and with apologies to Thomas Jefferson, I fear we cannot take them to be self-evident. Human history provides enormous evidence for their contestability; commitment to these beliefs has been (and remains) unusual rather than usual. Outside the West, social hierarchies and restrictions of freedom are commonplace (and Western societies derided for their commitments to liberty and equality); and even within Western democracies, beliefs that would limit liberty (e.g., within certain forms of fundamentalist religions) or challenge equality (such as racist or sexist views) are far more widespread than many would like to admit. If so many people can fail to see the warrant for these values, doesn't the burdens-of-reason argument force us to conclude (however much we may dislike to do so) that it is reasonable (albeit, in our view, incorrect or immoral) to believe otherwise? If Rawls were to persist in calling the rejection of these values unreasonable, wouldn't his use of that term be just as ill-supported as, say, the claim made by a fervent religious believer that it would be unreasonable not to admit God's existence?

I must be careful to note that I like Rawls's rhetoric here; but this is because I have morally informed notion of reason. If I were to say "Senator Jesse Helms is unreasonable to reject homosexuals' rights," I would understand 'unreasonable' here to be informed by moral ideas that are surely contestable but in which I have great faith. If the admission of a belief into the overlapping consensus rests solely upon its lack of contestability by fully reasonable and rational people who have nonetheless had access to different evidence, and whose experience with life yields different ways of judging and evaluating the world around us, I do not see how the values of freedom and equality pass that test. On the other hand, if Rawls is prepared to accept that his notion of reasonableness is morally informed, then (at least in my view) he is right to argue that the rejection of human freedom and equality is unreasonable. But clearly this position is a theoretically partisan one, and if it were openly embraced by a liberal society, that society could not claim to be neutral with respect to a variety of different forms of religious or philosophical beliefs that exist not merely in the world but within Western democratic societies themselves.

Maybe the difficulties I am pointing to arise because, without realizing it, Rawls actually uses two notions of reason in his recent work. In the burdens-of-reason argument in DPOC he asks, "Given who a person is and what he knows, what is it reasonable for him to conclude?" And he is surely right that there are all sorts of conclusions that individuals can reach, while adhering to standards of rational belief formation, about various religious, moral and political issues in virtue of their differing background and evidence. (Even the most hardened atheist could not fairly call a woman raised in the Mennonite tradition in Pennsylvania "unreasonable" or "irrational" because she believed in God, although he could certainly consider her wrong so to believe.) But Rawls himself is famous for asking a different kind of question in his earlier work, namely, "If a person could be placed in a moral Archimedean point, what would he be rational to conclude about moral matters?" Or (to use T. M. Scanlon's formulation), "what would a person be unreasonable to reject as the basis of informed, unforced general agreement?"[24] This sort of question asks not whether the beliefs of real people satisfy standards of rational belief formation but, rather, what beliefs would be rational if an individual had a morally ideal perspective. The beliefs about justice that a man on the street would hold might be perfectly rational beliefs given his upbringing, but they might not be the *right* beliefs as determined by that ideal reasoning procedure.

So there is ideal reasoning – reasoning in morally and epistemically ideal circumstances – and there is reasoning in real, less than ideal circumstances. When Rawls makes his burdens-of-reason argument, he is clearly talking about real reasoning, but when he insists that reason mandates a belief in human freedom and equality he appears to have shifted (as one might predict a Kantian contractarian would do) to an appeal to the conclusions of (what he takes to be) ideal human reasoning. But clearly conceptions of what ideal reasoning is like are informed by a whole variety of normative ideas that are eminently disputable by individuals who have grown up in a world that is not ideal. So to the extent that Rawls's theory is informed by these ideals, it is, in his own terms, a partially comprehensive view, and were it to be used in a liberal society, that society would be theoretically partisan rather than neutral.

IV. The reasonable as the presently acceptable

Rawls might still insist that there is some middle ground that the preceding arguments failed to recognize: If he interprets his reasonableness test as relying not on what are taken to be objectively authoritative normative notions (either moral or epistemic) or on what people happen to accept, given their experience and available evidence, but on what are taken to be the commonly accepted standards of reasonable and rational belief formation in a society, then he might be able to maintain that an overlapping consensus embracing the values of tolerance and his theory of justice can be constructed (only) from those beliefs held by people in modern Western democracies that are called 'reasonable' by virtue of the fact that those who hold them have conformed to the standards of belief formation in our society. If he maintains that belief in human freedom and equality is, in this sense, "reasonable" for us, and a denial of freedom and equality unreasonable given our standards of belief formation, Rawls might argue that no person who rejects these values can legitimately feel unfairly coerced if these values are foisted upon her by a political power. So on this view, the term 'reasonable' is informed not by any comprehensive moral theory or epistemological view but by commonly accepted assumptions in our society about what are taken to be reasonable ways of forming beliefs, producing what he calls "considered convictions" or "fixed points of our considered judgements."

This conception of what counts as 'reasonable' might appear to give acceptable results for Western societies, where most of the official political rhetoric assumes that we are free and equal. But I shall now argue that this interpretation of what is reasonable can fail in two ways: In certain circumstances, it can give warrant to illiberal beliefs, and in other circumstances it can fail to give warrant to liberal ones.

Consider, first, that this position would pressure Rawls to say it is not unreasonable, given their histories and culture, for governments in non-Western nondemocratic societies to use political power to run roughshod over people in violation of the ideals of freedom, equality, and tolerance. Such governments can correctly deny that democratic values have ever prevailed in their societies, and insist that commonly accepted ways of forming beliefs in their societies (which might include an appeal to inegalitarian religious faiths or "commonsense" views defining relative social status) sanction political policies that are intolerant, inegalitarian, or freedom-denying. If Rawls understands the "reasonable" as picked out by commonly accepted standards of belief formation, then he has no reply to such governments. This would mean he was without resources to criticize the political policies of such countries as South Africa, China, or Chile, whose leaders can smugly note that their nondemocratic histories can be taken to generate a conception of what is reasonable that licenses everything from torture to severe discrimination. And how can a responsible liberal condone practices (e.g., the torture of political prisoners, or the tolerance of clitoridectomy) in non-Western societies that inflict what we would call "serious rights violations" if they were performed in a Western democracy?

However, even those of us within Western democracies have reason to reject this position. Those people who come from groups in these democracies whose members still suffer discrimination will insist that their experience disputes the idea that there is universal or even widespread acceptance of "acceptable belief formation"; such discrimination is strong evidence that many members of these societies either reject, or disagree about how to understand, the values of freedom, equality and tolerance. Hence, the assumption of this position that the public charter of our society must be built out of the beliefs people actually hold can be chilling for those who are the target of attack by opponents of liberal values, and who may therefore have cause to worry about the extensiveness or the tenacity of Rawls's understanding of these values in their society.

Objectivist liberals can also argue that this kind of interpretation of what counts as a 'reasonable' (and hence permissible) belief can actually lead to violations of Rawls's own principle of legitimate political coercion. To see this: Suppose we are in a society in which everyone is committed to the values of human freedom and equality in a way that makes his commitment "free-standing" in either of the senses I defined earlier. If 'reasonable' is defined as "acceptable given common standards of belief formation," we can decide to include these values in the public charter for either of two reasons: first, because, as it happens, we all accept them and believe the public charter must be constructed out of the actual (reasonable) beliefs of the citizenry; or second, because we all believe and agree that they are the right political values (even though we may disagree about why they are right) and we believe the public charter must include only values or principles that are right.

If we take the first position, we are motivated, as Rawls says we should be, by the thought that political coercion can be legitimate only if based on ideas that all can reasonably accept. But what if a group in the society reasonably comes to believe that it does not share those ideas? In this case the public charter must be renegotiated, so that all can come to accept it once again. However, such renegotiation might be along lines that would strike any liberal as unjust, and thus the legitimacy of the use of power to enforce such a charter would be undermined in her eyes. In fact it seems that such a society would not be governed by a conception of justice at all but only by a modus vivendi that allowed groups differing in beliefs to live in some sort of harmony. Now, Rawls might vigorously deny that any group could *reasonably* come to disagree with basic liberal values: But, as discussed earlier, none of us possesses an airtight argument for these values, and none of us can plausibly maintain that they are self-evident as they stand. Thus there exists the possibility of reasonable disagreement on these values – where 'reasonable' is understood nonmorally and describes views that are perfectly possible given the available evidence (albeit, perhaps, morally offensive, given the comprehensive moral views many of us hold). And once that disagreement occurs, Rawls's principle of political legitimacy would require that the overlapping consensus be reconstructed so that it did not foist upon some members of the population liberal values they could not accept. An objectivist liberal is going to reject such a compromise with her political enemies, seeing it as a way of creating an unjust charter for her political society.

So if Rawls is adamant that such injustice must not be allowed, he might try taking the second position. Indeed, much of Rawls's rhetoric in DPOC suggests it. On this view Rawls would insist that if a group within the society came to reject a belief in human freedom and equality, the rest of the citizenry could insist that doing so defied this society's commonly accepted standards of reasonable and rational belief formation and refuse to renegotiate the charter, understanding it to be informed only by reasonable views and thus definitive of justice and the legitimate use of political power (so that if the society were to renegotiate it, that legitimacy would be lost).

But, as I have repeatedly asked, is it plausible to say that liberal understandings of freedom, equality, and tolerance are the *only* reasonable views one can have about human nature, relative human standing, and acceptable political practices? By saying this, Rawls is saying (as objectivist liberals would wish) not merely that antiliberals are wrong, but also that they do not meet the canons of acceptable reasoning. It is one thing to call your opponents wrong; it is quite another to say they hold their incorrect views only because they have been unable to form their beliefs in a fully rational and reasonable way. Such a position is far more insulting to the opponents of liberalism than is an objectivist liberal position, which admits the possibility that the opponents of liberalism can be reasonable and still disagree with them.

But even more worryingly, this position is reminiscent of the sort of position powerful groups eager to suppress the views of their opponents always take to justify their oppression (e.g., the Catholic Church in Spain during the Inquisition). It is easy for any powerful group to insist that its society's standards of what is reasonable and rational justify only its views of the world. Indeed, if nonliberal groups were to come to power in a society, couldn't they use their powerful position to insist that only their nonliberal views were reasonable – if necessary (in Hobbesian fashion) using the power of the state to encourage a reinterpretation, or even a refashioning, of the accepted standards of belief formation? Ultimately the most fundamental problem with the second position is that, by making the conception of what is 'reasonable' depend merely on what is supposed to be "commonly accepted" rather than on what is supposed to be "right," Rawls allows political rulers to understand or construct what is commonly accepted in accord with their own lights – which may be antiliberal.

So the middle ground Rawls sought to define has disappeared once again. Either Rawls defends his theory of justice in a way that is genuinely morally neutral by arguing that the ideas from which it is deduced are accepted by the populace – in which case the public charter of the society turns into a mere modus vivendi based on beliefs that happen to be held by the people today and that they might abandon tomorrow; or he defends them as correct (and for that reason worthy of being accepted), in which case his defense of liberal values presupposes the truth of a comprehensive metaphysical view that includes them, and implicitly rejects the idea that a liberal democratic society can take a neutral stand on every value-issue.

V. Liberalism and neutrality

There is a theme in all of the preceding arguments: Over and over again they show that Rawls must choose between a political theory that is morally neutral but impossible to justify apart from an appeal to what people happen to believe, or else a political theory for which there is a powerful justification but which, for that reason, cannot be morally neutral. There is no middle ground between those two choices. The search by Rawls (and others)[25] for a neutral but genuinely legitimating form of liberalism is quixotic. So the subterranean point of my comments on Rawls's work is that there is no such thing as a theoretically consistent form of "neutrality liberalism."

Some people (particularly critics of liberalism) might believe that these arguments therefore highlight a real paradox in liberal doctrine. As Thomas Nagel has discussed, liberals are so fundamentally committed to toleration that it would seem they would have to tolerate even those who would challenge (and use violence to oppose) their principle of toleration; or to paraphrase Robert Frost, it appears that their commitment to tolerance forces them not to take their own side in an argument.[26] But while it may be possible to formulate liberalism so that it generates such paradoxical results, one needn't do so. There are many objectivist forms of liberalism developed in modern times, for instance, those that assume the existence of human rights, and those founded on utilitarian reasoning. This kind of theory embraces a number of values, including tolerance, which its defenders take to be right,[27] but it does not tolerate, at the level of political legislation and enforcement, beliefs or theories that attack it. Proponents of these forms of liberalism try to argue for them without appealing to controversial religious or moral beliefs; nonetheless, they admit unabashedly that their theory is itself a philosophical position that cannot be indubitably proved but that they still take to be right.

So liberalism in this form eschews neutrality. It may prescribe tolerant attitudes generally, but it is intolerant of, and eschews neutrality with respect to, those normative beliefs that it takes to be definitive of justice and that define it. Indeed, when Rawls suggests that his "reasonableness" principle of legitimating political coercion is derived from the assumptions of human freedom and equality, his rhetoric suggests his (in my view legitimate) intolerance of the views of those who would repudiate these assumptions.

We should stop to dwell on the role of the principle of political coercion in Rawls's arguments: As I noted in the preceding section, it is that principle which, paradoxically, puts pressure on Rawls to respond "liberally" to the nonliberal views of a political society. But what is the justification of this principle itself? Note that the principle certainly doesn't follow from the mere fact of pluralism. After all, Hobbes agreed with Rawls that pluralism in belief is inevitable in most areas of human

life, given the limits of our intelligence and the difficulties of compre-
hending the world; yet Hobbes's recommendation for dealing with this
pluralism is the dictatorial enforcement of one point of view, not the
tolerance of many views. Rawls's argument for the latter response must
therefore presuppose premises that, taken together, would prohibit the
Hobbesian solution and mandate tolerance. Rawls never specifies what
these premises are, saying only that in modern Western democracies
people believe it is "unacceptable" to use force to annihilate pluralism.
But on reflection it would seem these premises must be moral ones
proscribing force in such circumstances, for instance, because force
compromises individual autonomy or because, given the contestability
of the facts, it is somehow unfair. How should Rawls justify these
premises? If, consistent with his other arguments, he maintained that in
our society only the acceptance of these beliefs is reasonable, and their
denial unreasonable, then his opponents would surely object, insisting
that the evidence available to human experience allows for the reasonable disputing of these ideas. If Rawls dismisses such opponents as
unreasonable, they would conclude that he was defending his political
principle using contestable moral notions, and the political enforcement
that such a defence legitimates would rest upon an attitude of intolerance toward those who would contest those notions. Now, from an
objectivist liberal standpoint there is nothing wrong with such intolerance, insofar as, on that view, intolerance of illiberal views that are
wrong and potentially highly damaging to oneself and others is entirely
justified. But Rawls and other "neutrality liberals" would wince at any
charge that they were intolerant, insofar as they appear to think that the
holy grail of the thoroughgoing liberal is to find some way of defending
liberalism so that no controversial and seemingly intolerant claims
directed against opponents need be made. Moreover, Rawls's burdens-
of-reason argument might be thought to provide the basis for just such a
defense of the principle of toleration, if not of other liberal values.

But although I, at any rate, take it to be a powerful defense of the
need to adopt tolerance toward a variety of views, my argument in this
essay is at odds with it with respect to normative beliefs central to the
liberal conception of justice. For although I do not see how the values
of freedom and equality basic to liberalism *have to be* embraced, no
matter their heritage or experience, by all fully reasonable and rational
people, nonetheless I think that a society would be unjust if it did not
insist on and enforce them against all challengers.

Although objectivist liberalism is the form of liberalism that has
heretofore undergirded the political life of Western political societies, it
remains to be seen whether or not it can continue to bind them together

as the populations of these societies become increasingly diverse in philosophical and religious beliefs. Perhaps the fear that it cannot is one of the reasons Rawls tries to create another, neutral form of liberalism.[28] For better or worse, however, liberalism cannot remain liberalism once it is defended on the basis of what is commonly accepted rather than what morality requires in a political context. One can only conclude that the growing literature purporting to develop a "neutral" form of liberalism is deeply misguided.

Notes

1 The two most important recent articles setting out this view are "Justice as Fairness: Political not Metaphysical," *Philosophy and Public Affairs* 14 (1985): 223–51, and "The Idea of An Overlapping Consensus," *Oxford Journal of Legal Studies* 7 (1987): 1–25.

2 For example, see Joseph Raz, "Facing Diversity: The Case of Epistemic Abstinence" in *Philosophy and Public Affairs* 19, no. 1 (Winter 1990): 3–46, and Jean Hampton, "Should Political Philosophy Be Done Without Metaphysics?" *Ethics* 99 (July 1980): 791–814.

3 John Rawls, "The Domain of the Political and Overlapping Consensus" (hereafter DPOC), in this volume. Page numbers are from the edition in *New York University Law Review* 64, no. 2 (May 1989): 233–55 – in this case, p. 234.

4 According to Rawls, a fully comprehensive view, when it covers all recognized values and virtues, does so in one precisely articulated scheme of thought; whereas a partially comprehensive doctrine includes some, but not all, nonpolitical values, and is rather loosely articulated. See DPOC, p. 240.

5 See Raz's discussion, pp. 4–15.

6 See "The Idea of an Overlapping Consensus," p. 1.

7 DPOC, p. 242.

8 Milton Gordon, *Assimilation in American Life* (New York: Oxford, 1964).

9 As Kallen put it, "the United States are in the process of becoming a federal state not merely as a union of geographical and administrative unities, but also a cooperation of cultural diversities, as a federation or commonwealth of national cultures." From "Democracy Versus the Melting Pot," *The Nation*, February 18 and 25, 1915, reprinted in Horace M. Kallen, *Culture and Democracy in the United States* (New York: Boni and Liveright, 1924), p. 116; quoted by Gordon, p. 143.

10 See Hampton, "Should Political Philosophy Be Done Without Metaphysics?"

11 DPOC, p. 240.

12 DPOC, p. 250.

13 For Hobbes, any doctrine is part of "science" if it cannot be contested because there is a conclusive demonstration of it. Any thesis that cannot be so demonstrated is contestable and so liable to disturb the peace of the

commonwealth unless a sovereign is given authority to decide the matter. See his "Six Lessons to the Professors of Mathematics . . . in The University of Oxford" (1956), Epistle Dedicatory, in *The English Works of Thomas Hobbes*, ed. W. Molesworth (London: John Bohn, 1840), 7: 183–4, and *De Homine*, chap. 10, sections iv–v, pp. 41–3, in *Man and Citizen*, ed. B. Gert (New York: Humanities Press, 1972).

14 DPOC, p. 236.

15 DPOC, p. 243.

16 DPOC, p. 244.

17 See DPOC, fn. 3, p. 234: "This idea [a reasonable comprehensive doctrine], when joined with suitable companion ideas such as the burdens of reason . . . and the precepts of reasonable discussion . . . imposes an appropriate limit on the comprehensive doctrines we may reasonably expect to be included in an overlapping consensus."

18 DPOC, p. 244.

19 Ibid.

20 DPOC, pp. 247–8.

21 E.g., DPOC, p. 245.

22 DPOC, p. 245.

23 Consider, for example, Russell's puzzlement about how to reconcile his outright moral condemnation of cruelty toward animals with his moral skepticism, discussed by John Mackie in *Ethics: Inventing Right and Wrong* (Harmondsworth: Penguin, 1977), pp. 34–5.

24 T. M. Scanlon, "Contractualism and Utilitarianism," in *Utilitarianism and Beyond*, ed. A. Sen and B. Williams (Cambridge: Cambridge University Press, 1982), p. 117.

25 I am referring to the body of literature that now exists purporting to define and defend a "neutral" liberalism. See, e.g., Nagel's article, cited in note 26.

26 See Thomas Nagel, "Moral Conflict and Political Legitimacy," *Philosophy and Public Affairs* 16 (1987): 215–40.

27 See Hampton, "Liberalism, Retribution and Criminality," in *Essays in Honor of Joel Feinberg*, ed. J. Coleman and A. Buchanan (Cambridge: Cambridge University Press, in press).

28 And would this brand of liberalism justify the prohibition of immigrants from societies which have a substantially nonliberal, nondemocratic political culture?

7

Constituting democracy

DAVID GAUTHIER

1. To the foreign student of political thought, the American intellectual landscape contains an unexpected feature – the Constitution. That the Constitution should be a fundamentally important element in political practice is unsurprising, even if, to the foreigner, the way in which the Constitution enters may at times seem strange. But that the Constitution should be fundamentally important in political thought is a quite different matter. Yet the foreigner may and should reflect that, to its founders, the United States is a nation founded in revolution, not only in the actual circumstances of its birth, but also, and more importantly, in the idea which informs it. That idea, expressed in the Declaration of Independence, is that "Governments [derive] their just Powers from the Consent of the Governed." The Constitution not only affirms this idea in its opening words, but applies it in the institutions and rights it determines. The Constitution, then, is to be read, not merely as defining a particular political practice, but as defining a *form* – indeed, in its time, a *new* form – of political practice, in which the powers of government are legitimate because they are established through and limited by the consent of "We, the People."

But how does the Constitution define a new form of political practice? Frank Michelman began a recent lecture with the claim, "In American constitutional argument the premise is standard, if often tacit, that all legitimate authority, hence all law, is ultimately traceable to a popular will."[1] Towards the end of the lecture he said, "In the American constitutional understanding – to take up, now, where I began – the thought is inescapable that the Constitution's authority, as judicially enforceable higher law, derives from its popular origin as 'our' law."

Earlier versions of this essay have been presented as lectures in the John M. Olin program in normative political economy at Duke University, and to the Society for Ethical and Legal Philosophy. I am grateful for the discussion on those occasions. The present version is reprinted from the text of the 1989 Lindley Lecture with the permission of the Philosophy Department of the University of Kansas. I also want to thank Christopher Morris for his comments on the initial version, and Jamie Titus for her advice throughout.

(M.) Between those two statements lies at least part of the problem I want to address. How does the Constitution come to be, not merely the embodiment, but the *privileged* embodiment, of the popular will? How does it come to be binding *higher* law?

The Constitution stands in a dual relation to popular will. It is expressive of that will; only so does it have authority. But it is also constitutive of that will. The Constitution determines what shall and shall not be expressive of popular will. And so we find ourselves asking, not only why the Constitution should have *any* authority – why we should see it as embodying the popular will – but why it should have the higher authority of defining the popular will, or of being, as we might say, its constitutive expression. I want to approach this question in the light of a distinction Michelman makes in elucidating constitutional argument, between deliberative and strategic politics.

"*Deliberative* politics connotes a reasoned interchange among persons who recognize each other as equal in authority and entitlement to respect, jointly directed towards answering some questions of public ordering . . . all remain open to the possibility of persuasion by others and . . . a vote, if any vote is taken, represents a pooling of judgments. *Strategic* interaction . . . appeals to one another's several self-interests by conditional offers of cooperation and forbearance . . . Strategic outcomes, whether formally embodied in votes or in contracts, or just informally carried out in social behaviors, represent not a judgment of reason but a vector-sum in a field of forces." (M.) I have made one significant alteration in Michelman's characterization of deliberative politics, in omitting reference to the constraints of "justice, right, and the common good" which he imposes on the reasoned interchange. Michelman's characterization treats these as exogenous to a reasoned interchange; I shall claim rather that a concern with justice and the common good are ensured by the very idea of such an interchange, properly conceived.

Michelman argues that to treat the constitution as binding higher law requires that we consider constitutional law-making as deliberative, rather than strategic. "If the Constitution is just another strategic political power play, why would or should we feel in the least bound by its authority?" (M.) But if this points to an explanation of why we consider the Constitution binding, it does not yet suggest why we consider it binding *higher* law. And here, we must invoke the idea that ordinary law-making – let us say legislative politics – typically rests on a strategic power play. The Constitution affords the perspective of deliberation, of reasoned judgement about the public ordering, for evaluating the day-to-day decisions taken about particular aspects of that ordering. If we were confident that these day-to-day decisions were themselves deliberatively reached, we should have no need of *higher* law.

2. My primary concern is to explore the deliberative/strategic distinction as a clue to understanding the role of a constitution in political interaction. So let us ascend, or at least abstract, from actual to ideal political interaction. And let us begin by considering the presumption against the justificatory force of strategic interaction which underlies Michelman's defence of the constitution as higher law. I want to ask – why deliberative politics? Why not accept the fruits of strategic interaction – interaction in which each person advances his or her own interests? The paradigm of successful strategic interaction is, of course, the market. Each advances her own interests, and the result is mutually beneficial – no one could do better without someone else doing worse. The market shows us the workings of Adam Smith's Invisible Hand. But the harmony of the market is neither natural nor universal. A market-like structure emerges only in the absence of opportunities for force and fraud; it succeeds only in the absence of occasions for free-riding, for escaping or displacing costs. Force, fraud, and free-riding are the ills that blight the fruits of strategic interaction.

Politics may now appear as the remedy for those ills. We may appeal here to the view of James Buchanan, who distinguishes the *protective* state, which seeks to eliminate coercion and deception from the relations of human beings, from the *productive* state, which aims at the cooperative provision of those public goods that are inefficiently realized in market competition because of free-riding possibilities for evading or displacing costs.[2] One way of characterizing this view of the role of politics is to represent it as making possible market success (by eliminating force and fraud), and remedying market failure (by eliminating free-riding). But the reference to market success and market failure might misleadingly suggest the subordination of the political realm to the economic. I am not proposing that we think of persons as concerned exclusively or necessarily even primarily with what are normally considered economic goods, so that they would view politics simply as instrumental to their economic ends. The rationale of politics is to supplant or constrain strategic interaction, whenever, left to itself, it would result in an outcome that although individually stable would be mutually disadvantageous – stable, in that no person can benefit by unilaterally changing her behavior, but disadvantageous, in that all persons could benefit were each to change her behavior. This failure represents the fundamental structural problem in interaction. It can arise whenever different persons value outcomes differently – whenever our conceptions of the good may lead us to opposed evaluations of the possible outcomes of our interaction. We need not be economic men – or economic women – identifying our good with the size of our individual commodity-bundle, to face the problems of strategic interaction, and to need the remedies of politics.

Consider, then, persons whose conceptions of the good lead them, in the absence of constraints, into mutually disadvantageous interaction. We need assume no deep hostility or conflict among these persons. To be sure, such conflict is possible – as between two persons, castaways on a very small and ill-favored island, each rightly viewing the presence of the other as a threat to his own survival. In these unfortunate circumstances, strategic interaction may result in a conflict assuredly fatal to one if not both of the persons; the logic is that of Hobbes's natural condition of humankind. Each may recognize this conflict to be disadvantageous, not only to himself but to his fellow, and yet peace may escape them. And the best they can even hope for is an uneasy truce. I mention this situation only to contrast it with the very different context that invites politics – the context of persons each of whom welcomes the presence of the others as potential participants in, to borrow Rawls's useful phrase, "a cooperative venture for mutual advantage," (R. p. 4)[3] but who recognizes also that individual differences in the evaluation of possible outcomes threaten to deprive each of the fruits of such a venture, and to do so despite each person's best efforts to advance her own interests. These persons seek, not only to avoid the costs of interference that even enemies might wish to avoid, but to gain the benefits that may be realized from the complementarity of resources and the division of labor. For such persons, and only for such persons, is there a *political* good.

I have contrasted two contexts of interaction; we should, however, consider the possibility of passage from one to the other. The interaction of those who would prefer not to interact, each of whom regards the presence of the others as a cost, may, in the most favorable circumstances, result in a *modus vivendi*. Now it may be that, having acquiesced in such a situation, the participants come over time to regard it differently, to realize that the others afford opportunities as well as imposing costs. The others are, if not yet welcome, nevertheless useful, their presence accepted and not merely and grudgingly tolerated. Persons who were once enemies, now find themselves allies. At first, their only bonds are those of convenience. And if opportunities for mutual benefit are seen to arise only in limited areas of life, and to be restricted to activities that are valued merely instrumentally, then the bonds between persons may remain ones of mere convenience. But as wider opportunities for mutual benefit come to be appreciated, so that each views her fellows as sharing in a way of life, then, provided that each finds those fellows willing to ensure that her place in their activities is a fair and reasonable one, they come to be seen as public friends, their presence now welcomed rather than merely accepted. What were bonds of convenience become ties of mutual civic concern.

3. Public or civic friendship is a key idea in my discussion. It expresses a distinctive form of concern with other persons, which is neither instrumental nor affective, although it does not exclude either or both of these. Civic friends need feel no emotional attachment to the good of their partners, but they affirm each other's good in willingly making and honoring whatever commitments are needed to make their mutual activities successful from each partner's perspective. To be sure, a merely instrumental partnership already requires agreement to constrain or redirect the strategically rational actions of each partner towards their mutual benefit. Civic friendship does not supplant this need, but supplements it with the further demand that the agreement assure equal respect.[4] Each of the partners retains her own conception of the good; their friendship requires, not that each submerge her identity and her aims in the common cause of a collective, but rather that each respect the identity and aims of her fellows, willingly according them equal place in their common affairs with her own. The more each feels secure in the place accorded by her fellows, the more each seeks to secure them in their places. To bring about this security, then, the partners face the task of designing institutions and practices that are the visible sign of their intention of friendship, so that by structuring their interaction in a way that manifests their mutual regard, they ensure that their friendship will endure. I shall, for convenience, speak of the design of appropriate institutions and practices as the formation of a constitution to regulate the interactions of persons regarded now as members of a society.

The constitution represents a shared good among the members of the society. This is to be understood in two related but distinct ways. First, in making possible cooperation and preventing unreasonable interference, it enables each better to realize his own good than would be possible in the "state of nature" characterized by universal strategic interaction. But second, and again in making possible cooperation and preventing interference, it enables each to express his friendship in performing actions that further the good of his fellows, and in refraining from other actions that would diminish their good. Thus persons are enabled to advance their own aims and interests in ways that exhibit respect for the aims and interests of each. I shall say that this constitutes the political good. It is possible only for persons who view each other as welcome partners in cooperative interaction, and it is realized by creating the conditions under which they can translate that welcome into practice.

Beginning with persons, each with his or her own conception of the good, who recognize that these distinct conceptions of the good create the possibility that individual rational strategic behavior will be mutually costly, I have narrowed my focus to exclude those for whom the very presence of their fellows is itself a source of disadvantage. I have supposed that those who first see others as useful will, as they share a wider range of activities, come to see those others as companionable, and will seek ways to regulate their interaction to secure mutual benefit and express mutual respect. These ways are embodied in their constitution. Note that this constitution expresses no good of its own; there is, or at least need be, no communal good beyond what arises from the individual goods of the members of society.[5] The idea is that the constitution should bring about those conditions that are optimally responsive to these individual goods, which are left quite open; each member of society is free to form and to carry out a life plan of her own. The only, but crucial, principled constraint imposed on each person's plan is that it be compatible with her receiving and being received by her fellows in welcome partnership.

4. I come now to the idea of deliberative politics. Let me quote again Michelman's characterization: "a reasoned interchange among persons who recognize each other as equal in authority and entitlement to respect, jointly directed towards answering some question of public ordering." (M.) The primary question of public ordering is to be answered by the constitution; what are the optimal conditions under which the members of a society may interact for their mutual advantage and to express their equal respect? How shall this question be answered? My concern here is, not to determine the answer, but to ascertain the method – the way in which one might arrive at an answer. And my suggestion is that we consider the primary question of public ordering as itself addressed to the public who stand to benefit from the ordering. The content of this question embraces *all* of the interactions of the members of society. But addressing this question to the public introduces a *particular interaction* taking as outcome a *public answer*. How shall this interaction be ordered? It might seem that we are faced with a circle – that we must know how social interaction may best be ordered so that we may best order the particular social interaction required to provide a public answer to the question how social

interaction may best be ordered. But, I suggest, this is not the case. The conditions for optimally ordering the particular interaction required to answer the question of optimal public ordering, may be made directly explicit by reflecting on the two standards that the ordering must satisfy – the standards of mutual advantage and equal respect.

We think then of a reasoned interchange. A deliberative politics is characterized procedurally. The appropriateness of the answers it yields to public questions is established, not by any appeal to assumed expertise, but by the assurance that the manner in which it is conducted is informed by the standards that the answer must satisfy. It begins from a question about the public ordering that all want answered, because the answer establishes standards or conditions of interaction from which all benefit, in relation to the benchmark set by individual strategic choice. It seeks an answer to which all can agree, since it is reached from a debate in which each is able, freely and fully, to offer his reasoned judgment under rules that treat no person as privileged and no answer as presumptively favored. The pressure to reach agreement arises solely from its desirability, which is felt equally by the members of society, and not from any differences in capacity or temperament or position, which might bear differentially on the members, and so benefit some at the expense of others. Since each is able to present his reasoned judgment, each is able to ensure that the mutual advantage realized in the answer embraces his own good. Since no one is privileged, each is able to ensure this only by equally embracing the good of his fellows, and so demonstrating his equal respect for them and their endeavors. A reasoned interchange, in which all seek an answer to which all must agree, results in unanimity. The procedure of deliberative politics is thus informed by the standards that its outcome must satisfy. Through deliberative politics, therefore, we are able to provide the public answer demanded by the primary question of optimal public ordering.[6]

5. I mentioned previously that in characterizing a deliberative politics, I altered Michelman's account by omitting the requirement that the reasoned interchange give an answer compatible "with the dictates of justice, right, and the common good." (M.) It is now time to bring these elements in to my account. We give content to both justice and the common good by establishing a constitution through the procedures of deliberative politics. Considered as structuring interaction to promote, or to enable the promotion of, mutual advantage, the institutions established in the constitution embody the common good. The recognized authority of these institutions is an important component of public capital. The value of this public capital is, of course, to be measured by

its enhancement of the individual goods of the members. The attainment of supposed national objectives, not themselves found in the equal recognition of these individual goods, is no part of the common good as I am characterizing it.

Considered as structuring interaction to exhibit, or to ensure the exhibition of, full and equal respect for persons, the institutions established in the society embody justice. In requiring that agreement on these institutions be reached through a reasoned interchange, deliberative politics offers each person the opportunity to advance whatever proposal he pleases, but requires him to submit it to the critical consideration of his fellows, so that its adoption depends on his being able to give it a reasoned grounding that must either speak equally to the life-plans of all of the participants, or establish the parity of the proposal with similar and compatible proposals that, taken together, reflect equally their several life-plans. Thus no one, after giving his consent, has any basis for complaining that he was unable either to advance or to defend his concerns in ways available to any of his fellows. Now I take this to ensure the *ex ante* fairness of the institutions chosen. But the ideal of justice manifested in such a choice is essentially negative. It is, we might say, the justice of mutual convenience – of relationships among persons who, in Rawls's useful phrase, "are conceived as not taking an interest in one another's interests." (R. p. 13) This is essentially the weak conception of justice I develop in *Morals by Agreement* and elsewhere, representing "the virtue of the self-interested . . . that curbs self-interest."[7] But I said earlier that, beginning from relationships of convenience, if each of the participants can see her share of benefits to be a fair and reasonable one, then the others may come to be no longer merely accepted but instead regarded as friends, and so as persons in whom one takes an interest. If, as I am supposing, a constitution is an affirmation of civic friendship, and not a mere treaty or compact of alliance, then we may expect the ideal of justice it embodies to require, not merely equitable opportunities for individuals to advance their own life-plans, but a positive affirmation of those life-plans as equally and fully entitled to the support of society. Since civic friendship does not rest on or require personal affection, this conception of justice is compatible with a purely *personal* indifference among individuals, but it reflects and requires a positive *political* or *civic* concern of each for his fellows.

The unanimist procedure of deliberative politics may remind us of Rawls's idea of choice in the original position. But for Rawls, unanimity is reached through subordinating the differences among persons to the veil of ignorance, rather than by coordinating those differences in mutual agreement. And Rawls distinguishes the choice of the principles of justice from the choice of a constitution; he supposes that the latter proceeds "subject to the constraints of the principles of justice." (R. p. 196) He insists, "In framing a just constitution I assume that the two principles of justice already chosen define an independent standard of the desired outcome. If there is no such standard, the problem of constitutional design is not well posed." (R. p. 198) In subordinating the choice of a constitution to that of principles of justice, Rawls's account differs markedly from the one I have developed. As I have characterized deliberative politics, principles of justice are not the subject of a prior or independent choice, and constitutional choice is not subjected to any principled constraint established by prior choice. The expectation that the constitution will promote mutual advantage and manifest equal respect is assured directly by the manner in which it is chosen.

My claim is that the outcome of deliberative politics is *constitutive* of justice among individuals. Concretely, a constitution may be said to constitute the political institutions of a society; abstractly, it may be said to constitute justice and, as we have seen, the common good. Rawls says, "Just as each person must decide by rational reflection what constitutes his good, . . . so a group of persons must decide once and for all what is to count among them as just and unjust." (R. pp. 11–12) I shall comment on "once and for all" presently. Here my concern is with the *decision* on what is to count as justice. In identifying that decision with the choice of a constitution, I emphasize the idea that a constitution is legally foundational as the *privileged* act of popular will. Behind the popular will expressed in the constitution are only the particular and multifarious goods expressed in the life-plans of the individual members of society. Justice can not be found by mere reflection on them. But from our awareness of the costs of strategic interaction based on these life-plans, we face the question of an optimal public ordering; the answer is, in effect, the determination of what is to count as just and unjust.[8] In giving this answer constitutional status, we represent it as a single, shared, public understanding.

6. I have developed the idea of deliberative politics as a constraint on strategic interaction. But as I recognized at the outset, within politics itself there is a strategic dimension, so that the day-to-day workings of the political system may be seen as exhibiting the very form of behavior that, I have claimed, the deliberative politics of the constitution exists to control and redirect. And we may find this view of strategic politics expressed in American Constitutional thought, which, as Michelman notes, accepts "the doctrine that treats state-based power as more

dangerous than market-based power," and does this, he argues, because of "a vision of the public, political process of regulatory law-making as predominantly strategic rather than deliberative in character." (M.) The Constitution[9] addresses, from the deliberative standpoint, the politics of later society, and finds it wanting. Thus the Constitution strictly limits this politics.

To understand the relation between deliberative and strategic politics, I shall first focus again on the relation between the two modes of interaction. In strategic interaction, each person seeks directly to advance her own good. Agreements are made, and kept, to the extent to which they are perceived to be maximally beneficial from each agent's perspective. Now one might think of deliberative interaction in the way in which Rawls describes R. B. Perry's account: as maximally "promoting the ends reached by reflective agreement under circumstances making for impartiality and good will." (R. p. 148) Agreement then is not limited to a coincidence of what is maximally beneficial from the differing perspectives of individuals. This may seem to correspond to the idea of "a reasoned interchange among persons who recognize each other as equal in authority and entitlement to respect." Impartiality and good will are implicit in the idea, underlying my argument, of persons as "welcome partners in cooperation."

Rawls's criticism of Perry, insofar as it is relevant to our concerns, turns on identifying good will with "a benevolent concern for one another's interests," (R. p. 141) and supposing that this makes an account of agreement unmanageably complex. But whether or not this is a fair criticism of Perry, in relating good will to civic friendship I understand its role rather differently. I do not suppose that good will requires persons to be personally benevolent, or to take any interest, *as individuals*, in the interests of others, although of course it is compatible with and perhaps even conducive to taking such interest. Rather, I understand good will as involving openness and good faith – the willingness to acknowledge the nature and strength of one's true concerns in the process of reaching agreement, and the subsequent willingness to adhere or keep to whatever is agreed. Within the framework of agreement, each must exhibit a positive concern for impartiality and mutuality.

In deliberative interaction persons may, and must be expected to, seek to advance their own good. The reasoned interchange that it demands should be understood, not as opposed to the mode of strategic interaction, but rather, I suggest, as an idealized form of the "conditional effects of cooperation and forbearance" that Michelman considers strategic. Here I appeal to one of the main themes of *Morals by*

Agreement. Under full information, the factors that lead ordinary bargaining to fall short of a reasoned interchange are absent. I say in my book, "In ordinary bargaining persons may conceal significant features of their circumstances, or the full range of their options, may misrepresent their preferences, or the strengths of their preferences. . . . In ordinary bargaining persons may bluff, especially if they are also able to conceal or misrepresent factors, so that others have uncertain or mistaken expectations about what the bluffers are willing to do. . . . In ordinary bargaining persons may make threats, but among fully rational persons threats are useless; no one will believe anyone who claims that he will act in a non–utility-maximizing way should others not comply with this threat, and to say that one will act in a utility-maximizing way is not to threaten. Our bargainers have no psychological strengths to exploit, or psychological weaknesses to be exploited. And we assume that . . . no one need come to a decision without full consideration; bargaining is unpressured. Thus each bargainer can employ only his own rationality to appeal to the equal rationality of his fellows. In addition to rationality, there are only each person's preferences and possible actions to consider, and it is about these that everyone bargains."[10] We regard each bargainer as serving as an ideal representative of the particular person he will be in the social world to be shaped by the constitution on which all agree.[11]

Deliberative agreement may thus be treated as strategic bargaining under full information, in circumstances designed to remove the effects of all differential pressures and capacities on reaching agreement.[12] Michelman's claim that "strategic outcomes . . . represent not a judgment of reason but a vector-sum in a field of forces" offers a false dichotomy; reason and force coexist in all human interaction. For force is the exercise of power, and without power, defined by Hobbes as an agent's "present means, to seek his future apparent good,"[13] there would be no place for practical reason, for deliberation on using one's power to attain that good.

7. Deliberative *politics*, however, demands a closer characterization in relation to strategic interaction. For we may say that in deliberative or constitutional politics, human beings seek, through an appropriately conditioned strategic interaction, to direct and constrain their future interaction, which they anticipate to be largely strategic. They seek to remedy the failure of strategic interaction to yield outcomes affording fair mutual advantage. I want to distinguish and focus on two parts of this remedy. The first addresses the mode of decision. In pure strategic interaction, outcomes result from the independent decisions of indi-

viduals. There is no social decision determining a social outcome. Under some circumstances, of which the perfectly competitive market is our favored example, this decentralized mode of decision-making proves efficient, and leads to outcomes in which individual benefits are proportionate with individual costs. But where this natural harmony of interests is lacking, we may seek a centralized mode of decision-making that will bring about an artificial harmony. In a democratic society, the choice of this mode becomes itself the object of interaction among individuals. We seek then a decision-making institution, within which individuals may be expected to interact in strategically rational ways, but which structures their interaction so that its product – the social decision – yields a fair and optimal state of affairs. Such an institution may be envisaged as arising from unanimous agreement, since it is acceptable, and equally acceptable, to all. Each sees the opportunity for advancing her interests commensurately with those of her fellows in determining the decisions of society.

Typically, this institution – the primary institution of government itself – is largely majoritarian, as seems practically necessary if it is to combine efficacity with democracy. But any majoritarian decision procedure poses a constant danger to the unanimist foundations of the constitutional order. For if persons are bent on strategic behavior, then chance alone will almost surely give some opportunities for exploiting the procedure of majoritarian decision to gain benefits while displacing some costs, which of course entails that others pay costs without gaining compensating benefits. If we focus exclusively on the dangers of majoritarian decision, we may be led to impose severe constitutional restraints on its scope, and so on the scope of governmental authority. We shall leave large areas of society to the decentralized decision-making represented by free individual interaction. But to restrain government in these areas is in effect to unleash the market, and insofar as government serves as a remedy for the failure of the strategic interactions characteristic of the market, to restrain government is in effect to accept a greater measure of market failure without remedy. To be sure, we do not want the power of government to extend to interference with market *success*. We do not want to replace the strategic interaction of free individuals, in those circumstances in which they are able to achieve optimal outcomes in which benefits are matched to costs, with the strategic interaction of an unrestricted majoritarian politics, which can by no means be expected to yield either optimal or fair outcomes. In effect then, we want to achieve a constitutional balance between two modes of strategic activity – market and government.

The second part of the political remedy concerns, not so much the mode of decision – individual or social, but the mode of reasoning. Here I may usefully quote Thomas Hobbes, while recognizing that he is not to be understood as a recruit to constitutionalism. In replying to Bishop Bramhall, Hobbes says, "because neither mine nor the Bishop's reason is right reason fit to be a rule of our moral actions, we have therefore set up over ourselves a sovereign governor, and agreed that his laws shall be unto us, whatsoever they be, in the place of right reason, to dictate to us what is really good."[14] Law, for Hobbes, provides a *public reason*, authoritative over the private reason of each individual. Hobbes's account of the need for public reason is a version, albeit an extreme version, of the general argument I have given in support of deliberative politics – unconstrained strategic interaction among individuals, in which each is guided by his own reason, leads to that most awful of strategic failures, the war of all against all. But we need accept neither his dismal vision, nor his insistence on a "sovereign governor," to adapt Hobbes's thought about law to my purpose.

Throughout my discussion, I have taken unconstrained and unstructured strategic interaction among persons as a base line. Now we may think of law as affecting that interaction in two very different ways. On the one hand, we may think of law as *structure*. This is how I have understood a constitution, as providing a framework for social decision in those areas in which, even if we assume that individuals interact strategically within the social framework, the outcome is likely to be mutually more advantageous than if matters are left to individual decision. But on the other hand, we may think of law as *constraint*. We may think of law as specifying a standard of *reasonable* conduct for each member of society, based on what those members would deliberatively acknowledge. Each then is expected to curb the pursuit of her own interests to conform to the requirements of law, and to do so because the law derives from a reasoned interchange to which she is party. It is in this sense that we may understand the law as a standard of *public* reason, overriding the exercise of private judgment and directing persons to their mutual advantage, and we may agree with Hobbes that "this *right reason*, which is the law, is no otherwise certainly right than by our making it so by our approbation of it and voluntary subjection to it."[15] My claim, then, is that the law is entitled to serve this constraining role because its authority derives from the deliberative politics of constitution-making, which finds its expression in the idea of "We, the People."

8. And in returning to the people I return from my abstract discussion of ideal politics. I must ask whether my argument has any application to

the real political and legal realms. I face an obvious objection: does not my entire argument gain the appearance of relevance by deliberately confusing an ideally reasoned interchange with a particular set of political events? I have defended the claim that a constitution would be justifiably enforceable as higher law, were it the product of an exercise in deliberative politics – of a reasoned interchange among persons in circumstances sufficient to afford each the expectation of mutual advantage and equal respect. But can any actual constitution be represented as the product of reasoned interchange? Can any actual political or judicial decisions be shown to be justifiably enforceable, by representing them as made in accordance with procedures that are the outcome of reasoned interchange?

There is a further problem – the problem of binding posterity. Suppose that we could defend an actual constitution as the product of a real-world approximation to a reasoned interchange. We might then suppose that its provisions might justifiably be enforced over the parties to the agreement. But if, as with the American Constitution, the reasoned interchange took place two hundred years ago, then why may its provisions be justifiably enforced on Americans today? The preamble speaks of "our posterity," but how is posterity brought within the Constitution's scope? How can the Constitution be chosen "once and for all"?

These are familiar problems with attempts to offer a contractarian understanding of a political system. Such an understanding requires more than showing that actual political and judicial institutions and practices, or the particular decisions to which they give rise, are those that would follow, directly or indirectly, from a reasoned agreement or interchange among citizens. To be sure, such a demonstration serves a justificatory role.[16] But it does not show that the institutions and practices take their *rationale* from the idea of a reasoned interchange. And this is essential to a full contractarian understanding. Recall that I began by referring to the importance, surprising to foreigners, of the American Constitution in political thought, and to the idea that it defines a new form of political practice, in which legitimacy derives from the will of "We, the People." By interpreting the Constitution as the outcome of a reasoned interchange among Americans, we connect the *fact* of the Constitution to the way in which the invocation of popular will yields political legitimacy.

Such an interpretation requires both an actual and an ideal ground. The actual ground comprises the adoption, judicial interpretation, and amendment of the American Constitution. The ideal ground is a unanimous rational agreement on the fundamental terms of political association. We ask whether the former may be interpreted as a reasonable approximation to the latter, and so whether it may be taken as the constitutive expression of popular will.[17] I can not, of course, carry out this enquiry here. I can only suggest the sort of argument that, if successful, would show why the American Constitution might be supposed to give legitimacy to the workings of the American political and legal systems, by expressing the rational will, not only of those who participated in its formation and adoption, but of their fellows and descendants.

9. Suppose then that we find an *actual* agreement, concluded in circumstances that, while no doubt falling far short of those that would permit a fully reasoned interchange on a fair basis among all the members of a society, may nevertheless be seen as intended to realize a practicable and reasonable approximation to such an interchange – or, perhaps more realistically, may be seen as making possible an interchange among a limited number of persons, the *outcome* of which might approximate to the outcome of a fair universal interchange. We think of the agreement as concluded by persons who take themselves to be representing, to the best of their ability, the members of their society, and to be seeking the terms that those members would find reasonable to accept. So that if the agreement begins "We, the People," we find the claim made in those words credible. And if the agreement continues by enumerating a set of objectives, the first being "to form a more perfect union," we may understand the agreement as speaking to the primary question of public ordering, so that it represents itself as the expression of the people's will about how their will shall be defined.

But these words may be expressions of pious sentiment – or even impious, uttered to mislead. They contain no guarantee that what follows them will express the people's will. Indeed, we may consider it unreasonable to suppose that any procedure of representation can guarantee an outcome approximating to that of a fair universal reasoned interchange. And we must expect any actual attempt at representation to be limited by both the circumstances and the understandings of its time. The framers of the American Constitution deliberated from the fixed existence of the distinct states and their established forms of government; they accommodated the historical reality of black slavery, and even where slavery did not exist, they could not be said to have represented free blacks. Nor of course did they represent women. But, although we should be concerned with the circumstances that limit the scope of the deliberations through which a constitution is adopted, we may find that, over time, their biasing effect on a fair and free interchange is offset by the actual political and legal practices that stem from the adoption of a constitution. We should look at the political and judicial institutions and their decisions, and ask if, over time, they may be interpreted as the reasonable workings of a society aiming at mutual advantage and equal respect among its members. That is, we should ask if the political practice created by an actual constitution is best understood as an endeavor to satisfy the standard set by our ideal of a reasoned interchange. Insofar as the American Constitution may be so understood, we may suppose that if it bound those who concluded it as their actual agreement, it may have come to bind their contemporaries and posterity because they may see it as concluded on their behalf. They may treat the agreement of the Founders as if it were their own.

But if the Constitution is to be seen as the expression of posterity's will, then that will must be involved more directly than through interpretation of the agreement of the Founders. I noted earlier that Rawls speaks of a group of persons deciding "once and for all what is to count among them as just and unjust." But no human agreement can establish the conditions of mutual advantage and equal respect once and for all. The development of our moral, political, and economic understanding, and of our technological capacities to shape our environment, calls for continuing accommodation. Thus if the Constitution is to remain congruent with a reasoned interchange for posterity, posterity must be able to adapt it to their altered understandings and powers. An agreement, to be truly ongoing, must be amendable, and amendable by a procedure that endeavors, to the fullest extent possible, to yield an outcome that might approximate to that of a fair universal rational interchange. Thus the process of amendment, like the process of adoption, must aspire to the status of deliberative politics.

The American Constitution was declared in effect on March 4, 1789. Speaking now from my foreign perspective, it seems to me that the best two hundredth birthday present that Americans could give their Constitution would be to devise a more determinate procedure for amendment. Whatever the merits of the failed Equal Rights Amendment, the procedure for ratification, with states ratifying and then seeking to deratify, with Congress setting a five year period and then, when the amendment remained unratified, extending the period to ten years, is a failure from the standpoint of deliberative politics. Although the constitutional ideal must be unanimity – an agreement fair and beneficial to all, so acceptable by all – yet in the real world, a unanimist procedure invites a descent from the deliberative to the purely strategic, as each wields his individual veto. What must be sought, and what is in principle sought by the requirement of concurrent two-thirds majorities in

Congress and ratification by three-fourths of the States, is consensus. What the amending procedure fails adequately to recognize, as the attempted ratification of the Equal Rights Amendment showed so clearly, is that consensus requires simultaneity – that Congress and the State should, in one period of time, accept the amendment. Even five years is here too long. The Equal Rights Amendment did not secure that consensus; had it been adopted by a controverted procedure that avoided true consensus, much harm would have been done to the constitutional ideal.

10. But the failed Equal Rights Amendment may itself be situated as part of an historical development of constitutional understanding that lends itself to a contractarian account. The more substantive amendments to the Constitution – the Bill of Rights, the Reconstruction Amendments, the amendments relating to suffrage – together with the more significant interpretative activity of the Supreme Court, may be seen as responses to recognized lacunae in the constitutional text, as judged in the light of evolved understandings and developed powers, and from the perspective of mutual advantage and equal respect. The failed Equal Rights Amendment was itself such a response, but one that ran aground on the apparently unresolved task of finding a judicial language that affirms sexual equality as it affirms racial equality, without presuming that legal acceptance or rejection of sexual categories must correspond to that of racial categories. Put very bluntly, there is yet no consensus on how to define the terms of civic friendship between men and women.

On a contractarian interpretation, the Constitution sets Americans an ongoing task. The canonical status claimed for its text requires that it be both expressive and constitutive of popular will. But insofar as popular will could be fully embodied only in the outcome of a fair reasoned interchange among all the members of the polity, a permanent tension exists between the actual text and the ideal text that would be such an outcome, could it be realized. To the extent that the historical process of interpreting and amending the Constitution is responsive to this tension, the fallible text is shown to be perfectible, and so to constitute, in the second-best circumstances of real politics, the standard of legitimate authority. But the responsiveness of the historical process is a matter of actual respondings by political actors. The canon is never closed; the legitimacy of the Constitution is always subject to the legitimating activity of relating it to the ideal standard of a deliberative politics.

And so I return to Michelman's starting point: "In American constitutional argument the premise is standard, if often tacit, that all legitimate authority, hence all law, is ultimately traceable to a popular will." (M.)

How shall we understand that will? My answer has been that we shall understand it as an agreement among the people, to overcome the failure endemic in human interaction, even when that interaction satisfies the standard of strategic rationality. We see the end for restructuring that interaction – to form, then, "a more perfect Union." That restructuring, I have argued, requires the establishment of justice. And we may take the other objectives in the Preamble to the American Constitution as abstract specifications of the main forms of public good – domestic tranquility, common defence, general welfare – concluding with "the blessings of liberty" to be secured to the citizens and their posterity. In this latter phrase, we may find the idea of a community in which each freely pursues her own good in a manner compatible with being welcome as a participant in the Union that the constitution establishes.

11. My conclusion is that, strange as it may initially seem to the foreigner, Americans are right to think that their Constitution defines a new form of political practice. For it is the first, and I believe arguably the most successful document to be plausibly represented as an expression of popular will determining what shall and shall not be expressive of that will. More than any other constitution, it has come to be accepted as the public expression of mutual agreement on the just powers of government. To be sure, we may expect to find, in any democratic polity, some recognition that the powers of government are legitimate because they are established and limited by "We, the People." The political practice codified in the Constitution has become the democratic norm, implicit in societies that lack the constitutional tradition that would make it explicit. And since the Constitution is the pioneering attempt to define that practice, we might find, in some democratic polities, laws and institutions that fit better as possible outcomes of a fair universal rational interchange than those of America. But such comparative questions are not my concern. For political thought, understanding the American Constitution, asking for the rationale of its text, reveals what we mean by constituting democracy.

Notes

1 Frank Michelman, "Conceptions of Democracy in American Constitutional Argument: The Case of Pornography Regulation," typescript; quoted by permission of the author. Further quotations from this lecture are identified by (M.).
2 See James M. Buchanan, *The Limits of Liberty* (Chicago: The University of Chicago Press, 1975), pp. 68–70. However, Buchanan's distinction between

constitutional and postconstitutional contract is not part of the present argument.

3 References prefixed by R. are to John Rawls, *A Theory of Justice* (Cambridge, Mass.: Harvard University Press, 1971).

4 Why is civic friendship needed in political society? Jules Coleman has suggested in conversation that *if* my argument in *Morals by Agreement* (Oxford: Clarendon Press, 1986) is sound, then a merely instrumental partnership should provide a sufficient base for the constraints needed to redirect individual actions to mutual benefit. (See especially chs. V–VII.) But without civic friendship, and the equal respect it engenders, some persons will almost certainly find themselves relatively disadvantaged by actual social arrangements, which they can not be expected to accept willingly, so that the society will tend to be both coercive and unstable. Coleman rightly questions both the basis of and the role for civic friendship in a rational contractarian theory; neither of these matters can be adequately treated in the confines of this lecture.

5 Thus political institutions, like the market, require no agreement on ends. However, political institutions do constrain each person in the pursuit of her ends, whereas the market does not. Thus the stable operation of the market does not require any analogue to civic friendship.

6 We may clarify this analysis by reminding ourselves of the distinction among perfect, imperfect, and pure procedures. (See R. pp. 85–6) Think of a procedure as employed to reach an outcome satisfying a certain standard. If the procedure ensures that the standard is satisfied, and the standard is specifiable independently of the procedure, then the procedure is perfect. If the procedure ensures that the standard is satisfied but the standard is not specifiable independently of the procedure, then the procedure is pure. If the procedure does not ensure that the standard is satisfied, so that the standard must be specifiable independently, then the procedure is imperfect. How are we to classify the procedure of deliberative politics, as determining outcomes that satisfy the standards of mutual advantage and equal respect? It may seem to be clearly imperfect. Even if agreement is reached in a manner informed by the demands of mutual advantage and equal respect, there would seem to be no guarantee that the institutions agreed to will in fact make possible optimal cooperation under conditions requiring each to demonstrate respect for his fellows. But we should, I think, introduce here the distinction between expectation and outcome. The institutions selected by the procedures of deliberative politics may in fact fail. But they must be expected to succeed, and expected because, and solely because, of the manner in which they are chosen. There is no criterion for *expected* advantage, or for *expected* equal respect, independent of the agreement of persons under the conditions of deliberative politics. In this respect, I suggest, deliberative politics is comparable to other procedures for decision and choice. It should then be classified as *ex ante* pure, and *ex post* imperfect.

7 The quote is from my paper "Three Against Justice: The Foole, the Sensible

Knave, and the Lydian Shepherd," in *Midwest Studies in Philosophy* VII (1982), p. 11. For the account of justice in *Morals by Agreement*, see especially ch. V.

8 A second contrast with Rawls's thought arises from my treatment of deliberative politics as determining what is to count as just and unjust. In recent writings, such as "Justice as Fairness: Political not Metaphysical" (*Philosophy and Public Affairs* 14, 1985, pp. 223–251) and "The Idea of an Overlapping Consensus" (*Oxford Journal of Legal Studies* 7, 1987, pp. 1–25), Rawls develops an account of justice not, as in *A Theory of Justice*, as a part of rational choice contractarianism, but rather as "a regulative political conception . . . that can articulate and order in a principled way the political ideals and values of a democratic regime" and "such that there is some hope of its gaining the support of . . . a consensus in which it is affirmed by the opposing religious, philosophical and moral doctrines likely to thrive" in the society. ("The Idea . . .," p. 1) This conception, of "'justice as fairness' . . . can be seen as starting with the fundamental intuitive idea of political society as a fair system of social cooperation between citizens regarded as free and equal persons." (Ibid., p. 7) I want rather to appeal beyond any *presupposed* moral ideas, whether of fairness or of freedom and equality, to the underlying rationale for political society captured by Rawls himself in the phrase, quoted above, "a cooperative venture for mutual advantage," where 'advantage' is understood in terms of the individual goods of the members of society. Such a venture, I have argued, invites civic friendship, which introduces (rather than presupposes) the moral idea of equal respect. Then, as I have argued, mutual advantage and equal respect provide the standards for determining an optimal public ordering, and so what is to count as just and unjust.

9 I employ the capitalized form here to indicate that it is now the American Constitution to which I refer, and not the abstract constitution that for some time I have been discussing.

10 *Morals by Agreement*, pp. 155–6.

11 The idea of bargainers as ideal representatives is found in my paper "Justice as Social Choice," in D. Copp and D. Zimmerman (eds.), *Morality, Reason and Truth: New Essays in the Foundations of Ethics* (Totowa, N.J.: Rowman & Allanheld, 1984); see pp. 257–8.

12 Additionally, bargaining must proceed from an appropriate base point if it is to be considered deliberative. In *Morals by Agreement* I introduce a modified Lockean proviso to ensure that the base point does not incorporate force, fraud, or free-riding. (See especially pp. 201–5) Here, however, the concern to manifest civic friendship through the expression of equal respect is intended to safeguard against these ills. The question, pressed on me especially by Bruce Ackerman, is whether this concern may not also rule out inequalities in the base point that would be permitted by the proviso. I think not. Mutual advantage and equal respect do not require that the parties begin from an equality of condition. But the issue is too large to pretend to settle here.

13 Thomas Hobbes, *Leviathan* (London: 1651), ch. 10.

14 *The English Works of Thomas Hobbes*, ed. Sir William Molesworth (London: 1839–1845), vol. V, p. 194.

15 Ibid., p. 193.

16 Some thinkers have claimed that hypothetical agreements lack justificatory significance. See for example Ronald Dworkin, "Justice and Rights," in *Taking Rights Seriously* (Cambridge, Mass.: Harvard University Press, 1977), pp. 150–2. That you would have agreed yesterday to sell me the painting on your wall for $100 does not entitle me to give you $100 today and make off with it, now that you have learned that it is not the cheap 19th century copy you took it to be, but actually from the workshop of Tintoretto. But contractarian justification in politics relates to a context in which actual universal agreement is not possible. We recognize the need for political and legal order – the need to ensure mutual benefit in our interactions. Since this is a shared need, it should be possible for rational persons to come to agreement on a political and legal order, despite initial disagreement about which order. But if persons can not come to such agreement *in medias res*, they nevertheless need to have political and legal institutions and practices in place. Therefore, that they would rationally have agreed to certain institutions and practices, in circumstances that would have given everyone an equal opportunity to advance her concerns and an equal requirement to accommodate the concerns of others, may be part of the best justification available for the political and legal order that they constitute.

17 Thus my account here treats a constitution, and the question of its justification, very differently than does Rawls's. For Rawls, "a just constitution is one that rational delegates . . . would adopt for their society." (R. pp. 200–201) The adoption is hypothetical. My account of the adoption of a constitution, although presenting the procedure of adoption abstractly, does not treat it as merely hypothetical. The constitutional fact plays a key role in the argument. Of course, it would be absurd to suppose that such a fact is *necessary* for democratic legitimacy. In a fuller treatment than is possible here, it would be important to consider how one would account for political legitimacy in democratic polities that lack a constitutional fact. Here an appeal to the "constitution . . . that rational delegates . . . would adopt for their society" might be expected to be essential to legitimating authority. But there would be nothing approximating to the constitutive expression of popular will. It would seem that in the absence of a constitutional fact, a contractarian justification of political authority would fall short of a full contractarian understanding of political institutions and practices.

On contractarian
constitutional democracy

CHRISTOPHER W. MORRIS

The protagonists of *Morals by Agreement*[1] are, in many respects, new-comers to the repertoire of characters known to students of Western moral philosophy, as they combine features rarely possessed by the same actors. They are moral conventionalists, understanding the requirements of justice to be, not part of the furniture of the world, or of the mind (of a single individual), but norms based in rational agreement. They are utility maximizers, like their neoclassical economic brethren; yet they are moved not only by considerations of preference satisfaction but also by rational constraints requiring counterpreferential choice, impossible for mere "economic men" or "straightforward maximizers." They are rather abstract creatures (to use a Hegelian term), for they are moved by utility-based reason alone, without appeal to sentiment or passion,[2] and they have no essential communal or national identities, much less religious allegiances, that would separate one from another.

What are such beings to make of their world when they emerge from their idealized interactions, constitutive of their "morals by agreement," to find themselves in late-twentieth-century democratic America? Possessing the understanding that cultural distance permits, the rational contractors, like their Canadian creator, would note some of the striking features of American political culture, in particular, the distinctive role of the Constitution in American political thought and discourse. The widespread respect of Americans for their constitution is remarkable, the more so that it is often unnoticed and taken for granted. To my knowledge, in no other culture does one encounter in political discussion the phrase "but that is unconstitutional!" – much less expect it to have argumentative force. Americans integrate the Constitution into their moral landscape in another way: They distinguish with difficulty the Constitution, in particular the Bill of Rights, from the equally famous statement of American political morality, Jefferson's Declaration of Independence.[3] The distinctively American reverence for the Constitution, reflected in the (often parochial) work of American historians and constitutional scholars, is indeed remarkable.[4] What are the "constrained maximizers" of morals by agreement to make of this political culture?

David Gauthier suggests that the U.S. Constitution "is to be read, not merely as defining a particular political practice, but as defining a *form* – indeed, in its time, a *new* form – of political practice, in which the powers of government are legitimate because they are established through and limited by the consent of 'We, the People.'"[5] Viewing the Constitution thus enables us, he argues, to understand how it comes to be binding *higher* law. But how can the neo-Hobbesian author of *Morals by Agreement*, hostile as he must be to the natural law tradition, do this? Further, how is this understanding of American politics possible after, say, the skeptical impact of Arrovian social choice theory and Virginia Public Choice?

Gauthier distinguishes, after Frank Michelman, between *deliberative politics* and *strategic interaction*. The latter is basically the mode of interaction of straightforward maximization, resulting in "a vector-sum in a field of forces," to use Michelman's phrase (p. 2). An admirer of the benefits of strategic interaction realized by competitive markets, Gauthier reminds us that "force, fraud, and free-riding are the ills that blight the fruits of strategic interaction" (p. 3). Deliberative politics, by contrast, as characterized by Michelman, "connotes a reasoned interchange among persons who recognize each other as equal in authority and entitlement to respect, jointly directed towards answering some questions of public ordering . . . all remain open to the possibility of persuasion by others and . . . a vote, if any vote is taken, represents a pooling of judgments" (p. 2). The purpose of deliberative politics for Gauthier, as one would expect, is to remedy the ills of strategic interaction. Its character, again as one would expect, is that of rational agreement that culminates in (*ex ante*) mutual advantage (pp. 4–5). The law that emerges from deliberative politics specifies a standard of *reasonable* conduct, of "right reason," for members of society, one that acquires its authority from its mode of derivation (pp. 13–14).

What is novel in the contractarian political tale that David Gauthier now tells is the attitude that members of a society founded on deliberative politics come to have toward one another. "As wider opportunities for mutual benefit come to be appreciated," Gauthier claims,

so that each views her fellows as sharing in a way of life, then, provided that each finds those fellows willing to ensure that her place in their activities is a fair and reasonable one, they come to be seen as public friends, their presence now welcomed rather than merely accepted. What were bonds of convenience become ties of mutual civil concern. (pp. 4–5)

Civic friendship is neither affective nor instrumental concern, but instead is that whereby individuals "affirm each other's good in willingly making and honoring whatever commitments are needed to make their mutual activities successful from each partner's perspective" (p. 5). To do this, agreement must assure equal respect. The design of basis institutions and practices to regulate the interactions of members of a society, institutions that both express and support civic friendship, is the task of forming a constitution (p. 5). Such a constitution is for its members a shared good. It makes possible mutually beneficial cooperation, and it permits the expression of civic friendship. As such, Gauthier claims, it constitutes *the political good* (pp. 5–6), offering an account that may be contrasted to utilitarian and Aristotelian alternatives.

The second novel idea, after that of civic friendship, is the particular implication Gauthier draws from this understanding of a constitution. Insofar as a society's institutions structure interaction "to exhibit, or to ensure the exhibition of, full and equal respect for persons," they embody justice (p. 8). That is, "the outcome of deliberative politics is *constitutive* of justice among individuals" (p. 9). Linking this understanding of the constitution as determining justice for a society to the idea of its affirmation of civic friendship, Gauthier infers a particular ideal of justice, liberal in the contemporary American sense of the term, an ideal that requires "not merely equitable opportunities for individuals to advance their own life-plans, but a positive affirmation of those life-plans as equally and fully entitled to the support of society" (p. 8).

In *Morals by Agreement* there is little talk of government or of law, albeit considerable discussion of a variety of forms of social and political interaction. It is reasonable, one would think, to attribute to the author of that work a distinction, denied by Hobbes, between state and society. For constrained maximizers, cognizant of the principles of justice that morals by agreement generate,[6] can form social arrangements independently of government and law. The difficulties they face are primarily informational; when the number of individuals is large, constrained maximizers will not always know whether others have preferences and dispositions characteristic of the Prisoners' Dilemma or of the assurance games. Justice, then, is to a large extent prior to and independent of government and of law. Thus, it would not be unreasonable to understand the implicit constitutionalism of morals by agreement to permit, indeed to require, the priority of justice to the constitution. But this is not the view that Gauthier now defends.

Contrasting his position to that of John Rawls in *A Theory of Justice*, Gauthier makes clear the manner in which he wishes to be understood.

Rawls, as one would expect of a contractarian *moral* theorist,[7] distinguishes the choice of a constitution from that of principles of justice, the choice of the former being subject to the constraints of the latter. This would not be an unreasonable view, as one of the typical aims of contractarian moral theorists is the generation of principles for the (moral) evaluation and justification of government. And this had been the manner in which I had hitherto understood morals by agreement. Gauthier, however, wishes to be understood differently:

In subordinating the choice of a constitution to that of principles of justice, Rawls's account differs markedly from the one I have developed. As I have characterized deliberative politics, principles of justice are not the subject of a prior or independent choice, and constitutional choice is not subjected to any principled constraint established by prior choice. The exception that the constitution will promote mutual advantage and manifest equal respect is assured directly by the manner in which it is chosen.

My claim is that the outcome of deliberative politics is *constitutive* of justice among individuals. Concretely, a constitution may be said to constitute the political institutions of a society; abstractly, it may be said to constitute justice and, as we have seen, the common good. (p. 9)

"Constituting Democracy" also introduces a third idea, albeit one that is implicit in *Morals by Agreement*. In late medieval and early modern *political* theory, it was not uncommon to understand the "social contract," which was supposed to justify political relations among individuals, to have the form of an explicit promise. The ancestors of such an act presumably were the oaths of allegiance that bound vassals and lords, princes and kings. This tradition is one of the sources for contemporary contractarianism. Another is an older tradition in *moral* theory, to be found in the thought of some of the Sophists and of Epicurus. This is a conventionalist tradition, which understands the norms of justice to be second-best, mutually beneficial conventions among individuals equally vulnerable to harm or injury. This tradition is the other main source of contemporary hypothetical contractarianism.

In the first tradition, where the original contract is understood to be some sort of *actual* commitment, there are two elements that may be understood to form part of the justification of the institutions (or relations) in question. First, these are (*ex ante*) advantageous or agreeable, or else, one may presume, one would not have agreed to them. Second, one is bound or committed to these institutions, for one has agreed to them; that is, one has bound oneself to them by an act of *will*. In actual contractarianism, benefit and will appear to perform justificatory tasks. In hypothetical contractarianism, the older tradition attacked by Plato in the *Republic*, there is no actual agreement, so the second element cannot have a justificatory function. The will cannot, in hypothetical agreement, bind, for it is not there present.

Now, just as Gauthier, through his understanding of the constitution as determining of justice, is agreeing with Hobbes that the latter is not prior to the former, so he appears to be identifying with actual contractarianism, whereby agreement serves the two roles described above. Without wishing to require that the founding agreement must not be merely hypothetical, Gauthier seems to want to derive part of the justificatory force of rational agreement from engagement of the will. A contractarian understanding of a political system, he claims,

> requires more than showing that actual political and judicial institutions and practices, or the particular decisions to which they give rise, are those that would follow, directly or indirectly, from a reasoned agreement or interchange among citizens. To be sure, such a demonstration serves a justificatory role. But it does not show that the institutions or practices take their *rationale* from the idea of a reasoned interchange, and this is essential to a full contractarian understanding. (p. 14)

These three elements – civic friendship, constitutional justice, and the will as source of legitimacy – form the basis for my critical remarks. The first, that of civic friendship, has its roots in Gauthier's reflections on the "liberal individual" in the last chapter of *Morals by Agreement*. Here there are three aspects to be considered in turn. First, civic friends keep their commitments (p. 5); they are constrained maximizers. This represents no departure from earlier work. Second, civic friends come to welcome, rather than merely accept, the presence of their fellows, and they end by respecting one another (pp. 4–5). Third, this respect is to be understood as *equal* respect; civic friends – perhaps this is implicit in the notion of friendship – respect each other equally. I shall treat the last two parts together.

Whence equal respect? If respect is merely compliance with fair agreements, it is not problematic for morals by agreement. But the equality condition and the element of acceptance of the ends of others are problematic for a conventionalist moral theory that, unlike the tradition to which Michelman and many contemporary American liberals appeal, makes no fundamental normative assumptions about respect or equality. Hobbes is explicit about his understanding of equality: By nature, humans lack the differentiating attributes that many Aristotelian and medieval thinkers took to be evidence of natural moral superiority and desert. Natural equality was to be understood, like natural right, as nothing more than the absence of natural or nonconventional moral inequalities and of classical natural laws. Indeed, what else could a radical moral conventionalist claim? In civil society, humans ought to strive to treat each other equally "because men that think themselves equall, will not enter into conditions of Peace, but upon Equall termes, such equalitie must be admitted. . . . The breach of this Precept is Pride."[8] Hobbes' reasoning here clearly differs from that, say, of Ronald Dworkin; humans care about relative status – "every man looketh that his companion should value him, at the same rate he sets upon himselfe"[9] – and equal respect is merely instrumental in preserving peace. Why equality, rather than some unequal but stable arrangement? Presumably considerations of salience favor equality.[10]

Jules Coleman rightly challenges the necessity of civic friendship for the conclusions that Gauthier wishes to defend. The latter reports Coleman as suggesting that "*if* my argument in *Morals by Agreement* is sound, then a merely instrumental partnership should provide a sufficient base for the constraints needed to redirect individual action to mutual benefit" (p. 19n). One would have thought so; equal respect at best appears unnecessary, at worst incompatible with the general framework, unless derived from more fundamental considerations. But Gauthier disagrees. "But without civic friendship, and the equal respect it engenders, some persons will almost certainly find themselves relatively disadvantaged by actual social arrangements, which they can not be expected to accept willingly, so that the society will tend to be both coercive and unstable." Considerations of instability, however, are supposed to be handled by the constraints on the baseline for bargaining imposed by the Proviso and the rights on initial acquisition.[11] This answer begs the question.

Another way of defending equal respect is by appeal to the assumption of *equal rationality* that plays such an important role in Gauthier's bargaining theory of justice.[12] But this assumption, taken over from classical game theory, is as problematic as that of equal respect, whatever the chances of deriving the latter from the former.[13]

We turn next to Gauthier's view of the constitution as constitutive of justice. As already mentioned, this is not the position one would have expected to find derived from morals by agreement; instead, it would have been natural to expect something like Rawls's view. The reason for this expectation is fairly simple.[14] Suppose that the account of morality provided by *Morals by Agreement* is roughly correct. And suppose further that all agents in our and other communities are fully rational, although not necessarily fully informed. (Suppose also that all are in the circumstances of justice.) Then what role does government have? It would seem that its tasks would be merely coordinative (in the Schelling–Lewis sense).

Relax the condition of full rationality so that straightforward maximizers enter our world. Then we would want governments to provide defense and adjudicative services. (Adjudication here is different from the arbitration that agencies might provide for constrained maximizers faced with honest disagreement.) Government on this view is a second-best institution for worlds in which not all agents are constrained maximizers.

Now fully rational agents in the world depicted by Gauthier would want standards of justice. These standards they would generate, via collective agreement, before establishing government, the need for which has not yet been established. If it turns out that everyone is a constrained maximizer, then everything needed is in place. If it turns out that there are many straightforward maximizers, then the others should set about devising and agreeing about the institutions required to keep peace. In either world – the one without and the one with straightforward maximizers – justice is prior to the institutions of government. Why then make the constitution constitutive of justice?[15]

Gauthier's motivation seems to be practical:

In identifying [the decision on what counts as justice] with the choice of a constitution, I emphasize the idea that a constitution is legally foundational as the *privileged* act of popular will. Behind the popular will expressed in the constitution are only the particular and multifarious goods expressed in the life-plans of the individual members of society. Justice can not be found by mere reflection on them. (p. 9)

The last sentence suggests the practical motivation for the identification: How else, Gauthier seems to be saying, to determine what justice is except by actual reasoned agreement?

There is, however, an alternative, and it is proposed in *Morals by Agreement* and restated in "Constituting Democracy."[16] The alternative to actual, constitutionally constrained agreement is the ideal, informed bargain of morals by agreement, issuing in the principle of minimax relative constraint. Why does that exercise not determine justice and do so prior to and independently of constitutional choice?[17]

The third element in Gauthier's contractarian constitutionalism, the role of will in legitimating government, is also problematic. The classical challenge to hypothetical contractarianism, repeated by Dworkin against Rawls, is that hypothetical agreements don't bind. This challenge worries Gauthier, and he attempts to address it. The answer I have always favored is simple: Hypothetical agreements have at most a *heuristic* role, as pure procedures for determining principles. They do not bind in the way that ordinary promises, contracts, or commitments do. Gauthier's answer is different, presumably because he wishes to retain the will as a legitimating element. I quote at length:

> But contractarian justification in politics relates to a context in which actual universal agreement is not possible. We recognize the need for political and legal order – the need to ensure mutual benefit in our interactions. Since this is a shared need, it should be possible for rational persons to come to agreement on a political and legal order, despite initial disagreement about which order. But if persons can not come to such agreement *in medias res*, they nevertheless need to have political and legal institutions and practices in place. Therefore, that they would rationally have agreed to certain institutions and practices, in circumstances that would have given everyone an equal opportunity to advance her concerns and equal requirement to accommodate the concerns of others, may be part of the best justification available for the political and legal order that they constitute. (n. 16, pp. 20–1)

The argument is puzzling. That something might be the best justification for some arrangement is compatible with its being, in fact, no justification at all. The question how we are to understand the hypothetical engagement of the will as binding has not really been addressed.

   Let me conclude with some reflections connecting these issues with some of the recent political developments in Central and Eastern Europe. Many observers have noted the significant role of nationalism in these developments. While the contributions of democratic sentiments, and the attractions of various ideals of human rights, are not to be underestimated, the importance of nationalism remains to be appreciated. In the contexts of the debate over German reunification, however, appeals to nationalism have, for obvious historical reasons, been criticized and repressed. What is then to be the substitute for the sentiments of loyalty and attachment that enable individuals to make extraordinary sacrifices for one another? The recent answer of some Germans has been *Verfassungspatriotismus*, the postwar German constitution being, it is thought, a suitable object of loyalty. The nationalism of Americans is, it may be argued, very much of a form of "constitution-patriotism," and Gauthier's analysis reflects this. It too may be a beneficial substitute for the nationalism that has wrought so much harm in this century and the last.

   We may think of much of the current revival of classical republican ideals of civic friendship in this light, as a substitute for nationalism. But is it a substitute, or the same in disguise? Consider the notion of "a people" in Gauthier's discourse. In contemporary English this notion has lost, it would appear, some of its old eighteenth- and nineteenth-century connotations. Consider instead *le peuple* or *das Volk*. These do not designate mere aggregates; rather, they are collections of individuals tied by cultural, linguistic, and national bonds. In the German debate, the notion of *das Volk* is as taboo as that of nation. One reason is that the peoples of East and West Germany composed but two proper subsets of the German *Volk*; talk of "unification" of the German *Volk* would suggest incorporation of Austria, if not Silesia.

I should like to suggest, then, that finding the source of legitimacy in the will of the people, especially if their will is to be the sole source of justice, is reactionary. Classical eighteenth-century notions of popular sovereignty are as dangerous as earlier notions of state sovereignty. What we do not need today are ways of understanding justice and legitimacy that divide the globe into separate (and unequal) nations, united internally by relations of justice and civic friendship, but separated one from another, in a larger state of nature, with all of the classical problems thereof.

Notes

1 David Gauthier, *Morals by Agreement* (Oxford: Clarendon Press, 1986).
2 Sentiment, however, moves a second generation of Gauthier's rational contractors. See Gauthier, "Value, Reasons, and the Sense of Justice," in *Value, Welfare, and Morality*, ed. R. G. Frey and Christopher W. Morris (Cambridge: Cambridge University Press, in press).
3 I sometimes ask my philosophy-of-law students at the beginning of term to list some of the rights granted by the Constitution, and I regularly find that those of "life, liberty, and the pursuit of happiness" are on students' lists, alongside free speech and the right to bear arms. Several years ago, the very week that I performed this exercise, President Ronald Reagan referred to "our constitutional rights" of life, liberty, and pursuit of happiness, as did an English professor in an op-ed-page article in the student newspaper.
4 In other political cultures, it is not unusual to identify the current constitution, or republic, by its place in a sequence of political arrangements (e.g., Fifth Republic, Third Reich). But no one would think of referring to "the Constitution" as the Second Constitution, which is precisely what it is, if one remembers the Articles of Confederation. One must ask, in the contexts of our present discussion, whether a clear-eyed understanding of the origins of the (second) U.S. Constitution would impede our attempt to view it in the manner proposed by Gauthier, as expressive and constitutive of the popular will.
5 David Gauthier, "Constituting Democracy," in this volume (p. 1). All parenthetical page references are to this essay as it originally was published as the Lindley Lecture for 1989 by the University of Kansas.

6 The main principle of justice in *Morals by Agreement* is that of minimax relative concession (Chapter 5). The moral rights and the Proviso on initial appropriation, which constrain the bargain that established this principle, may be understood to form additional parts of justice (Chapter 7). The latter are "Lockean" only in their *priority to* agreement, for they are not, as they could not be in a Hobbesian theory, *independent of* agreement. Constrained maximization, of course, is the mode of reasoning that enables rational agents to secure otherwise unstable arrangements (Chapter 6).

7 I distinguish here and in the paragraphs that follow contractarian *moral* theory from contractarian *political* theory. The distinction is between contractarian accounts of moral norms (e.g., principles of justice) and of political arrangements (e.g., governments, legal systems). While the distinction is not deep, it is important for the question of the possible priority of moral principles to law.

8 *Leviathan* (1651), Part I, chap. 15.

9 *Leviathan*, Part I, chap. 13.

10 Note "the remarkable frequency with which long negotiations over complicated quantitative formulas or *ad hoc* shares in some costs or benefits converge ultimately on something as crudely simple as equal shares." Thomas Schelling, *The Strategy of Conflict* (New York: Oxford University Press, 1963), p. 67.

11 *Morals by Agreement*, Chapter 7.

12 See Gauthier, "Constituting Democracy," p. 11.

13 Several commentators on *Morals by Agreement* have noted the crucial but problematic status of the assumption of equal rationality. See Gilbert Harman, "Rationality in Agreement: A Commentary on Gauthier's *Morals by Agreement*," *Social Philosophy and Policy* 5 (1988): 1–16, and Jody Kraus and Jules Coleman, "Morality and the Theory of Rational Choice," *Ethics* 97 (1987): 715–49.

14 The paragraphs that follow are taken, with small modifications, from comments made on an early draft of "Constituting Democracy."

15 I ignore the implications of this move for international justice.

16 *Morals by Agreement*, chap. 5; "Constituting Democracy," pp. 11 and 7.

17 James Buchanan would be sympathetic to Gauthier's identification of justice with constitutional reasoned agreement. But his agreement would stem from his skepticism about the determinate results that may be derived from abstract, idealized bargaining theory. Additionally, Buchanan often espouses an Austrian account of value or utility, claiming that prior to (actual) choice, no one, including the agent, can say what someone's values are – hence Buchanan's antagonism to the use of the Kaldor–Hicks criterion of efficiency or "optimality."

Part IV

Democracy and economics

8

The possibility of market socialism

JOHN E. ROEMER

I

Since the fall from power of the ruling parties in Eastern Europe, in 1989, most commentators in the West and the East alike have proclaimed the death of communism. The inference that these commentators implicitly make is that socialism, too, is a dead letter. I shall argue here for the feasibility of market socialism, a politicoeconomic system in which firms are publicly owned, the state has considerable control of the "commanding heights" of the economy, all private goods are traded on markets, and there is democratic control over society's use of its economic surplus.

The failed "communist" experiment was characterized by the following three features:

1. Public or state ownership of the means of production
2. Noncompetitive (i.e., single party) politics
3. Command–administrative allocation of resources and commodities

The inference that those proclaiming the death of *socialism* have made is that, since (1), (2), and (3) imply economic failure, therefore *all* of (1) through (3) must be negated to achieve a successful economic system. This is, of course, a false inference: All we can infer from the failure of (1) + (2) + (3) is that at least one of the three characteristics must be changed to achieve economic success. What I outline below is an economic mechanism in which (2) and (3) are, indeed, negated – there will be democratic, competitive politics, and market allocation of most commodities and resources – but public ownership of the principal

I thank my collaborators I. Ortuño-Ortin and J. Silvestre, who have given me permission to report in this essay some of our joint work on investment planning. I am deeply indebted to J. Silvestre for our many discussions on market socialism, which have been basic in forming the views I currently hold. As well, I am grateful to the many people who have commented on these ideas as they have been presented in various seminars and conferences.

means of production is maintained. Put slightly differently, my claim is that markets are necessary to achieve an efficient and vigorous economy, but that private ownership is not necessary for the successful operation of markets. It is the failure of both the right and the left to disambiguate the concepts of private ownership and market equilibrium that has led to the premature obituaries of socialism.

II

Market socialism is not a new idea: it was formulated by Oskar Lange, Wlodzimierz Brus, and Alec Nove,[1] among others. Brus gives a useful history of the concept in *The Palgrave Dictionary of Economics*.[2] The challenge is to design an economic mechanism in which (1) markets are used to allocate resources, (2) firms are publicly owned, and (3) the state, with a democratic mandate, controls the "commanding heights" of the economy. (1) and (2) might seem to be mutually exclusive, as might (1) and (3). By the commanding heights of the economy, I mean *the pattern and levels of investment in the major sectors of the economy*. By a publicly owned firm, I mean one *the distribution of whose profits is determined by political means*. In centrally planned economies, many details of the operations of publicly owned firms were also *controlled* by the government. That will not be true in the market socialist model put forth in sections III and IV. The public property right in my nomenclature extends only to the *allocation of profits*, not to control of the firm by the state.

A necessary condition of democratic socialism is that the allocation of profits of public firms be an issue for democratic decision *and* that society decide to distribute these profits more or less equally to all households. I have tried to defend the desirability of an egalitarian distribution of profits elsewhere, and will not be further concerned with that here,[3] except to explain why I do not advocate distribution of profits in proportion to the value of labor performed, a formula many view as socialist par excellence. First, the value of labor performed will vary a great deal across people, owing to differential skills. I do not support a desert or rights principle asserting that people either deserve or have a right to a share of the social product proportional to the value of their labor contribution, because I do not believe that individuals are mainly responsible for the market value of skills they have acquired. Second, there would be severe efficiency problems associated with a decentralized (i.e., market) economic system in which it were announced that the distribution of social profits would be proportional to the value of labor expended. Oskar Lange correctly recognized that the formula for the distribution of the social dividend to citizens must be independent of actions citizens can take in the market – he recommended a distribution of profits in proportion to family size, as a proxy for need, ignoring the theoretically possible perverse effects such a formula might have for population growth.

Although the reason to distribute profits equally is primarily ethical, the reasons to authorize state control of the sectoral pattern and level of investment are mainly economic, if such a distinction can be made. The market unaided will not achieve a socially desirable distribution of investment. One may list various reasons. (1) There are both positive and negative externalities associated with investment, and markets do not achieve an efficient allocation of resources in the presence of externalities. The negative externalities (e.g., pollution) are widely known; I shall therefore concentrate on positive externalities. Investment, especially in human capital, brings about increased possibilities for technological innovation, both because a more highly trained work force exists to operate sophisticated technology, and because highly trained people will engender more innovations. Education also improves social welfare directly because there are massive positive consumption externalities for people living in a society with other well-educated people. Thus, investment in education and in goods that are intermediate inputs into the educational process is typically too low without state intervention. (2) Many investments are worthwhile only if certain complementary investments are also made. The unfettered market allocation may result in neither of a pair of complementary investments being made, instead of both being made. (3) More generally, there is a *market failure* which may cause underinvestment, to wit, futures markets do not exist for most goods, and lacking these, investors may react to any uncertainty in the economy by choosing to keep their assets liquid rather than commit themselves to investment, even when more investment would be socially optimal. Something like this underlies the Keynesian view that recessions in capitalist economies are caused by a failure of investment, itself due to the "animal spirits" of capitalists. These spirits might be less dramatically described as risk-averse reactions to uncertainty when a complete set of markets is lacking.[4]

One should note that the view that the state should have the authority to influence the pattern and level of investment is not in itself radical: Mainstream economists, such as Lester Thurow, argue that the poor performance of the U.S. economy vis-à-vis the Japanese economy is due to America's refusal to allow substantial government interference in the private sector's investment plan and Japan's reliance on it. So public control of investment is not sufficient to characterize socialism, although it is necessary.

Finally, I should remark on what the state does *not* plan in this conception of market socialism: the consumption goods that are produced and consumed by the citizens, the prices of commodities and labor, the allocation of labor, and the output of firms.

III

To permit a fairly precise description of the design of a market socialist mechanism I must first describe in some detail the model of a prototypical *economic environment*. In describing this environment, I do not presuppose any economic mechanism, capitalist or socialist; I simply describe the temporal and physical nature of production and investment. Imagine a society that exists for two periods, with a population of citizens who work and consume in each period. There is one sector that produces the economy's single investment good (say, steel), and a number of sectors, say N, that produce the different consumption goods. There are a number of firms in each sector; perhaps different firms in a single sector have different technologies. Citizens supply labor to firms, and consume the N consumption goods in each period: Each shall try, under any economic mechanism, to consume that pattern of consumer goods over his lifetime that maximizes his particular utility, subject to whatever budget constraint he faces. During the first period, all firms must produce with whatever capital stock they have, but they may place orders for the investment good during the first period, which they use to augment their capital stock in the second period. The volume of investment is most proximately determined by the division of society's labor in the first period between the production of consumption goods and the production of the investment good. The more investment good is produced and invested, the greater will be the production capabilities of the economy in the second period, when only consumption goods are produced. Thus, a decision to invest more is a decision to trade off present consumption for future consumption.

Now impose a capitalist economic mechanism on this environment, which amounts to specifying that the firms are privately owned, that there is some particular distribution of ownership of firms, and that markets allocate resources. Each citizen owns the right to a certain fraction, perhaps zero, of the profits of each firm. If this economy is anything like actual capitalist economies, there is a large class of people who own no rights to positive fractions of the profits of any firm: In the

United States, 85 percent of the population own no corporate stock, and the richest 0.5 percent own 50 percent of all corporate stock. We study the capitalist economy in a state of market equilibrium, also known as a *Walrasian equilibrium*.[5]

A Walrasian equilibrium can be described, briefly, as follows. First, consider markets and prices. There is a price for each consumer good in each period, for the investment good in the first period (that's a total of $2N + 1$ prices so far), and for each kind of labor in each period. Say there are K qualities of labor, or types of skill, in the economy. In addition, there is an interest rate at which citizens can save and firms can borrow. Thus there are $2N + 2 + 2K$ prices in this economy. I shall assume that all citizens and firms know today's prices, and either know or correctly forecast the prices of the second period. Facing any vector of these $2N + 2 + 2K$ prices, economic actors – firms and citizens – behave as follows:

1. Each consumer-good firm demands amounts of the various kinds of labor and an amount of investment good, and supplies amounts of its output in both periods so as to maximize its total discounted profits over the two periods at given prices. We assume that each firm is small relative to its market, so that it need not take into account the effect of its production on the price of output: it behaves as a price-taking competitor;

2. The investment-good firm chooses an amount of the investment good to supply and an amount of each kind of labor to demand, to maximize its profits (in the first period), at given prices;

3. Each citizen has a lifetime budget consisting of her wage income from supplying her labor endowment in the two periods to firms, plus her profit income from firms, derived from her ownership shares. Given this lifetime budget, she decides on an amount to save or borrow in the first period, and an amount of each consumer good to demand in each period, to maximize her utility subject to her lifetime budget constraint. Savings in the first period are returned with interest in the second period;

4. The timing of economic activity is as follows. Firms pay out the profits at the end of each period to shareholders, and pay wages to workers at the end of each period. Every firm sells its output at the end of the period in which it is produced. Thus firms retain no earnings, and must borrow to pay for the investment good that they purchase at the end of period one, but which is not counted as a cost of production until period two.

Such is the behavior of every economic actor in this economy facing any vector of prices. A price vector is a *Walrasian price equilibrium* if:

5. The total demand for each commodity and each kind of labor equals the total supply for each commodity and each kind of labor, and the total supply of savings equals the demand for investment. That is, all markets clear at these prices.

It is a deep and important theorem of neoclassical economics that, under suitable conditions on the nature of preferences or utilities of the citizens and on the nature of firms' technologies, a Walrasian price equilibrium exists. We now take the leap of asserting that the normal state of a capitalist economy is to be at such an equilibrium, and we infer aspects of resource allocation in a capitalist economy from aspects of the resource allocation at a Walrasian equilibrium of the model. In particular, there will be some particular *pattern of investment* at a Walrasian equilibrium. Total investment of firms will equal total savings of consumers. A consumer decides how much to save based only on trying to maximize his lifetime utility, facing the given prices of consumer goods and the interest rate, and knowing his budget (in particular, we assume that he correctly predicts the profits of each firm in which he has an interest, as his shares of these constitute part of his budget); each firm decides on its investment only with an eye to maximizing the present value of profits, not with an eye to satisfying the demands of consumers.

Notice that the distribution of income will be unequal in this economy for two reasons: Some citizens will be endowed with qualities of labor that are more valuable, at equilibrium wages, than others', and profits might be distributed in a highly unequal fashion. Note also that there are no taxes in this economy – in order to simplify the analysis, I have made the unrealistic assumption that there are no transfer payments or public goods of any kind for which taxes would be needed. We are examining a simple prototype of an economy where everyone is able-bodied, or can otherwise survive on his income, and all final goods are private goods.

I shall now outline how a market socialist mechanism could allocate resources in this same economic environment, while addressing itself to the unequal distribution of profits and the perhaps undesirable pattern of investment of the Walrasian equilibrium. There is a democratic process that elects a party empowered to implement its economic program. This program consists of two planks: a proposed distribution of the after-tax profits of all (public) firms among the citizens, and a proposed level and pattern of investment for the economy. There is a manager of each firm whose job it shall be to maximize profits of that firm, facing market prices. Each citizen's income will consist of her wage income, from selling her labor power to firms in both periods, and her social dividend, that is, her share of total profits of public firms, after taxes. In the particular mechanism – one variant of possible market socialism – that I now describe, there will be taxes collected by the government only on the profits of firms.

The instruments the government will use to influence the pattern of investment are discounts and surcharges on the market interest rate. The central bank will be empowered to lend money to firms, with a specific interest rate discount for each consumer-good sector. A firm in a particular sector can borrow at its specific discount; citizens save or borrow at the market rate. I now define a *Lange equilibrium* for this economy, named after the economist who first proposed that interest rates be used by the socialist government to regulate investment, as a set of prices for all goods in each period $(2N + 1)$, a set of wages in each period $(2K)$, an interest rate, a set of discounts on the interest rate (N), and a set of tax rates on corporate profits (N), at which the following happens:

1. Each consumer-good firm demands an amount of labor of each quality and an amount of the investment good, and supplies an amount of its output in both periods that maximizes the present value of profits over two periods. In particular, note that it will be relatively more profitable for firms receiving higher interest rate discounts to invest, since investment is financed by loans;

2. Each investment-good firm demands labor and supplies its output in those amounts that maximize profits;

3. Each citizen calculates her budget as the sum of her labor income and her social dividend, which is the share of after-tax corporate profits she receives. She chooses the pattern of consumption over two periods, and the amount she saves or borrows, that maximizes her utility subject to her budget constraint;

4. The central bank pays out interest to citizens in the second period at the market rate, and it collects interest from firms at various discounted rates. Even if savings equals investment, as it will in equilibrium, the receipts and payments of the central bank will not balance because of the difference in interest rates. Taxes collected from corporate profits must exactly cover the central bank's deficit;

5. The total supply of every good and each kind of labor equals the total demand for every good and each kind of labor, and the total supply of savings of citizens equals the total value of investment goods demanded by firms.

Using the techniques of general equilibrium theory, I. Ortuño, J. Silvestre, and I have studied this economic mechanism, and have proved that many Lange equilibria exist.[6] Suppose the government wants to implement a particular pattern of investment in the economy. If this vector of investment levels lies in a certain well-defined set, then there are interest rate discounts that the government can announce and corporate tax rates such that a Lange equilibrium exists at which the investment levels in sectors are precisely the levels of that vector. Just as one assumes that the market finds the Walrasian equilibrium in a capitalist economy, so we assume that the market will find this Lange equilibrium in the market socialist economy described. One assumption is as robust as the other.

Let me qualitatively describe how the government sets interest rate discounts to influence the investment levels that firms demand. Suppose it wants all sectors to invest more than they would at the laissez-faire Walrasian equilibrium. It wants citizens to save more and firms to invest more. It announces discounts on the interest rate at which firms can borrow. This will increase the demand for investment by firms, in different amounts, depending on how big the discount is by sector. But now investment demand will outstrip savings of citizens, and so the market interest rate will rise. At equilibrium, if one exists, savings equals investment, and so the central bank will suffer a deficit, since it borrows at the market rate (from citizens) and lends at a low rates (to firms). The deficit is financed by corporation taxes. This is only a very approximate explanation of what happens, since in general all other prices will change to equilibrate markets when the market interest rate changes from its value at Walrasian equilibrium. That is why a mathematical argument is necessary to prove that such Lange equilibria in fact exist, and to understand what they look like.

From the viewpoint of the theory of economic planning, what is of interest is that what I have called the Lange mechanism – the use of interest rate discounts and surcharges to guide investment – is essentially as powerful a method for influencing investment as are some other methods that would involve much deeper intervention in the economy by the central planning bureau. Consider two other methods. In the first, which we call the *command–market* mechanism, the center commands each firm to purchase a certain specified amount of the investment good. After these commands have been issued, there is no further intervention; markets reach an equilibrium at which all orders are realized and all other markets clear. All firms maximize profits in this model, although it may be that some firms realize negative profits at the equilibrium. (They are not allowed to shut down, for this would entail investing a zero amount, less than the amount they were ordered to invest.) These losses will be covered by subsidies from the center, financed out of total corporate profits. The second mechanism we call the *direct investment* mechanism. In this case, the center issues no commands, but it purchases the investment good on the open market and gives it to firms in specified amounts. Firms are free to purchase more of the investment good if they wish, but they may not sell their government grants of investment to other firms. Again, a market equilibrium is reached.

It may seem that the government would be able to implement a larger class of investment vectors using the command–market mechanism or the direct investment mechanism than by using the Lange mechanism, since it appears to intervene more deeply or directly in the economic process under those two mechanisms. But we have proved that this is not the case. The Lange mechanism can implement more investment vectors than the direct investment mechanism, and exactly the same set of investment vectors as the command–market mechanism, while maintaining nonnegative social dividends for all citizens. Furthermore, the Lange mechanism is superior to the other two mechanisms on grounds of informational simplicity. For to give firms the correct commands under the command–market mechanism, or the correct investment grants under the direct investment mechanism, the center must know the technology of *each* firm; whereas to use the Lange mechanism, the center need only monitor the total investment orders in an industry, and adjust the interest rate discounts or surcharges accordingly, much as the Federal Reserve adjusts the interest rate it charges to banks. Guiding the economy by the use of interest rates requires less knowledge on the center's part. We therefore view the theorem described as an important one for the establishing the possibility of market socialism, that is, for replacing a system of deep central intervention with a market system without giving up on the goal of investment planning.

In a Lange equilibrium, citizens' incomes are more equal than in a capitalist Walrasian equilibrium because the profits of firms are distributed more equally. Total incomes, however, will not be equal: Differences due to differential values of labor remain, as wages are determined by the market. If we want to alter further the distribution of income, we must introduce further taxation and transfer payments. Let us note some other properties of Lange equilibria. The state sets no quantities, and arranges for the delivery of no firm's output to any retail outlet, nor does it arrange any investment transactions. All orders, demands and supplies, are decentralized to the firm level; firms acquire all inputs and dispose of all outputs on markets. Firms maximize profits, facing market prices and interest rates, and no firm is subsidized by the government. The center sets no prices, except the interest rate discounts. In the Soviet Union, there were approximately ten thousand prices set by the center – not to speak of the quantities that are also set, for example, the planned output of every large firm.

What about efficiency? The Walrasian equilibrium of the capitalist economy is Pareto efficient: There exists no technologically feasible allocation of resources that gives all citizens a higher utility than they enjoy at a Walrasian equilibrium. This, at least, is the case if there are no public goods or externalities. It can be proved that a Lange equilibrium enjoys the following kind of Pareto efficiency: There is no technologically feasible allocation of resources that can bring a higher utility to every citizen, given that society will invest as it has. It is perhaps worthwhile to emphasize that this kind of efficiency comes about because the public firms are maximizing profits; were firms controlled by workers who decided to maximize income per worker, rather than profits, the interest rate mechanism would not lead to the kind of efficiency characteristic of Lange equilibria.

Having now explicated a model of market socialism, I should comment on an inconsistency between it and the motivation I gave earlier for investment intervention. I said that it might be desirable to modify the Walrasian investment vector because of externalities, but externalities do not appear in the model I described, which is, therefore, too simple to reflect properly some of the motivating concerns. All I can say is that we conjecture that in a more complex model – with public goods, more than one generation, finite natural resources, externalities, and incomplete markets – there will be a similar result in regard to central control of investment by means of interest rates; namely, that the Lange mechanism is essentially as powerful as the mechanisms that involve more intensive central intervention and knowledge.

Another criticism – not of the model but of its philosophy – is this. I have proposed that citizens choose the investment vector to be implemented through a democratic political process: Why should such a pattern of investment be any more socially desirable than the one they would vote for in the market, with their dollars, at a Walrasian equilibrium? Why not just distribute profits as social dividends, and then allow an unregulated capital market? Suppose citizens' market behavior does not reflect their interests (for example, they do not save as much as they should for the future). Will they be guided by their interests or their "utilities" in the voting booth? Suppose their economic behavior does not sufficiently take into account the welfare of future generations. Will their political behavior reflect more of an interest in future generations? I propose to answer both questions with a qualified yes. A democratic political process is, as well, an educational process. (Here, one must refer to Habermas.) There is evidence that people view voting as a civic act (it is notoriously difficult to explain why *homo economicus* should vote): People may well vote their "moral preferences," which are not the same as the utilities they use when deciding on personal savings and consumption.[7] Finally, with regard to public goods and externalities, voting is surely a way in which citizens may solve the problem of providing public goods, which they cannot solve through decentralized economic behavior. A typical citizen may well vote to increase taxes to finance a public project, while at the same time filling out his tax form in a way that minimizes what he must pay. This behavior should not be mysterious to us.

IV

Perhaps the most important criticism against the coherence of the model of market socialism here proposed is that there will be no way to motivate firm managers to maximize profits unless firms are privately owned by shareholders who can trade shares on a stock market. More generally, where will entrepreneurial spirit come from in such an economy, and how will technological innovations take place? Critics will say that the kind of static efficiency that the Lange model enjoys, even if firms maximize profits, is a rather unimportant achievement. Capitalism's important achievement is dynamic vigor, which comes from entrepreneurs and technological innovation. Can an economy in which firms are not privately owned achieve that vigor?

Let us first take up the question of managerial discipline. Stories abound about corrupt and incompetent management of firms in socialist economies: Recall the famous *Krokodil* cartoon of the manager of a Soviet nail factory who, to meet a quota of one ton of nails, produces a one-ton nail. It is wrong to conclude from the experience of firms in a command economy what publicly owned firms will be like in a market economy. Managerial culture in the Soviet Union was demoralized, to say the least: Often managers could get the inputs they needed only by bribery and barter. This culture would be very different if inputs and outputs could be bought and sold on markets. But culture, of course, cannot be the complete answer to the challenge. Most finance economists maintain that the only reason that managers pursue the interests of shareholders, which require maximizing profits, rather than their own selfish interests, is the threat of losing their jobs. The discipline is provided via the stock market. If a firm is being poorly managed, its profit prospects will darken, and its stock price will fall. It will become an attractive target for a takeover by investors who will buy the firm cheap, change the management, and return the firm to a profit-maximizing path, thus increasing the value of their investment. Guaranteeing vigorous firms requires having a market for corporate control; this is the stock market in a capitalist economy, and there is no such market, thus far proposed, under market socialism. It is noteworthy that finance economists believe that private ownership of firms is insufficient to guarantee profit maximization. There must be *highly concentrated* private ownership, they maintain, with a few very large stockholders in whose interests it is to monitor the management closely. It is also large investors who organize takeovers. If this is so, the quandary for market socialism is real: How can an economy whose firms distribute profits diffusely to the population devise a mechanism to monitor firm management?

Indeed, Janos Kornai, one of the most informed students of actually existing socialism, argues that market socialism can never succeed, because the government will never allow publicly owned firms to compete in the ruthless way necessary to produce cost minimization and technological innovation: Management will be able to avoid the hard choices involved in carrying out these tasks by making deals with the state bureaucrats responsible for the performance of the firm.[8] His arguments, however, are based on experiments with aspects of market socialism in Hungary and Yugoslavia, where political competition did not exist and firms remained controlled, in many respects, by the center. To answer Kornai's criticisms, a model is necessary in which the government is not the body to which the firm management is ultimately responsible.

A clue to a possible solution comes from the experience of Japanese capitalism, where the stock market was relatively unimportant until recently. Firms are organized into groups, called *keiretsu*, each associated with a main bank, whose responsibility it is to lend to the firms in its group, and to monitor the firms' managements. The investment projects proposed by firms are evaluated by the staff of the bank, and in this way the bank is able to monitor the firms' behavior. Ironically, main banks also defend firms in their group against takeovers from firms outside the group, which might seem to protect inefficiency. But the system appears to have been very successful. There is no market for corporate control in Japan – at least, it does not take the form that it has in the United States, and capital is not directed to its most profitable uses by the stock market. This last point is worth emphasizing, for another plank of capitalist or, let us say, Chicago ideology is that bureaucrats cannot decide how to allocate capital: That is best done by a stock market, where millions of people express their opinions by voting with their dollars. Yet in Japan, apparently the accountants, economists, and industrial experts working for the big banks are sufficiently savvy to pass good judgment on investment proposals of firms.

Pranab Bardhan[9] has proposed a system wherein firms in the kind of market socialist economy I have outlined could be organized into groups modelled after the Japanese keiretsu. Say firms W, X, Y, and Z are in one group, with bank B. Each firm would own some shares of the other firms in the group, and the bank would also own some shares of each firm. The board of directors of a firm would consist of representatives of its shareholders, that is, of the various firms and banks in the group. That part of profits of firm W, for instance, not going to the bank, the other three firms, or directly to W's own workers, would go to the state and would be distributed to all citizens as part of the social dividend. The fraction of firm W's profits going to firms X, Y, and Z by virtue of their ownership of shares of W, would constitute a significant other part of the social dividend of the workers of X, Y, and Z. Thus, every worker in the economy would receive his social dividend from two sources: a centralized dividend from the government, comprising a small share of profits of all firms in the economy, and a decentralized part, consisting of a fraction of the profits of the other firms in his group. The function of this decentralization would be to give firms X, Y, and Z an interest in monitoring the behavior of firm W. In particular, if firm X thinks firm W is not profit-maximizing, then it can demand that the bank buy its shares of W. This in turn puts pressure on the bank to force W's management to do better.

Bardhan's proposal is not equivalent to introducing a stock market; it is a mechanism for decentralizing the accountability of firm management to a small number of institutions, in this case, other firms and banks, that are capable of monitoring the management. Complete equality in the social dividend received by different households would be compromised to create a mechanism for decentralizing the monitoring of firms. For although the centrally disbursed part of the social dividend would be equal across households, the decentralized part would not be.

Concerning innovation, it would again be wrong to conclude from the experience of firms in command economies that firms that are not privately owned will not innovate. I think that if there is sufficient competition, innovation will occur in market socialist firms. To the extent that innovation in capitalist economies takes place in organized research and development divisions in large firms, it can just as well take place in a socialist firm. It might be said that the kind of innovation that would not occur under market socialism would be that of the lonely entrepreneur, who, spurred on by the prospect of becoming a multimillionaire, invents a new kind of computer. Under capitalism, these people, if they succeed, form small firms and are in almost all cases eventually bought out by large firms. I suggest that such private firms be permitted in market socialist economies. They should be nationalized, with proper compensation to their owners, at some given size. The government, instead of IBM, would buy out the small computer firm. Or the publicly owned IBM could buy out the small firm, subject to the usual antitrust considerations, which would be necessary under market socialism as well. This mechanism should provide almost as much material incentive to the entrepreneurial spirit as capitalism provides.

Another variant of market socialism involves a larger scope for the stock market. The government would issue to citizens vouchers entitling them to purchase shares of firms, or of mutual funds that held firms' stocks, at prices denominated in voucher units. People could trade freely the stock in one firm (or mutual fund) for stock in another – but all trades would be made with voucher currency. The voucher price of stocks would be determined by the stock market. Vouchers could not be purchased with money, nor could money purchase shares of firms or mutual funds. Under this system, the (voucher) price of a firm's stock would signal to the banks (and investors) how well a firm was perceived as doing: It is in order to have this signal that the stock market is introduced, as well as to give citizens more choice, than under the Bardhan scheme, in the portfolio of risky assets they wish to hold. Each firm would continue to have a main bank responsible for arranging loan consortia for the firm, and the bank would be the firm's main monitor. If the stock price of a firm fell, the bankers would quickly step in and investigate the firm's management. All financing of firms would be through bank loans. Voucher holders would provide no equity capital to the firm; the voucher system would be only a way of allocating the firms' profits to citizens. This system would maintain a distribution of profits among citizens that would be much more egalitarian than the typical capitalist distribution. At death, a person's voucher holdings of stock would return to the state treasury to be distributed to the current cohort of young adults.[10]

V

Will a market socialist society be a just society? Will it maximize the potential for self-realization of its citizens? It is wrong, in my view, to maintain that any market system, with or without capitalists, allocates resources and incomes justly. What perfectly working competitive markets do is pay people according to the evaluation that other people in society place on their "contribution." In a capitalist economy, a person's contribution consists not just of her labor contribution, but also of the contribution of her capital. Leftists have usually attacked the justice of the capitalist income distribution on the grounds that capitalists are not the rightful owners of their capital, and hence their receipt of profits is an injustice, and, moreover, constitutes exploitation of those to whom the capital should rightly belong. The problem with this argument is that it does not go far enough. For I do not think it is correct to say that a distribution of income in which each is paid the value of her labor contribution to the rest of society is just either, as I have indicated earlier.

I view the differential wages that will accompany a market socialist system as justifiable for only one reason: Such wages are a by-product of using a labor market to allocate labor, and there is no known way to allocate labor more efficiently in a large, complex economy than by use of a labor market. Now, there are various ways to reduce real income differentials among workers that could be used by a market socialist society – to the extent, of course, that a democratically controlled society condones using them. One practice of the social democracies, obviously not precluded under market socialism, is to tax income sharply and progressively, and to redistribute it by providing some goods, such as health services, on an equal basis to all at no fee.

If some inequality is one undesirable feature of market socialism, a second is, as G. A. Cohen has written, that the market "motivates contribution not on the basis of commitment to one's fellow human beings and a desire to serve them while being served by them, but on the basis of impersonal cash reward."[11] Indeed, one should not idealize the behavior of people in a market socialist economy. Firms might advertise deceptively, and try, as they do under capitalism, to create in people tastes for goods by exploiting their feelings of insecurity and incompetence. Workers would need unions to protect them from overzealous managers, even if they had the power to remove management. More generally, conflicts between different groups of people based on their different economic interests would continue to exist. Environmentalists and workers in the lumber industry might continue to clash.

VI

In the model discussed thus far, there is no unemployment at equilibrium, since all prices, including the wage, are market clearing. But because unions will form, and will be necessary under market socialism, wages might be sticky, just as they are in a unionized capitalist economy. It would appear, that is, that wages would not adjust to market-clearing levels in the labor market, and unemployment would result. I will offer two arguments to support the claim that unemployment would be lower in a market socialist economy than in a capitalist economy.

The first has already been offered: to the extent that recessions are induced by the "animal spirits" of capitalists, they can be prevented by the mechanism of investment planning.

The second argument addresses the cause of wage stickiness in a capitalist economy with trade unions. Suppose that a capitalist economy is operating near full employment, and then a bad shock occurs – say, the price of some important input, such as oil, jumps up. Given the new price for the input, the full employment equilibrium for the economy will now require a fall in the real wage. If unions are strong, workers have a choice: to allow the real wage to fall, or to maintain it at its old level. It will, in general, be in the interest of large groups of workers to maintain the old wage – if the probability of their becoming unemployed is sufficiently small. This probability will usually be quite small for many workers, and indeed, for workers who may be powerful in unions (those with seniority, skills, etc.).

Now consider the situation in a market socialist economy, which experiences the same shock. A worker's income consists of two parts: her wage and her social dividend, which, let us say, is her per capita share of total profits in the economy. Suppose, for simplicity, that all workers in the economy are identical. Then each worker receives, as her total income, exactly her per capita share of the total product of the economy – for each receives the same wage and the same share of profits. It turns out that *it is always in the interest of such a worker to allow the real wage to fall to its new full employment level after a shock*, roughly because the total product of society will be greater with full employment than without it, and the worker receives roughly her per capita share of the *total* product.[12]

Thus, a market socialist economy has a built-in stabilizer that pushes it in the direction of maintaining full employment in the face of negative shocks. This is mindful of the property of Martin Weitzman's "share economy," although the mechanism is completely different. In the share economy, full employment is maintained because firms always have an interest in hiring unemployed workers, but in the market socialist economy, it is maintained because workers generally do not have an interest in maintaining real wages that are so high as to produce unemployment.

VII

Thus far, the only role stipulated for democracy has been to determine the economic platform of the government, in particular, the formula for the distribution of the social dividend to citizens and the investment plan. I have assumed that the distribution formula chosen would be egalitarian, but that is not necessary for the viability of the economic mechanism I have discussed. Citizens might vote to tilt the social dividend more in the direction of need, on the one hand, or desert, on the other; I indicated that some, but not all, such proposals could have deleterious effects on economic efficiency.

With respect to the democratic control of investment planning, one may express, besides the Chicago point indicated in note 7, the fear that different interest groups in society would expend a great deal of resources to influence the electorate, or the relevant parliamentary committees, to increase the planned investment level in their industry or region. In the jargon, placing the investment decision in the electoral arena would open the door to wasteful rent-seeking activity. I do not deny that such resources would be expended; I question, however, the wastefulness of the expenditures. A public debate with interest groups trying to make the best case to the rest of society for investment subsidies that would be in the groups' immediate self-interest may be a good thing, and worth its cost to society.

There are at least two kinds of parochialism that are harmful to a democratically run society that, I think, would be at least partially alleviated under market socialism. The first is worker parochialism: As just suggested, workers in a declining industry would try to influence the government and electorate to subsidize their firms, when, from the point of view of social welfare, these firms should be allowed to die. This parochialism can be alleviated, to some extent, by aggressive retraining and placement programs for such workers, as is practiced, for example, by Sweden.

The second kind of parochialism is, in my opinion, the major problem with capitalist democracy: Capitalists, or captains of industry, try to influence the electorate and the electoral process in the interest of the profitability of their particular firms. More generally, and more aptly for the late twentieth century, capitalist society is divided into substantially two groups:[13] a large fraction of citizens whose income consists almost entirely of wages, and a small fraction whose income consists mainly of profits. The interests of these two groups are not the same, and it is the small fraction that has the financial resources to unduly influence policy through the electoral and parliamentary process. Under market social-ism, these two groups would not exist: Everyone would receive a large fraction of his income from wages and a smaller fraction from profits – in the United States, the typical ratio would be about 4:1, if we are to judge by the current national income accounts. In particular, there would be no one whose fortune depended so dramatically on the profits of any one firm, or small group of firms, as there is in capitalist society.

The exception to this statement is the firm manager, who may receive wage incentives that depend on the profitability of the firm, or even if not, who may identify his success with the success and size of the firm. Is it not possible that firm managers would form a class that would attempt to influence state policy through the democratic process, much as capi-talists and those whose income comes primarily from profits do under capitalism? It would be brash to claim that the market socialist society I have described could have foolproof insurance against this eventuality. It is at this point that worker control over management can become important: Either workers in the firm would elect management, or the management would be chosen by the board of directors of the firm, which, under the Bardhan scheme, would consist in the main of repre-sentatives of workers of other firms. Clearly, to the extent that workers have parochial interests in the profitability of their own firm and firms in their *keiretsu*, they would support management's efforts to use political influence to increase the firm's profits. But these workers would not depend so substantially on the profits of the firm or firms as capitalists do, and hence the kind of politics they would support would differ from capitalist politics. For example, managers who fought against the intro-duction of pollution-control laws would less likely be supported under democratic market socialism than under capitalism: for, while a substan-tial shareholder of a capitalist firm will take a huge loss in income with the introduction of costly pollution control, a worker in market social-ism, who would receive only a small fraction of her income from the profits of a particular firm, even one in her *keiretsu*, would not. It may well be worth her while to sustain that relatively small loss in income for the public good, whereas the capitalist must make a huge sacrifice to create the same amount of public good.

Clearly these thoughts on socialist democracy are sketchy and debat-able. The conjecture I have tried to motivate is that the character of democracy would be quite different in a society where there is no small class whose members, by virtue of their ownership of the means of production, have both the resources and the motive to influence state policy in a parochial direction.

VIII

The Bolshevik revolution was, in the beginning, a utopian experiment: Its designers inherited from Marx an antipathy toward the market mechanism, and believed they could replace it with a system of central allocation. That was not their most devastating error. Worse was the strangulation of all opposition, which made almost impossible the rectification of errors in general. There were advocates of market socialism, in some aspects, throughout Soviet history, from Nikolai Bukharin in the twenties, to Leonid Kantorovich (the only Soviet recipient of a Nobel prize in economics) and Evsey Liberman in the sixties and seventies. But by that time, the ideological blinders of the labor theory of value, on the one hand, and the physical entrenchment of a class of state and party authorities deriving their power largely from the absence of markets, on the other, combined to render almost nil the prospects for a transition to market socialism, or, as many would say, to socialism.

Despite this assessment, I am not one who celebrates the demise of the Soviet experiment. For it made massively viable, for the first time in modern history, the ideology that there exists an alternative to greed as the cement of society. I guard against underestimating the effect, on hundreds of millions of people throughout the world, of the Soviet and Chinese experiments, the good effect of making live for them the possibility of organizing a society based on cooperative and egalitarian principles.

What the left should learn from the last seventy-five years is not that socialism is impossible, or even that planning is unnecessary or harmful, but, rather, that the transition to socialism will be less dramatic than our ideological grandparents had hoped. The transition to a society based on cooperation and equality will take a long time and, tritely, must begin with people as they are. What some will consider bad news is that socialism will require markets. The good news is that markets do not require capitalists, that is, the concentration of economic power and wealth in the hands of a small class. The bad news is that an economic structure based on markets will make the transition to "the socialist person" a more protracted process than the utopian Bolsheviks and Maoists had hoped. The good news is that without a capitalist class, and in a democratic setting, people will be able to think more autonomously about, and act in their true interests, than under capitalist democracy. Marx was a great teacher of the nature of capitalism; he was not competent to instruct us on how to construct socialism, a lesson we must learn from the history, both capitalist and socialist, of the twentieth

JOHN E. ROEMER

century. Others, such as Léon Walras, the pioneer of the theory of general economic equilibrium of a market economy, and coeditor of *Le Travail*, a review dedicated largely to the cooperative movement of his time,[14] will eventually take their place beside Marx in the socialist pantheon.

Notes

Oskar Lange, *On the Economic Theory of Socialism* (Minneapolis: University of Minnesota Press, 1938); Wlodzimierz Brus, *The Market in a Socialist Economy* (London: Routledge & Kegan Paul, 1972); Alec Nove, *The Economics of Feasible Socialism* (London: George Allen & Unwin, 1983).
W. Brus, "Market Socialism," in J. Eatwell, M. Milgate, and P. Newman, eds., *The Palgrave Dictionary of Economics*, vol. 3 (London: Macmillan, 1987), p. 337.
3 J. E. Roemer, "The Morality and Efficiency of Market Socialism," *Ethics*, 102 (1992), 448–64.
4 I thank Joaquim Silvestre for this formulation.
5 After the late-nineteenth-century French economist Léon Walras, who first formalized the concept of general economic equilibrium.
6 I. Ortuño, J. Roemer, and J. Silvestre, "Investment Planning in Market Socialism," in S. Bowles, H. Gintis, and B. Gustafsson, eds., *Democracy and Markets: Participation, Accountability, and Efficiency* (Cambridge: Cambridge University Press, in press).
7 This is to be contrasted with the view of Chicago economists, such as George Stigler, who maintain that a citizen's voting behavior is irresponsible, unlike her market behavior, because she pays the cost of her market decisions but not of her voting decision. (This last is so because a person's vote has only a minuscule probability of affecting the outcome of the election.) For a view contrary to the Chicago one, however, see Cass Sunstein, "Preferences and Politics," *Philosophy and Public Affairs* 20, (1991); 3–34. For a discussion of the evidence, see D. R. Kinder and D. R. Kiewiet, "Sociotropic Politics: The American Case," in R. G. Niemi and H. F. Weisberg, eds., *Controversies in Voting Behavior* (Washington D.C.: Congressional Quarterly Press), and David Sears et al., "Self-interest vs. Symbolic Politics in Policy Attitudes and Presidential Voting," *American Political Science Review* 74 (1980).
8 Janos Kornai, *The Socialist System* (Princeton, N.J.: 1992).
9 Pranab Bardhan, "On Tackling the Soft Budget Constraint in Market Socialism, in P. Bardhan and J. Roemer, eds., *Market Socialism: The Current Debate* (Oxford: Oxford University Press, in press).
10 More details of this proposal, and simulations comparing its performance to that of a standard capitalist economy, are presented in J. E. Roemer, "Can there be socialism after Communism?" in P. Bardhan and J. Roemer, eds., *Market Socialism: The Current Debate* (New York: Oxford University Press, in press).

11 G. A. Cohen, "The Future of a Disillusion," *New Left Review* No. 190 (November–December, 1991).

12 It is assumed that unemployed workers continue to receive the social dividend. The adjective "roughly" is necessary because there is some discretion in the amount of wage replacement the unemployed would receive.

13 I do not call these groups "classes," as they are not identical to classes whose membership is defined by relationship to the labor process. See J. Roemer, *A General Theory of Exploitation and Class* (Cambridge, Mass.: Harvard University Press, 1982).

14 Donald Walker, "Léon Walras," in *The Palgrave Dictionary*, vol. 4, p. 852.

Alternative conceptions
of feasibility

MICHAEL S. McPHERSON

Disambiguation

John Roemer aims to discuss the *feasibility* of socialism in a way that
disentangles certain features that are sometimes definitionally attached
to it. This is a particularly worthy effort in a field where proponents of
competing ideological views too often attempt to defend their claims by
definitional fiat rather than by careful theoretical and empirical argument. In this comment, I want to argue for the value of carrying this
effort at disambiguation even farther than Roemer does. My main
suggestion is to sharpen a distinction among conceptions of feasibility
that is, in fact, already present in Roemer's essay. This suggestion then
leads to the observation that disambiguating some notions about private
property regimes may help in much the same way that Roemer's distinctions among features of socialism(s) do.

Feasibility

Let me, in fact, draw two different sets of distinctions concerning what is
meant by feasibility. The first of these, between what I will call "Walrasian" and "institutional" feasibility, plays, at least implicitly, a rather
large role in Roemer's treatment. The second, between "attainability"
and "sustainability" as feasibility concepts, is of major importance, I
think, in regard to the larger political-economic issues at stake here, but
is not a central feature in Roemer's discussion.

Institutional versus Walrasian feasibility

Walrasian feasibility, as I define it, establishes the range of economic
equilibria that is available within, to use Roemer's terminology, a particular
"economic environment." Certain stylized institutional facts are introduced
in characterizing the institutional setup – for example, whether property is
publicly or privately owned – but much of the institutional and behavioral

context is set by the Walrasian framework within which the problem is investigated. Analysis, that is, proceeds on "standard" motivational assumptions about firms, individuals, and governments, accompanied by assumptions about perfection of information, completeness of markets, and market clearing. The idea is to compare economic performance under alternative institutional arrangements, basing all comparisons on the same (or analogous) idealized assumptions.

"Institutional feasibility" I will define somewhat vaguely as comparative analysis based on weaker versions of some or all of the idealized assumptions employed in the Walrasian formulation. The idea here is to take account of differences in the political and motivational dimensions of different regimes that cannot be captured in the Walrasian framework. Roughly the first half of Roemer's essay reports formal results concerning the Walrasian feasibility of a market socialist economic environment, while the rest takes up less systematically a number of topics involving institutional feasibility. Among the important assumptions considered under the latter head are these:

Behavioral tendencies of governments. For purposes of Walrasian analysis, Roemer treats the government as an ideal planner in a market context, asking if there exists a set of parameters (in particular, an interest rate) that the government can establish to produce a desired Walrasian equilibrium. The question of whether an actual democratically elected government would seek to establish the "correct" parameters is one of institutional feasibility.

Imperfections in markets and information. As Roemer notes, part of the economic interest in a market socialist regime is the possibility that such a regime could deal better with problems of externalities and informational and other market failures than a private property regime would. Although in principle he hopes to extend the reach of (what I call) Walrasian feasibility analysis formally to attack these questions, at this point he treats the subject more informally, as a set of departures from the Walrasian assumptions.

Motivational problems with workers and managers. The Walrasian program assumes efficient behavior by owners and managers – in particular, that managers maximize profits. Whether this is a reasonable institutional assumption in the market socialist (or indeed the capitalist) context Roemer treats as a problem in institutional feasibility.

"Attainability" versus "sustainability"

I have in mind here distinguishing two different ideas about what it means for a particular set of arrangements to be feasible. One might ask, on one hand, whether these arrangements, once attained, would inevitably unravel of their own accord or would produce results that are economically (or in some other way) unacceptable. On the other hand, one might ask, starting from some given actual reality, whether there exists a path that will lead to the attainment of the given set of arrangements. The first of these is feasibility in the sense of "sustainability"; the latter concerns "attainability."[1]

Roemer's discussion focuses almost exclusively on problems of sustainability, and there is a good argument that this is the more fundamental category. In practical discussion, however, issues of attainability are critical to problems of strategy and judgment in deciding what kinds of change to push for. Difficult moral questions arise if a particular regime appears to be sustainable and to be better than the existing arrangements, but where all paths to that regime seem to require either violating some people's rights or enduring a period where things get worse. I will suggest in the conclusion that some of our thinking about the events in Eastern Europe may be illuminated by this distinction.

Significance of these distinctions

How do these distinctions map onto Roemer's essay? As I just indicated, he is not much concerned, except inferentially, with "questions of attainability," mostly, rather, with sustainability of equilibria once attained.

The formal part of Roemer's essay, like the work of Oskar Lange that inspired it, studies Walrasian feasibility. The agenda for this research is to ask whether in principle a state that owns all or most productive property can accomplish democratically determined goals regarding resource allocation without detailed interference with markets. A major part of the project for Roemer is to compare the potential effectiveness of alternative models of socialism, and to show in particular that a well-motivated socialist government can have the same impact on key features of resource allocation through central setting of interest rates that it can have through more detailed intervention in markets. A second purpose is to compare the potential efficiency of private property with that of market socialism, within the limitations of the Walrasian framework. Roemer succeeds admirably in putting these parts of the debate between "private property" and "socialism" on a more systematic footing, and his extensions and corrections of Lange are reassuring for those whose doubts about market socialism concern its Walrasian feasibility. The project of extending these modeling exercises to more realistic specifications of economic environments is certainly promising, although it has proved notoriously difficult in neoclassical economics to get powerful results when relaxing the informational and motivational assumptions that lie at the heart of the Walrasian research program.

My own sense, for what it is worth, is that many of the most interesting and challenging questions regarding the feasibility of market socialism lie in the realm of "institutional feasibility" – the range of political–economic questions that lies beyond the framework of assumptions defining the Walrasian agenda.[2] The points Roemer makes in these contexts – for example, about the motivations of managers under both capitalism and market socialism – seem to me illuminating and important, but as he recognizes, they fall well short of a systematic treatment. Another quite thoughtful but rather more pessimistic assessment of the prospects for democratic market socialism is available in a recent book by Przeworski (1991). These differences of view remind us how much we have to learn about such problems.

As Roemer recognizes, there are tensions between the parts of his essay that deal with Walrasian and with institutional feasibility. Most obviously, the potential economic advantages of central direction of investment planning depend on features of the economy (externalities and informational problems) that do not exist in the version of the Walrasian framework in which the theorems Roemer reports are proved. It seems to me that the following important question will arise as Roemer extends his formal investigations to economic environments that incorporate these imperfections: How will the government's knowledge be modeled? Simply to assume that the government possesses the information needed to attain a Pareto optimum – information, for example, about the extent of interfirm external economies – would be to beg a key question. (One reason private markets ignore such externalities is that they are hard to identify and measure.) Yet to model governmental processes of information acquisition convincingly looks to be quite difficult.[3]

There is also tension, as Roemer acknowledges, between the assumptions about firms' behavior in the Walrasian model and in Roemer's informal intuitive discussion. Roemer's Walrasian models assume that managers maximize firms' profits. Roemer emphasizes that this assumption is critical to the findings he reports. Yet the institutional discussion, in arguing for the superiority of market socialism to private property in terms of promoting democracy, emphasizes the democratic advantages of worker-controlled firms.

Disambiguating "private property"

In considering the feasibility of socialism, Roemer does well in sorting out alternative conceptions of that ambiguous term. There may be value in doing some analogous work on notions of private property regimes. Roemer builds into his definition of market socialism the assumption that the returns to social property will be divided more or less equally. He also assumes that in fact (although not as part of the definition) "capitalist" or "private property" regimes will concentrate the returns to property in a small and restricted class.[4] Now, as a matter of Walrasian feasibility, this latter assumption is plainly unwarranted. It is, in fact, a principal result in neoclassical welfare economics that suitable distributions of property rights will allow a market economy with private ownership to achieve any desired distribution of incomes or consumption without efficiency loss. At this idealized formal level, there is nothing to choose between socialism and private property on distributive grounds.

It is, however, a very important question whether the claim that private property regimes must be highly unequal is justified on grounds of institutional feasibility. Is it a necessary feature of any private property regime with a more or less egalitarian distribution of property that it will unravel over time into a more familiar kind of capitalism with highly unequal ownership? Or that it will be highly inefficient? The question is important not only because of the economic significance of inequality but because of the close ties between economic and political inequality.

Thus, the main reason why Roemer claims that a market socialist regime will be more effectively democratic than capitalism is the more egalitarian distribution of returns to property. ("Everyone would receive a large fraction of his income from wages and a smaller fraction from profits.") Plainly a private property regime that could sustain a (more or less) egalitarian distribution of property would have this same feature. It would presumably be more effectively democratic than our present society, although whether it could be as effectively democratic as the best feasible socialist regime is less clear.

Is an egalitarian private property regime feasible? Plainly not without substantial government regulation to provide a framework of rules that would either discourage or redistribute large accumulations of property over generations. It is reasonable to assume away such redistributive and regulatory arrangements in analyzing Walrasian feasibility, but not in analyzing institutional feasibility. As J. S. Mill argues in his *Principles of Political Economy*, it is necessary to compare ideals to ideals and actuals to actuals. Presumably the list of private-property-based institutional schemes should involve various kinds of "reformed" or "regulated" capitalism, including ones that might be modeled on Scandinavian and other "social democratic" models, as well as more abstract schemes like James Meade's "property-owning democracy." No existing private property regime is close to the degree of equality in property holdings that Roemer envisions for market socialism, but they do vary a lot. The issue is how much egalitarianism is feasible institutionally for a private-property-based regime.

Roemer's discussion of managerial incentives raises an important economic worry about egalitarian private property. Is diffusely held property compatible with an efficient private capital market? As Roemer notes, some finance economists now argue that concentrated private property is needed to overcome free-rider problems in capital markets. If so, those arguments would tell against schemes in which corporate stock is diffusely held by individuals (such as Meade's). Various kinds of corporatist schemes, however, in which stock is held in large pension funds or mutual funds, or is managed by trade unions, might be able to respond to this problem. (And, of course, these finance economists may be wrong!)

A second major issue is the difficulty of maintaining effective political regulation of property inequalities over time. An argument against the sustainability of egalitarian private property is that as soon as property inequalities start to emerge, their beneficiaries will use their nascent economic advantage to gain unequal political power and thus undermine the needed regulation. Against this, however, is the consideration that the hypothesized regime would start with highly equal property and hence a strong democratic interest in preserving egalitarian regulations. Again, institutional designs that involve some kind of collective administration of corporate stock may differ in their political tendencies from more individualistic regimes.

In trying to come to a judgment on the feasibility of reformed private property, it is important to distinguish between the *attainability* and the *sustainability* of an egalitarian private property regime. It is extremely hard to envision how we might go from existing highly unequal property to an egalitarian property regime (just as it is extremely hard to envision a path from where we are to market socialism). This may lead us to think such a regime infeasible. Yet that is plainly a different question from the one Roemer asks about socialism: If such a regime could be attained, would it be sustainable? Is it a feasible equilibrium once you get there?

In my judgment we are far from having adequate answers to these questions, just as we are far from having a good grip on judgments about the institutional feasibility of market socialism. Roemer's essay points the way toward the hard analytical and empirical work that is needed to make progress on these questions.

374	MICHAEL S. McPHERSON

Notes

1 It is tempting to equate "sustainability" with some notion of "equilibrium" feasibility and "attainability" with some notion of "dynamic" feasibility, but these words arise in a number of other contexts in assessing the feasibility of economic environments (in particular concerning the growth tendencies of alternative environments), so I have tried to avoid them. There is a close connection between this distinction and issues that arise in discussing "stability" in John Rawls's *Theory of Justice*. For further discussion, see Krouse and McPherson 1987.

2 It is not clear to me whether there is in principle any sharp dividing line between what I have styled the "Walrasian" and "institutional" aspects of the problem of feasibility. Just as Roemer proposes to relax the informational assumptions of the Walrasian models he discusses earlier, one could in principle develop equilibrium models that explicitly analyzed voting behavior and its effects on resource allocation in a Walrasian spirit. However, many of the features that Roemer insists in his informal discussion are important in politics – such as its educational dimensions and its tendency to bring forth nonselfish dimensions of citizens' concerns – are likely to prove hard to introduce into equilibrium models in an illuminating way.

3 This is not so much a problem in comparing central planning to market socialism, where the question would be how effectively the government can use whatever information it has. It's a more pressing question in comparing the effectiveness of market socialist and private property regimes.

4 Theorists like Marx and Weber made the holding of property by a restricted class part of the definition of capitalism and would not have called an egalitarian regime of private property "capitalist." With some reluctance, I follow Roemer and many contemporary economists in using the terms interchangeably.

References

Krouse, Richard and Michael McPherson. "On Rawlsian Justice in Political Economy: Capitalism, 'Property-owning Democracy,' and the Welfare State," in Amy Gutmann, ed., *Democracy and the Welfare State*. Princeton: N.J.: Princeton University Press, 1987.

Meade, James. *Efficiency, Equality and the Ownership of Property*. London: George Allen & Unwin, 1964.

Mill, John Stuart. *Principles of Political Economy*. Toronto: University of Toronto Press, 1965.

Przeworski, Adam. *Democracy and the Market: Political and Economic Reforms in Eastern Europe and Latin America*. Cambridge: Cambridge University Press, 1991.

Rawls, John. *A Theory of Justice*. Cambridge, Mass.: Harvard University Press, 1971.

9

A political and economic case for the democratic enterprise

SAMUEL BOWLES and HERBERT GINTIS

1. Introduction

We consider two reasons why firms should be owned and run democratically by their workers. The first concerns *accountability:* Because the employment relationship involves the exercise of power, its governance ought on democratic grounds to be accountable to those most directly affected. The second concerns *efficiency:* The democratic firm uses a lower level of inputs per unit of output than the analogous capitalist firm.[1]

These claims are not obvious. If labor is transferred to an employer through a voluntary exchange in a competitive market, how can the employment relationship exhibit a well-defined power relationship? If the democratic firm is more efficient, what prevents the capitalist from replicating it and reaping the profits? And if capitalist firms cannot capture the efficiencies of democratic firms, why have democratic firms not simply outcompeted capitalist firms?

The existing theoretical literature on the democratic firm has argued strongly against its viability. In seminal contributions, Ward (1958), Domar (1966), and Vanek (1970) modeled the worker-controlled firm as maximizing net revenue per worker rather than profits, and proved that such firms would hire too few workers and, furthermore, would respond perversely to price changes, decreasing output when prices increase and vice versa. Meade (1972) showed that different but equally inefficient results follow if the democratic firm is prohibited from adjusting its employment in response to economic conditions. Furubotn and Pejovich (1974), and later Jensen and Meckling (1979), showed that the absence of competitive capital markets would lead democratic firms to allocate investment resources irrationally. In particular, if workers have no ownership rights to the capital stock when they leave the democratic firm, such firms will systematically underinvest, favoring the full distribution of potential investment funds to worker members.

We thank Philippe van Parijs and John Roemer for helpful comments on an earlier draft of this chapter.

But these studies have suffered from serious methodological biases, treating the capitalist firm as embedded in an environment free from market failure, and the democratic firm as embedded in an environment of contrived restrictions leading to systematic inefficiencies. Each of the above perversities of the democratic firm arises because of some restriction placed on the democratic firm that limits its ability to achieve optimal allocations, but is not entailed by any general prerequisites of democratic governance. Dow (1986), Drèze 1989), and others have pointed out that where market failures are absent and both forms are equally unrestricted the two institutional forms are *indistinguishable in their behavior*. Indeed, this is the gist of Paul Samuelson's (1957) provocative remark that in "a perfectly competitive model it really does not matter who hires whom," since an economy of workers renting machines is indistinguishable from an economy of capitalists owning machines and hiring workers.

A more evenhanded and insightful treatment of the capitalist versus the democratic firm would begin by identifying the central market failures that *both* types of firms face, and then analyze their comparative performances.[2] We follow such a strategy in this paper, identifying failures in labor and capital markets inherent in all market economies, and to which capitalist and democratic firms can be expected to respond in systematically different ways.

Our approach differs from the existing literature on the democratic firm primarily in that it addresses problems of motivation, incentives, discipline, malfeasance, and opportunism. Surprisingly, these issues are absent in most theoretical treatments by economists. Yet many consider these concerns central to the evaluation of governance structures and property rights. More technically, our approach focuses on agency problems. An agency problem exists when a principal A cannot costlessly control the behavior of an agent B, but would like B to take some action that B would otherwise not undertake. The market failures that differentiate the performance of the democratic and capitalist firm arise because of agency problems in labor and capital markets.

In addition to realism, our focus on market failures arising from agency problems bears two main advantages unattainable in approaches that abstract from these issues. First, our focus on the agency problems associated with the regulation of labor intensity – the so-called labor discipline problem – allows us to define precisely the exercise of power of employers over workers in a competitive capitalist economy. This concept of power in turn motivates our claim that on democratic grounds firms ought to be governed by their workers.

Our concept of power is as follows: Agent A has power over agent B if, by imposing or threatening to impose sanctions on B, A is capable of affecting B's actions in ways that further A's interests, while B lacks this capacity with respect to A. Thus the advantageous and asymmetric exercise of sanctions is a sufficient condition for the existence of a power relationship.

We use this concept to advance specifically democratic criteria for the evaluation of the organization of the firm, and to demonstrate the superior efficiency characteristics of the democratic firm. Neither the political nor the efficiency argument can be sustained in a framework – such as the standard neoclassical model – that ignores agency problems. Indeed, the elimination of agency problems by assumption, typical of much of the literature on worker self-management, reduces the case for the democratic firm to the curious claim that it would mimic the capitalist firm. But if, as this view implies, the political structure of the enterprise is politically noncoercive and economically irrelevant, the reasons for preferring democratic firms over their capitalist counterparts must be sought elsewhere. Neither democratic nor efficiency arguments would be germane.

Second, by providing a unified treatment of agency problems arising in labor and capital markets, we can assess the strengths and weaknesses of the democratic firm more adequately than when labor and capital markets are treated in isolation, or when general equilibrium approaches that abstract from agency problems are adopted. In particular, we can offer a coherent explanation of the failure of the democratic firm to outcompete its capitalist counterparts despite its efficiency advantages, and we can analyze what we believe to be the major weakness of the democratic firm: its tendency to engage in insufficient levels of risk-taking and innovation.

The efficiency gains associated with the democratic firm arise from three sources, all related to market failures arising from the employment relationship and the problem of labor discipline: (1) a correct social rather than private accounting of the costs of regulating the intensity of labor and consequently an optimal mix of monitoring costs and wage incentives, (2) an increased effectiveness of monitoring of the labor process owing to the incentive for workers to report private information on the activities of their fellow workers, and (3) improved incentive compatibility concerning the intensity of labor. The effectiveness of all three mechanisms derives from the residual claimancy status of workers. The first two operate irrespective of the size of the work team, and the third diminishes in importance as the work team becomes larger. The resulting efficiency gains may be expressed either as Pareto improvements or as increases in output per unit of input.

If market failures arising from the agency problems in the labor market confer an efficiency advantage on the democratic firm, market failures arising from agency problems in the capital markets place the democratic firm at a competitive disadvantage in a capitalist economy. Capitalist owners, who are asset-rich, are better able to address capital market failures than are worker owners, who are generally asset-poor: Even in perfectly competitive credit markets asset-poor workers cannot borrow funds on terms equivalent to those available to asset-rich borrowers. The result is both a competitive disadvantage for the worker-owned firm, and a tendency toward conservatism by worker managers. In light of the tendency of the democratic firm to undertake a suboptimal level of innovation and risk, the preferred ownership structure of the democratic firm takes account of the tendency of external ownership to promote innovation and risk taking, and of worker ownership to promote labor effort. It consequently involves a balance of internal and external residual claimancy and control.

Two limitations of our argument should be highlighted at the outset. First, we confine ourselves to a comparison of the capitalist firm and the democratic firm, thereby considering only in passing other institutional forms that might also foster greater accountability, efficiency, equality, and the formation of a democratic culture. We do not address the issue, for example, of whether a system of collective bargaining at both the firm and the economy-wide level, perhaps embedded in a social democratic institutional framework, would in some respects outperform an economy with a widespread network of democratic enterprises.

Second, our capitalist and democratic firms may be considered somewhat utopian versions of the real thing. Here we forgo a number of arguments in favor of the democratic firm. These include the lesser propensity of the democratic firm to engage in some dangerous and environmentally destructive practices because workers are often the most adversely impacted by these practices. The argument clearly applies to local environmental effects but not to such global problems as greenhouse gas emissions. Further, democratic firms are less likely to pursue global mobility strategies, which often enhance the profits of a capitalist firm while relocating production to regions with lower productivity, thus reducing global economic efficiency.

Conversely, we abstract from a number of problems likely to confront the democratic firm. For instance, while we take account of the work-monitoring costs in both types of firms, we abstract from the costs of democratic decision-making, expressed both in the time spent by participants and in the possible drawbacks of cyclicity in voting, unresponsiveness, and susceptibility to manipulation.

2. The employment relationship and contested exchange

The classical theory of contract used in most of neoclassical economics holds that the enforcement of claims is performed by the judicial system at negligible cost to the exchanging parties. We refer to this third-party enforcement assumption as *exogenous enforcement*. Where, by contrast, third-party enforcement of claims arising from an exchange is infeasible or excessively costly, the exchanging agents must themselves seek to enforce their claims. In the presence of *endogenous enforcement*, exchange is a strategic, nonanonymous relationship, in the sense that the terms of exchange depend on the power of the exchanging parties to enforce favorable outcomes and are continually subject to de facto respecification (Bowles and Gintis, 1993).

Consider agent A, who purchases a good or service from agent B. We call the exchange *contested* when B's offering possesses an attribute that is valuable to A, is costly for B to provide, yet is not adequately specified in an exogenously enforceable contract. Exogenous enforcement is absent under a variety of quite common conditions: when there is no relevant third-party (as when A and B are sovereign states); when the contested attribute can be measured only imperfectly and at considerable cost (e.g., in work effort or the degree of risk assumed by a firm's management); when the relevant evidence is not admissible in a court of law (such as an agent's eyewitness but unsubstantiated experience), when there is no possible means of redress (e.g., when the liable party is bankrupt); or when the nature of the contingencies concerning future states of the world relevant to the exchange precludes writing a fully specified contract. In such cases the *ex post* terms of exchange are determined by the bonding, monitoring, sanctioning, and other mechanisms instituted by A to induce B to provide the desired level of the contested attribute.[3] As endogenous enforcement is ubiquitous in labor markets, credit markets, and even some goods markets, we consider it to be a fundamental aspect of the capitalist economy.

We shall here analyze only one, but an extremely important, endogenous enforcement mechanism: *contingent renewal*. Contingent renewal obtains when A elicits performance from B by promising to renew the contract in future periods if satisfied, and to terminate the contract if not. For instance, a manager may promise an employee reemployment contingent upon satisfactory performance, or a lender may offer a borrower a short-term loan, with the promise of rolling over the loan contingent upon the borrower's prudent business behavior. The labor market is a case in point.

An employment relationship is established when, in return for a wage, the worker agrees to submit to the authority of the employer. The worker's promise to bestow an adequate level of effort and care upon the tasks assigned, even if offered, is for the most part legally unenforceable. At the level of effort expected by management, work is subjectively costly for the worker to provide, valuable to the employer, and difficult to measure. The manager–worker relationship is thus a contested exchange in the sense just defined. The endogenous enforcement mechanisms of the enterprise, not the state, are thus directly responsible for ensuring the delivery of any particular level of labor services per hour of labor time supplied.[4]

We assume effort is costly for the worker (B in the above scenario) to provide above some minimal level. The employer, A, knows that B (one of a team of employees) will choose a level of effort in response to both the cost of supplying effort and the penalty that A imposes if dissatisfied with B's performance. In particular, unless threatened with penalties, B will not supply more than the minimum level of effort. For simplicity we assume the sanction A will impose is the nonrenewal of the employment relationship – that is, dismissing the worker.

The worker seeks to avoid the sanction because the loss of the job is costly to her, in the following sense. We define the *value of employment* as the worker's future income stream, and we define the worker's *fallback position* as her future income if she loses her job – perhaps a future stream of unemployment benefits, or the income from some other job, or more likely a combination of the two. We call the difference between the value of employment and the fallback position the *enforcement rent*, or the *cost of job loss*. The key observation is that A's threat of dismissal is costly to the worker only if the cost of job loss to B is positive.

The necessity of a positive cost of job loss can be recast in terms of the wage rate, as follows: Let us define the *reservation wage* as the wage the employer would have to pay the worker to reduce the cost of job loss to zero, in other words, to render the worker indifferent between holding and losing the job. Then a positive cost of job loss implies that the wage exceeds the reservation wage.

Two important results follow from an employer's offering a wage yielding a positive cost of job loss. First, in the resulting equilibrium B provides a level of effort greater than would have been the case in the absence of the cost of job loss, so A's enforcement strategy is effective (otherwise A would be unwilling to pay the excess of the wage over the reservation wage). Second, because the wage exceeds the reservation wage, the labor market does not clear in competitive equilibrium: Excess supply, or unemployment, exists. Thus, workers holding jobs are not indifferent to losing them, and there are workers identical to B either involuntarily unemployed, or employed in less desirable jobs.

As this argument hinges critically on the fact that the capitalist will choose a wage rate yielding a positive cost of job loss, and, indeed, that such a wage will also be the competitive equilibrium wage, we should explore whether the following might not be the case. In making a wage offer, the capitalist balances two effects working in opposite directions: An increase in the wage will enhance worker effort, raising output and firm revenues; but at the same time a wage increase is costly. The rule allowing the employer to find the wage that maximizes the firm's profits is: "Start with the reservation wage and then increase the wage as long as the gains from increased effort are greater than the cost of the wage increase itself." As long as the gains to a wage increase exceed the direct costs of the increase when the capitalist is offering the reservation wage, a higher wage rate will be offered, and the cost of job loss will be positive, sustaining our argument.

If, counter to our argument, the capitalist were to offer the reservation wage, the worker would do exactly as she pleases at work, putting in what we call the "whistle while you work" level of effort (or on-the-job leisure, as the case may be). Under what conditions could this be optimal for the capitalist? Two suggest themselves. First, the worker could be *income-satiated*, so that increases or losses in income have little or no effect on her behavior; in this case the cost of job loss would be ineffective as a sanction. Second, the worker could be *unalienated*, wishing voluntarily to work at such a high pace that little increase in the intensity of labor could be induced, even by powerful incentives.

Although these two conditions leading to a zero cost of job loss and hence a clearing labor market are imaginable, they are not plausible as a general rule, and in any case the suggestion that the labor market clears is empirically contradicted not only by data on the unemployed but by evidence that the cost of job loss is indeed substantial for most workers. Further, less direct confirmation is suggested by the fact that employers regularly hire supervisors to monitor the labor process; yet this expenditure would be irrational if the employer had already conceded that there existed no means of affecting the behavior of the employee, as would be the case for either the income satiated or unalienated worker.

3. Short-side power and democratic accountability

The analysis of the labor market as a contested exchange motivates our claim that in a capitalist economy the employment relationship gives the employer power over the worker, that on democratic grounds this power should be democratically accountable, and that a workplace democracy is a means toward securing this democratic accountability.

We begin by asking, Does the employer indeed have power over the worker? In a neoclassical competitive equilibrium, no sanctions may be imposed through the private actions of noncolluding agents, and hence there is no power in our sense of the term, accountable or otherwise. Prices in this model implement each agent's constrained optimum and simultaneously eliminate excess supply or demand in all markets, thus resulting in clearing markets. In competitive equilibrium, if agents A and B exchange, B's gain exactly equals the gain from her next-best alternative. For if this were not the case – if, for example, B's gain exceeded her next-best alternative – there would be some third agent C currently receiving the same (lower) value as B's next-best alternative, and who would benefit from occupying B's current position. Agent C could thus have offered A a contract superior to that offered by B, blocking B's exchange with A. Because this did not occur, no such C exists, and B's next-best alternative must be at least as valuable as the exchange with A. On the other hand, B's next-best alternative cannot have greater value, or B would not have entered into the current contract with A. We conclude that B's gain from trading with A exactly equals the gain from B's next-best alternative, so A's threat of non-renewal of contract with B forcing B to her next-best alternative imposes no costs on B, and hence gives A no power over B.

In the neoclassical model, it follows, the locus of sovereignty within the enterprise – its political structure – has no effect in competitive equilibrium, and hence is irrelevant to the study of power. But if this were so, the conversion of a firm from capitalist to democratic rule would be without consequence. The neoclassical model, however, is based on the dubious assumption that claims are enforceable at zero cost to the exchanging parties. In contested exchanges characterized by endogenous enforcement, by contrast, equilibria are characterized by a well-defined distribution of power.

Consider our model of the employment relationship: Does A (the employer) have power over B (the worker)? First, there is a range of wage rates from which A can choose, any of which would be acceptable to B, but the choice of which affects B's well-being (as measured by the value of employment). Additionally, A may dismiss B, reducing B's welfare to the reservation position. Hence, A can apply sanctions to B. Second, A can use sanctions to elicit a preferred level of effort from B, and thus to further A's interests. Finally, although B may be capable of applying sanctions against A (e.g., B may be capable of burning down A's factory), B cannot use this capacity to induce A to choose a different wage, or to refrain from dismissing B should A desire to do so. Should B make A a take-it-or-leave-it offer to work at a higher than equilibrium wage, or should B threaten to apply sanctions unless A offers a higher wage, A would simply reject the offer and hire another worker. For as we saw in the preceding section, in equilibrium there will exist unemployed workers identical to B who would prefer to be employed. Thus A has power over B.[5]

This power is based on A's favorable location in a nonclearing market. We say that the employer A, who can purchase any desired amount of labor and hence is not quantity constrained, is on the *short side* of the market. Where excess supply exists – as in the labor market – the demand side is the short side, and conversely.[6] Suppliers of labor are on the *long side* of the market; some of them cannot sell all the labor time they would like to at the going wage (or perhaps not at all).

When contingent renewal is operative, the principle of *short-side power* holds: Agents on the short side of the market have power over agents on the long side with whom they transact. Long-side agents are of two types: those such as B who succeed in finding an employer and receive a rent that constrains them to accept the employer's authority; and those such as C who fail to make a transaction and hence are rationed out of the market.[7]

Two objections to our interpretation may be raised. First, it might appear that A has expressed a preference for power and has simply traded away some income – the enforcement rent – to gain power. But this is false: A is assumed to be indifferent to the nature of the authority relationship per se and is simply maximizing profits.

Second, it may be argued that B has power over A, if not in our formal sense, then in the sense that B has the capacity to induce A to offer an enforcement rent over and above the amount needed to induce B to enter into the transaction. But the fact that B receives a rent, while certainly conferring a distributional advantage to B as compared to a no-rent alternative, does not involve "power" in the sense of a capacity that can be strategically deployed toward furthering one's interests; it is therefore not relevant to the issue of democratic accountability. To see this, note that A's power to dismiss B is a credible threat, whereas B can issue no credible threat. Rather than attribute the fact that B receives a wage in excess of the reservation wage to "B's power over A," we might better say that the enforcement rent derives from B's autonomy, that is, from the inability of A to dictate B's level of effort costlessly.

The conclusion that the employer A does indeed have power over the worker B is the basis of our claim that A should be democratically accountable to B and other members of the team of workers. It is far from obvious, however, that the appropriate remedy for concentrating short-side power in the hands of the employer is to give a democratic voice to the employed long-siders through workplace democracy. A menu of alternative remedies suggests itself. The most obvious, the abolition of employment relationship itself and its replacement by self-employment, is prohibitively costly except in those lines of work not characterized by economies of large-scale production.

A second remedy might be to redesign the nature of work and to alter the process of human development to make working more intrinsically rewarding, so that the work intensity freely chosen by the worker would be sufficiently high as to make labor-disciplining strategies unnecessary, or possibly counterproductive. As we have seen, these conditions would support a labor market–clearing equilibrium, thereby eliminating the short side of the market and with it, of course, short-side power. If the preceding remedy, abolishing team production, could be termed the "yeoman's utopia," this approach is utopian socialist in flavor. We do not doubt that changing property rights and altering the structure of control over labor could render the process of work considerably less unpleasant; but we doubt that any feasible program of disalienation of labor can eliminate the problem of work discipline except in a minority of jobs.

A more promising remedy would seem to be elimination of short-side power through the assurance of costless exit to employees. This could be accomplished either through the pursuit of macroeconomic policies to eliminate all but frictional unemployment or by granting of unemployment benefits at or near the level of the going wage. Compelling objections, however, may be raised against the strategy of assuring costless exit: It is neither feasible nor desirable. The elimination of employment rents entailed by the free-exit strategy is impossible because independently of the level of unemployment benefits or the macroeconomic environment, it will generally be cost-minimizing for the employer to offer a wage such that employment is preferable to the worker's next-best alternative. Attempts to eliminate the employment rent will redistribute income from capital to labor, and possibly foster inflation, but cannot eliminate the employment rent. The elimination of employment rents is also undesirable, for the only wage at which exit could become costless is the worker's reservation wage, which, if offered, would elicit the worker's reservation level of work effort (the effort that is preferred by the worker independently of the effect on output or reward). But a work-incentive scheme that places no value on output per hour of work is clearly irrational.

Economies of scale in production and the resulting team nature of production, the infeasibility of basing labor exclusively on intrinsic reward, and the efficacy of contingent renewal strategies of endogenous enforcement thus all strongly disfavor the strategy of addressing the problem of concentrated short-side power, by abolishing the employment relationship, by eliminating the coercive element in work, or by ensuring costless exit from employment. Lacking attractive strategies for obviating the problem of short-side power, we propose that on democratic grounds short-side power ought to be accountable to work team members. We offer four arguments in support of this claim, each based on standard and widely accepted arguments in political philosophy for a democratic state.

Keep in mind that our claim for democratic accountability refers not to the *administrative* but, rather, to the *political* structure of the enterprise. The former refers roughly to its organizational chart, whereas *political* refers to the locus of final accountability. We might envisage, for example, a bureaucratic administrative structure combined with a democratic political structure, all members of the firm electing a chief executive officer who then enjoys broad organizational authority. This system is democratic compared to an organization with the same administrative structure and a political structure according to which the chief executive officer is accountable to no one. Democratic accountability logically entails neither participatory decision making nor nonhierarchical administrative structures, although accountability may in some circumstances be enhanced, functionally speaking, by those participatory and nonhierarchical attributes often mistakenly considered to *define* the democratic firm.

Our four arguments for democratic accountability of the employer follow.

First, where one group has the capacity to tyrannize another – as, for example, a state elite might tyrannize a citizenry – democratic institutions have been advocated as a protection against despotism. Indeed, this is the traditional argument for democratic governance of the state. Does it apply to the firm? Our deliberate use of the terms "tyrannize" and "despotism" may suggest not, but this impression is false. We may strengthen our claim somewhat, drawing on Robert Dahl's recent treatment of democratic and property rights in firms: Any compelling argument for democratic governance of the state entails democratic governance of firms as well, and arguments that deny the legitimacy of democratic governance of firms equally oppose democratic governance of the state.

A modern restatement of the classical argument for democracy as a defense against tyranny is this: When decisions of major importance (perhaps including matters of life and death) are binding on parties not directly involved in the decision making, the decision makers should be accountable to those directly affected. There can be little doubt that employers make important (even life-and-death) decisions affecting workers. But are the decisions binding? If the cost of job loss is high – with financial distress, loss of medical insurance, disruption of one's family, having to relocate, and the like as consequences of leaving one's job – the firm's decisions must be taken as binding on the worker in the same sense that government decisions are binding. Of course, citizens may leave their nations and workers may leave their work. But, Robert Dahl asks:

is not "exit" (or exile) often so costly, in every sense, that membership is for all practical purposes compulsory – whether it requires one to leave a country, a municipality, or a firm? If so, then the government of a firm looks rather more like the government of a state than we are habitually inclined to believe: because exit is costly, membership in a firm is not significantly more voluntary or less compulsory than citizenship in a municipality or perhaps even in a country. (Dahl 1985:115)

Some who would agree that membership in the firm is perhaps more compulsory than membership in a municipality might balk at applying the analogy to the nation. But in view of the fact that democratic governance of localities is widely advocated, does not even this limited view support the claim for democratic governance of firms?

Our first argument is in no way compromised by the incontestable observation that the employees are better off employed than not employed, and better off employed in the face of a cost-of-job-loss threat than without the threat. This objection confuses the administrative structure of the firm with its political structure. It is, of course, conceivable that workers running a democratic firm might choose to erect a hierarchical administrative structure making use of penalties for less than adequate work. Indeed, the democratic firm we have modeled does just this.

Standard neoclassical economic arguments – such as those offered by Oliver Williamson (1984) and Armen Alchian and Harold Demsetz (1972) – support the notion of sanctions and hierarchy. But they in no way justify a lack of democratic accountability. Alchian and Demsetz, in fact, go to some lengths to convince their readers that a team of equal workers might have freely chosen to appoint one of their number to monitor them. But they provide no reason why the monitor might not be subject to periodic reelection.

A second argument for democratic governance is that it produces better decisions by exploiting both the superior information structures and motivational environments made possible by involving those directly affected in making decisions. Our argument concerning mutual monitoring is an example of such reasoning. While we support workplace democracy, this argument gives us reason to reject the position of those who concede that employers have power over workers but insist that such power should be made accountable through the democratic election of states with regulatory powers over employers.

A third argument (originally suggested by John Stuart Mill) is that democratic governance is a school for the formation of democratic citizens capable of collective self-rule. This human-development argument for the democratic firm begins with the observation, often overlooked in economic theory, that *the economy produces people*, their experiences as economic actors strongly affecting their personal capacities, their attitudes, and the character of their interpersonal relations. Democratic social relations foster forms of social development that are desirable in their own right and also supply the skills allowing individuals to control their political and community lives. The undemocratic structure of the capitalist enterprise, by virtue of the everyday experiences it fosters and the cultural forces mobilized in its defense, thus thwarts the development of a fully democratic culture (Almond and Verba 1963; Kohn 1969; Pateman 1970). Indeed, we have suggested that the sharp contrast between the democratic character of political life and the authoritarian character of primary and secondary education in contemporary liberal democratic societies, flows from the requirement of the educational system to prepare youth for their future positions in an authoritarian workplace (Bowles and Gintis 1976). A greater diversity in the political organization of firms would, according to this logic, allow the educational system to foster more participatory social relations without undermining the dominant culture of the workplace.

A final argument (proposed by R. H. Tawney, T. H. Marshall, and others) is that democratic accountability of the state is essential to assuring the equal dignity of citizens. This argument holds that unaccountable relations of power establish master–servant relations inimical to self-respect and mutual recognition among citizens. If our first argument concerning the compulsory nature of membership in the firm – stemming from our analysis of the power of the employer – is accepted, this fourth argument clearly applies to the governance of the firm, although we would want to stop short of prohibiting capitalist employment relationships as contrary to democratic citizenship.

As this last remark suggests, we do not think that the case just discussed requires that in any real economy all employment relationships be made democratically accountable. Some employment relationships may exhibit such ease of exit that the tyranny argument does not apply, for example. In others the costs of democratic governance might be exceedingly high, suggesting a compromise of democratic governance in favor of economic efficiency. And one might on libertarian grounds wish not to restrict unduly the freedom to contract for the sale or purchase of labor time.

The argument for democratic governance, not surprisingly, is thus one among possibly competing arguments. Among the competing claims often advanced is the proposition that democratic governance of firms would lead to economic inefficiency. We shall see that although such a conflict might obtain in special cases, democratic firms are likely to be more efficient, at least in the static sense of maximizing output per unit of inputs.

4. Market failures arising from contested exchange

Our efficiency evaluation of the democratic and capitalist firm will focus on the ability of each to address the market failures associated with the two agency problems arising from the noncontractible aspects of work effort and risk taking. Ideally, economic institutions would generate a structure of incentives such that potential investments would be evaluated purely on the basis of their social rate of return, irrespective of their risk, and work intensity would be regulated such that the marginal productivity of effort would be equated to the worker's cost of supplying effort.

Feasible institutions – democratic, capitalist, or other – generally fail to achieve these optima. Where production takes place in teams virtually any institutional arrangement will result in the level of work effort falling short of the optimum, for feasible pay schemes insufficiently reward the effort contribution of the individual member of a work team. Whether residual claimants or not, team members have an incentive to free-ride by reducing effort. The level of risk taking, on the other hand, may exceed or fall short of the social optimum. Where authority over risk-taking decisions is assumed by borrowers who are residual claimants with limited liability, the level of risk will generally exceed the social optimum. In this case, the decision maker benefits from large gains as a residual claimant but is protected from large losses by her limited liability status. Conversely where risk taking is assumed by agents who are not residual claimants but who must bear the costs in case of project failure (e.g., managers), the level of risk will generally be suboptimal.

One's (correct) intuition is that while in coping with the effort determination problem the democratic firm has significant advantages stemming from the residual claimancy status of workers, in dealing with risk taking, the concentration of assets implied both by worker ownership and by the fact that workers are unable to diversify their labor-related assets will tend to render the democratic firm unduly conservative. By contrast, the classic equity-financed capitalist firm insulates the risk-taking decision from workers, who hold the most concentrated assets, placing it in the hands of managers, who may be responsive to the more nearly risk-neutral objectives of residual claimant owners. Thus, by locating residual claimancy in capital, the easily diversified asset, risk taking is promoted while the capitalist firm forgoes the superior work incentives available through the residual claimant status of workers in the democratic firm.

The central market failure resulting from the labor agency problem is that when the capitalist firm chooses a profit-maximizing wage, the resulting equilibrium wage and effort levels are less efficient than some combination of a higher wage and a greater level of work effort.[8] The implied improvements are infeasible, however, while the employer remains residual claimant, since the worker's promise of providing more effort for a higher wage is unenforceable.

Turning to the problem of risk taking, we shall identify two additional market failures. The first and most obvious market failure occurs when a residual claimant owner, highly diversified and hence risk-neutral, employs a manager to make decisions concerning the level of risk. The manager's assets (an income stream with the firm, a reputation) are highly concentrated in the firm and tied to its survival. The manager may thus prefer a lower level of risk taking than the more diversified owner. To address this conflict of interest, the owner may offer the manager in addition to a fixed salary, a share of firm profits, setting both such that the manager may expect to receive an income in excess of her next-best alternative, thus giving the owner short-side power over the manager (other means of influencing the manager may, of course, be used, but we ignore them here).

The manager will thus choose a welfare-maximizing level of risk, taking account of the income on the job and the likelihood that overly conservative risk choices will result in the loss of the job. The owner will offer a payment scheme for the manager designed to maximize expected profits, which will vary (over the relevant range) positively with the level of risk and negatively with the manager's income. At the resulting equilibrium, the owner would be willing to pay the manager more if a higher level of risk taking could be secured (a first order–second order argument of the type presented in note 8 again shows that this is true), but there is no way to enforce such an agreement.

Our final market failure arises when a borrower is residual claimant on an income stream the level of which depends on the borrower's choice between risky and less risky projects. An obvious conflict of interest arises because the borrower (as residual claimant) stands to gain from high return but risky projects, whereas the lender gains nothing from the greater returns of these projects and stands to lose should the project fail.[9]

For simplicity, let us assume that collateral cannot be posted so that the lender relies solely on a contingent renewal enforcement strategy: The borrower would like to continue the relationship with the lender, who offers an enforcement rent in the form of a greater amount of credit or a lower rate of interest than the borrower can expect to enjoy elsewhere.[10] But the lender may terminate the relationship should the borrower engage in excessively risky business practices. For any interest rate offered by the lender, the borrower thus maximizes her welfare by choosing a risk level to balance the expected gains from high-risk projects against the probability that risky strategies will be detected by the lender and the loan not be renewed in subsequent periods. The result is an inefficiency, in which the lender would like to offer a lower interest rate if he could induce the borrower to take less risky choices, but there is no way of enforcing such an arrangement. (Once again, a first order–second order argument demonstrates this point.)

The market failures we have identified, concerning insufficient wages and effort, and either insufficient or excessive risk-taking, suggest a number of respects in which even under highly competitive conditions democratic firms might allocate resources differently than capitalist firms. We turn first to the advantages of the democratic firm in regulating the pace of work.

5. The efficiency of the democratic firm in regulating work

Consider two firms, one owned by its workers and governed by their elected representatives, the other owned by a nonworker and governed by the owner or an owner-designated manager. We assume that workers direct the managers of the democratic firm to select a payment scheme to maximize the workers' welfare. We assume that both firms employ identical workers, produce with identical technologies, and make use of a dismissal-based system of labor discipline. We shall identify three reasons to think that the democratic firm will be more efficient than the capitalist firm in the sense that it uses less of at least one input to produce the same output.

First, the worker in the democratic firm is both the residual claimant on a share of the firm's income and a member of a sovereign body of members of the firm. It seems likely that workers thus integrated by both property and political process into the firm will experience work as less onerous at the margin and therefore, if faced with a given wage, will work harder than they would in a capitalist firm. Our reasoning is simply that the alienation of the worker from the capitalist firm – specifically, the exclusion of the worker from managerial decision making and from ownership of the products of labor – and the contrasting integration of the worker in the democratic firm (even if quite imperfect) give the democratic firm important motivational advantages. We refer to this as the *participation effect* entailing greater efficiency in the democratic firm.

The participation effect is easily confused with what might be termed the *direct residual claimancy effect*. This effect arises because the worker, as a residual claimant, will take account of the effect of working harder on total firm income. thereby reducing the incentive incompatibility in the employment relation. Although it may be an important consideration in small work teams, the direct residual claimancy effect is too small to provide a major motivational basis for increased work intensity in work teams of reasonable size. As we shall see, however, it may be sufficiently large to provide a motivation allowing for a superior monitoring system even in the largest firms.

Our second reason for the superior efficiency of the democratic firm is that the residual claimancy status of workers provides such a firm with monitoring mechanisms unavailable or prohibitively expensive for the capitalist firm. Abstracting from the participation and direct residual claimancy effects, one might think that the worker would have no less incentive to free-ride on the democratic firm than on the capitalist firm by pursuing on-the-job leisure. But this view is mistaken. Workers frequently have virtually costless access to information concerning the work activities of fellow workers, and in the democratic firm each has an interest in the effort levels of other workers. The residual claimancy status of workers thus provides a motive for mutual monitoring.[11] The democratic firm could thus deploy a considerably more effective monitoring structure at less cost than could the capitalist firm. We refer to this as the *mutual monitoring effect*.

Our third reason for the technical efficiency of the democratic firm is that the wage offered in the capitalist equilibrium is too low and monitoring expenditures too high. The reason is that the capitalist firm faces two prices in selecting its enforcement structure. One, the price of monitoring, correctly measures a social marginal cost, for the use of monitoring equipment or personnel entails real opportunity costs. But the other price, the wage, does not measure a real social cost. The payment of a higher wage is redistributive; it does not entail the greater use of scarce resources with alternative uses in production. Not surprisingly, then, the capitalist firm uses too little wage incentive and too much monitoring relative to an efficient alternative.[12] We refer to the potential gain to the democratic firms the *wage incentive effect*.

Converting the capitalist firm to a democratic firm would thus improve efficiency. Indeed, it would be possible to compensate the former owners at the level of their previous claim on the surplus, and pay out the reduced monitoring input costs to members of the firm. The former owners would be no worse off and the worker members would be doubly better off: They would experience less disutility of labor and would receive a payment corresponding to the reduced monitoring expenditures.

This efficiency gain associated with the democratic firm is, however, still not socially optimal, because even apart from the free-riding problem, workers in the democratic firm maximize their welfare, which takes account of the probability that they will lose their jobs. The social optimality criterion, by contrast, is indifferent to which workers hold jobs. Workers in a democratic firm thus have a job retention incentive to work hard corresponding to no social benefits.

The participation, direct residual claimancy, mutual monitoring, and wage incentive effects work together to improve the efficiency of the democratic firm over its capitalist counterpart.

6. Impediments to the success of the democratic firm in a competitive capitalist economy

Why do democratic firms, while more efficient in regulating work than their capitalist counterparts, nonetheless operate at a competitive disadvantage and hence not flourish in a capitalist economy? Furthermore, why can the efficiency gains associated with workplace democracy not be reaped by a capitalist firm?

Three general answers may be considered. First, learning to govern a firm effectively through democratic means takes time, and requires a work force schooled in common deliberation and decision making. Unless the efficiency gains associated with the democratic firm are considerable, the costs of learning, as well as the lack of a pool of workers experienced in democratic management, may be prohibitive.

We call this the *democratic capacities constraint*. This constraint may be a particularly strong impediment to the proliferation of democratic firms to the extent that the experience of work in capitalist firms and the process of formal schooling orients human development toward capacities that are more functional in the context of hierarchical rather than reciprocal relationships and that discourage the development of cognitive capacities needed to govern production (Bowles and Gintis, 1976).

Second, the conditions favoring the competitive viability of the democratic firm may be more likely to obtain in an economy with many such firms, and similarly for the capitalist firm. Thus, an economy composed primarily of capitalist firms might sustain and foster general economic conditions precluding the viability of the democratic firm, while an economy of democratic firms would also preclude the viability of the capitalist firm. We call this the *economic environment constraint*. For instance, Levine and Tyson (1990) argue that the variability of demand, the level of unemployment, and the general inequality of income differentially favor the capitalist over the democratic firm in a capitalist economy, but would change in a direction favorable to the democratic firm in an economy composed primarily of democratic firms. Thus, using the terminology of evolutionary biology, it is possible that a population of capitalist firms would be uninvadable by a small number of democratic firms, and a population of democratic firms would also be uninvadable by a small number of capitalist firms. Both types would thus be evolutionarily stable, in the sense that homogeneous populations both of capitalist firms and of democratic firms would constitute stable evolutionary equilibriums.

One less speculative reason for the paucity of democratic firms is that workers face serious wealth constraints: The firm's capital requirements are generally not within the means of workers, nor would risk-averse workers rationally choose to concentrate their wealth in a single asset. Unable to finance the democratic firm directly, and lacking even the collateral required for borrowing the necessary funds, workers may find the democratic firm an unattractive option despite its superior efficiency. We refer to this as the *wealth inequality constraint*.

Of course, were capital markets like those depicted in the neoclassical model, wealth constraints would not exist, since workers could borrow whatever amount was needed to finance the firm on terms no more costly than for the wealth-holding capitalist. But in fact capital markets are as much arenas of contested exchange as are labor markets: The promise to repay a loan is enforceable only if the borrower is solvent at the time repayment is due and, as we have seen, the borrower's promise to remain solvent is not third-party enforceable.

394 SAMUEL BOWLES and HERBERT GINTIS

Of course, the lender can devise contracts that induce more favorable performance than borrowers would spontaneously exhibit. Among the most effective is that of requiring the borrower to post collateral. Since this collateral is forfeited in case of borrower insolvency, the incentive incompatibility between borrower and lender is attenuated: A highly collateralized borrower has objectives closer to the lender's. But collateral by its nature must involve the borrower's own wealth, and cannot (except through subterfuge) itself be borrowed without undermining the collateral's enforcement effect.

7. Conclusion: the agency problems of a democratic economy

We have argued that on democratic grounds firms ought to be worker-run and that capital market imperfections account for the competitive disadvantage of the democratic firm, despite its superior ability to deal with the labor agency problem. There is thus a prima facie case on both political and economic grounds for considering some form of subsidy for the democratic firm.

For a firm to be considered "democratic," and hence to enjoy such a subsidy, it might be required to conform to several conditions: (1) The firm must have a democratic constitution guaranteeing fair elections among worker members subject to the protection of minority rights, freedom of speech, information, and political activity, plus whatever additional conditions are required to facilitate substantive democratic decision making; (2) new workers must be extended equal rights of political participation within a reasonable period of their admission to the firm; and (3) the firm must follow due process in hiring, dismissal, and promotion procedures. Associations not meeting these requirements, while not otherwise disadvantaged, would be obliged to forgo privileged access to credit.

Suppose, then, that credit were made available to the democratic firm on the same terms as to its capitalist counterpart, thus eliminating its competitive disadvantage. How would we then assess the democratic firm's ability to handle the twin agency problems surrounding labor and risk taking?

Concerning the labor agency problem, we expect the democratic firm to benefit from the participation, direct residual claimancy, and mutual monitoring effects. The wage incentive effect, however, is more problematic. It is well known that unless returns to the firm's capital stock are correctly allocated among firm members, the democratic firm will hire too little labor and undertake a suboptimal level of investment.[13] The logical solution to this problem is to create a financial instrument, the "worker stock," that is purchased by an incoming worker as a condition of employment, and that must be sold when the worker leaves the firm, at prices reflecting the capital value of the firm.[14] Assuming such a mechanism is in place, the wage incentive effect will be inoperative unless the democratic firm is subsidized in a manner favoring it over the capitalist firm (e.g., through a wage subsidy or lower profits tax). The efficiency gains associated with the wage incentive effect would appear to favor this subsidy as an efficiency-enhancing form of egalitarian redistribution.

Is there any reason, however, to believe that democratic firms would provide an adequate solution to the choice of risk and innovation? As we have seen, it is socially optimal that firms act in a risk-neutral manner, whereas economic agents tend to be risk-averse, and more so the larger the portion of their wealth involved in a particular project. Capitalist firms mitigate this problem in two ways: They vest control in relatively wealthy and hence less risk-averse agents, and they are financed through institutions, such as banks and stock markets, capable of inducing firms to innovate and take risks.

The capitalist solution is probably too conservative. But the internally financed democratic firm can be expected to act in an even more risk-avoiding manner on both counts: Its members are not wealthy and are not compelled by outside interests to take risks. Indeed, members of the democratic firm, even were they risk-neutral, would have an additional reason to shun high-risk, high-return projects: Since workers earn enforcement rents, they incur additional bankruptcy costs (the loss of job rents) not imposed on their capitalist counterparts (Gintis 1989a).

From the democratic perspective the problem of innovation raises the following dilemma: Some degree of external control of the firm by those who are not worker members is justified by its contribution to a socially optimal level of risk taking; but external control of the firm compromises the principle of democratic accountability.[15] Yet the democratic argument for workers controlling their conditions of employment does not extend to creditors controlling the conditions under which their assets are used, since creditors are not generally long-side agents facing short-siders who wield power over them.

Notes

1 See Elster and Moene (1989) for a broader set of criteria.
2 We say a "market failure" occurs when uncoordinated market interactions lead to results that are inferior by comparison to some other technically feasible outcome.

3 Our analysis is limited to the case where enforcement problems are present on only *one side* of the exchange. By addressing cases in which one side of the exchange provides a monetary payment (the costs of monitoring of which are assumed to be zero), we set aside the more general problem of "bilateral endogenous enforcement," in which both parties to the exchange exercise strategic power.

4 The analysis presented in this section is developed in Gintis (1976), Bowles (1985), and Gintis and Ishikawa (1987). Related models have been developed by Calvo (1979), and Shapiro and Stiglitz (1984). The reader will recognize its affinities with Marx's analysis of the extraction of labor from labor power.

5 Readers familiar with noncooperative game theory might wonder, if the cost to the employer of replacing a dismissed worker is positive, whether the threat to dismiss is credible, in the sense that it is in the employer's interest to carry out this threat when actually faced by a shirking worker. If the employer's disciplinary actions are observable by other (present and future) workers, then a "reputation effect" argument shows that this is the case. See Bowles and Gintis (1990) for details.

6 More generally: The short side of an exchange is located where the total amount of desired transactions is least, on the demand side if there is excess supply and on the supply side if there is excess demand.

7 A more extended treatment would take account of agents who attain some level of transactions, but less than they would have chosen at the prevailing price or wage.

8 This assertion can be understood using a "first order to second order argument (for details, see Bowles and Gintis, 1990). Because the worker chooses effort to maximize welfare, she suffers only second-order losses from a small increase in effort in the neighborhood of the chosen level. By contrast, the employer enjoys first-order benefits, equal to the marginal product of effort. Thus, were it possible for the employer to contract with the worker for a small increase in effort, the cost to the employer of compensating the worker for this small increase in effort would be an order of magnitude less than the benefits. But as effort itself cannot be contracted for, this generally beneficial bargain cannot be struck.

9 This conflict of interest has been explored by Stiglitz and Weiss (1981).

10 If collateral is allowed, a distinct market failure arises from the fact that agents capable of posting collateral need not coincide with agents having access to fruitful investment opportunities. For an analysis of this situation, see Bowles and Gintis (1990).

11 It may be argued that mutual monitoring introduces sufficient discord within a work team to undermine the positive effect of participation on worker productivity. Although we cannot point to empirical studies in this area, we believe that mutual monitoring in a democratic setting should strengthen the participation effect, in part by enhancing the perception of equal contribution among members, and hence of reducing the incentive to free-ride.

12 An analogy makes this reasoning clear. Imagine a trucking company choosing between a shorter route over a toll road or a somewhat longer route without tolls. The two prices in question are the operating cost per mile and the road tolls. The trucking company would treat the two prices as equivalent, perhaps avoiding use of the shorter toll road. But the toll does not represent a real social cost, while the operating costs on the truck (fuel, wear and tear) do. The choice of the longer road, like the choice of lower wages and more intense monitoring, is cost-minimizing but socially inefficient.

13 By the return to capital being "correctly allocated," we mean that each worker shares in the change in the value of the capital stock that occurred during her tenure with the firm, and that new firm members be required to purchase an appropriate share of the firm's capital stock.

14 For an analysis of the literature addressed to this problem, see Bonin and Putterman (1987). The solution was proposed by Sertel (1982), and is analyzed in Dow (1986).

15 To complicate the picture, it is likely that a democratic firm would require a considerably *greater* degree of external influence to achieve the same level of risk taking as a managerially controlled enterprise, since the external owners and creditors of a capitalist firm can focus their risk-enhancing incentives (e.g., bonuses and stock options) on a small group of agents (the managers), whereas to induce a majority of workers to act in the same manner would generally require that such incentives extend to a majority of the firm members (Gintis 1989b). Under some plausible conditions, dual worker–outsider ownership is also unstable (Ognedal, in press).

Bibliography

Alchian, Armen, and Harold Demsetz. "Production, Information Costs, and Economic Organization," *American Economic Review* 62 (December 1972): 777–95.

Almond, Gabriel, and Sidney Verba. *The Civic Culture: Political Attitudes and Democracy in Five Nations*. Princeton, N.J.: Princeton University Press, 1963.

Bonin, John P., and Louis Putterman. *Economics of Cooperation and the Labor-Managed Economy*. New York: Harwood, 1987.

Bowles, Samuel. "The Production Process in a Competitive Economy: Walrasian, Neo-Hobbesian, and Marxian Models," *American Economic Review* 75, no. 1 (March 1985): 16–36.

Bowles, Samuel, and Herbert Gintis. *Schooling in Capitalist America: Educational Reform and the Contradictions of Economic Life*. New York: Basic Books, 1976.

Bowles, Samuel, and Herbert Gintis. "Contested Exchange: New Microfoundations of the Political Economy of Capitalism," *Politics and Society* 18, no. 2 (1990): 165–222.

Bowles, Samuel, and Herbert Gintis. "The Revenge of *Homo Economicus*:

Post-Walrasian Economics and the Revival of Political Economy," *Journal of Economic Perspectives*, Winter 1993.

Calvo, Guillermo. "Quasi-Walrasian Theories of Unemployment," *American Economic Review* 69, no. 2 (May 1979): 102–7.

Dahl, Robert. *Preface to the Theory of Economic Democracy*. Berkeley, Calif.: University of California Press, 1985.

Domar, Evsey. "The Soviet Collective Farm as a Producer Cooperative," *American Economic Review* 56 (September 1966): 743–57.

Dow, Gregory. "Control Rights, Competitive Markets, and the Labor Management Debate," *Journal of Comparative Economics* 10 (1986): 48–61.

Drèze, Jacques H. *Labour Management, Contracts, and Capital Markets*. Oxford: Basil Blackwell, 1989.

Elster, Jon, and Karl Moene. "Introduction," in Jon Elster and Karl Moene (eds.), *Alternatives to Capitalism*. Cambridge: Cambridge University Press, 1989.

Furubotn, Eirik G., and Svetozar Pejovich. *The Economics of Property Rights*. Cambridge, Mass.: Ballinger, 1974.

Gintis, Herbert. "The Nature of the Labor Exchange and the Theory of Capitalist Production," *Review of Radical Political Economics* 8, no. 2 (Summer 1976): 36–54.

Gintis, Herbert. "Financial Markets and the Political Structure of the Enterprise," *Journal of Economic Behavior and Organization* 1 (1989a): 311–22.

Gintis, Herbert. "The Principle of External Accountability in Financial Markets," in Masahiko Aoki, Bo Gustafsson, and Oliver Williamson (eds.), *The Firm as a Nexus of Treaties*. New York: Russell Sage, 1989b.

Gintis, Herbert, and Tsuneo Ishikawa. "Wages, Work Discipline, and Unemployment," *Journal of Japanese and International Economies* 1 (1987): 195–228.

Jensen, Michael C., and William H. Meckling. "Rights and Production Functions: An Application to Labor-managed Firms and Codetermination," *Journal of Business* 52 (1979): 469–506.

Kohn, Melvin. *Class and Conformity: A Study in Values*. Homewood, Ill.: Dorsey Press, 1969.

Levine, David I., and Laura d'Andrea Tyson. "Participation, Productivity, and the Firm's Environment," in Alan Blinder (ed.), *Paying for Productivity*. Washington, D.C.: Brookings, 1990.

Meade, James E. "The Adjustment Processes of Labour Co-operatives with Constant Returns to Scale and Perfect Competition," *Economic Journal* 82 (1972): 402–28.

Ognedal, Tone. "Unstable Ownership," in Samuel Bowles, Herbert Gintis, and Bo Gustafsson (eds.), *The Microfoundations of Political Economy: Participation, Accountability, and Efficiency*. Cambridge: Cambridge University Press, in press.

Pateman, Carole. *Participation and Democratic Theory*. Cambridge: Cambridge University Press, 1970.

Samuelson, Paul. "Wages and Interests: A Modern Dissection of Marxian Economics," *American Economic Review* 47 (1957).

Sertel, Murat R. *Workers and Incentives*. New York: North-Holland, 1982.

Shapiro, Carl, and Joseph E. Stiglitz. "Unemployment as a Worker Discipline Device," *American Economic Review* 74, no. 3 (June 1984): 433–44.

Stiglitz, Joseph, and Andrew Weiss. "Credit Rationing in Markets with Imperfect Information," *American Economic Review* 71 (June 1981): 393–411.

Vanek, Jaroslav. *The General Theory of Labor-managed Market Economies*. Ithaca, N.Y.: Cornell University Press, 1970.

Ward, Benjamin. "The Firm in Illyria: Market Syndicalism," *American Economic Review* 48 (September 1958): 566–89.

Williamson, Oliver E. "The Economics of Governance: Framework and Implications," *Journal of Institutional and Theoretical Economics* 140 (1984): 195–223.

Contested power

KARL OVE MOENE

While democratic governance is occupying new territory in Eastern European politics, most firms in the West are still governed like command economies in miniature. But in view of the fact that democratic governance in politics is widely accepted, why does it not automatically apply to firms? Bowles and Gintis think it should. Governance should be accountable to those most directly affected, they argue, and worker-owned firms are recommended as a way to obtain this. They make a good case for their view based on a uniform theory of production, distribution, and the exercise of power in a competitive capitalist economy. Their essay implies that a better understanding of the present system is needed to identify fully the possible gains from a conversion to worker ownership. Accordingly, Bowles and Gintis devote most of their discussion to conflicts, power, and inefficiencies in traditionally owned enterprises, and I shall do so as well. My comments will concern mainly the robustness of the theory of contested exchange as a guide to the understanding of power relations.

Short-side power

The basic arguments of the essay by Bowles and Gintis follow from the theory of contested exchange that explains how the market can assure contractual performance. Contracts are renewed only as long as the agent performs according to the wishes of the principal. To elicit good performance, the agent has to earn excess rents that give rise to a nonchearing market equilibrium. Thus, with repeated transactions market failures easily follow from the requirements of endogenous contract enforcement.

To model the effort bargain within this approach the employer is assumed to determine the wage followed by the workers' determination of their individual effort levels. Effort is not directly observable and can be monitored only randomly by the employer. Yet the more effort the worker puts in, the higher is the probability of keeping the job in future periods. But since effort is costly to the worker, the employer has to raise the wage above the going rate to stimulate effort. Hence, in equilibrium workers work hard to keep jobs that offer them a positive employment rent. But every employer cannot pay better than the average. So no equilibrium occurs before unemployment is sufficiently high to discipline workers. Macroeconomic waste is therefore needed to obtain microeconomic efficiency. Bosses can exercise power because they can incur the costs of job loss to workers who do not obey their orders.

I am not convinced this story captures the most important or typical instances of power abuse by capitalists. In one variant or another the underlying efficiency wage considerations, initiated in part by the work of Gintis and Bowles in the 1970s, are by now included in mainstream labor economics. The criticism that can be raised against this theory is also well known. Employers may sometimes obtain better work performance by utilizing promotions rather than the sack as a disciplining device. Moreover, contingent renewal of employment does not necessarily lead to unemployment, since the excess rent that workers earn need not be pecuniary. Because of friendships on the job (social bonding) workers may be afraid of losing their jobs even though similar jobs with equal pay are easy to obtain elsewhere. Finally, the decision-making structure inherent in the model does not apply to all types of jobs. Sometimes the speed of work is determined by the speed of the machines controlled by the employer. Monitoring of work effort may be easier in some jobs than in others, and so on. Thus, the essay offers a general theory of a special case.

In addition, the job situations where the model does apply are not necessarily bad from the workers' viewpoint. Employers, I believe, can be much more powerful under circumstances where the model does not fit. The employer may, for example, determine both the wage and the effort level. The workers are then left with the option to accept or reject as in the neoclassical approach to the effort bargain. But in the neoclassical setup unilateral wage and effort determination are combined with an implicit assumption that the contract can be enforced by a third party *ex post*. If this is the case, no power rests with the employer after the worker has agreed to work for him. The competitive level of workers' utility is determined by market clearing where workers' utility levels most likely are bid up above what workers obtain when unemployed (the reservation level). Thus, if the labor contract were not binding, employers could have obtained higher profits by squeezing more effort out of their workers.

Worker lock-in

In reality it is almost impossible to write complete labor contracts that can be enforced by a court. Details of job content and work assignments have to be left to the employer. He can therefore often control work effort after the worker is employed. When this is the case, employers can exploit workers until workers' utilities are reduced to the reservation levels. Faced with moving costs, however small they may be, workers have no credible threats against such employer behavior. A worker cannot improve his situation by threatening to work for another employer who, after hiring him, will be equally exploitive. He will be no better off by threatening to become unemployed. Hence, his best option is to stay with his present employer, which means that he is locked in, to some extent.

In this case, further analyzed by Alan Manning (1988), workers' utilities are driven down to the reservation levels independently of the state of the labor market.

The result arises because once workers have agreed to work for an employer, the employer faces an inelastic supply of labour at a utility level below the competitive level. Ex post, each employer is like a monopsonist. Furthermore, because of the employer's control over the effort bargain, s/he can exploit this ex post monopsony power. The perfectness requirement on employer's decisions mean that this opportunity will always be exploited. There is no credible way that employers can offer a higher utility level by offering a higher wage, as this will simply mean that a higher level of effort will be chosen in the second stage of the labour contract. (Manning 1988, p. 1803)

The differences from the model of Bowles and Gintis are worth noticing. In the worker–lock-in model, excess demand is the normal state of the labor market, while contingent renewal leads to unemployment. Effort with worker lock-in is too high in the sense that the members of a labor-managed twin might choose to work less. Effort with contingent renewal is too low as the workers would have worked harder if they received the whole surplus as under labor management. It is therefore more difficult for a worker cooperative to compete in an otherwise capitalist industry dominated by worker–lock-in firms as compared to contingent-renewal firms.

A common framework

It is possible to derive the two models as special cases of a common framework. In both cases the worker can be viewed as maximizing the present value of expected utility, given the perceived relation between effort and the probability of job loss. In the Bowles-and-Gintis case, this probability is decreasing in the level of work effort. The resulting effort choice by the worker therefore balances the disutility of work with expected future gains from keeping the job. In Manning's case, the probability of job loss is equal to one as long as effort is below a critical value e^* determined by the employer. Effort levels equal to or higher than e^* are associated with a zero probability of job loss. Thus, when the worker optimizes he chooses an effort level equal to e^*. The utility level he will obtain can, by a suitable choice of e^* *ex ante*, be pressed as close to the reservation value as the employer wishes.

Which of the two models provides the more reasonable description? As we have seen, the crucial points are the monitoring technology and who controls the job content. I would find it very surprising if radical economists should claim that over the history of capitalism the control over work effort rests primarily with the workers. The rise of the factory system was to a large extent associated with the tyranny of bosses. Unions have, since the beginning, made substantial efforts to reduce employer authority at the workplace. Skilled workers, in particular, have gained some job control. Over time we may very well have moved from a situation that is best described by Manning's model to a situation that is better captured by the model of Bowles and Gintis. This change should then be considered a step toward less abusive capitalist power.

The increased use of autonomous work groups in Scandinavia has, for example, reduced the authority of employers and increased the welfare of workers. As far as I can understand, this is also the prediction of the contingent renewal model. Employees' welfare goes up with worker control over effort, as does the employment rent. Thus, the disparity between the long side and the short side of the market increases as unemployment rises. It is unclear to me whether this should be interpreted as an increase in capitalists' short-side power as well.

Be this as it may, most people would agree that employers are most powerful when monitoring is perfect. Imperfect monitoring protects workers and reduces the direct authority of bosses at the workplace. The notion of short-side power is therefore of questionable interest, being too closely tied to the existence of privileges of the putatively powerless agents. The most salient aspects of power, perhaps, are hidden in the process that leads to a situation wherein the employer has to bribe his workers to obtain command over them. Could one not just as easily view the existence of employment rents as a result of threats against the employer?: "We shirk unless the wage is higher." Hence, the workers are capable of influencing their adversary's offer in a way that furthers their interests, and one could equally well talk about their having power over the employer as the other way around.

Consumer power with contested exchange

Before leaving the question of who has power over whom, we should consider whether anybody has short-side power over firms. Are firms located on the short side of all market transactions in which they are involved? It is well known that when product quality is not immediately observable, market clearing with price-taking firms that earn zero profits cannot be sustained as an equilibrium (Klein and Leffler 1981). When profits vanish, firms start exploiting consumers by lowering the quality of the product.

The firm can profit, however, by increasing the price above marginal cost to signal a high-quality product. Consumers have reason to believe that high prices guarantee good quality, since the corresponding high profits make firms afraid of losing their customers. Again, the market mechanism can be used to enforce contracts. A sufficiently high price seems to ensure good performance by the firm.

At a price higher than marginal cost, however, firms are willing to increase sales as long as there is effective demand for their products. Hence, consumers end up on the short side of the product market and have power in the sense that if the firm is not performing in accordance with consumer preferences, the consumers can punish the firm by exiting. Indeed, the theory of contingent renewal fits nicely with the Chicago style of reasoning where market forces, in the end, ensure contractual performance to the benefit of consumers.

Managerial problems

Bowles and Gintis's discussion of managerial incentives is also based on the principle of contingent renewal. They write that "the owner may offer the manager in addition to a fixed salary, a share of firm profits, setting both so that the manager may expect to receive an income in excess of her next best alternative, thus giving the owner short-side power over the manager."

This description may fit for some closely held enterprises. In other stock companies, however, the failure of internal control is more widespread. Most stockholders are passive investors with little or no knowledge of the firms they own. Even when stockholders have some information, there are all sorts of free-rider problems among them when it comes to monitoring the manager and in taking actions to correct his behavior.

As Andrei Shleifer and Robert Vishny emphasize, the board of directors has the nominal power "to block major corporate projects. In practise, however, boards of directors are rarely effective in stopping non-value-maximizing behavior of managers. As a rule managers control the election of directors" (p. 8). Control is therefore increasingly separated from ownership, and more and more power is collected in the hands of the managers.

A share of profits in addition to a fixed salary to managers seems to be an insufficient incentive to maximize net present value of future profits. Most top managers do not stay for long with any particular corporation, but move from one firm to another. Moreover, a top manager does not merely run his own show, he is also likely to be found on the boards of directors of many other companies. Hence, the boards elect their managers and within the boards, managers elect managers. Indeed, managers constitute the nomenclatura of the West, and it is no wonder that their salaries have increased in relation to wages and profits.

Even though collectively they have great power, the success of one particular manager depends on how other managers evaluate his performance. The decisions managers make in their companies are tests of their leadership talent. A manager's perceived talent, based on short-run comparisons between corporations, determines his future opportunities. This induces shortsightedness and biased incentives: The best, of course, is to do well when others fail, and the worst is to fail when others do well. To follow the others is a safe strategy in these circumstances, because each manager then does not reveal whether he is talented or not. David Scharfstein and Jeremy Stein (1990) argue that "managers simply mimic the investment decisions of other managers, ignoring substantial private information. Although this behavior is inefficient from a social point of view, it can be rational from the perspectives of managers who are concerned about their reputations in the labor market" (p. 466). The result of this herd behavior is an unstable market economy.

I therefore think that Bowles and Gintis miss the point when they indicate that owners in general have short-side power over corporate leaders. The study of power in this connection should be directed more toward understanding how top managers protect their positions in the market for corporate control and how this may depend on the ownership structure. In fact, democratic enterprise reforms may have a positive effect in this connection. Worker ownership combines democratic governance with long-run commitments and a sufficiently concentrated holding of assets to overcome the free-rider problems of traditional share ownership. Moreover, worker owners have more local knowledge about their firm than absentee owners have, and because they are present at the workplace, it is easier for them to check the daily activities of their manager.

Conclusion

Even though I disagree with some of the arguments in their essay, I am in sympathy with the conclusion Bowles and Gintis offer. In fact, I think the case for worker ownership is made stronger by not tying all the arguments so closely to the theory of contested exchange. Bowles and Gintis emphasize one class of agency problems and the corresponding market failures but overlook other, equally important problems. There is a body of empirical literature that supports their claim that worker-owned firms are not only more democratic but also more efficient than capitalist enterprises. (See, e.g., Blinder [1990] and the literature referred to therein.)

References

Blinder, Alan S., ed. 1990. *Paying for Productivity*. Washington D.C.: Brookings Institution.

Klein, Benjamin, and Keith B. Leffler. 1981. "The Role of Market Forces in Assuring Contractual Performance," *Journal of Political Economy*, 89:615–41.

Manning, Alan. 1988. "A Model of the Labour Market with Some Marxian and Keynesian Features," *European Economic Review*, 32:1797–1816.

Scharfstein, David S., and Jeremy C. Stein. 1990. "Herd Behavior and Investment," *American Economic Review*, 80:465–79.

Shleifer, Andrei, and Robert W. Vishny. 1983. "Value Maximization and the Acquisition Process," *Journal of Economic Perspectives*, 2:7–19.

Part V

Democracy: case studies

10

Capitalist development and democracy

Empirical research on the social origins of democracy

JOHN D. STEPHENS

Introduction

Capitalism and democracy go hand in hand. This claim of Western journalists and politicians has come to be accepted at face value all the more in the wake of the collapse of Eastern European communism. According to this view, capitalist development – economic development driven by capitalist interests in competition with one another – will bring about political freedom and democratic participation in government. Ironically a quite similar view was held by Lenin and his followers, albeit with a very different slant of evaluation. They too considered "bourgeois democracy" the constitutional form that perfectly fits the capitalist economic order. But, in their view, capitalism and democracy go hand in hand because democracy, while proclaiming the rule of the many, in fact protects the interests of capital owners. The authors of classics of nineteenth-century political theory also tended toward the view that the transformations wrought by capitalist development would bring democracy. But their reactions to this prospect were not at all what one might expect from the thought of their twentieth-century heirs. Tocqueville and J. S. Mill were not alone in being apprehensive about the consequences of full-fledged democracy. By contrast, at the left of the political spectrum, Marx saw in universal suffrage a major step in the transition from capitalism to socialism. His "dictatorship of the proletariat" was not so very different from Tocqueville's "tyranny of the majority," except that for Marx this was a vision of hope while for Tocqueville it was one of disaster.

The relation between capitalist development and democracy has not

This is a revised version of a paper prepared for the conference on democracy sponsored by the Program of Economy, Justice, and Society at the University of California, Davis, May 4–5, 1990. Some of this material appeared in chapters 4 and 6 of Rueschmeyer, Stephens, and Stephens's *Capitalist Development and Democracy* (Cambridge: Polity, and University of Chicago Press, 1992).

been the object of political argument and broad speculation in political philosophy alone. For several decades it has been subjected to careful and systematic empirical research in sociology, political science, and history. The findings of this research are not conclusive, however. In this essay, I summarize the main findings of a recently completed study by Dietrich Rueschemeyer, Evelyne Huber Stephens, and myself that attempts to resolve this controversy (Rueschemeyer, Stephens, and Stephens, 1992). The definition of democracy used in virtually all of these empirical studies (and in the present essay as well) is a formal one that leaves open the question of the extent to which formally democratic societies approach real political equality. I define a polity as democratic if it is characterized by government resting on responsibility to parliament (possibly complemented by direct election of the head of the executive), regular free and fair elections, freedom of expression and association, and universal suffrage.

Two research traditions

Two distinctive traditions of research, which employed different research strategies and methods, have come to quite different and as yet unreconciled results about the relation between capitalist development and the chances of democracy. Quantitative cross-national comparisons of many countries have consistently found a positive correlation between development and democracy. They thus come to relatively optimistic conclusions about the chances of democracy in the developing countries of today. By contrast, comparative historical studies emphasizing qualitative examination of complex sequences tend to trace the rise of democracy to a favorable historical constellation of conditions in early capitalism. Their conclusions are therefore far more pessimistic about today's developing countries. The contradictory results of the two research traditions represent a particularly difficult problem precisely because they derive from different methods. Given contrasting methodologies, it is difficult to decide by which criteria to evaluate the inconsistent findings.

Lipset's *Political Man* (1960) defines one tradition of empirical research as it combines cross-national statistical analysis with a modernization or structural-functional theoretical framework. The main theme of the modernization literature on the development of democracy is that socioeconomic development increases the likelihood of political democracy. Lipset begins by observing that greater economic affluence is generally associated with democracy in writings on the subject. He goes on to demonstrate a correlation between democracy and industrialization, urbanization, education, literacy, and per capita income and consumption. Education (and literacy), he contends, broadens one's outlook, increases tolerance, restrains one from adopting extremist doctrines, and increases one's capacity for making rational electoral choices. This is true not only between but also within countries: The more educated strata are more tolerant and thus more supportive of democracy. Increased wealth moderates the politics of the lower classes and thus makes them more prone to accept gradual change. Moreover, there is generally more inequality in poorer countries and this makes the rich hostile to democracy, as it may threaten their privileges. The rich may see it as morally wrong to let the poor participate, an arrogant attitude that feeds the resentment of the poor. Thus, in Lipset's analysis the middle class emerges as the main prodemocratic force. In sum, he argues that industrialization leads to increases in wealth, education, communications, and equality, which in turn are associated with a more moderate lower and upper class and a larger middle class (which is by its nature moderate); and this increases the probability of stable democratic politics.

Subsequent cross-national studies using a broader range of countries, more complex operationalization of the dependent and independent variables, and more sophisticated statistical techniques repeatedly confirmed Lipset's original findings: The level of development and political democracy were consistently correlated (Cutright 1963; Cutright and Wiley 1969; Bollen 1979, 1983; Bollen and Jackman 1985a, 1985b). Moreover, responding to the criticism of Lipset's essay, these studies demonstrated that this correlation held even if the analysis was limited to late-developing countries, dependent capitalist countries, or specific world regions. The interpretations given to this statistical correlation invariably followed Lipset, and thus the studies were taken to confirm a key theoretical proposition of modernization theory. These studies also demonstrated that a number of social, historical, and economic characteristics of countries exhibited stable correlations with democracy, prominent among them the positive relations of democracy with Protestantism and a legacy of British colonialism, and the negative relations with ethnic heterogeneity and economic dependence. Except for the dependence findings, the other statistical relations were interpreted as confirming the predictions of structural-functionalist sociology. A legacy of British colonialism was hypothesized to promote democracy because it resulted in the diffusion of British governmental institutions and values to the colonies. Ethnic diversity was assumed to undermine societal consensus and social cohesion and thus discourage democracy. Protestantism, it was argued, promoted individualist values and thus was conducive to democracy.

The other research tradition combines comparative historical analysis with a political economy or class analytic approach. It is perhaps best exemplified by Barrington Moore's *Social Origins of Dictatorship and Democracy* (1966) and Guillermo O'Donnell's *Modernization and Bureaucratic Authoritarianism* (1973). Based on his analysis of six cases (England, France, the United States, China, Japan, and India) and in-depth research on two more (Russia and Germany), Moore argues that there is no necessary relation between development and democracy. Economic modernization may lead to dictatorship or democracy. The critical condition for the development of modern capitalist authoritarianism is the cementing of a powerful coalition of large landholders, the state, and a politically dependent bourgeoisie of medium strength. The maintenance of peasant agriculture under landlords oriented to the market but employing political rather than market control of labor – labor-repressive agriculture, as Moore calls it – into the modern era is one essential feature of the path to authoritarianism. The method of labor control provides the strong antidemocratic impulse of the land-holding class. The bourgeoisie is kept in a politically dependent position as industrialization is aided, and to some extent directed, by the state through protection, development of infrastructure, state credits to industrialists, development of industry later handed over to the private sector, and military procurements. Finally, peasant revolutionary potential must be low[1] or else the whole process would have broken down at an earlier point in history.

O'Donnell (1973, 1979) seeks to explain authoritarian developments in South America during the 1960s and 1970s. Argentina, Brazil, Uruguay, and other countries turned away from democratic constitutional forms at fairly high levels of development and, he argues, for reasons precisely related to their comparatively advanced stage of development. Thus, he directly contradicts the central finding of the cross-national quantitative studies. O'Donnell argues that late developers could not follow the same path of political development as that of core capitalist countries, and he contends that the economic and political dependence of late-developing countries on the developed core of the capitalist world economy changed the structure of the economy and the alignments of classes and state actors in a manner that made authoritarian solutions attractive to the economic and political elites.

In *Social Origins*, Moore states that he agrees with "the Marxists" on one point: "no bourgeoisie, no democracy" (Moore 1966:418). The traditional Marxist explanation of the origins of "bourgeois democracy" is that it is the work of the bourgeoisie, that as that class becomes stronger because of growing dominance of the capitalist mode of production, it is able to eliminate progressively feudal and absolutist political forms and introduce democratic ones. If one follows the standard definition of democracy as entailing universal adult suffrage, responsible government, and freedom from intimidation in exercising rights to assemble, speak, vote, and so on, then such a position would appear to be at variance with Marx's own view as he saw the achievement of universal suffrage as the role of the working class (Marx 1852; Marx and Engels 1848:504). Recently one Marxist scholar, Therborn (1977), rediscovered this insight of Marx's in a comparative historical analysis of the development of democracy in advanced capitalist countries. He contended that the working class was the single most important actor in pressing for democracy.

Our theoretical approach and research strategy

For reasons just discussed, the empirical research on the relation of political democracy and capitalist development would appear to be at an impasse: The two different research traditions come to diametrically opposite conclusions based on different methodologies and theoretical frameworks. In *Capitalist Development and Democracy*, Dietrich Rueschemeyer, Evelyne Huber Stephens, and I attempt to resolve this debate. We argue that the cross-national quantitative findings are correct: Capitalist development is not only correlated to the development of democracy, it is causally associated with it. However, we explain the relationship within the political economy frame of reference of the cross-national studies. Our theoretical approach to the explanation of the social and historical origins of democracy and authoritarianism is an attempt to combine the insights of Moore, the dependency approach, and the working-class–strength perspective. We combine Moore's emphasis on agrarian class relations and landlord-bourgeois-state coalitions with attention to the size and organizational strength of the working class to produce a "relative class power model." Our central hypothesis is that capitalist development is associated with the rise of democracy in part because it is associated with a transformation of the class structure that strengthens the working class and weakens the landowning classes. In addition, we argue that certain configurations of state power and international constellations of power are more (or less, as the case may be) conducive to democracy (to be discussed farther on).

Pluralists and modernization theorists have often argued that democracy is facilitated by the development of relatively autonomous social groups based in a differentiated social structure (e.g., see Huntington 1984:202–3). This idea is closely paralleled in the Marxist literature by

Gramsci's contention that rule through consensus is made possible by the development of a "dense civil society" that is a by-product of the development of capitalism. Civil society, in this conception, is the totality of social institutions and associations, both formal and informal, that are not strictly production-related, governmental, or familial in character.[2] Density refers to the relative frequency of such associations and social interactions. While increased density of civil society per se does facilitate the development of democracy, it is hardly a one-to-one relation, because as Gramsci emphasizes, in the absence of a working-class movement, civil society acts as a conduit to spread the ideological hegemony of the propertied classes. In our view, it is the growth of working-class counterhegemony developed through the organization and growth of trade unions and working-class parties that is critical for the promotion of democracy. However, even in the absence of relatively strong labor organization, a strong civil society may contribute to an eventual democratic breakthrough by establishing a counterweight to state power and facilitating the development of middle-class inclusion.

Our research strategy is to combine the strengths of comparative historical and cross-national quantitative analysis: We employ comparative historical analysis but analyze a large number of cases, including nearly all the countries of Latin America and the Caribbean, as well as advanced capitalist societies. The case selection seeks to accomplish specific analytic purposes. The set of cases examined represents the areas with the most extensive democratic experience. At the same time, there are many examples of stable nondemocratic regimes as well as of breakdowns of democratic political systems that can be analyzed comparatively side by side with instances of democratization and stable democratic rule. In the present essay I present selections of the comparative historical account (on Europe and Central America and the Caribbean) to give an overview of the central argument. I shall focus on the reinterpretation of the findings of the cross-national studies on the relation of democracy not only to capitalist development but also to Protestantism, British colonialism, and ethnic divisions.

Europe

The cases analyzed in this section are the universe of Western European nations that experienced some period of democracy before World War II. The focus is on the period after 1870, as all but one of these countries experienced the transition to democracy in this period of rapid and intense industrialization that transformed the economic and class structures of Europe.

Therborn's (1977) study of the transition to democracy in the advanced capitalist world emphasizes the role of the working class, as represented by working-class parties and unions, and the role of geopolitics, especially foreign wars. Both factors appear in our theory. Lipset's more general statements on the relationship between development and democracy, on the other hand, would lead one to hypothesize that the European industrial spurt of 1870–1914 was associated with democracy because it enlarged the middle class.

Because they seek to make broad generalizations from a universe of cases, these studies do not explain deviations from the central tendency, such as highly developed countries that were nevertheless authoritarian. I follow Moore (1966), arguing that the critical condition for the development of modern capitalist authoritarianism is the development of a coalition of large landholders, the crown (the monarch, bureaucracy, and military, i.e., the state) and the bourgeoisie.

To foreshadow my conclusions briefly: I shall underline the role of the organized working class in the final push for democracy but shall demonstrate not only that the working class needed allies in other classes in this final push but also that other social classes were, in many instances, more important in earlier extensions of suffrage and struggles for parliamentary government. One can account for the variation in such class coalitions in the push for democracy and the causes of the interwar breakdowns by examining the dominant class–state coalitions of the late nineteenth century. The existence of a large landed class created a set of alliance possibilities for other classes that impeded the development of democracy in the first place and, once democracy was established, facilitated its eclipse by authoritarian forces. The course of domestic events took place in the context of, and was heavily influenced by transnational structures of power, which had its most dramatic impact in the form of wars and depressions.

In 1870, only one country in Europe was democratic by the criteria just laid out. By 1920, the overwhelming majority were. Two decades later, democratic rule had been eclipsed in a number of these countries. Let us now look more closely at the processes that brought democracy to these countries and at the factors that separated the democratic survivors from the cases of breakdown in the interwar period. Moore's analysis focuses heavily on the type of agricultural arrangements and labor-force control adopted by the landed aristocracy. Had Moore included the smaller European countries, his focus would certainly have begun with the existence of (or absence thereof) a politically powerful landlord class. This, in turn, is largely a product of the pattern of concentration of landholding itself: In all of the small countries, there

Late nineteenth-century strength of agrarian elite and political
outcomes in Europe

Political outcome	Weak agrarian elite	Strong agrarian elite
Democracy survives in interwar period	Sweden Denmark Norway Switzerland Belgium Netherlands France	Britain
Authoritarian regime established		Austria-Hungary Spain Italy Germany

were too few large estates to support the development of a politically significant class of landholders. This one factor prevents the development of the class coalition that is fatal for democracy. In fact, the correlation between the strength of large landlords and the survival or breakdown of democracy in the interwar period as shown in the accompanying table indicates that this one factor provides a powerful explanation for the survival or demise of democracy.

Britain stands out as a deviant case in terms of landholding, and resort to Moore's emphasis on the type of commercialized agriculture as an explanatory factor is necessary to bring this case into line. British landlords turned to sheep raising and, from the enclosure movement on, could rely on market mechanisms to supply the necessary labor (e.g., see Brenner 1976, 1977). In contrast, it is also accurate to classify the three authoritarian cases not discussed by Moore (Italy, Spain, and Austria-Hungary) as cases of dominance of "labor-repressive" agriculture. In other words, in these three countries as in Germany, agriculture was labor-intensive and landlords relied on nonmarket "political" mechanisms to assure themselves of an adequate supply of cheap labor. Still, although the correlation presented here suggests the causes of breakdown, we must examine the individual cases to uncover what social forces actually brought in democracy and what forces and dynamics appear to explain the relation between landed-class strength and breakdown.

By the eve of World War I, a handful of countries had become democratic: Switzerland (1848) was the trailblazer, followed by France (1877) and Norway (1898). In 1915, Denmark joined this group.[3] These are all nations of smallholders, urban petty bourgeoisie, and with a significant though not nearly dominant industrial sector (and therefore significant working and capitalist classes) at the time of democratization.

The first breakthrough to democracy came in Switzerland. The most clearly identifiable date for the achievement of full democracy is the adoption of the Constitution of 1848. However, the roots of Swiss democracy reach relatively far back and are grounded in Swiss social structure. From the origin of the Swiss confederation in 1291, Swiss history is punctuated with successful intervention of family farmers in political developments. As we shall see repeatedly in this section, such autonomous and successful intervention on the part of small farmers only occurs in countries without a powerful landed upper class, and it is certainly this characteristic of the social structure of the Swiss countryside that was responsible for early political influence of farmers. Under the political arrangements of 1815, the cities were privileged vis-à-vis the countryside. The politically dominant groups under this system were the guild masters and merchants in most cantons, together with patrician families in some cantons, notably Bern. This political system came under attack canton by canton beginning in the 1820s by a loose association of social and political groups joined together in what Gruner (1977:73–89) calls the *Freisinnige Grossfamilie*, the extended family of Liberals. Originally they included the entire array of the social structure, from industrial entrepreneurs, professionals, intellectuals, and artisans to farmers and workers, all of whom stood to gain from a reduction in the economic power of the guild masters, merchants, and patricians. Given that the beneficiaries of the traditional restrictions also held political power, the Liberal program called for extension of suffrage and representative and open government (Gitermann 1941:441).

As we shall see, Switzerland was unusual in that the industrial bourgeoisie joined other groups in support not only of economic liberalism but also of full democracy. There appear to be three primary reasons for this posture: First, as in other countries, the bourgeoisie shared an interest with groups in the liberal movement in sweeping away the restrictions on economic activity. Second, since industry was largely located in rural areas, the bourgeoisie belonged to those politically disadvantaged by the dominant position of the towns under the Restauration political arrangements. Finally, the Swiss bourgeoisie in this period faced not only no socialist labor movement, which would not develop for decades, but no industrial labor organization whatsoever. Moreover, as this was before the development of Chartism, there was no world-historical precedent of threat to bourgeois interests from organized industrial labor.

In France, the various Republican factions of the late 1860s and

1870s, who were the carriers of the final push to democracy, were supported by the working class, the petty bourgeoisie, segments of the peasantry (depending on local economic organization, clerical presence, and Revolutionary traditions), and segments of the bourgeoisie, especially in the provinces. The events of the late Second Empire clearly built on earlier democratic advances, especially 1848, which, though rolled back, continued to influence the course of events. In these developments, the bourgeois influence was weaker and rebellions of the largely artisanal working class played a much larger role (Elwitt 1975; Anderson 1977, Aminzade in press).

In the two Scandinavian countries, the working class organized in unions and political parties played some role in the drive for democracy. In Norway, the working class contributed to the final push for universal suffrage (embodied in various laws passed between 1898 and 1913), although earlier suffrage extensions were largely the work of the peasantry, with the help of sections of the urban middle class (Rokkan 1966; Derry 1973). In Denmark, an alliance of the working class, small and medium farmers, and urban middle-class segments as represented by the Social Democratic–Venstre coalition pressed through the 1901 introduction of parliamentary government. The driving force behind the 1915 introduction of universal suffrage was the Social Democrats and the Radikale Venstre, representing the working class, small farmers, and segments of the middle class (Miller 1968; Dybahl 1969; Christiansen 1988).

In the rest of Europe, but particularly among the antagonists in World War I, the social dislocations caused by the war contributed to the breakthrough of democracy. The war and its outcome changed the balance of power in society, strengthening the working class and weakening the upper classes. The ruling class was discredited, particularly in the defeated countries. Labor support was necessary at home for the production effort, and on the front for the first mass-mobilization, mass-conscription war of this scale and duration. Finally, the war economy and mass conscription strengthened the hand of labor in the economy, enabling it to extract concessions for the coming period of peace. One indicator of the change in class power was the swell in labor organization from an average prewar level of 9 percent of the labor force to a postwar peak of 30 percent in the antagonists, which experienced the transition to democracy in this period (1918 or 1919). Organization more than doubled in the two nonparticipants (Sweden and the Netherlands), which experienced the same transition at this time (Stephens 1979:115). In all these countries the working class played a key, usually the key, role in the transition to democracy. But, as

Therborn (1977) notes, the working class was not strong enough alone. It needed allies or unusual conjunctures of events to effect the introduction of democracy. As an indicator of this it could be pointed out that in no case did the working class parties receive electoral majorities, even after the introduction of universal suffrage.

It can be argued that in England, Sweden, Belgium, and the Netherlands, the war only accelerated the introduction of democracy. In each country, the prodemocratic coalition at the party level and the underlying alignment of social forces had formed or was in the process of formation. In most cases, the coalition had been responsible for previous suffrage extension, such as the 1907 reform in Sweden or the 1893 reform in Belgium.

In Sweden (as well as in Belgium and the Netherlands), the agrarian elites were too weak to be a significant political force. The independent peasantry played an important role in the introduction of democracy in Sweden. There, as in Norway and Denmark, it was split on the question of universal suffrage. It was the Liberals, who were based in the urban middle classes, dissenting religions and in small farmers in the north and west, who joined the Social Democrats in the push for suffrage extension. Several decades of political pressure (through strikes, demonstrations, parliamentary obstruction) by the Social Democrats and the trade unions in cooperation with segments of the Liberals resulted in the introduction of male suffrage, but not parliamentary government, in 1907.

Citing the examples of Scandinavia and the north and west of the United States, Rokkan has observed that strong temperance movements only develop in Protestant smallholding societies and are presumably another manifestation of the tendency to rural self-organization in these societies. Dissenting Protestant sects also find fertile grounds in such societies. Although the case of England shows that Protestant sects can develop elsewhere, certainly their strength in Scandinavia as compared to Germany is in part due to the rural social structure. The Lutheran and Anglican churches were important conduits of ruling-class hegemony, and escaping their hold either into the Protestant sects or into the secularism of the labor movement represented an important step in preparing the ground for the development of a democratic counterhegemony.

In Belgium, the Workers' Party, after decades of struggle including six general strikes, found support in the Social Christian wing of the Catholic party, which was based among working-class Catholics (Lorwin 1966; Therborn 1977:12, 25; Fitzmaurice 1983). In the Netherlands, similar divisions in the religious parties and the liberals produced alliance possibilities for the Social Democrats (Daalder 1966:203–11). It is worth underlining that the accounts of the transition in both of the low countries make it clear that the growing importance of the working class in society created the pressures that moved these nonsocialist parties toward a more democratic posture. In part, this pressure was transmitted by workers and artisans already mobilized by self-help societies and trade unions who joined these parties, and, in part, the pressure was a result of the efforts of these parties to compete with the Social Democrats for the loyalties of unmobilized workers.

The establishment view of suffrage extension in the British case argues that the "peculiarities of English history" (variously specified) meant that segments of the British upper classes had settled into a pattern of peaceful political competition by the mid-nineteenth century and this competition extended to competition for working-class votes that resulted in the suffrage extensions of 1867 and 1884. On deeper examination this view appears to be flawed. As Johnson (1976) argues in his critique of Moore's view of the British route, these reforms were in large part a response to working-class pressure beginning at least as early as the Chartist movement, whose main demand was universal suffrage, and extending throughout the nineteenth century. After forcefully suppressing the immediate threat represented by Chartism, the established parties, under the pressure of electoral competition, later responded to the working-class challenge with attempts to co-opt segments of the working class by politically incorporating them. Moreover, Harrison (1965) contends that in the case of the 1867 reform, the immediate agitation by the working-class political organizations, most notably the Reform League, beginning in 1864 and culminating in the Hyde Park demonstration of May 6, 1867, had a significant effect on the 1867 reform. The British case bears some resemblance to the French case, as the transition to democracy was in part a delayed response to earlier working-class agitation that predated the formation of late nineteenth-century social democratic parties.

Nonetheless, it is peculiar that the final political initiation of the reforms came from upper class–led parties without a strong working-class base. Part of the explanation of this lies in the late development of the Labour party itself. The Liberals and the Tories were only willing to extend the right to vote to workers because they hoped to benefit from the votes of the newly enfranchised workers. Had a substantial Labour party already commanded the loyalty of workers, the threat perceived by the elites certainly would have made the established parties more reluctant to make such a move. If this argument is correct, it also suggests that the absence of a significant socialist working-class party in

France in the late 1860s and 1870s may have contributed to the willingness of significant sections of the bourgeoisie to support parliamentary government based on universal male suffrage. The support of the Swiss industrial bourgeoisie for democracy, which occurred under conditions of little working-class organization, further reinforces this generalization.

Finally, the reform of 1918 in Britain, which established male suffrage and eliminated all but minor provisions for multiple voting, was the culmination of the Labour–Liberal cooperation that led to the rise of the Labour party. No one would deny the important role of the working class in this reform.

This survey leaves us with our breakdown countries as cases where the war may have influenced more than the timing of the introduction of democracy. But before moving on to them, we should take stock of what can be learned from the development of democracy in Europe as we have outlined it. One obvious lesson, stressed by Therborn (1977), is the important role played by the working class, that is, by its organizational representatives, the trade unions and the socialist parties. In the Swiss, French, and British cases, one can add the role of artisan agitation and early craft unions and, in Britain, Chartism. Workers also played a role in the confessional parties in the Netherlands and Belgium, in pressing those parties toward a more democratic posture. The rapid development of industrial capitalism in the second half of the nineteenth century stimulated working-class organization that, first gradually and then, with the war and its outcome, decisively changed the balance of class power in all these countries; indeed, it changed the balance of class power in the entire core of the world capitalist system. The change in the underlying class structure as indicated by labor force figures is significant enough: Between 1870 and 1910, the nonagricultural work force grew in these countries by one-third to one-half to an average of 61 percent. The change at the level of class formation and class organization was even more significant: In no country in 1870 were the socialists a significant mass-based party, and the trade unions organized a minuscule proportion of the labor force: By the eve of World War I, the parties affiliated with the Second International garnered an average of 26 percent of the vote (despite suffrage restrictions in a number of countries) and the trade unions organized an average of 11 percent of the nonagricultural labor force. In the immediate postwar elections, the socialists' electoral share increased to an average of 32 percent while trade union organization grew spectacularly, increasing two and a half fold. The organized working class was also the most consistently prodemocratic force in the period under consideration: At the onset of World War I, European labor movements, all members of the Second International, had converged on an ideology that placed the achievement of universal suffrage and parliamentary government at the center of their immediate program (Zolberg 1986).

This interpretation supports our theory and turns on their head Lipset (1960) and all the cross-national studies that followed; the working class, not the middle class, was the driving force behind democracy. It also contradicts Moore, most Marxist analysts, and many liberal social scientists (e.g., Dahrendorf 1967) who argue that the primary source of democratic impulses was the bourgeoisie. However, Therborn's (1977) focus on the last reforms in the process of democratization leads to an exaggeration of the role of the working class. First, in the two agrarian democracy cases (Switzerland and Norway), the role of the working class was secondary even in the final push to democracy. Second, in other cases, not only did the working class need allies in the final push, in earlier democratic reforms, multiclass alliances were responsible for the success of the reform (France, Britain, Denmark, Sweden, and Belgium).

As the authoritarian cases demonstrate, however, none of these other social classes was as consistently prodemocratic, both across countries and through time, as the working class.[4] The urban middle class and/or segments of the peasantry provided the mass base for authoritarianism in the breakdown cases. The bourgeoisie, whose role in the introduction of democracy has been emphasized in so many accounts, from Marxist to liberal, played a positive role in only three cases: Switzerland, Britain, and France. Moreover, in Britain and France it was only segments of the class that cooperated in the push for democracy, and then only after earlier histories of popular agitation for democracy and bourgeois resistance to it. In all of the others, the bourgeoisie was one of the centers of resistance to working-class political incorporation. It did make an indirect contribution to the outcome, however. In the cases discussed so far, the bourgeoisie sought entry into the corridors of power and in all cases, except for Denmark and Sweden, it supported the drive for parliamentary government. Bourgeois political forces established parliamentary government with property, tax, or income qualifications for voting – that is, democracy for the propertied – a true "bourgeois democracy" in contrast to the bourgeois democracy of Leninist Marxism. This system then was opened up by successive organized groups demanding entry into the system: the peasantry, the middle class, and finally the working class. There is a certain amount of truth to the extremely crude interpretation that each group worked for its own incorporation and was ambivalent about further extensions of democracy. The positive contributions of the bourgeoisie were to push for the introduction of parliamentary government and then to capitulate to pressures for further reforms rather than risk civil war.

As we saw, the working class needed allies; its power alone was insufficient. At this point we can turn to Moore's thesis on the characteristics of the authoritarian path for the social and historical conditions that foreclosed or created the possibilities for alliances. In the cases of coalitions of the landed upper classes, the state, and the bourgeoisie, no alliance strong enough to overcome their opposition could be constructed. It was only the change in the balance of class power caused by the war that allowed for the democratic breakthrough. But, as Maier (1975) argues in his study of Germany, France, and Italy, this surge in the strength of labor and the political left was quickly, though not completely, rolled back. A quick glance at union membership and voting statistics indicates that this was a general European pattern. In the cases where this surge of working-class strength was the essential ingredient in the transition to democracy, the working class and its allies (where it had any) were unable to maintain democracy when a new conjuncture presented new problems (e.g., depression, worker or peasant militance) and new alliance possibilities for the upper classes moved the bourgeoisie and the landlords from passive to active opposition to the democratic regime.

In each of the four authoritarian cases, the landlord–state–bourgeois coalition was crucially implicated in (1) the weakness of the push toward democracy outside of the working-class movement before World War I and (2) the events that led to the demise of democracy in the interwar period. In Italy and Spain, direct intervention by landlords to protect traditional methods of labor control played a pivotal role in the eclipse of democracy in the interwar period. In Germany and Austria, the social democratic parties were the only consistent supporters of full democracy in the prewar period. The historical experience of these two countries shows the weakness of the pluralist view of the relationship of the strength of civil society (or "secondary groups") to democracy. Both countries were relatively advanced societies, and historical research has shown that the organizational life in both was very strong. However, middle-class organizations in them became conduits for ruling-class ideologies. In Austria, it was primarily the network of organizations connected to the Christian Social party that helped make authoritarianism popular. In Imperial Germany, the landed upper classes and heavy industry conducted separate efforts, seen most clearly in the activities of the Agrarian League and the Naval League, to make militarism and authoritarianism popular. As Allen's (1984) in-depth study of a German

town shows, these efforts were successful and created enduring ideologies in the middle classes that made them susceptible to the appeals of
the Nazis in the interwar period. By contrast, the working class–social
democratic subcultures in both Austria and Germany insulated their
followers from ruling-class ideology, and relatively few workers supported the mass authoritarian movements in these societies. Thus, it is
not the density of civil society per se that is important for the development of democracy but, rather, its articulation to the class structure.

In sum, the comparative historical analysis of European political
development confirms our contention that the correlation between economic development and democracy found in the quantitative cross-
national studies is more accurately explained by our political economy
approach than by modernization theory. My discussion of religion and
civil society in Scandinavia contains the seeds of a similar alternative
explanation for the correlation between Protestantism and democracy
found in the quantitative studies. In these studies, this correlation is also
explained by concepts and relationships derived from structural-
functionalism. Again, Lipset's early essay is the source of this explanation of the correlation. He contends that "Protestantism's emphasis on
individual responsibility furthered the emergence of democratic values
in these countries" (Lipset 1960:57), an assertion cited by Bollen and
Jackman (1985a:31).

The Scandinavian cases point in another direction: What was important about the dissenting religions was not the values they promoted but
the sectarian organization; that is, they were autonomous organized
communities whose development strengthened civil society. Furthermore, they were organized in opposition to the state church and the
state so their existence insulated their members from ruling-class hegemony. State churches, Lutheran and Anglican as well as Catholic, were
conduits for ruling-class hegemony. The parties developed by these
state church–class–state coalitions (Lipset and Rokkan 1967) were
opponents of democracy. Parties with strong bases in dissenting sects
were always more liberal, supporting civil liberties and suffrage expansion and, in some cases, full democracy. Thus, we argue that the critical
distinction here is state church versus sect, not Protestantism versus
others as indicated by the cross-national analyses.

There is no question that doctrine does reinforce the political tendencies of churches and sects. Lutheranism shares with Catholicism authoritarian features: Although members are encouraged to read the Bible,
the church retains a monopoly on the authoritative interpretation of it.
Luther also strongly emphasized obedience to political authority (Sanders 1964). However, comparative historical evidence from the Euro-

pean cases indicates it was the political situation of the church that was crucial in determining the political posture of the party allied with it: Where the church was not allied with the state and was also a minority, the allied political party (e.g., the German Zentrum) was a relatively democratic force and the church's subculture did insulate its followers from authoritarian ruling-class hegemony.

Central America and the Caribbean

The development and survival of political democracy in the English-speaking Caribbean make that group of countries remarkable in comparison to other countries at similar stages of socioeconomic development. By contrast, the Central American countries conform to the norm of authoritarianism at their level of development, but the intensity of social strife and the strength of revolutionary challenges as well as of repression make them exceptional also. This section attempts to explain the emergence of both types of regimes through comparative historical analysis. I compare the ex-British West Indies to the ex-Spanish plantation economies in the region in order to examine what characteristics of the political economies and histories of these two groups appear to be connected with the markedly different political destinies of the two groups of countries. In the process, I develop an alternative interpretation of the effect of British colonialism on democracy to the diffusionist interpretation offered in the current literature and cited in the statistical studies. The section concludes with a brief analysis of Guyanese developments, both to explain why this country deviates from the British West Indian pattern and to suggest an alternative interpretation to the structural functionalist one for the ethnic diversity and democracy correlation.

The West Indies and Central America contrasted

Some additional comments on the arguments concerning the relationship between British colonialism and democracy prevalent in the literature are in order before we develop our analysis. The quantitative studies hardly do more than mention the diffusionist argument in passing, but several other recent studies (Huntington 1984; Weiner 1987; Diamond 1989) argue that British colonialism left a legacy favorable for democracy because it provided for a period of tutelary democracy before independence. The evidence offered by Weiner (1987:20) is that "every country with a population of at least 1 million (and almost all the smaller countries as well) that has emerged from colonial rule since

World War II and has had a continuous democratic experience is a former British colony." His explanation points to the enduring legacy of the establishment by the British colonial authorities of bureaucratic structures and the rule of law, and of representative institutions and periodic elections. Because of their socialization in these institutions, local elites internalized the norms of democratic procedure and developed organizational and other political leadership skills.

Caribbean and Central American countries share some socioeconomic characteristics that cross-national statistical studies have shown to be inimical to democracy. As already pointed out, their levels of development in 1970 were too low to be favorable for democracy. Their economies were traditionally plantation economies, with some mining and industrialization, and tourism in the Caribbean, superimposed in the post–World War II period. This means that the societies were traditionally very hierarchical and the economies highly dependent on foreign trade and foreign investment. Thus, low economic development, high inequality, rapid social change, and the extremely high dependence on U.S. interests all militated against the installation and consolidation of democratic regimes in the region.

Not surprisingly, then, all but two of the Spanish-speaking countries in the Caribbean basin were ruled by authoritarian regimes in the sixties and seventies, and the seventies saw increasingly violent confrontations between these regimes and reformist or revolutionary forces. The exceptions were Costa Rica and, from 1978 on, the Dominican Republic. In contrast, all but two of the English-speaking Caribbean countries had democratic regimes from the time of their independence in the 1960s throughout the 1970s. Guyana and Grenada were the exceptions. The question is why democracy could flourish in some countries, whereas in others economic elites and military establishments resorted to increasingly violent repression not only of revolutionary movements but of democratic reformist forces as well.

The antecedents of the different situations of the West Indies and Central America in the 1960s and 1970s lie in the developments in the 1930s. The depression brought great disruptions to the extremely export-dependent societies in the region. In response to decreasing real wages and increasing unemployment, attempts at labor organization and labor protests emerged in all societies. The reactions of the economic elites to these protests and organizing attempts were universally negative, but the reaction of the state varied widely. Here, British colonialism was important, insofar as it constituted an alternative to landlord or military control of the state and thus the use of the coercive forces of the state to repress the protests as well as the emerging labor unions and allied political parties. Consequently, the 1930s marked the beginning of organized political life and opened the way for the subsequent consolidation of civil society in the Caribbean, whereas in Central America they set the precedent for the primacy of the coercive apparatus of the state and for state control over, and repression of, civil society, exercised either by landowner–military coalitions or by the military alone. Costa Rica, the deviant case in Central America, resembled the Caribbean insofar as the large landowners were not in firm control of the state apparatus and consequently unions and political parties were allowed to consolidate their organizations.

To explain why the economic elites or the military controlled the state in Central American countries and the Dominican Republic in the 1930s and used this control to squash emerging social forces, two interdependent sets of factors are crucial, namely, the economic strength of the large landowners and their relations with the state, and the extent of U.S. economic presence and direct political intervention. To underline the theoretical point that the strength of the landed class is not the only critical variable but, rather, that the role of the state and foreign forces has to be considered, one can distinguish two basic types of class–state constellations in Central America in the first three decades of this century (or three types, if one takes Costa Rican exceptionalism into account). In one type, exemplified by El Salvador and Guatemala, the large landowners were very prosperous, having established commercial and financial holdings as well (El Salvador), or having merged with originally merchant elites (Guatemala). They formed an oligarchy in the true sense of the word, controlling the state directly or via military officers. In the other type, exemplified by Honduras, Nicaragua, and the Dominican Republic, the landowners were not as prosperous because historically the territories had been sparsely populated, had suffered many military invasions, and, particularly in Nicaragua, had seen fierce fights among different factions of landowners. Also, foreign capital had a strong presence, dominating the financial system and, in Honduras, the crucial export sector, bananas. Thus, the landowners as a group were not in control of the state; rather, military strongmen, sometimes in alliance with an elite faction, exercised political power. Moreover, these three countries were the object of repeated U.S. military intervention and occupation in the first third of the twentieth century, which further impeded the establishment of civilian control over the state apparatus. The U.S. legacy in Nicaragua and the Dominican Republic was a U.S.-trained and -equipped security force that was to perform the function of keeping peace and order after the withdrawal of U.S. troops. In both cases, these forces were used by their commanders as stepping stones to the establishment of dictatorial rule and economic fortunes for their families.

In the early 1930s, growing unemployment and falling real incomes caused popular protests and attempts at labor organization in all the Central American countries. The response was repression of varying intensity and the establishment or consolidation of dictatorial regimes. Under the dictators of the thirties and their successors in the forties and fifties, activities of unions and political parties were heavily restricted and their growth was stifled. The degree of repressiveness of the governments varied between countries and over time, but even where parties and unions were allowed to exist, they were not able to acquire any significant organizational strength and socioeconomic or political influence. Organizations of subordinate classes did not develop as significant counterweights to the economic domination of the large domestic landowners and the foreign corporations, nor did civil society develop as a significant counterweight to the state. On the contrary, the imbalance between state and civil society was aggravated after World War II, as the state apparatus, particularly its coercive arm, was strengthened through U.S. military aid. As a consequence, the military developed the capacity for increasingly autonomous political action.

The real exception to the pattern prevailing in Central America was Costa Rica. The crucial factors setting it apart, which had their roots in colonial times, were the relative weakness of the oligarchy and the relative strength of the rural middle class. For this reason, by the time the depression generated significant popular protests, the large landowners were no longer in full control of the state apparatus, nor could they successfully appeal to the military to reestablish such control. Rather, popular organization continued to grow. The National Republican party (PRN), a moderately reformist party, grew in strength in the 1930s, partly by presenting itself as the more moderate alternative to the communists, and it won the elections in 1936, 1940, and 1944. Reformist but increasingly corrupt, the PRN government was thrown out by a successful rebellion led by Jose Figueres. The rebellion was carried out in the name of democracy, and thus did not constitute a radical break with previous political institutions. Arguably the most important outcome of the civil war for the survival of democracy in the longer run was the dismantling of the army by Figueres. In sum, Costa Rica entered the period of rapid transformation in the sixties and seventies with a comparatively well-consolidated labor movement, party system, and political institutions, and without a largely autonomous repressive arm of the state.

In the British Caribbean, the general pattern of state–society relations at the onset of the 1930s was direct colonial (crown colony) rule over a weakly articulated civil society. Local assemblies, usually with a mix of appointed and elected members, and with property and/or income and literacy qualifications for the franchise, continued to exist, but their powers were subject to those of the governor. Between 1934 and 1938, a wave of labor rebellions swept the Caribbean. From this unrest emerged a number of labor and political leaders, mostly of middle-class origin, who played crucial roles in the formation of unions and allied political parties. Although security forces, reinforced by British troops, were deployed to put down mass demonstrations and riots, the repression did not nearly approach the levels prevalent in Central America. Rather, the colonial government left unions intact and allowed for the formation of new political parties in the aftermath of the disturbances. The parties that emerged in alliance with trade unions out of this conjuncture became for the most part the driving forces in the nationalist movement, pushing for democratic rule and increased local autonomy.

The critical feature that prevented the formation of the Moorian coalition of landlords, state, and bourgeoisie in the British West Indies was that the local elites did not control the state apparatus. It was in the hands of the imperial power. This is not to argue that planter interests were not overwhelmingly dominant under crown colony rule as well as in the earlier periods of greater (upper class) self-government (e.g., see Lewis 1968; Lutchman 1974; Hoyos 1978). There is no question, however, that beginning at least with emancipation in the 1830s, the imperial power was a brake on the exploitative aims of the planter class.

This raises the question, of course, of why the British colonial administration responded comparatively mildly to the labor rebellions and why it was willing to make political concessions thereafter. One core element of our argument is that the relative balance of class power within Britain was a very important factor determining the action of the British state and thus colonial policy. The industrial capital interests that were the dominant force in Britain in the last half of the nineteenth century did not require the kind of labor repression that plantation agriculture did. Also, the rising strength of the labor movement, first organizationally in the trade unions and then politically, decisively changed the balance of class power in the country and resulted first in the transition to democracy (1918) and then in extensive social reform (see above and Stephens 1979).

The British had already acted as a brake on West Indian planters' interests in the nineteenth century. The rise of Labour and the introduction of democracy made themselves felt both in changing the general political climate that helped to legitimate the struggles for democracy and self-rule in the colonies and also in specific actions of the government. Most important, it is widely conceded that the Labour government of 1945–51 was critical in taking major steps toward democracy and decolonization in the West Indies and elsewhere (Ryan 1972:71; Spinner 1984:25; Hintzen 1989:31).

We can identify some similarities to, and differences from, the analysis of the emergence of democracy in South America and Europe. First, the planters, like the large landowners engaged in labor-intensive agriculture in South America and Europe, were strongly opposed to any concessions to the subordinate classes. Second, neither was the bourgeoisie a proponent of democracy and independence. Moskos's (1967:42) interviews with a systematic sample of West Indian leaders in 1961–2 found that 94 percent of businessmen opposed independence.

The driving force behind democratization and decolonization was an alliance of the working class and the middle classes. This cross-class coalition usually took the form of a party–trade union alliance similar to that in northern European social democracy, but it had greater middle-class support and was more heavily middle class in its leadership than in Europe.[5] Most of these alliances adopted Fabian socialist principles in their early years, but by the 1950s the more socialist (as opposed to welfarist) elements were all but abandoned. Thus, these parties constituted no immediate threat to either the domestic economic elites or foreign capital, neither one of which openly and actively opposed democratization and independence at that point. Although historical evidence, and the interviews already referred to, indicates strong reservations on the part of businessmen about seeing political power pass to local democratic governments, the economic elites were isolated on this issue and, most important, could not enlist any allies in the state apparatus to block progress in this direction. The telling exception is Guyana, where the radical nature of the program of the dominant nationalist party galvanized the domestic economic elites, foreign capital, the U.S. government, and the British colonial authorities into an alliance that undermined the emergence of democratic self-government. In sum, then, one can say both the strength of working- and middle-class organization in unions and political parties and the moderation of these organizations favored completion of the process of constitutional decolonization and consolidation of democratic rule.

In the 1960s and 1970s, Central America and the Caribbean underwent similar spurts of economic growth, leading to economic and social diversification. Because growth in both areas was taking place under dependent capitalism, it increased inequality and unemployment in rural and urban areas, although the severity of rural dislocation varied.

The political reactions to these economic developments were widely different, however. In the Caribbean, newly emerging groups were for the most part absorbed into the party–union blocs. Except in Guyana and Grenada, democracy survived, even where economic and political conflict put it under heavy strain, as in Jamaica in the seventies. In Central America, in contrast, newly emerging groups met with repression of varying intensity. The results of this ranged from successful to stalemated revolution and military-dominated highly restricted democracy; the achievement of full democracy became ever more remote.

In the 1960s, both import substitution industrialization and export agriculture grew considerably in Central America. Spurred by the Central American Common Market, U.S. private investment and U.S. aid for the military and infrastructure, production and construction increased. These processes created the conditions for growing middle- and working-class organization, and they also increased rural unrest as land concentration deprived more and more families of their traditional subsistence. However, the repeated stifling of unions and political parties through internal oligarchic–military alliances or external intervention in the previous decades, together with massive U.S. military aid, had left the societies with an extreme imbalance between the organizational power of the middle and lower classes on the one hand and the economic power of elites and the repressive power of the state apparatus on the other hand. Accordingly, channels for the peaceful expression of discontent resulting from dislocation were largely ineffective, and efforts to make them more effective and change the power imbalance by strengthening popular organization met with continued repression.

Costa Rica stands in stark contrast to the other Central American cases. The repressive apparatus of the state was emasculated and the economic power of the elites was to some extent counterbalanced by the organizational power of the middle and working classes. The economic growth of the sixties provided resources for further expansion of the social welfare system and public sector employment. The economic and social inclusion of the majority of the population supported their political inclusion and thus helped strengthen democratic institutions.

The situation in the Caribbean islands after independence resembled the Costa Rican one with respect to the repressive apparatus; in other words, the military was of minimal strength. The organizational base of the middle and working classes in the party–union complexes was for the most part even stronger than in Costa Rica. Progress in national insurance systems, education, and health services similarly contributed to popular loyalty to the parties and the democratic system of government. Elites had learned before independence to work with and through the established parties, using financial contributions and control over print media as major sources of leverage. Rapid economic growth also led to further social diversification, but the emerging forces were for the most part absorbed by existing unions or integrated into the political parties through patronage.

A comment on Grenada, one of the two West Indian countries that did turn to authoritarianism, is in order because it qualifies the apparently universally positive role working-class forces play in the development of democracy. Eric Gairy, who established a personalistic dictatorship on the tiny island by the mid-1970s, rose to power as a charismatic trade-union leader, and it was on the basis of the votes of the working class and peasantry that he originally came to office. The difference between Grenada and the other countries examined here lies in the ideology of persons or forces that organized the labor movement. The organizational force of the working class in each case was harnessed in the service of the movement (or persons) who first succeeded in organizing it and advancing its material demands. Given the structural position of the working class in authoritarian capitalist societies, it is not surprising that these movements most often have democratic ideologies, since political democracy will ensure the freedom of workers to organize and advance their demands and may even give the workers' movement a share of political power. The example of Grenada, however, shows that workers can develop loyalties to authoritarian movements if they advance workers' material interests. Moreover, Peronism in Argentina demonstrates that one is not simply dealing with an idiosyncrasy of a microsociety here. These ideologies, socially constructed and constituted at a particular historical moment, last for generations.

In sum, the analysis of the Caribbean and Central America confirms the central finding of the European study on the relationship of capitalist development to democracy: Capitalist development is related to democracy because it creates subordinate groups that organize and demand political inclusion. As in the European cases, where democracy was successfully installed (the West Indies and Costa Rica), it was the work of middle-class–working-class coalitions. In all cases, the bourgeoisie opposed democracy before its installation. Again, as in Europe, large landlords were yet more consistent and intense in their opposition to democracy.

However, in contrast to Europe, the existence of a significant large landholding class engaged in labor repressive agriculture was not sufficient to block the development of democracy or lead to a breakdown of democracy once it was established. The large landed class or allies in the military had to control the state in order to set political development on an authoritarian course. This is where British colonialism made a crucial contribution to the development of democracy. By responding to the 1930s labor rebellion with political reform and tolerance of popular organization instead of the repression desired by the plantocracy, the colonial government set the conditions for the gradual transition to democracy based on the growing strength of the working and middle classes in the form of labor unions and political parties.

Two other related contrasts to the European cases present themselves. First, transnational structures of power were more important in this region populated by small states in the backyard of a single great power. Intervention by the United States contributed to the development of authoritarianism primarily by strengthening domestic militaries but also by direct intervention to overthrow or undermine democratic governments. In only one case, the Dominican Republic in 1978, did the United States make a pivotal positive contribution to the development of democracy, and there it was simply undoing what it had done with the invasion thirteen years before. Second, in large part because of external support from transnational actors, the state or, more specifically, the military played a larger role in the Central American countries than it did in Europe.

Ethnic diversity and democracy: the case of Guyana

Democracy did not survive the first postindependence decade in all countries in the English-speaking Caribbean. By the late 1970s, the electoral process in Guyana was sufficiently corrupted that it is fair to say it was impossible for the opposition to win an election and displace the government. Moreover, opposition parties, unions, and newspapers were subject to considerable harassment.

Cross-national statistical research has shown that ethnic diversity is negatively related to democracy. Guyana fits this generalization, as virtually all observers of Guyana agree that the ethnic division between East Indians and Africans contributed to the development of authoritarianism in that country. But the existence of this ethnic cleavage was hardly a sufficient cause, as Trinidad demonstrates.

There are strong similarities in the class–ethnic divisions in Trinidad and Guyana. With emancipation, the African[6] population left the sugar estates as soon as possible and the planters brought in East Indian indentured servants to work the fields. Sugar workers in both countries are still overwhelmingly East Indian. Increasingly, Africans left not only the plantations but rural life altogether and the East Indian population became the dominant group in the peasantry (rice in Guyana; cocoa, cane, and market gardening in Trinidad). Owing to discrimination in employment, the upwardly mobile East Indians gravitated to the free professions and small business. Africans dominated the urban working-class occupations, mining (Guyana), oil fields (Trinidad), and the civil service, especially the police. Thus, the two racial–ethnic groups are not only occupationally but also geographically segregated, which helps preserve the separate cultures and impedes social mixing. The upper classes in both countries were drawn from various European and Middle Eastern nationalities. By the time of the postwar events of concern here, the independent sugar plantocracy was a thing of the past and sugar production was dominated by multinational corporations.

Hintzen (1989:3) certainly points to the core of the answer to why democracy collapsed in Guyana when he observes that the People's National Congress (PNC) "was brought to power by relying not only upon mobilization of the black and mixed masses but, perhaps more importantly, upon the fact of black domination and preeminence in the colonial and post-colonial state bureaucracy including its armed branches." What differentiated Guyana from Trinidad was that the ethnic group dominating the state was a minority or fast becoming one in Guyana, whereas it was a substantial majority in Trinidad.[7] In addition, one needs to add the very important role of the Cold War and the actions of the two relevant core capitalist powers without which the PNC's initial ascent to state power might not have been possible.

The anticolonial movement in Guyana split into two parties in the late 1950s: the People's Progressive Party (PPP), which was East Indian based and led by the Marxist–Leninist Cheddi Jagan, and the PNC, which was African based and led by Forbes Burnham.[8] The PPP won the elections of 1957 and 1961, both with a minority of votes owing to the disunity of the opposition (in 1961, 43 percent of the vote and twenty of thirty-five seats to the PNC's 41 percent and eleven seats, with the conservative United Force taking the remaining seats). The policies of the Jagan governments disproportionately benefited East Indians as they heavily favored agriculture over urban development, helped small to medium business (and thus East Indians) at the expense of large business, recruited and promoted East Indians in civil service jobs, and passed educational reforms benefiting East Indian teachers and children (Spinner 1984:74–81; Despres 1967:232–52; Hintzen 1989:49–50).

The beginning of the end of the Jagan government (and, retrospectively, Guyanese democracy) came with a general strike in February 1962, launched by government employees and supported by the PNC and the UF. A mass demonstration by the government's opponents degenerated into a riot, arson, and looting of East Indian businesses.

The police and paramilitary units looked on and Jagan was forced to rely on the intervention of British troops to quiet the situation. Two years of disorder followed, the high point being an 80 day general strike, covertly financed by the CIA and AFL-CIO. In the end, the PPP was forced to accept the introduction of proportional representation, a solution favored by the PNC, the UF, and Washington. Thus, the capitulation was forced by a coalition of the domestic upper and middle classes, the black urban lower classes, the state apparatus, and metropolitan interests.

In 1964, the Guyanese people participated in the last honest election in the country's history. The PNC polled 41 percent and the UF 12 percent, and these two parties formed a government that took Guyana into independence in 1966. Through judicious use of patronage, the PNC managed to get enough parliamentary crossovers to dispense with the coalition. The PNC then moved to ensure their victory in the 1968 election through massive fraud. Once in power, Burnham greatly increased the size of the security forces. Thus, when the economy began to deteriorate badly in the middle and late 1970s and the source of patronage began to dry up, the government came increasingly to rely on coercion and shows of force to control the country.

This brief historical overview makes it clear that more than ethnic conflict and lack of societal consensus were necessary components of the breakdown of Guyanese democracy. The alliance with the domestic upper classes and the metropolitan powers was essential for first placing the PNC in power, given the minority position of its race and class base. The PNC then established authoritarian rule, a move that would have been impossible without an initially strong base in the security forces, and subsequently consolidated it by expanding the security forces and ensuring their loyalty. Thus, the way in which ethnic divisions were articulated in the state made the state's coercive arm an instrument of political elites representing one of the ethnic groups in its quest for state power. The quest for power of these elites, who initially lacked a decisive power base of their own because their ethnic group was a minority and composed of subordinate classes, was successful because of support from external forces and domestic economic elites.

Conclusion

Summary of findings

The centrality of class power to the process of democratization was repeatedly confirmed in the comparative studies presented here as well

as those on other advanced capitalist societies and Latin America included in the larger study. The organized working class appeared as a
key actor in the development of full democracy almost everywhere, the
only exception being the few cases of agrarian democracy in some of the
smallholding countries. In most cases, organized workers played an
important role in earlier extensions of political inclusion as well.

How the working class affected events was highly variable. Even in
Europe, where the main effect of working-class organization came in the
form of the parties of the Second International and affiliated unions, it
also expressed itself through independent artisanal agitation, delayed
responses to defeated movements, and pressure from the working-class
wings of confessional and liberal parties. In the West Indies, working-
class pressure expressed itself first in the form of the labor rebellions of
the 1930s that led the colonial authorities to introduce some measure of
self-government, and then in the form of unions and multiclass parties.
In Latin America, unions and parties of varying ideological persuasions
and with at least some base in the working class were essential parts of
alliances that introduced full democracy. In all regions, however, pressure from the organized working class alone was insufficient to bring
about the introduction of democracy; the working class needed allies.

Large landlords, particularly those who depended on a large supply of
cheap labor, consistently emerged as the most antidemocratic force in
the comparative studies. If an economically significant class of labor-
dependent landlords had control or, at least, very significant influence
on the state in a given period, the state resisted demands for the
expansion of democratic rights. When ongoing capitalist development,
often in conjunction with immediate political or economic crises, stimulated a surge in the demands of the masses for political inclusion and
economic amelioration, the state responded – immediately or at a later
point, when the crisis had subsided – with political exclusion and repression. This key element of Moore's pioneering study has borne the test of
repeated examination across the countries studied.

The orthodox Marxist and liberal social science view of the role of the
bourgeoisie as the primary agent of democracy has not stood up under
scrutiny. Though clearly not as antidemocratic as landlords, capitalists
and the parties they primarily supported rarely pressed for the introduction of full democracy. Our comparative analyses uncovered cases in
which the bourgeoisie, in contrast to labor-dependent landed upper
classes, did support a political arrangement that entailed significant
extensions of suffrage to the lower classes. Nineteenth-century suffrage
reforms in Switzerland, Britain, and France spring to mind as examples.
It is important to note that in these cases the threat posed by the
working class was small because of the absence of socialist organization

in the class. A much more frequent contribution of the bourgeoisie to democracy has been to accommodate to it and even support it once it is established. Yet this is hardly a universal response: All of our comparative studies were riddled with examples of the bourgeoisie supporting the termination of democratic regimes once new conditions increased its motivation to do so or presented it with allies in such a project.

The contrasting posture of the landed upper class and the working class contains the core of our argument as to why capitalist development and democracy are related: Capitalist development weakens the landed upper class and strengthens the working class as well as other subordinate classes. The respective positions of the bourgeoisie and the working class show that capitalism creates democratic pressures in spite of capitalists, not because of them. Democracy was the outcome of the contradictory nature of capitalist development, which, of necessity, created subordinate classes, particularly the working class, with the capacity for self-organization. Capitalism brings the subordinate class or classes together in factories and cities where members of those classes can associate and organize more easily; it improves the means of communication and transportation facilitating nationwide organization; in these and other ways it strengthens civil society and facilitates subordinate class organization. Although the working class has not proved to be the gravedigger of capitalism, it has frequently been capable of successfully demanding its own political incorporation and an accommodation of at least some of its substantive interests. No other subordinate class in history has been able to do so on anywhere near the same scale. As Przeworski (1985, 1988) has frequently argued, democratic capitalism rests on a class compromise between labor and capital in which the interests of both sides are to varying extents accommodated.

The comparative studies showed that a key source of variability across countries at a given level of development was the posture of the middle classes. Indeed, it can be said that because the working class nowhere was strong enough to push through democracy alone, the middle classes assumed a pivotal role in the development of democracy. Their role was ambiguous, however: It varied owing to different relations with the dominant classes as well as to variations in the middle classes' own interests. Moreover, because of their intermediate position in the class structure and their internal heterogeneity, the interests of the middle classes were subject to a greater variety of social interpretation and construction. For this reason, even the urban middle classes were much more likely to come under the influence of dominant classes, sometimes supporting political movements that opposed their objective interests, by almost any interpretation of what those interests were.

The influence of the dominant classes on the politics of rural middle classes, poor peasants, and the agricultural proletariat was, in general, even greater than in the case of the urban middle classes. Although peasants and rural workers shared an interest in democracy with the urban proletariat, they acted much less frequently in support of it, in part because they followed the lead of large landlords and in part because they had much greater difficulty organizing themselves. However, to assert that the rural lower and middle classes were always backward, always on the receiving end of history, or always manipulated by other actors is a distortion of history. Our comparative studies demonstrated that in predominantly smallholding countries (e.g., the small European countries), family farmers, and in some cases poor peasants, acted as an independent, usually self-organized force and largely in favor of democracy. In the Caribbean and Central America, the plantation proletariat also organized and usually weighed in as a democratic force.

In contrast to the relative consistency of class behavior, we found systematic variation in the role of the state and international constellations of power across the regions studied. In the segment presented in this essay, the effects of both factors were most striking in the Caribbean region. Moreover, they were interrelated. In the British West Indies, the dominant class did not control the state because the islands were still under colonial rule, and this turned out to have favorable consequences for the development of democracy. By contrast, in Central America, direct intervention or financial and technical support for the military by the United States had the result of building up or strengthening the coercive arm of the local states. In some instances, this provided local oligarchies with powerful allies to repress popular forces; in others, particularly after the 1950s, it made the military relatively autonomous from civil societies and capable of imposing authoritarian rule on the countries.

To return to the theme of alternative explanations for the findings of cross-national statistical studies introduced at the outset of this essay, I have argued that the relationship between capitalist development and democracy can be better explained in a political economy than in a functionalist theoretical framework. The evidence presented does support the political economy explanation. Capitalist development is associated with the rise of democracy in large part because it is associated with a transformation of the class structure strengthening the working class, as measured by both its relative size and its degree of organization, and weakening the landed upper class. This contradicts the functionalist interpretations provided by the authors of the cross-national studies.

I have also presented some evidence here on three other factors that have been shown to correlate consistently with political democracy: Protestantism, the British colonial experience, and the absence of ethnic diversity. In each case, my interpretation stands in contrast to the structural-functional interpretation provided by statistical analysts.

My analysis of Protestantism indicates that the statistical relationship found in the cross-national studies is based on an improper operationalization of the independent variable. It was not Protestantism but, rather, Protestant sectarianism that encouraged the development of democracy. The Protestant sects, which were autonomous groups formed, in most cases, in opposition to state churches, strengthened civil society, whereas the state churches were conduits for ruling-class hegemony.

As we have seen, the dominant theme in the literature on the pro-democratic effects of British colonialism is the role of "indirect rule," which supposedly tutored the indigenous elites in the exercise of power and left them better prepared for independence. By contrast, the experience of the Caribbean indicates that the main contribution of the British to democracy was to refuse to align with the colonial plantocracy and to concede reforms when local pressures were great enough to make it a choice between reform or escalation of disorder in the colony. One can certainly argue that there was an element of political learning in the parliamentary game in the postwar transition to democratic self-government, but a comparative perspective suggests that the growth of civil society and the lack of a significant coercive apparatus were the greater contributions to democracy.

The functionalist view of why ethnic divisions contribute to the development of authoritarianism is that they undermine social integration and societal consensus. The Guyanese case demonstrates that this perspective is not without its merits, but it is hardly the whole story. Nor is the hypothesis that democracy is compatible with oppression of ethnic minorities by majorities (e.g., the United States and Northern Ireland) but not vice versa (South Africa). The Guyanese case (and the contrast to Trinidad) argues that one must examine the entire interrelationship among ethnic divisions, the class structure, and the state to understand the political consequences of the ethnic divide.

Reflections

What relation has formal democracy to the ideal of political equality? What is its relation to substantive social justice, to the improvement of the conditions of life for those that are socially and economically disadvantaged? Some findings of our study give these questions particular urgency, since they indicate that the development or stabilization of democracy was facilitated by keeping such issues off the agenda or, where they were on the agenda, from becoming policy. This essay has shown that if working-class parties raised radical demands, this created a reaction among the propertied classes that delayed or prevented the development of democracy or led to its termination. In the Latin American portion of the broader study (Rueschemeyer, Stephens, and Stephens, 1992: chap. 5), we found that the existence of strong right-wing parties and other political mechanisms that serve to protect elite interests facilitated the development and stabilization of democracy. This could be taken as evidence to support the Leninist position: Formal democracy is a sham; it does not give the lower classes political influence (not to speak of political equality) and thus does not improve their material condition.

I think this is a misreading of the historical evidence. Although I do not believe that the ideal of democracy in the sense of complete political equality will ever be realized, I do contend that significant progress toward greater political equality and substantive social justice not only is possible in the context of formal democracy, but also that important steps in that direction have been made in some democracies in the past. The two goals are tied together: In order to reduce political inequality, it is necessary that the distribution of wealth, status, and socioeconomic power become more equitable. Moreover, precisely the same kinds of shifts in class power relations that were responsible for the development of democracy in the first place were also responsible for the achievements in the areas of political equality and substantive social justice.

The actually existing democracies of today – defined by regular free and fair elections, responsibility of the state apparatus to elected representatives, and protection of civil liberties – vary a great deal in the degree to which they really give the many a voice in the determination of collective decisions. On the one hand, even if we exclude sham democracies, in some formal democracies the economically powerful are able to exert sufficient control over the political process that political decisions rarely challenge their interests. The masses respond by failing to show up at the polls to make electoral choices that appear to them to make little difference in the policy output of the government. On the other hand, other formal democracies are characterized by vibrant participation not only in elections but also in various organizations whose aim is to determine public policy and that arguably have proved to have some influence on policy. These differences appear if one examines not only the policy-making process but also the outcomes of

that process. At one extreme, there are cases where formally democratic processes barely modify the distribution of power and economic
resources. At the other end of the spectrum, the actual political power
of the many has over time made a real difference in the distribution of
scarce social and economic resources – of income and wealth, of power
and influence, of honor and respect – and thus, in turn, improved the
bases of political equality. Changes away from a merely formal democracy toward the latter pole of the continuum represent qualitative
advances both of democracy and of substantive social justice.

The same factors that advance the chances of democracy in the formal
sense of the term, then, also make democracy more real. The more the
balance of class power favors subordinate class interests, and the more a
dense civil society aids in giving organizational expression to these
interests, at the same time constituting a countervailing force against
unrestrained and autonomous state power, the greater the chances not
only of installing democratic institutions and making them stable but
also of increasing the real weight of democratic decision making. The
greater weight of the subordinate classes in the political process should
express itself in state policies that redistribute resources from the privileged to the underprivileged. This, I assert, is what has happened.
Although social democracy has nowhere achieved its original goal of
democratic socialism, it is becoming increasingly difficult for its detrac-
tors to deny that in countries in which trade unions are strong and social
democratic parties have been in power for extended periods of time, its
achievements have been substantial.[9]

What of the reversals of democracy stimulated by radical working-
class demands already cited? In my view, such cases do not demonstrate
that democratic institutions cannot be used to advance the substantive
interests of the lower classes or even that there is some limit to the
degree that those interests can be advanced in the context of formal
democracy. Rather, they are generally cases in which the working class
parties pressed demands which were impossible to realize given the
power balance in civil society. This is most clear in the Chilean case in
the 1970s in which the left gained control of the powerful presidential
office with a minority of the popular vote. Moreover, radical transformation needs very broad based support to overcome elite opposition,
so a slim majority, like that achieved by the Spanish left in 1936, is not
sufficient to sustain such a project.

Thus, in conclusion, it can be said that formal political democracy
does not guarantee progress toward political equality and substantive
justice. However, it does make it possible by setting two necessary

conditions for such progress: civil liberties which give the lower classes the right to organize, and universal suffrage and representative political institutions which make it possible for the lower classes to translate organization into influence on public policy.

Notes

1 Moore discusses the causes of variation in "peasant revolutionary potential" in his chapter on communism. I do not discuss this section of the work here, as it is not relevant to my cases, with the possible exception of Nicaragua.
2 I say "production-related" rather than "economic," as only relationships and activities strictly necessary to the production and distribution of goods and services are excluded from civil society. Trade unions and employers' associations are part of civil society. To take some Caribbean examples, civil society includes everything from the informal darts group at the local rum bar to the trade union, from the cricket club to the political party, from the yacht club to the chamber of commerce.
3 It should be noted that the following discussion of the transition to democracy is based not only on the final reform establishing democracy as we have defined it but also on previous steps that resulted in suffrage extension to the majority of the working class or the establishment of cabinet responsibility to parliament (e.g., the 1884 suffrage extension in Britain or 1901 establishment of parliamentary government in Denmark).
4 In the interwar period this generalization about the working class is harder to sustain, since the splits in the working class induced by the war and the Russian Revolution created antidemocratic minorities, above all the Communist parties, whose political posture clearly contributed to the breakdown of democracy.
5 These generalizations also apply to the smaller British West Indian islands not analyzed here (see Lewis 1968:118–43 and Henry and Stone 1983). In general, the middle-class component was better organized and played a more important role in the larger islands, especially Jamaica, than it did in the smaller ones.
6 I use "Africans" here to refer to both the black and brown (i.e., mixed, colored, or mulatto) populations of the two countries.
7 The population in Trinidad was 56 percent black and mixed and 40 percent East Indian in 1970 (Hintzen 1989:3). The Guyanese population was 44 percent East Indian in 1946 and 51 percent in 1970. The corresponding figures for black and mixed were 48 percent and 41 percent respectively (Greene 1974:174).
8 The colonial power, supported by the United States, played an important role in the early events, by suspending the PPP government of 1953, which enjoyed multiracial lower-class support (on the grounds that it was near communist), and encouraging Burnham to split with the PPP and form his own party.

9 The literature supporting this assertion is now voluminous; e.g., see Stephens 1979; Korpi 1982; Myles 1984; Esping-Andersen 1985, 1990; Buhmann 1988; Kohl 1988; Palme 1988, 1989; Smeeding and Torrey 1988; Kangas 1990; Kangas and Palme 1990.

References

Allen, William S. 1984: *The Nazi Seizure of Power: The Experience of a Single German Town 1922–1945* (rev. ed.). New York: Franklin Watts.

Aminzade, Ronald. In press: *Ballots and Barricades: Republican Visions, Urban Politics, and Capitalist Development in Mid-nineteenth Century France.* Princeton, N.J.: Princeton University Press.

Aminzade, Ronald. Forthcoming: *The Origins of Democratic Institutions: Political Parties and Class Formation in France.*

Anderson, R. D. 1977: *France 1870–1914: Politics and Society.* London: Routledge & Kegan Paul.

Bollen, Kenneth A. 1979: "Political Democracy and the Timing of Development." *American Sociological Review* 44(4): 572–88.

Bollen, Kenneth A. 1983: "World System Position, Dependency, and Democracy: The Cross-national Evidence." *American Sociological Review* 48(4): 468–79.

Bollen, Kenneth A., and Robert Jackman. 1985a: "Economic and Noneconomic Determinants of Political Democracy in the 1960s." In Richard G. Braungart (ed.), *Research in Political Sociology.* Greenwich, Conn.: Jai Press.

Bollen, Kenneth A., and Robert Jackman. 1985b: "Political Democracy and the Size Distribution of Income." *American Sociological Review* 50(4): 438–57.

Brenner, Robert. 1976: "Agrarian Class Structure and Economic Development in Pre-industrial Europe." *Past and Present* 70: 30–75.

Brenner, Robert. 1977: "The Origins of Capitalist Development: a critique of neo-Smithian marxism." *New Left Review* 104 (July–August): 25–92.

Buhmann, Brigitte, Lee Rainwater, Günther Schmaus, and Timothy M. Smeeding. 1988: "Equivalence Scales, Well-Being, Inequality, and Poverty: Sensitivity Estimates Across Ten Countries Using the Luxembourg Income Study (LIS) Database." *Review of Income and Wealth* 34:155–42.

Christiansen, Nils Finn. 1988. "The Role of the Labour Movement in the Process of Democratisation in Denmark 1848–1901." In Bo Stråth (ed.), *Democratisation in Scandinavia in Comparison.* Gothenburg: Department of History, University of Gothenburg.

Cutright, Phillips. 1963: "National Political Development: Measurement and Analysis." *American Sociological Review* XXVIII (April).

Cutright, Phillips, and James A. Wiley. 1969: "Modernization and Political Representation, 1927–1966." *Studies in Comparative International Development* 5:23–44.

Daalder, Hans. 1966: "The Netherlands: Opposition in a Segmented Society."

In Robert Dahl (ed.), *Political Oppositions in Western Democracies*. New Haven, Conn.: Yale University Press, 188–236.

Dahrendorf, Ralf. 1967: *Society and Democracy in Germany*. Garden City, N.Y.: Doubleday.

Derry, T. K. 1973: *A History of Modern Norway 1814–1972*. Oxford: Clarendon Press.

Despres, Leo A. 1967: *Cultural Pluralism and Nationalist Politics in British Guyana*. Chicago: Rand McNally.

Diamond, Larry. 1989: "Introduction: Roots of Failure, Seeds of Hope." In Larry, Diamond, Juan J. Linz, and Seymour Martin Lipset (eds.), *Democracy in Developing Countries: Africa*. Boulder, Colo.: Lynne Rienner, pp. 1–32.

Dybdahl, Vagn. 1969: *Partier og Erhverv*. Aarhus: Universitetsforlaget.

Elwitt, Sanford. 1975: *The Making of the Third Republic: Class and Politics in France 1868–1884*. Baton Rouge: Louisiana State University Press.

Esping-Andersen, Gøsta. 1985: *Politics Against Markets: the social democratic road to power*. Princeton, N.J.: Princeton University Press.

Esping-Andersen, Gøsta. 1990: *The Three Worlds of Welfare Capitalism*. Cambridge: Polity Press.

Fitzmaurice, John. 1983: *The Politics of Belgium: Crisis and Compromise in a Plural Society*. New York: St. Martin's.

Gitermann, Valentin. 1941: *Geschichte der Schweiz*. Thayngen: Augustin-Verlag.

Greene, J. E. 1974: *Race vs. Politics in Guyana*. Mona, Jamaica: Institute of Social and Economic Research, University of the West Indies.

Gruner, Erich. *Die Partien in der Schweiz*. Bern: Francke Verlag.

Harrison, Royden. 1965. *Before the Socialists*. London: Routledge & Kegan Paul.

Henry, Paget, and Carl Stone (eds.), 1983: *The Newer Caribbean: decolonization, democracy, and development*. Philadelphia, Pa.: Institute for the Study of Human Issues.

Hintzen, Percy. 1989: *The Costs of Regime Survival: Racial Mobilization, Elite Domination, and Control of the State in Guyana and Trinidad*. Cambridge: Cambridge University Press.

Hoyos, F. A. 1978: *Barbados: A History from the Amerindians to Independence*. London: Macmillan.

Huntington, Samuel. 1984: "Will More Countries Become Democratic?" *Political Science Quarterly* 99(2): 193–218.

Johnson, Richard. 1976: "Barrington Moore, Perry Anderson and English Social Development." *Working Papers in Cultural Studies* 9:7–28.

Kangas, Olli. 1990: "The Bigger the Better? Left Power, Social Rights, and Expenditures in Sickness Insurance." Paper delivered at the International Sociological Association meetings, Madrid, July 9–13.

Kangas, Olli, and Joakim Palme. 1990: "Statism Eroded? Labour Market Benefits and the Challenges to the Scandinavian Welfare States." Paper delivered at the International Sociological Association meetings, Madrid, July 9–13.

Korpi, Walter. 1982: *The Democratic Class Struggle*. London: Routledge & Kegan Paul.

Lewis, Gordon. 1968: *The Growth of the Modern West Indies*. New York: Modern Reader.

Lipset, Seymour Martin. 1960: *Political Man*. Garden City: Doubleday.

Lipset, Seymour Martin, and Rokkan Stein. 1967: "Cleavage Structures, Party Systems, and Voter Alignments: An Introduction." In S. M. Lipset and S. Rokkan (eds.), *Party Systems and Voter Alignments*. New York: Free Press, 1–64.

Lorwin, Val. 1966: "Belgium: Religion, Class, and Language in National Politics." In Robert Dahl (ed.), *Political Oppositions in Western Democracies*. New Haven, Conn.: Yale University Press, 147–87.

Lutchman, Harold Alexander. 1974: *From Colonialism to Co-operative Republic: Aspects of Political Development in Guyana*. Rio Piedras, Puerto Rico: Institute of Caribbean Studies, University of Puerto Rico.

Maier, Charles. 1975: *Recasting Bourgeois Europe*. Princeton, N.J.: Princeton University Press.

Marx, Karl. 1852: The chartists. In T. B. Bottomore and M. Rubel (eds.), *Karl Marx: selected writings in sociology and social philosophy*. New York: McGraw Hill, 1964.

Marx, Karl, and Friedrich Engels. 1848. "Manifesto of the Communist party." In *Karl Marx and Friedrich Engels, Collected Works VI*. New York: International Publishers, 1976.

Miller, Kenneth E. 1968. *Government and Politics in Denmark*. Boston: Houghton Mifflin.

Moore, Barrington. 1966: *The Social Origins of Dictatorship and Democracy*. Boston: Beacon Press.

Moskos, Charles C. 1967: *The Sociology of Political Independence*. Cambridge: Schenkman.

O'Donnell, Guillermo A. 1973: *Modernization and Bureaucratic Authoritarianism*. Berkeley, Calif.: Institute of International Studies.

O'Donnell, Guillermo A. 1979: "Tensions in the Bureaucratic Authoritarian State and the Question of Democracy." In David Collier (ed.), *The New Authoritarianism in Latin America*. Princeton, N.J.: Princeton University Press.

Palme, Joakim. 1988: "The Determinants of Old-Age Pensions in 18 OECD Countries 1930–1980." Paper delivered at the Workshop on Comparative Social Research in Social Policy, Labour Markets, Inequality, and Distributional Conflict, Stockholm, August 25–8.

Palme, Joakim. 1989: "Models of Pension and Income Inequality: A Comparative Analysis." Paper delivered at the Conference on the Welfare State in Transition, Bergen, August 24–7.

Przeworski, Adam. 1985: *Capitalism and Social Democracy*. Cambridge: Cambridge University Press.

Przeworski, Adam. 1988: "Capitalism, Democracy, Pacts: Revisited." Paper delivered at the Conference on the Micro-Foundations of the Democracy, University of Chicago, April 29 – May 1, 1988.

Rokkan, Stein. 1966: "Norway: Numerical Democracy and Corporate Pluralism." In Robert Dahl (ed.), *Political Oppositions in Western Democracies*. New Haven, Conn.: Yale University Press, 70–115.

Rueschemeyer, Dietrich, Evelyne Huber Stephens, and John D. Stephens. 1992: *Capitalist Development and Democracy*. Cambridge: Polity Press.

Ryan, Selwyn. 1972: *Race and Nationalism in Trinidad and Tobago: A Study of Decolonization in a Multiracial Society*. Toronto: University of Toronto Press.

Sanders, Thomas G. 1964: *Protestant Concepts of Church and State: Historical Backgrounds and Approaches for the Future*. New York: Holt, Rinehart & Winston.

Smeeding, Timothy M., and Barbara Boyld Torrey. 1988: "Poor Children in Rich Countries." *Science* 242:873–77.

Spinner, Thomas J. 1984: *Political and Social History of Guyana 1945–1983*. Boulder, Colo.: Westview.

Stephens, John D. 1979: *The Transition from Capitalism to Socialism*. Urbana: University of Illinois Press.

Therborn, Göran. 1977: "The Rule of Capital and the Rise of Democracy." *New Left Review* 103:3–41.

Weiner, Myron. 1987: "Empirical Democratic Theory." In Myron Weiner, and Ergun Ozbudun (eds.), *Competitive Elections in Developing Countries*. Washington D.C.: American Enterprise Institute, 3–34.

Zolberg, Aristide R. 1986: "How Many Exceptionalisms?" In Ira Katznelson, and Aristide R. Zolberg (eds.), *Working Class Formation: Nineteenth-Century Patterns in Western Europe and the United States*. Princeton, N.J.: Princeton University Press, 397–455.

Comments on John D. Stephens, "Capitalist Development and Democracy"

PRANAB BARDHAN

I agree with much of the empirical or comparative historical analysis and the political-economy emphasis of John Stephens's essay. Going beyond the usual cross-national statistical studies of democracy, Stephens provides a convincing causal explanation of the association of democracy with capitalist development, drawing on (though not entirely endorsing) the insights of Barrington Moore (1966) and Göran Therborn (1977). Capitalist development facilitates the rise of democracy, Stephens claims, by transforming the class structure, weakening the landlord class and creating a large working class and facilitating its organization. He gives many examples to make his point that historically the working class acted as the driving force of democracy (except in the cases of smallholder agrarian economies like Switzerland and Norway), but in most cases they needed allies in the final push for democracy, particularly allies in the middle classes (more in the Caribbean than in Europe). The capitalist class, in this account, has not been an active or consistent supporter of democratic reforms, except in Britain, France, and Switzerland (even in these cases, the support came before the capitalists felt threatened by working-class organizations). The accommodating policy of the British colonial administration in the Caribbean toward liberal or union organizations against the inclinations of the plantation plutocracy helped democratic formations, whereas in Central America (with the exception of Costa Rica) the military–landed oligarchy alliance, often with support and intervention from the United States, sealed their fate.

Let me now briefly refer to points of detail where I have some disagreement or different emphasis (in this I shall take a broader range of country examples):

1. Capitalist development has not always led to strong working-class organization and mobilization, even in this century. There are many examples of this, not just in East Asia (Japan, Korea, etc.), where it is glaring, but also in South and Central Europe.

2. The working class has not always been prodemocratic (even in

countries where a strong communist movement did not distract their loyalty). The author notes, in passing, the case of Peronism in Argentina but fails to discuss its structural context. There are other cases (e.g., Mexico or Mussolini's Italy). One would like a fuller discussion of this issue, which is central to the author's theme.

3. Notwithstanding Moore, I have not quite understood why the landowning class is characterized as "labor-repressive" and interested in political control of workers but the capitalist class is not. There is no reason why monopoly capital should be less interested in a political control of the labor process. It is possible labor repression is more difficult to carry out in the factory setting than in remote, scattered farms. Interwar Japan and Korea in the more recent military regimes provide examples of authoritarianism under a coalition between the state and a labor-repressive monopoly capitalist class in countries where agriculture is largely in small farms – this is a contrasting case to the authoritarianism in Central Europe and Central America under a state-landed oligarchy coalition.

4. The author, I think, underplays the cases of the rise of democracy as a strategic outcome of social processes, where the extension of democratic rights emerged as a consequence, sometimes unintended, of the rivalry of the upper classes. The classic examples of this in the extension of suffrage in nineteenth-century Britain and France, before the formation of working-class organizations are, somewhat unconvincingly, explained away by the author as "a delayed response to earlier working-class agitation" (like the Chartist movement in Britain). In France, Louis Napoleon actually used the universal (male) suffrage to give the vote to the conservative peasants as a check against the militants in the cities. (He even reportedly advised the Prussian government in 1861 about this advantage of universal suffrage; see Anderson [1972], p. 115.)

5. The author distinguishes between the role of middle classes (often prodemocratic) and that of the bourgeoisie (often, though not always, resisting working-class political incorporation) in the rise of democracy. This leads to questions about the usually contradictory class location of many members of the middle classes. This particularly applies to the increasingly important group of professionals, who are often large owners of human capital. It is important to resolve this issue because in most movements for democracy (most recently in Eastern Europe and South America), professionals play the key role.

6. On the basis of Guyana and other cases, the author finds a definite *negative* relation between ethnic divisions in society and democracy. But the world's most diverse society – in terms of ethnicity, language and

religion – is also the world's largest democracy: India. Maybe the explanation lies in the fact that unlike in the case of social polarization in Guyana, in India there is a plurality of dominant social and economic interest groups, with no individual group powerful enough to hijack the state. Democracy persists in India, not because the subordinate classes are organized but possibly because the divided elite groups have found in democracy the least arbitrary rule of negotiation and bargaining among themselves. For an analysis of the resilience of Indian democracy on these lines, see Bardhan (1988).

References

M. S. Anderson, *The Ascendancy of Europe, 1815–1914*, Longman, London, 1972.

P. Bardhan, "Dominant Proprietary Classes and India's Democracy," in A. Kohli (ed.), *India's Democracy: An Analysis of Changing State–Society Relations*, Princeton University Press, Princeton, 1988.

B. Moore, *The Social Origins of Dictatorship and Democracy*, Beacon Press, Boston, 1966.

G. Therborn, "The Rule of Capital and the Rise of Democracy," *New Left Review*, 1977.